D1499947

After the Irish
An Anthology of Poetic Translation

After the Irish
An Anthology of
Poetic Translation

Edited by

GREGORY A. SCHIRMER

CORK
CUP
UNIVERSITY
PRESS

First published in 2009 by
Cork University Press
Youngline Industrial Estate
Pouladuff Road, Togher
Cork, Ireland

British Library Cataloguing in Publication Data

After the Irish : an anthology of poetic translation.
    1. Irish poetry.   2. Irish poetry--Translations into
English.
    I. Schirmer, Gregory A.
    891.6'21008-dc22

    ISBN-13: 9781859184387

Typeset by Tower Books, Ballincollig, Co. Cork
Printed by Athenaeum Press, UK

www.corkuniversitypress.com

Grant aided by

For Jane

Contents

The Nineteenth Century

Modern Ireland

Contemporary Ireland

Introduction

The premise governing this anthology is that verse translation from the Irish, a practice that has been going on steadily in Ireland for nearly three centuries, constitutes a significant body of Irish poetry in its own right. The anthology is not, in other words, designed primarily to provide an historical record of verse translation, nor, what is more common in bilingual anthologies in Ireland, to give readers with little or no Irish access to the tradition of poetry written in the native language. As its subtitle declares, *After the Irish* is an anthology of *poetic* translation. Brendan Kennelly has said that a good verse translation 'is also a completely new, autonomous poem in English,'[1] and it is this wealth of new and autonomous poems written in English but based – sometimes closely, more often quite loosely – on poems written in Irish that this anthology represents.

The anthology's one hundred and fifty poetic translations, representing the work of seventy one poets and stretching as far back as Jonathan Swift's 'The Description of an *Irish Feast*' written in 1720 and as far forward as a translation by Seamus Heaney published in 2006, were selected, accordingly, on the basis of their stature as achieved poems in English. As will be clear to anyone who reads through the anthology, and especially to anyone who compares the poetic translations with their sources, the writers doing the translating represented in these pages were decidedly more conscious of their work as poetry than as scholarly or literal translation. Indeed, a number of them had little working knowledge of Irish, and many have been reluctant to use the term translation to describe what they were doing; Austin Clarke labelled his poems based on the work of the eighteenth-century poet Turlough Carolan 'free variations', Tom MacIntyre called his poetic translations 'versions and adaptations', and James Stephens referred to his as 'Loot and Plunder'. A number of the verse translators represented in this anthology also freely reworked the forms and conventions of English verse to reflect the very different forms and conventions of poetry written in Irish, a practice that often produced markedly poetic translations, and that also has had a significant effect on much Irish poetry written in English apart from translations.

Although this anthology is intended primarily to argue for verse translation as poetry, it is organised chronologically, and so inevitably reveals something of the development of verse translation from the Irish over the past three centuries, and some of the ways in which translation has reflected and contributed to the long and complex relationship between Ireland's two principal literary traditions. One can also see at work in this collection certain political and cultural issues, many of which have to do with Ireland's colonial and post-colonial status. As Declan Kiberd has argued, one root meaning of 'translate' is 'conquer',[2] and colonisation generally requires, to some degree at least, the translation of the native culture into the terms of the presumably superior colonising culture. This certainly happened in Ireland, the first of England's colonies. But translation in a colonial context always works in two directions: while it enacts and encodes the colonisation of the native culture, it also inspires, whatever the intention of a particular translator, resistance to colonisation by validating the worth of that culture. Translations from the Irish produced by cultural unionists like Charlotte Brooke in the eighteenth century and Samuel Ferguson in the nineteenth could be read, and were read, as sources of inspiration for political resistance to the English presence in Ireland.[3] More broadly, translation in any society, because it requires a crossing of boundaries often constructed on essentialisms of one kind or another, calls into question single-minded readings of history and culture; in Ireland, translation has worked in this way to undermine not only the essentialist assumptions of colonial conquest, such as the inherent superiority of the English language and its literary tradition, but also essentialist assumptions underlying the resistance effort, such as the idea of Gaelic purity. As Richard Kearney has said, the practice of translation in Ireland has made clear that there is no 'unitary master narrative of Irish cultural history, but a plurality of transitions between different perspectives.'[4]

What is probably the earliest verse translation from Irish into English appeared in 1635, from the hand of a scribe named Michael Kearney, from Ballyoskey, Co. Tipperary.[5] But verse translation from the Irish did not become a regular practice until the early years of the eighteenth century, when the necessary conditions were in place: a developing Anglo-Irish literature written in English and aimed primarily at an English audience, and a substantial and centuries-old literature written in Irish and aimed almost exclusively at an Irish audience. Moreover, in large part because of the establishment of Trinity College at the end of the sixteenth century, the various plantations in the sixteenth and seventeenth centuries, and the huge land transfers throughout the seventeenth century that created an English-speaking landed gentry in Ireland, the Irish language had lost enormous ground to English by the beginning of the eighteenth century. In this context, even the most sensitive and high-minded theories about translation as a means of salvaging the Irish-language tradition were inevitably anchored in colonialist assumptions, including the ability of the English-language tradition to absorb texts written in the native language. It is no accident that virtually all the verse translation from the Irish done in the eighteenth century essentially rewrote Irish-language texts into the alien forms of English verse; the attempt to reshape those forms to reflect the conventions and forms of Irish-language poetry would not come until the nineteenth century, when translation had taken on board the tenets of nationalism.

The views of Charlotte Brooke, one of the most important verse translators in the eighteenth century, reflect accurately the colonialist mentality that underpinned so much work in translation in the period. In the preface to her collection of translations, *Reliques of Irish Poetry* (1789), Brooke, the daughter of a distinguished Anglo-Irish man of letters, argued that translation from the Irish could generate mutual understanding between England and Ireland: 'The British muse is not yet informed that she has an elder sister in this isle; let us then introduce them to each other! together let them walk abroad from their bowers, sweet ambassadresses of cordial union between two countries that seem formed by nature to be joined by every bond of interest, and of amity.'[6] But as the very title of her work makes clear, the cordial union that Brooke envisioned depended on the assumption that the Irish-language tradition was already dead and buried, able to be revived only if translated into English. Also, Brooke's translations, even at their best, are very much the work of an eighteenth-century English literary sensibility unable to penetrate the culture from which it is translating.

Nevertheless, this view that verse translation from the Irish in the eighteenth century always served England's colonial ambitions vastly oversimplifies an undertaking that in fact had a variety of complex and often contrapuntal effects and implications. For one thing, there was a genuine interest among English-speaking people across the British Isles in what might be called the Celtic past, and it was not entirely or always colonial in implication. The enormous popularity of James Macpherson's bogus versions of the poems of Oisín, published in the 1760s – and the extended controversy, in Ireland particularly, about their authenticity – is one sign of this, as is the large readership for Dermot O'Connor's often politically radical translation into English of Geoffrey Keating's seventeenth-century compilation of fact and fantasy, *Foras Feasa ar Éirinn*, which went through at least twelve editions between 1723 and 1865. Brooke's

Reliques of Irish Poetry was also very well received, and circulated widely in Ireland and England. Moreover, for all its colonialist assumptions, Brooke's collection did in fact represent, and with some parity, both of Ireland's traditions; partly to counter Macpherson's fraudulent representations of Gaelic culture, Brooke provided her readers with the Irish-language texts of the poems that she was translating, and although few of her readers would have been able to read these texts (and they were often unreliable, in any case), they represent one of the earliest appearances in print of Irish-language poetry.[7] Also, not all verse translation in the eighteenth century came from writers with Anglo-Irish backgrounds and having English as their first language; there were a number of Irish-language poets publishing verse translations from the Irish at the time, represented in this anthology by Micheál Óg Ó Longáin, an Irish-language scribe born into a learned family from Co. Cork, and writing in Irish from a distinctly nationalist point of view.

A substantial flourishing of folk poetry, in both Irish and English, in the eighteenth century also offered significant points of contact between the two traditions, especially when mediated by translation, and these connections often had very little to do, at least overtly, with England's colonial ambitions in Ireland. Inside Irish-language poetry, the collapse of the bardic tradition in the seventeenth century meant that the strictly formal compositions associated with that tradition were increasingly replaced by more popular forms such as the ballad and song, and translations of this kind of Irish-language verse were quite common in the eighteenth century, as witness the many translations of the work of Turlough Carolan (including a number by Charlotte Brooke), and the considerable number of translations of Irish-language drinking songs, represented in these pages by Arthur Dawson's 'Bumpers, 'Squire Jones' and Henry Wilson's 'Aiombo and Umbo'. In 1796, just seven years after Brooke's *Reliques of Irish Poetry* appeared, Edward Bunting published the first edition of his influential collection of Irish folk songs, *A General Collection of the Ancient Irish Music*, which included verse translations into English by various hands.

Finally, although verse translators in the eighteenth century relied on forms of English verse for their translations, paying little attention to the forms and conventions of poetry in Irish, this practice was not always insensitive to the spirit of the original. Denis Woulf's version of Brian Merriman's eighteenth-century social satire 'Cúirt an Mheán-Oíche' ('The Midnight Court'), constructed around complaints of sexual frustration from young Irish women, is written in octo-syllabic rhyming couplets, very much an Augustan form, but Woulf's lively diction, along with his ability to imitate the rich internal assonantal patterns of the original, enable him to capture quite successfully the irreverent and vigorous character of Merriman's poem. The seventeenth-century ode 'Teagasc Fleath', a weighty poem about political governance, is rendered by Theophilus O'Flanagan in heroic couplets, but in O'Flanangan's hands this quintessentially English verse form validates the native culture by embodying not only the authority of the voice in the original, but also the poem's status as a piece of public discourse describing a politically sophisticated culture that is to be taken seriously. Moreover, verse translation in the eighteenth century did not always assume superiority for the English-language tradition; one frequently comes across translators in the period admiring the complexity of Irish-language poetry, and lamenting their inability to render it in English.

However one defines or qualifies the links between verse translation from the Irish in the eighteenth century and England's colonial occupation of Ireland, the rise of romanticism in the early decades of the nineteenth century brought about radical changes in verse translation, and in its cultural and political implications. For one thing, the kind of writers practicing verse translation tended to be different, coming very often from within the native Irish culture rather than from among the Anglo-Irish. For another, verse translation from the Irish began to embody, overtly or covertly, romantic-nationalist rather than colonialist views. At the same time, translators began looking for ways to make the forms of English verse take the impress of verse in Irish. First consciously undertaken in the early years of the nineteenth century by J. J. Callanan, a deeply romantic writer with deeply romantic ideas about Ireland, this poetic strategy had implications far beyond the aesthetic as it set about creating poetic translations into English that refused to be completely English, embodying an implicit resistance to the assumed ability of the English tradition to absorb the culture of its colony. Callanan's 'The Outlaw of Loch Lene', for example, presumably based on a poem from the oral tradition, is unlike any verse translation produced in the eighteenth century:

> O many a day have I made good ale in the glen,
> That came not of stream, or malt; – like the brewing of men.
> My bed was the ground; my roof, the greenwood above,
> And the wealth that I sought one far kind glance from my love.

Those striking assonantal links, wavering rhythms, and long, irregular lines – all rooted in Irish-language poetry – declare that Ireland's native tradition need not be totally sacrificed, even in translation into English, to the cultural dominance of England, that in fact the English tradition can be repossessed, in a way even colonised, by being re-formed to accommodate poetry written in Irish.

The politics of resistance implied in Callanan's translations are considerably more overt in the work of other nineteenth-century verse translators. Like Callanan, Edward Walsh was deeply conversant with the Irish-language folk tradition, and translated with genuine sensitivity from it, as can be seen in translations included here such as 'Have You Been at Carrick?', 'Flower of the Brown-Haired Maidens', and 'From the Cold Sod That's O'er You'. But Walsh was also a fierce nationalist, and the nineteenth-century fusion of antiquarianism and romantic nationalism is particularly clear in his collection of verse translations published in 1844, *Reliques of Irish Jacobite Poetry* (Charlotte Brooke's title with 'Jacobite' added), which brought the often insurrectionary political poetry of the eighteenth century, written in Irish, to the attention of English readers,[8] while enabling Walsh to express his own distinctly nineteenth-century nationalist views. Although the most significant figure on the landscape of verse translation in the nineteenth century, James Clarence Mangan, could hardly be described as a political writer – he did not openly embrace the nationalist cause until 1848, the fourth year of the famine and a year before his death – his verse translations from the Irish often mix personal suffering and cultural deprivation in ways that embody both a romantic sense of self and an implicitly nationalist politics, as in the remarkable 'Lament over the Ruins of the Abbey of Teach Molaga'. Mangan's well-known translation 'Dark Rosaleen', with its charged, often violent synthesis of religious imagery and the language of passionate love, certainly invites the nationalist readings that it has so often inspired.

Mangan also brought to the art of verse translation from the Irish a sense of creative inhibition rooted in romantic theories exalting the poetic imagination. In Mangan's translations, this poetic freedom is often manifested as a license to revise radically the forms of English verse into which he was translating. As a result, although he had little Irish himself, certainly not enough to produce scholarly versions of the poems he translated, Mangan produced poetic translations from the Irish that were as distinctly un-English in their forms and textures as were those produced by Callanan, who was probably a fluent Irish speaker. In 'O'Hussey's Ode to the Maguire', for example, Mangan takes extraordinary liberties with the original, which was written in 1600 by the chief bard to the Maguire clan in the extremely formal, highly compressed syllabic metre associated with the bardic schools. Mangan's version is marked by irregular rhythms (often spondaic in effect), long and varying lines, frequent internal assonance, and the romantic afflatus that characterises almost all his work:

> Where is my Chief, my Master, this bleak night, *movrone*!
> O, cold, cold, miserably cold is this bleak night for Hugh,
> Its showery, arrowy, speary sleet pierceth one through and through,
> Pierceth one to the very bone!

In the end, the gap between Mangan's translation and its original is arguably of less interest than is its distance from conventional English verse forms – a distance that indirectly embodies the kind of nationalist sentiments made remarkably overt in the final image of 'O'Hussey's Ode to the Maguire': '*But the memory of the lime-white mansions his right hand hath laid/In ashes warms the hero's heart.*'

This bending of the forms of English verse to accommodate the qualities of verse in Irish was not always tied to romantic-nationalist conviction in the nineteenth century. Samuel Ferguson was a Belfast Protestant with landed gentry in his background who in theory wanted to carry forward the cultural-unionist ideas about translation found in Charlotte Brooke in the previous century, hardened by a fierce anti-Catholic bias. But Ferguson produced impressive verse translations from the Irish that were sensitive to the native culture and implicitly validated it, while freely altering the forms of English verse in the process. Although Ferguson's knowledge of Irish was limited, he managed quite remarkably at times to express the poetic textures of the originals he was working from, in part because he decided to negotiate the significant differences between Irish-language and English-language poetry by using the line rather than the foot as his basic unit of measure. The effect of this can be seen in Ferguson's rendering of the folk poem 'Caisiol Múmhan', in which he abandons conventional English metrics, extending each line as far as necessary to encompass the substance of each corresponding line in the original:

> I'd wed you without herds, without money, or rich array,
> And I'd wed you on a dewy morning at day-dawn grey;
> My bitter woe it is, love, that we are not far away
> In Cashel town, though the bare deal board were our marriage-bed
> this day!

The lack of fulfilment expressed in these lines is typical of much of the folk poetry translated by writers like Ferguson, Mangan, Callanan, and Walsh. The grim realities of nineteenth-century Irish rural life no doubt largely account for this, but this note of despair also resonates with romantic obsessions with melancholy and grief – still another

way in which the romantic and the Gaelic were fastened together in
these years. While there are still drinking songs like John D'Alton's
'Why, Liquor of Life' and Matthew Graham's 'Captain Whiskey', and
comic and satiric poems like Mangan's 'The Woman of Three Cows'
and 'The Dame of the Slender Wattle', verse translations of poems
about loss and betrayal abound in the period, and the predominant
note is elegiac: young men are imprisoned (Callanan's 'The Convict of
Clonmel') or in exile (George Fox's 'The County of Mayo'), lovers are
buried (Walsh's 'From the Cold Sod That's O'er You') or hopelessly
separated by circumstances beyond their control (Walsh's 'Flower of
Brown-Haired Maidens'), amorous yearnings meet with indifference
(Thomas Furlong's 'Peggy Browne'), and nearly everywhere the past
casts a long, dark shadow over the present.

In the last years of the nineteenth century, with the advent of the
Irish literary revival, verse translation from the Irish began to
undergo more changes. For one thing, Irish writing in English became
dependent on translation in quite a practical way in the this period, as
many of the revival's architects had to rely on translation for access to
the Irish-language tradition that they saw as essential to their efforts
to create a new and distinctive Irish literature written in English. Also,
Yeats and other writers in the movement looked to the verse transla-
tions of nineteenth-century figures like Mangan and Ferguson, and to
the translations from Connacht folk poetry being done at the time by
Douglas Hyde, for models of poetry written in English but distinctly
Irish in form and texture. All this tended to close the gap between the
two traditions by putting verse translation in the service not of polit-
ical separatism, which usually sought to emphasize differences
between Irish-speaking Ireland and English-speaking Ireland, but of a
cultural nationalism constructed around the idea that the two tradi-
tions were interdependent.

At the same time, a number of verse translators working during the
revival sought to establish a broader understanding of the Irish-
language tradition, and thereby dismantle romantic-nationalist
representations of it found frequently in nineteenth-century discourse.
This effort was manifest not only in the practice of verse translation
itself, but also in the publication of various anthologies of translation.
The most important of these is George Sigerson's *Bards of the Gael and
Gall*, published in 1897. Starting with translations from Ireland's pre-
Christian tradition and proceeding chronologically to the eighteenth
century, *Bards of the Gael and Gall* attempts to construct the Irish tradi-
tion in pluralistic rather than nationalistic terms. 'It is not the Gael only
who mourns,' Sigerson wrote in the preface, in reference to the seven-
teenth century. 'A Norman Nugent feels the pang of exile as keenly as

the O'Neill.'[9] Of Scandinavian ancestry himself, Sigerson was at particular pains to challenge the conventional view of the Norse as marauders who destroyed Gaelic civilization. Sigerson also explicitly called into question any tendency to romanticise the Gaelic tradition. 'Those who want to associate Irish poetry with effusiveness of thought and luxuriance of language,' Sigerson said, 'will be surprised to find that bardic poetry was characterized by classic reserve in thought, form, and expression.'[10] Many of Sigerson's translations, especially of poems from early periods, are positively stark by comparison with much verse translation from earlier in the century. 'Winter's Approach', for example, based on an original dating back to the ninth or tenth century, is constructed around short lines, compressed imagery, specific description, and emotional reserve – all perfectly in keeping with the original, as Sigerson would be the first to point out:

> List my lay: oxen roar,
> Winter chides, Summer's o'er,
> Sinks the sun, cold winds rise,
> Moans assail, ocean cries.
>
> Ferns flush red, change hides all,
> Clanging now, gray geese call,
> Wild wings cringe, cold with rime,
> Drear, most drear, ice-frost time.

Eleanor Hull shared Sigerson's scepticism about the romanticisaton of the Irish-language tradition. In addition to producing a two-volume *Textbook of Irish Literature* in 1906, and helping establish the Irish Texts Society, Hull published her own anthology of verse translations from the Irish by various hands, including her own, *The Poem-Book of the Gael*, in 1913. In the preface, she took the same anti-romantic position that Sigerson had argued for a few years earlier: 'The reader who does not know Ireland or know Gaelic is ready to accept softness . . . what he is not prepared for is the sudden break into matter-of-fact, the curt tone that cuts across much Irish poetry. . . . He resents it, as he resents the tone of the "Playboy of the Western World"; yet it is the direct modern representative of the tone of mind that produced the Ossianic lays.'[11] Like many of those done by Sigerson, Hull's translations, including some of poems attributed to Oisín, strike a distinctly unromantic note at the same time that they follow the original quite closely. One year after Hull's anthology appeared, Alfred Perceval Graves published an ambitious anthology of Irish verse in English entitled *The Book of Irish Poetry* that included more than twenty of his own verse translations, most of them done in a spare, direct style that owed far more to Sigerson than it did to Mangan.

Verse translation from the Irish-language folk tradition during the revival also effectively called into question earlier representations of the Irish-language tradition. Douglas Hyde's insistence on the poetic merit of the colloquial voice differentiated his work sharply from much of the verse translation from the folk tradition that preceded him,[12] and in poetic translations such as 'My Grief on the Sea', 'Brow of Nefin', and 'Ringleted Youth of My Love' – all having to do with failed love, separated lovers, or sexual betrayal – Hyde sounds the same note of loss and grief found in much nineteenth-century verse translation, but with little if any romantic resonance. Hyde's rural realism also recognises the considerable violence and cruelty that marked the remote world of Irish-speaking Ireland at the end of the nineteenth century; before Hyde there is nothing in verse translation from the Irish anything like the irreverent and brutal fantasies found in Hyde's 'Bruadar and Smith and Glinn', a version of a traditional curse poem. Unlike Hyde, who was an Anglo-Irish Protestant, Padraic Colum wrote about post-famine melancholy and loneliness from the position of an insider. Colum was born in a Co. Longford workhouse – he once said he 'had the advantage of the disadvantages that Yeats and the others didn't have'[13] – and the straight-forward, candid language of his poetic translations describing the decidedly unromantic realities of Irish rural life at the end of the nineteenth century is deliberately stripped of any trace of Wordsworthian solace or Keatsian paradox.

Hyde and a number of other translators associated with the literary revival also were committed to bringing into their verse translations from the Irish the most striking formal quality of Irish-language folk poetry, the use of assonance. Hyde once said that his verse translations were to be distinguished from those of previous translators, including Mangan and Ferguson, because of his attempt 'to reproduce the vowel rhymes as well as the exact metre of the original poem'.[14] Thomas MacDonagh, who argued in his influential study *Literature in Ireland* (1916) for the development of an Irish poetry written in English but heavily inflected by Irish-language verse, put his theories into practice in verse translations that use rhyme and assonance to imitate the terminal, medial, and terminal-medial assonantal patterns found in much Irish-language poetry; the effect of this can be seen clearly in MacDonagh's translation of Cathal Buí Mac Giolla Ghunna's well-known drinking song about the yellow bittern:

> The yellow bittern that never broke out
>   In a drinking bout, might as well have drunk;
> His bones are thrown on a naked stone
>   Where he lived alone like a hermit monk.

O yellow bittern! I pity your lot,
> Though they say that a sot like myself is curst –
I was sober a while, but I'll drink and be wise
> For fear I should die in the end of thirst.

By the time that another revival figure, James Stephens, published his one collection of verse translations from the Irish, *Reincarnations*, in 1918, the revival was finished. Stephens's work in translation can in fact be seen as a bridge between the revival's efforts to temper the romantic assumptions and qualities of much nineteenth-century translation and a thoroughly modern scepticism. Stephens identified with the great Irish-language poets of loss and exile, Dáibhí Ó Bruadair and Aodhagán Ó Rathaille, and the rebellious, quarrelsome, acidly ironic tone of his poetic translations of the work of these two figures – and the fearless questioning of hierarchy that lay behind it – was to become a hallmark of much modern Irish writing. But for the writers who followed Stephens, the authority in question had undergone a substantial change from that which preoccupied Ó Bruadair and Ó Rathaille (and Stephens) – the power of England in Ireland. For writers like Austin Clarke and Frank O'Connor, the two most important verse translators in the middle decades of the twentieth century, the enemy of Irish freedom was not England but the newly empowered Irish Catholic Church, and the society that it dominated. Consciously appealing to the radical, anti-establishment nature of the Irish-language tradition, Clarke and O'Connor turned to verse translation as a vehicle for critiquing what they regarded as a destructively religious, provincial, conservative, and – witness the Censorship Act of 1929 – philistine society.

As is evident even from the selections included in this anthology, the Irish-language tradition generally approaches matters of the body and sexuality in a spirit of open-mindedness occasionally bordering, as in Merriman's 'Cúirt an Mheán-Oíche' and numerous love poems in the folk tradition, on the bawdy. Clarke, writing in part out of his own disturbing experience of Irish Catholicism – he once said that Joyce's *A Portrait of the Artist as Young Man* 'had long since become confused with my own memories or had completed them'[15] – found in one of the most frequently of all translated Irish-language poets in the eighteenth and nineteenth centuries, Turlough Carolan, the ideal vehicle for questioning the church's repressive attitudes toward sexuality. Clarke's interest in Carolan is nothing like the antiquarian interest that inspired Carolan's earlier translators, such as Charlotte Brooke in the eighteenth century or the contributors to James Hardiman's nineteenth-century collection of verse translations, *Irish Minstrelsy*; rather, Clarke converts Carolan's love songs in Irish into poems in English that are deliberately erotic, designed both to challenge the teachings of the church regarding sexuality, and to question attempts to construct Irish identity around the twin pillars of modern Catholicism and traditional Gaelicism by reinterpreting the Irish-language tradition to square it with the puritanical values of the church. And so in 'Mabel Kelly', where Carolan writes, 'Is sí is deise cos, bas, lámh, agus béul,/Péighre rosg a's folt ag fás léi go féur' [She has the prettiest foot, palm, hand, and mouth,/A pair of eyes and hair growing to the grass], Clarke translates: 'Foot, hand, eye, mouth, breast, thigh and instep, all that we desire,/Tresses that pass small curls as if to touch the ground'. Those small curls are certainly implied in Carolan, but Clarke is not about to leave that particular detail to his reader's imagination.

Clarke also was one of the most skilled of all Irish verse translators in the techniques of representing the formal qualities and textures of Irish-language poetry in English verse. But for Clarke this kind of poetic imitation was considerably more than a matter of what it had been for translators like Callanan and Ferguson, or Sigerson and Hyde – a way of promoting the qualities of Irish verse. Rather, Clarke's self-conscious and knowledgeable attempts to re-shape English-language poetry by making it take the impress of Irish-language poetry amounted to a crucial part of his critique of modern Irish society; in his view, the Irish-language tradition had to be rescued from efforts to force it into concord with the values of modern Irish Catholicism, and Clarke's poetic translations, in their very idioms, rhythms, and patterns of assonance, are constantly validating his credentials as the true spokesman for that tradition.

O'Connor, who produced a wide range of verse translations throughout his career, found an especially kindred spirit in Brian Merriman. As Carolan had done for Clarke, Merriman offered O'Connor a way of using the Gaelic tradition, in particular the often graphic and irreverent sexual comedy of 'Cúirt an Mheán-Oíche', to critique the Irish society of his day, and to undermine efforts to make the Irish-language tradition a prop for the conservative and puritanical values being promoted in that society.[16] As if to make O'Connor's point for him, the Censorship Board banned his translation of 'Cúirt an Mheán-Oíche' while the original was still available from the government's own printing office. 'I believe the best authorities hold that it is almost entirely my own work,' O'Connor commented, 'the one compliment Ireland has ever paid me.'[17]

If Clarke and O'Connor's use of verse translation to attack Irish society in the middle decades of the twentieth century constitutes one significant modern development in the history of verse translation, another is represented by the work of the English-born Robin Flower, who viewed verse translation as a way of revealing the connections between the Irish-language and English-language traditions, thereby calling into question not only the nationalist impulse to view the two traditions in terms of difference, but also the tendency in post-Free State Ireland to define Irish identity as distinct from anything having to do with England. Particularly in his translations from Irish-language love poetry of the sixteenth and seventeenth centuries, Flower emphasizes wit, irony, compression and arresting imagery – the translations read more like poems by John Donne than like any of the translations of native love poetry done earlier – to suggest that the Irish-language tradition needs to be read not in opposition to the work of Elizabethan, Jacobean, and Caroline poets in English, but rather in conjunction with it.

No writer of Clarke's and O'Connor's generation could have foreseen the radical changes that have taken place in Irish society in recent years, including material prosperity, urbanisation and suburbanisation, rapid population growth, immigration replacing emigration, a sharp decline in the influence of the Irish Catholic Church, and Ireland's sense of itself as a European nation. Nor could that writer have foreseen the extraordinary flowering of contemporary Irish writing, in all genres and in both languages, and the climate of imaginative and cultural freedom in which that writing has been taking place. In this environment, verse translation from the Irish has also flourished, but largely without the antiquarian or nationalist or socially subversive motives that defined it from the early decades of the eighteenth century to the middle decades of the twentieth. Rather, verse translation has emerged in recent years as another means, along with writing in English and writing in Irish, of addressing a variety of contemporary issues and experiences that often transcend differences between the two traditions. Indeed, one of the most striking contemporary points of view being expressed in both languages, and in translations from one to the other, is a profound scepticism about the validity of those differences, and of the nationalistic and religious ideas about Irish identity upon which they were built. Translations like Michael Hartnett's of Nuala Ní Dhomhnaill's deliberately shocking poem about the annunciation, 'Scéala', Dermot Bolger's version of Michael Davitt's, 'I gClochar na Trócaire,' in which the narrator attempts to seduce a nun, and Ciaran Carson's translation of Ní Dhomhnaill's 'The Shan Van Vocht', in which one of the most revered of nationalist icons appears as an 'old bitch' who is 'locked/Into self-pity', would have been inconceivable in an earlier age.

Verse translation from the Irish has also increasingly been seen in recent years as a way of insisting on the relevance of the Irish-language tradition to contemporary Ireland even as the pressures on the language have increased greatly with the emergence of relatively pluralistic and cosmopolitan ideas about Irish identity.[18] This insistence might seem surprising, given the speed and relative ease with which contemporary Ireland has cast off so many of the cultural markers that connect it to a distinctive past, but as the history of verse translation from the Irish makes clear, the Irish-language and English-language traditions have been vitally linked for centuries. Moreover, the Irish language, despite its status as a minority language and the rarity with which it is actually used outside the Gaeltacht, has managed something of a cultural comeback in recent years, as evidenced by the spread of Gaelscoileanna, the success of the Irish-language television station, the increasing interest in traditional Irish music, and, most important for verse translation, the extraordinary amount of poetry of high quality being written and published in Irish. Equally extraordinary is the visibility in the contemporary Irish literary landscape that Irish-language poets like Ní Dhomhnaill, Davitt, and Cathal Ó Searcaigh have achieved, and the kinds of audiences that they are reaching: essentially middle-class, largely urban, and often politically radical – more or less the same kind of audiences reached by contemporary Irish poets writing in English, and as different as could be from the readership of Irish-language poetry even one generation earlier, which tended to come from the Gaeltacht and be relatively conservative.[19] One sign of the perceived relevance of Irish-language writing to contemporary culture is the marked tendency of so many of today's poetic translators to turn to contemporary poets, rather than to poets from the past, for their sources. Of the forty-eight contemporary poetic translations represented in this anthology, for example, no fewer than eighteen are based on the work of contemporary poets writing in Irish.

When contemporary verse translators do turn to poets from the past, they tend to look for contemporary relevance. Seamus Heaney takes up the twelfth-century *Buile Suibhne* because he finds in the figure of Sweeney correspondences to his own position as a poet from Northern Ireland writing in the context of the sectarian conflict in the North. In the preface to his translation, Heaney describes Sweeney as 'a figure of the artist, displaced, guilty, assuaging himself by his utterance', and the poem as 'an aspect of the quarrel between free creative imagination and the constraints of religious, political and domestic obligation'[20] – every term of which applies to Heaney himself. Also, while contemporary poets like Heaney are committed, in translating older texts, to preserving what Michael Cronin calls their 'unsettling otherness',[21] they also work very often to make those earlier texts resonate with contemporary issues. Heaney's translation of part of Merriman's 'Cúirt an Mheán-Oíche', for example, casts the earlier poem into terms that advance specific criticisms of certain aspects of Irish society in the 1980s and early 1990s (the translation was published in 1993):

> It's goodbye to freedom and ancient right,
> To honest dealing and leadership;
> The ground ripped off and nothing put back,
> Weeds in the field once the crop is stacked.
> With the best of the people leaving the land,
> Graft has the under- and upper hand.
> Just line your pockets, a wink and a nod,
> And to hell with the poor! Their backs are broad.
> Alas for the plight of the underclass
> And the system's victims who seek redress:
> Their one recourse is the licensed robber
> With his legalese and his fancy slabber.
> Lawyers corrupt, their standards gone,
> Favourtism the way it's done,
> The bar disgraced, truth compromised,
> Nothing but kick-backs, bribes and lies.

For Ciaran Carson, to recover the Gaelic past is to re-view the sectarianism in the North through the lens of history. By deliberately injecting contemporary Northern-Irish diction into his translation of Merriman's 'Cúirt an Mheán-Oiche', Carson constructs bridges not only between past and present, between the Irish-language tradition and its English-language counterpart, but also between south and north, between Merriman's native Limerick and Carson's native Belfast, thereby working against divisive cultural stereotypes.

With some exceptions, Thomas Kinsella being the most important, contemporary verse translators have approached their sources, contemporary or historical, with a remarkable sense of creative freedom, very much part of the poetic environment in which they work. At times, this sense of liberty, in conjunction with the extraordinary range of distinctive voices and styles to be found among contemporary poets, runs the risk of displacing the original text rather than representing it. In Nuala Ní Dhomhnaill's collection *Pharaoh's Daughter*, published in 1990, her poems are accompanied by verse translations from no fewer than thirteen different contemporary Irish poets; in the end, Ní Dhomhnaill's own voice is often difficult to locate, and, read with a focus on the translations, the book threatens to become an anthology of contemporary poetry based on themes found in Ní Dhomhnaill, rather than a collection of Ní Dhomhnaill's poetry with translations.[22]

But this kind of free translation from one language into another has been going on a very long time in Ireland, at least as far back as the middle ages for translations into Irish,[23] and there is much to be said for it. Jonathan Swift's 'The Description of an *Irish Feast*' may have considerably more of Swift in it than of Aodh Mac Gabhráin, but it is a remarkable poem in any case; and only an extremely conservative view of translation would dismiss Mangan's 'Dark Rosaleen', or Hyde's 'My Grief on the Sea', or Clarke's 'Mabel Kelly', or Paul Muldoon's 'August' on the ground that they depart too freely from their sources. The truth is that over the course of three centuries, in translating poetry written in Irish into poetry written in English, poets in Ireland have managed far more than the resurrection of Irish-language poetry. They have in fact transformed one body of poetry into another body of poetry, one tied to the original but not too closely, dependent on it to some extent but also sufficiently independent of it to enable an extraordinary level of creative expression. One need only read through the poems in this anthology – and they are, first and foremost, poems– to see how verse translation from the Irish has enriched the tradition of writing in English in Ireland. 'A poet/translator, if he loves the original more than he loves himself,' Michael Hartnett has said, 'will get the poetry across.'[24] He will also, from time to time at least, produce that 'completely new, autonomous poem in English' described by Brendan Kennelly, a poem that would not exist were it not for the art of poetic translation.

Note on Irish-language texts and literal translations

In identifying sources for the poetic translations, every effort has been made to provide texts as close as possible to those from which the poets were presumably translating. At times the original is certain and readily available, but there are translations for which the only available version of the original seems unlikely to be what the poet had in front of him or her, or for which there are several different versions of the source to hand. In the latter instance, the version that seems closest to the poetic translation is quoted, and other versions are referred to in the endnote. For a few translations, it has not been possible to identify an original.

The originals are reprinted without editing or updating of spelling. There is, accordingly, considerable inconsistency, and some corruption, throughout the book in the Irish-language texts, but as the point of including the originals is to get as close as possible to the texts from which the poets were working, such inconsistency is inevitable, and might even be said to have its virtues.

The literal translations are intended to allow the reader unfamiliar with Irish to measure the distance between the originals and the poetic translations. I have tried to produce literal translations that come close to being word-for-word and line-for-line representations of the Irish, although it is, of course, impossible to translate a poem literally, especially one written in a language as different from English as is Irish. In the many situations in which a choice had to be made between accuracy with awkwardness or fluency with possible inaccuracy, accuracy with awkwardness was almost always chosen. Placenames and names of people have not been translated into English, except in the most obvious instances. Finally, although I bear full responsibility for the literal translations, I am indebted to the work of many earlier translators, especially those working with texts in Old and Middle Irish.

Abbreviations

AD	*An Duanaire: 1600–1900: Poems of the Dispossessed.* Ed. Seán Ó Tuama. Trans. Thomas Kinsella. Mountrath, Portlaoise: Dolmen Press, 1981.
CEÓL	*Ceól-Sídhe, I, II agus III.* Ed. Norman Borthwick. Dublin: Irish Book Company, 1912, 1913.
DÁNGRÁ	*Dánta Grádha: An Anthology of Irish Love Poetry.* Ed. Thomas F. O'Rahilly. Cork: Cork Univ. Press, 1925, 1926.
DG	*Duanaire Gaedhilge.* 3 vols. Ed. Róis Ní Ógáin. Baile Átha Cliath: Comhlacht Oideachais na h-Éireann, 1921.
FD	*The Field Day Anthology of Irish Writing.* 3 vols. Ed. Seamus Deane. Derry: Field Day, 1991.
FG	*Filidheacht na nGaedheal.* Ed. Pádraig Ó Carainn. Baile Átha Cliath: An Press Náisiúnta, 1942.
HYDE	*Abhráin Grádh Chúige Connacht: Love Songs of Connacht.* Ed. and trans. Douglas Hyde. London: T. Fisher Unwin; Dublin: Gill, 1893.
IM	*Irish Minstrelsy, or Bardic Remains of Ireland.* 2 vols. Ed. James Hardiman. London: Joseph Robins, 1831.
MURPHY	*Early Irish Lyrics: Eighth to Twelfth Century.* Ed. Gerard Murphy. 1956; Dublin: Four Courts Press, 1998.
ND-I	*Nua-Dhuanaire: Cuid I.* Eds. Pádraig de Brún, et. al. Baile Átha Cliath: Institiúid Ardléinn Bhaile Átha Cliath, 1971.
ND-II	*Nua-Dhuanaire: Cuid II.* Ed. Breandán Ó Buachalla. Baile Átha Cliath: Institiúid Ardléinn Bhaile Átha Cliath, 1976.
ND-III	*Nua-Dhuanaire: Cuid III.* Ed. Tomás Ó Concheanainn. Baile Átha Cliath: Institiúid Ardléinn Bhaile Átha Cliath, 1978.
NEESON	*Poems from the Irish.* Ed. Eoin Neeson. Cork: Mercier Press, 1967.
Ó-C	*Óir-Chiste: Duanaire Liricí do'n Aos Foghluma.* Ed. Séamus Ó hAodha. Baile Átha Cliath: Comhlucht Oideachais na hÉireann, 1922.
PPM	*The Poets and Poetry of Munster: A Selection of Irish Songs.* Ed. C.P. Meehan. Trans. James Clarence Mangan. Dublin: James Duffy, 1885; 1925.
SONGS	*Songs of the Irish.* Ed. and trans. Donal O'Sullivan. Dublin: Brown and Nolan, 1960.

Acknowledgements

I'm grateful to the Office of Research, the College of Liberal Arts, and the Department of English at the University of Mississippi for their generous support of this project in all its stages. I would also like to acknowledge the staffs of the Boole Library at University College Cork, the National Library of Ireland, and the University of Mississippi Library for their cooperation and assistance. I'm grateful to the following people for various kinds of help: Dermot Bolger, Greg Delanty, Peter Fallon, Tom Mac Intyre, Pauline O'Sullivan, and Kathleen Shields. Special thanks are due to Tom Dunne for his understanding and encouragement at a crucial moment in the development of this project, and to Máire Ní Shíocháin for her invaluable knowledge of the Irish language.

Midnight Court (Oldcastle, Co. Meath: Gallery Press, 2005). Reprinted by permission of Gallery Press and Wake Forest University Press.

Austin Clarke, 'The Scholar', 'The Blackbird of Derrycairn', 'Mabel Kelly', 'Peggy Browne', 'O'Rourke's Feast', from *Collected Poems* (Dublin: Dolmen Press, 1974). Reprinted by permission of R. Dardis Clarke, 17 Oscar Square, Dublin 8.

Michael Davitt, 'Luibh na bhFear Gonta', from *Freacnairc Mhearcair: The Oomph of Quicksilver: Rogha Dánta 1970-1998* (Cork: Cork University Press, 2000); 'An Scáthán' and 'Lunasa', from *Selected Poems/Rogha Dánta 1968-1984* (Dublin: Raven Arts Press, 1987); and 'I gClochar na Trócaire', from *The Bright Wave/An Tonn Gheal: Poetry in Irish Now*, ed. Dermot Bolger (Dublin: Raven Arts Press, 1986). Reprinted by permission of Moira Sweeney.

Seamus Deane, 'Why was I banished Cinaed, why', from *The Field Day Anthology of Irish Writing*, Vol. IV (Cork: Cork University Press, 2002). Reprinted by permission of the author.

Greg Delanty, 'Me', from *An Crann Faoi Bhláth: The Flowering Tree: Contemporary Irish Poetry with Verse Translations*, eds. Declan Kiberd and Gabriel Fitzmaurice (Dublin: Wolfhound, 1991). Reprinted by permission of Greg Delanty.

Peter Fallon, 'Inside Out', from *Pharaoh's Daughter*, by Nuala Ní Dhomhnaill (Oldcastle, Co. Meath: Gallery Press, 1990). Reprinted by permission of Gallery Press.

Gabriel Fitzmaurice, 'The Yellow Bittern' from *Poems I Wish I'd Written: Translations from the Irish* (Indreabhán: Cló Iar-Chonnachta, 1996); 'Just My Luck I'm Not Pig-Ignorant', from *Poems from the Irish: Collected Translations* (Cork: Merino, 2004). Copyright: 2004 Gabriel Fitzmaurice. Reprinted by kind permission of Mercier Press Ltd., Cork.

Robin Flower, 'The clear-voiced bell', from *The Irish Tradition* (Oxford: Clarendon Press, 1947). Reprinted by permission of The Lilliput Press.

Michael Hartnett, 'Pity the man who English lacks' and "A shrivelled-up skivvy . . .' from *O Bruadair* (Oldcastle, Co. Meath: Gallery Press, 1985). Reprinted by permission of Gallery Press. 'A sad and bitter story . . .', from *Haicéad* (Oldcastle, Co. Meath: Gallery Press, 1993). Reprinted by permission of Gallery Press. 'Annunciation', from Nuala Ní Dhomhnaill, *Selected Poems: Rogha Dánta* (Dublin: Raven Arts Press, 1986, 1988). Reprinted by permission of the Michael Hartnett Estate.

Seamus Heaney, 'Tonight the Snow is Cold', from *Sweeney Astray* (New York: Farrar Straus Giroux, 1984), by Seamus Heaney. Copyright © 1984 by Seamus Heaney. Reprinted by permission of Farrar, Straus, and Giroux, LLC; and by permission of Faber and Faber Ltd. Selection from *The Midnight Verdict* (Oldcastle: Co. Meath: Gallery Press, 1993), by Seamus Heaney. Reprinted by permission of Faber and Faber Ltd. 'Poet to Blacksmith', from *District and Circle* (New York: Farrar Straus Giroux, 2006), by Seamus Heaney. Copyright © 2006 by Seamus Heaney. Reprinted by permission of Farrar, Straus, and Giroux, LLC; and by permission of Faber and Faber.

Pearse Hutchinson, 'After Breaking My Own Foot in France', from *Done into English: Collected Translations* (Oldcastle, Co. Meath: Gallery Press, 2003). Reprinted by permission of Gallery Press.

Douglas Hyde, 'The Brow of Nefin', 'My Grief on the Sea', 'Ringleted Youth of My Love', 'My Love, Oh, She Is My Love', from *Abhráin Grádh Chúige Connacht: Love Songs of Connacht* (London: T. Fisher Unwin; Dublin: Gill, 1893); 'Bruadar and Smith and Glynn: A Curse' from *Abhráin Diadha Chúige Chonnacht: or The Religious Songs of Connacht*, Part I (Dublin: M. H. Gill, n.d. [1906]). Reprinted by permission of Douglas Sealy.

Brendan Kennelly, 'The Bell', from *A Drinking Cup: Poems from the Irish* (Dublin: Allen Figgis, 1970). Reprinted from *Familiar Strangers: New & Selected Poems 1960-2004* (Bloodaxe Books, 2004) by permission of Bloodaxe Books. 'The Wild Man and the Church', from *A Drinking Cup: Poems from the Irish* (Dublin: Allen Figgis, 1970). Reprinted by permission of Brendan Kennelly.

Thomas Kinsella, 'I Heard from a Decent Man the Other Day', 'Remember that Night', and 'Who Is That on My Grave?', from *An Duanaire: 1600-1900: Poems of the Dispossessed*, ed. Seán Ó Tuama (Mountrath, Portlaoise: Dolmen Press, 1981); 'Homage to John Millington Synge', from *The New Oxford Book of Irish Verse*, ed. Thomas Kinsella (Oxford: Oxford University Press, 1986). Reprinted by permission of Thomas Kinsella.

Michael Longley, 'Aubade', from *Pharaoh's Daughter*, by Nuala Ní Dhomhnaill (Oldcastle, Co. Meath: Gallery Press, 1990). Reprinted by permission of Gallery Press.

Donagh MacDonagh, 'The Day Set for Our Wedding' and 'A Hundred Men Think', from *The Hungry Grass* (London: Faber and Faber, 1947);

'The Jackeen's Lament for the Blaskets', from *A Warning to Conquerors* (Dublin: Dolmen Press, 1968). Reprinted by courtesy of the MacDonagh family.

Tom Mac Intyre, 'Cathleen' and 'On Sweet Killen Hill', from *Blood Relations: Versions of Gaelic Poems of the 17th and 18th Centuries* (Dublin: New Writers' Press, nd [1972]). Reprinted by permission of Tom Mac Intrye.

Medbh McGuckian, 'Nine Little Goats', from *Pharaoh's Daughter*, by Nuala Ní Dhomhnaill (Oldcastle, Co. Meath: Gallery Press, 1990). Reprinted by permission of Gallery Press. 'The Ebony Adonis', from *The Water Horse*, by Nuala Ní Dhomhnaill, trans. by Medbh McGuckian and Eiléan Ní Chuilleanáin (Oldcastle, Co. Meath: Gallery Press, 1999). Reprinted by permission of Gallery Press.

Máire Mhac an tSaoi, 'Black Eye-Brow', 'The Woman that I Loved the Most', and 'The Red-Haired Man Reproaches His Wife Who Has Left Him', from *Trasládáil* (Belfast: Lagan Press, 1997). Reprinted by permission of Máire Mhac an tSaoi.

Derek Mahon, 'The Race', from *Pharaoh's Daughter*, by Nuala Ní Dhomhnaill (Oldcastle, Co. Meath: Gallery Press, 1990). Reprinted by permission of Gallery Press. 'A Game of Cards', from *Harbour Lights* (Oldcastle, Co. Meath: Gallery Press, 2005). Reprinted by permission of Gallery Press.

John Montague, 'The son of the King of the Moy', from *The Book of Irish Verse: An Anthology of Irish Poetry from the Sixth Century to the Present* (New York: Macmillan, 1974). Reprinted from *Collected Poems*, by John Montague (Oldcastle, Co. Meath: Gallery Press, 1995; Winston-Salem, N.C.: Wake Forest University Press, 1995) by permission of Gallery Press and Wake Forest University Press. 'Sunset', from *The Great Cloak* (Dublin: Dolmen Press, 1978). Reprinted from *Collected Poems*, by John Montague (Oldcastle, Co. Meath: Gallery Press, 1995; Winston-Salem, N.C.: Wake Forest University Press, 1995) by permission of Gallery Press and Wake Forest University Press. 'Blodewedd', from *Pharaoh's Daughter*, by Nuala Ní Dhomhnaill (Oldcastle, Co. Meath: Gallery Press, 1990). Reprinted by permission of Gallery Press. 'St. John's Wort', from Michael Davitt, *Freacnairc Mhearcair: The Oomph of Quicksilver: Rogha Dánta 1970-1998* (Cork: Cork University Press, 2000). Reprinted by permission of John Montague.

Paul Muldoon, 'The Mirror', from *Quoof* (London: Faber and Faber, 1983); reprinted in *Poems 1968-1998*, by Paul Muldoon. Copyright ©

2001 by Paul Muldoon. Reprinted by permission of Farrar Straus, and Giroux, LLC; and by permission of Faber and Faber Ltd. 'August', from *Selected Poems/Rogha Dánta 1968-1884*, by Michael Davitt (Dublin: Raven Arts Press, 1987). Reprinted from *New Selected Poems 1968-1994*, by Paul Muldoon (London: Faber and Faber, 1996) by permission of Faber and Faber Ltd. 'The Black Train', from *The Astrakhan Cloak*, by Nuala Ní Dhomhnaill (Oldcastle, Co. Meath: Gallery Press, 1992; Winston-Salem, N.C.: Wake Forest University Press, 1993). Reprinted by permission of Gallery Press and Wake Forest University Press. 'Myself and Pangur', from *Hay* (London: Faber and Faber; New York: Farrar Straus Giroux, 1998). Copyright © 2001 by Paul Muldoon. Reprinted by permission of Farrar Straus, and Giroux, LLC; and by permission of Faber and Faber Ltd.

Eiléan Ní Chuilleanáin, 'You Are', from *The Water Horse*, by Nuala Ní Dhomhnaill, trans. by Medbh McGuckian and Eiléan Ní Chuilleanáin (Oldcastle, Co. Meath: Gallery Press, 1999). Reprinted by permission of Gallery Press. 'Kilcash', from *The Girl Who Married the Reindeer* (Oldcastle, Co. Meath: Gallery Press, 2001; Winston-Salem, N.C.: Wake Forest University Press, 2002). Reprinted by permission of Gallery Press and Wake Forest University Press.

Nuala Ní Dhomhnaill, 'An Casadh', 'An Rás', 'An Taobh Tuathail', 'An tSeanbhean Bhocht', 'Aubade', 'Blodewedd' from *Pharaoh's Daughter* (Oldcastle, Co. Meath: Gallery Press, 1990). Reprinted by permission of Gallery Press. 'An Prionsa Dubh' and 'Tusa' from *The Water Horse* (Oldcastle, Co. Meath: Gallery Press, 1999). Reprinted by permission of Gallery Press. 'An Traein Dubh' from *The Astrakhan Cloak* (Oldcastle, Co. Meath: Gallery Press, 1992; Winston-Salem, N.C.: Wake Forest University Press, 1993). Reprinted by permission of Gallery Press and Wake Forest University Press. 'Scéala', from *Selected Poems: Rogha Dánta*, trans. by Michael Hartnett (Dublin: Raven Arts Press, 1991). Reprinted by permission of Nuala Ní Dhomhnaill.

Flann O'Brien, 'Scel Lem Duib' and 'Domforcai Fidhbaidae Fál' (Copyright © Flann O'Brien). Reprinted by permission of A. M. Heath & Co Ltd.

Frank O'Connor, selection from 'The Lament for Art O'Leary', 'Fathers and Sons', selections from 'The Midnight Court', 'A Prayer for Recollection', from *Kings, Lords and Commons* (© Frank O'Connor 1959) are reproduced (territory: world excl. N. America) by permission of PFD (www.pfd.co.uk) on behalf of the Estate of Frank O'Connor; and by permission of The Jennifer Lyons Literary Agency, LLC, on behalf of Harriet O'Donovan Sheehy.

Sean O'Faolain, 'The Desire for Hermitage', 'Fand Yields Cuchulain to Emer', and 'The Cad', from *The Silver Branch: A Collection of the Best Old Irish Lyrics, Variously Translated* (New York: Viking, 1938). Copyright © Julia O'Faolain 1968. Reproduced by permission of the Estate of Sean O'Faolain, c/o Rogers, Coleridge & White Ltd., 20 Powis Mews, London W11 1JN.

Desmond O'Grady, 'Donnagha White', from *Off Licence* (Dublin: Dolmen Press, 1968). Reprinted by permission of Desmond O'Grady.

Gabriel Rosentstock, 'Think upon My Song of Love', from *Treasury of Irish Love Poems, Proverbs, and Triads* (New York: Hippocrene Books, 1998). Reprinted by permission of Hipppocrene Books.

Frank Sewell, 'For Isaac Rosenberg', from Cathal Ó Searcaigh, *Out in the Open* (Indreabhán: Cló Iar-Chonnachta, 1997). Reprinted by permission of Frank Sewell.

James Stephens, 'O woman full of wiliness!' 'Mary Ruane', 'Clann Cartie', 'Righteous Anger', and 'Skim-Milk' from *Reincarnations* (London: Macmillan, 1918). Reprinted by permission of the Society of Authors as the Literary Representative of the Estate of James Stephens.

Every effort has been made to trace copyright holders and secure permission to reprint. I would be grateful to hear from any copyright holder not acknowledged here.

The Eighteenth
Century

Original: 'Pléaráca na Ruarcach',   Literal translation:
        by Aodh Mac Gabhráin

Pléaráca na Ruarcach   The revelry of O'Rourke
    A ccuímhne an uile dhuine,   In the memory of every person,
Da ttiucaidh da bhfaicfeadh   Of those who will come, of those who would see,
    'S da ccluinfeadh go fóill.   And of those who would hear for a while.
Seacht bhfithchead muc,   Seven score pigs,
    Mart agus caora,   Bullocks and sheep,
Dá ccasgairt don ghasraidh,   Being slaughtered for the mob,
    Gach aon, ló,   Every single day,
Na céada pál uisge-beatha,   Hundreds of pails of whiskey,
    'Sna meadra dha líonadh,   And the wooden cups being filled,
Ag éirghe air maidin,   Rising in the morning
    Is againn a bhí an spóirt,   It is we who had the sport,
Do briseadh mo phiopasa,   My pipe was broken,
    Sladamh mo phócasa,   My pocket was robbed,
Guideadh mo bhrísdesi,   My breeches were stolen,
    Loisgeadh mo chlócasa.   My cloak was burnt.

Jonathan Swift
(1667–1745)

There are various theories as to how Swift, who had limited acquaintance with Irish, came to make this translation, first published in 1720. Most commentators agree that the original poem, 'Pléaráca na Ruarcach', was written by Aodh Mac Gabhráin (fl. 1715), a poet born in Co. Cavan and frequenting the circle of Irish-language scholars in Dublin centered around Tadhg Ó Neachtain. It's possible that Swift had some connections with this circle, and that Mac Gabhráin supplied him with a literal translation to work from.[1] Mac Gabhráin was also a friend of the poet and harper Turlough Carolan (1670-1738), and it has been suggested that Carolan set Mac Gabhráin's words to music, and that Swift, who knew and admired Carolan, came to the poem through him.[2] It has also been argued that Swift received significant assistance with the translation from at least one associate who had a stronger command of the Irish language than he had.[3] The original may describe a feast to mark the departure of the powerful Ulster chieftain O'Rourke for a visit to Queen Elizabeth. For other translations of 'Pléaráca na Ruarcach', see Charles Henry Wilson's version (pp. 35–39), published later in the eighteenth century, and Austin Clarke's twentieth-century translation (pp. 255–257).

'The Description of an *Irish-Feast*, translated almost literally
out of the Original *Irish*'

> O Rourk's noble Fare
> > Will ne'er be forgot.
> By those who were there,
> > Or those who were not.
> His Revels to keep,
> > We sup and we dine,
> On seven Score Sheep,
> > Fat Bullocks and Swine.
> *Usquebagh*[4] to our Feast
> > In Pails was brought up,
> An Hundred at least,
> > And a Madder[5] our Cup.
> O there is the Sport,
> > We rise with the Light,
> In disorderly Sort,
> > From snoring all Night.

3

Original: 'Pléaráca na Ruarcach' (cont.)	Literal translation (cont.):

Chaill me mo bhirréad,
  Mfallainn is mfilléad;
Ó dimigh na gairead,[a]
  Ar seacht mbeannacht leó,
Spreag air an cclairsigh sinn,
  Seinn an Pléaráca sin,
Prap dhuinn sgáird don digh sin:
  A, sí so, an chuirm chóir.
Lucht leanmhuna na Ruarcach
  Ag crathadh a ccleitighe,
Tra chuala siad turman,
  Is troipleasg a cheóil.
Gan aire air a ccoisreagadh,
  Ag éirghe as a leapacha;
Is a bhean féin ar leathlaimh
  Ag gach aon don chóip.
Budh láidir an seasamh,
  Don talamh, bhí fúthsa;
Gan réabadh le sodar
  Is glugar ann gach bróig.
Sláinte agus saoghal chugad
  A Mhaoileachluinn ui Aonagáin,
Dar mo laimh is maith adhamhsas tu,
  A Mhairsill ní Ghriodagain.
            . . .
Craith fúinn an tsráideóg sin,
  Leathnoigh oruinn an chátheóg sin,
An bugsa sin Aine is
  Graideóg[b] le na ól.
Athair na ngrása cé be,
  Chifeadh an ghasraidh,
Iar lionadh a ccroicne,
  Is ar lasadh san ól,
Bhi cnáimh-ruighead bachuird
  Ar fad ann gach sgín aca;
Ag stabadh 'sa gearradh
  Go leór, go leóir.
Céad aithshlisne darach air,
  Lasadh gabhail tríd na cheile;
Ag cnagadh, ag leagadh,
  Ag losgadh, 'sa doghadh,
A bhodaigh as é m'athairse,
  Chuir mainistir na Búille suas,
Sligeach is Gaillimh is

I lost my cap,
  My mantle and my fillet;
Since the friends left,
  Our seven blessings with them,
Urge on that harp,
  Play that Pléaráca,
Quick for us a squirt of that drink:
  Ah, this is the decent ale.
The refreshed people of O'Rourke,
  Shaking their feathers,
Once they heard the noise,
  And the clatter of music.
Without heed to their acts of blessing,
  Rising out of their beds;
And his own woman beside
  Every one of the gang.
Strong was the standing,
  For the ground, which was under them;
Without shattering with trotting
  And a squelching in of every shoe.
Health and life to you,
  Maoileachluinn ui Aonagáin,
By my hand it is well you dance,
  Mairsill ní Ghriodagain.
            . . .
Shake that pallet under us,
  Spread that rush mat on us,
That box, Áine, and
  A bowl for the drinking.
Father of grace, whoever
  Would see the mob,
After filling their skins,
  And burning with the drink.
A cubit of a carpenter's rule was
  The length in every knife they had;
Stabbing and cutting
  In plenty, in plenty.
A hundred strong oak slats there,
  Blazing, going confusedly;
Striking, knocking down,
  Scorching, and burning.
Lout, it is my father
  Founded the monastery of Boyle,
Sligo and Galway and

O how was I trick't,
    My Pipe it was broke,
My Pocket was pick't,
    I lost my new Cloak.
I'm rifled, quoth *Nell*,
    Of Mantle and Kercher,[6]
Why then fare them well,
    The De'el take the Searcher.
Come, Harper, strike up,
    But first by your Favour,
Boy, give us a Cup;
    Ay, this has some Savour:
O *Rourk*'s jolly Boys
    Ne'er dream't of the Matter,
Till rowz'd by the Noise,
    And musical Clatter,
They bounce from their Nest,
    No longer will tarry,
They rise ready drest,
    Without one *Ave Mary*.
They dance in a Round,
    Cutting Capers and Ramping,
A Mercy the Ground
    Did not burst with their stamping.
The Floor is all wet
    With Leaps and with Jumps,
While the Water and Sweat,
    Splish, splash in their Pumps.
Bless you late and early,
    Laughlin O Enagin,
By my Hand, you dance rarely,
    Margery Grinagin.
Bring Straw for our Bed,
    Shake it down to the Feet,
Then over us spread,
    The winnowing Sheet.
To show, I don't flinch,
    Fill the Bowl up again,
Then give us a Pinch
    Of your sneezing; *a Yean*.[7]
Good Lord, what a Sight,
    After all their good Cheer,
For People to fight
    In the Midst of their Beer:

Original: 'Pléaráca na Ruarcach'
(cont.)

Literal translation (cont.):

Carruig Dhrum-Rúsga fós.	Carrick-on-Shannon also.
Se Iarla Chilldara,	It is the earl of Kildare,
Agus biatach Mhuighnealta,	And victualler Moynalta,
Doil agus daltrom me,	Who reared and fostered me,
Fiosraidh do Mhóir.	Inquire of Mór.
Leagaidh an támad sin,	Lower that timber,
Búailidh an stráiméad sin	Strike that heavy blow,
Cick an sa tarr is	A kick in the belly and
Cuff an sa tsróin.[8]	A cuff on the nose.

---

[a] The literal translation assumes *caraid*, based on the textual variant *gcairead* in Ó Máille.
[b] The literal translation assumes *scálóg*, a textual variant in Ó Máille.

They rise from their Feast,
  And hot are their Brains,
A Cubit at least
  The Length of their Skeans.[9]
What Stabs and what Cuts,
  What clatt'ring of Sticks,
What Strokes on Guts,
  What Bastings and Kicks!
With Cudgels of Oak,
  Well harden'd in Flame,
An hundred Heads broke,
  An hundred struck lame.
You Churle, I'll maintain
  My Father built *Lusk*,[10]
The Castle of *Slain*,[11]
  And *Carrickdrumrusk*:[12]
The Earl of *Kildare*,[13]
  And *Moynalta*, his Brother,
As great as they are,
  I was nurs'd by their Mother.
Ask that of old *Madam*,
  She'll tell you who's who,
As far up as *Adam*,
  She knows it is true,
Come down with that Beam,
  If Cudgels are scarce,
A Blow on the Weam,
  Or a Kick on the A_se.[14]

Original: from *Foras Feasa ar Éirinn*, by Seathrún Céitinn	Literal translation:
Mil la mnaoi, leamhnacht la mac,	Honey with a woman, new milk with a child,
Biadh la fial, carna la cat,	Food with a ferret, flesh-meat with a cat,
Saor istigh agus faobhar,	A craftsman within and a sharp-edged instru-ment,
Aon la haon is ró-bhaoghal.[15]	One with one is too great a danger.

Dermot O'Connor
(fl. 1720)

Dermot O'Connor's translation of Geoffrey Keating's seventeenth-century compilation of fact and fantasy, *Foras Feasa ar Éirinn* (*The General History of Ireland*, as the title was translated by O'Connor) was as influential as it was controversial. By the time it was published, in 1723, O'Connor had drummed up more than 300 subscribers for the London edition and 400 for the Dublin edition, and the book went through at least twelve editions between 1723 and 1865.[16] Moreover, as it was the only available translation of Keating's work for nearly a century, it had a considerable effect on Irish literary culture for a long time. O'Connor described himself on the title page as 'Antiquary of the Kingdom of Ireland', and seems to have done considerable work in antiquarian research, often in the rather remunerative line of tracking family pedigrees. The accuracy of his translation, however, was questioned from the beginning – 'The grossest Imposition that has been ever yet obtruded on a learned age' was the judgment of one eighteenth-century Irish scholar[17] – although more recent readers have been kinder.[18]

Little is known about O'Connor's life. He was working as a scribe as early as 1712 in Limerick, and from 1719–1720 was in Dublin, where he became associated with the circle of Irish scribes centered on Seán and Tadhg Ó Neachtain. In 1720, O'Connor went to London, where he seems to have lived until his death (caused, according to one account, by syphilis), sometime after 1730.

'A girl, with honey by her plac'd'

(This poem about marital infidelity has to do with Partholanus, who supposedly arrived in Ireland 300 years after the flood. Told that his wife was being unfaithful to him, he confronts her, and her response takes the form of this verse.)

> A girl, with honey by her plac'd,
> Smells to the pot, and longs to taste;
> A child sweet milk will cry to eat;
> A cat will ne'er refuse her meat;
> A workman eagerly desires
> To use the tool his art requires;
> So man and woman, when alone,
> And the dull thing, a husband, gone,
> Will toy and trifle, till they prove
> The most endearing sweets of love.[19]

9

Original: from *Foras Feasa ar Éirinn*, by Seathrún Céitinn	Literal translation:
Gaedheal Glas cionnus do rádh	Gaedhael Glas, how was the naming
Ris in bhfear gcrithir gcomhlán?	Of the fearful, perfect man?
An ní ó bhfuil Gaedheal Glas,	The thing from which Gaedhael Glas is,
Is tearc ga bhfuil a sheanchas.	It is few who have its history.
Dar fhothruig ar an dtuinn dtréin	Being bathed in the strong wave
Gaedheal mac Niuil go ndeighmhéin;	Gaedheal son of Niul of sincerity;
Gur iadh an nathair 'n-a chneas,	The snake ate his skin,
Níor bh'furus é do leigheas.	It was not easy to heal.
An tí ghlas ní dheachaidh de	The grey spot did not go from him
Nó gur fhóir go maith Maoise;	Until Moses relieved it well;
Is eadh thuigid eolaigh as	The learned men understand from this
Gonadh de atá Gaedheal Glas.[20]	That it is from this that Gaedheal Glas is.

Original: from *Foras Feasa ar Éirinn*, by Seathrún Céitinn	Literal translation:
Deichneabhar cuibhreann an ríogh,	Ten persons the staff of the king,
Gan imreasain gan imshníomh;	Without controversy, without anxiety;
Eol damh a n-áireamh uile,	I know their number all,
Idir rígh is ró-dhuine.	Both king and noble.
Dleaghair i gcuibhreann ríogh raith,	Appointed to the staff of the king of grace are
Breitheamh is file is flaith;	A judge and a poet and a courtier;
An rí ag nach bia an tréidhe thall,	The king who does not have those three,
Ní dhligh Féine a eineaclann.	The landed freeholders do not owe their tribute to.
Anmchara ag foircheadal scéal,	A spiritual advisor for the instruction of doctrine,
Seancha leasuigheas gach léan;	A recorder who preserves every sorrow;
Oirfideach ré téadaibh thall	A musician with his strings also
Dlighidh íoc is eineaclann.	Payment and tribute are owed to.
Liaigh an ceathramhadh duine	A physician the fourth person
D'fhios ghalair gach aoin uile;	With knowledge of the diseases of everyone;
Triar friothólmha mbuidhneadh mbann	Three stewards attending a populous troop of soldiers
Sloinnfead do shluaghaibh Éireann.	I will tell of the hosts of Ireland.

'The hissing serpent, eager of his prey'

(This translation describes the naming of the prince Gadelas, or 'Gaodhal glas', from whom, Keating says, the Irish are called Clanna Gaodhal.)

> The hissing serpent, eager of his prey,
> Ascends the couch where sleeping Gadel lay;
> In winding mazes then himself he roll'd,
> And leap'd upon him in a dreadful fold,
> And shook his forked tongue, and then around
> His neck he twists, and gives a deadly wound;
> From his black gums he press'd the killing foam,
> And from his mouth the blasting vapours come.
> The subtle poison spreads through every vein,
> No art, no juice of herbs, can ease the pain,
> Till Moses, with his never-failing wand,
> Touch'd the raw wound, which heal'd at his command,
> But a green spot the tender skin distain'd.
> From hence the princely youth receiv'd his name,
> And was called Gaodhal glas.[21]

'Ten royal officers, for use and state'

(This translation describes the court of Irish kings.)

> Ten royal officers, for use and state,
> Attend the court, and on the monarch wait:
>   A nobleman, whose virtuous actions grace
> His blood, and add new glories to his race.
>   A judge, to fix the meaning of the laws,
> To save the poor, and right the injur'd cause.
>   A grave physician, by his artful care,
> To ease the sick, and weaken'd health repair.
>   A poet, to applaud and boldly blame,
> And justly to give infamy or fame;
> For without him the freshest laurels fade,
> And vice to dark oblivion is betray'd.
>   The next attendant was a faithful priest,
> Prophetic fury roll'd within his breast;
> Full of his god, he tells the distant doom
> Of kings unborn, and nations yet to come;
> Daily he worships at the holy shrine,
> And pacifies his gods with rites divine,
> With constant care the sacrifice renews,
> And anxiously the panting entrails views.

Original: from *Foras Feasa ar
Éirinn*, by Seathrún Céitinn (cont.)

Literal translation: (cont.)

An rí ag nach béidh sin uile
Ní dhligh i Réim Ríoghruidhe;
I dtigh Teamhra ní bhia a sheal,
An rí ag nach bia an deichneabhar.[22]

The king who will not have all those
Is not entitled to be in the Succession of Kings;
In the house of Tara shall not pass his time,
The king who does not have the ten.

To touch the harp, the sweet musician bends,
And both his hands upon the strings extends;
The sweetest sound flows from each warbling string,
Soft as the breeze of the breathing spring.
Music has the pow'r the passions to controul,
And tunes the harsh disorders of the soul.
          The antiquary, by his skill, reveals
The race of kings, and all their offspring tells,
The spreading branches of the royal line,
Traced out by him, in lasting records shine.
          Three officers in lower order stand,
And, when he dines in state, attend the king's command.[23]

Arthur Dawson
(1698–1755)

There is a story about how Arthur Dawson's 'Bumpers, 'Squire Jones' came to be written that raises some questions about its status as a translation. Dawson, an Anglo-Irishman of some distinction who attended Trinity College, and whose father built Dawson Street in Dublin, was visiting the house of one Squire Jones, in Moneyglass, Co. Antrim, sometime in the 1730s, along with the poet and harper Turlough Carolan. Carolan had retired to his room to compose a song in honour of his host. Dawson, whose room was next to Carolan's, apparently overheard Carolan at work, and turned up at breakfast the following morning with his own version of the song, complete with words in English, and, presumably as a joke, charging Carolan with piracy. According to one account, what Dawson heard in the next room was Carolan's melody along with words in English, which he then revised.[24] Other commentators, however, have suggested that the words that Dawson heard were in Irish.[25] The original text has not been identified; no poem in Tomás Ó Máille's edition of Carolan's poems corresponds to it.

'Bumpers, 'Squire Jones: Imitated from Carolan'

Ye Good-fellows all,
Who love to be told where there's claret good store,
Attend to the call
Of one who's ne'er frighted,
But greatly delighted,
With six bottles more:
Be sure you don't pass
The good house Money-Glass,
Which the jolly red god so peculiarly owns;
'Twill well suit your humour,
For pray what would you more,
Than mirth, with good claret, and bumpers, 'Squire Jones.

Ye lovers who pine
For lasses that oft prove as cruel as fair;
Who whimper and whine
For lillies and roses,
With eyes, lips, and noses,
Or tip of an ear:

15

Come hither, I'll show you,
How Phillis and Chloe,
No more shall occasion such sighs and such groans;
For what mortal so stupid
As not to quit Cupid,
When call'd by good claret, and bumpers, 'Squire Jones.

Ye poets who write,
And brag of your drinking fam'd Helicon's brook,
Though all you get by it
Is a dinner oft-times,
In reward of your rhimes
With Humphry the duke:
Learn Bacchus to follow
And quit your Apollo,
Forsake all the Muses, those senseless old crones:
Our jingling of glasses
Your rhiming surpasses,
When crown'd with good claret, and bumpers, 'Squire Jones.

Ye soldiers so stout,
With plenty of oaths, tho' no plenty of coin,
Who make such a rout
Of all your commanders
Who serv'd us in Flanders,
And eke at the Boyne:
Come leave off your rattling
Of sieging and battling,
And know you'd much better to sleep in whole bones;
Were you sent to Gibraltar,
Your notes you'd soon alter,
And wish for good claret, and bumpers, 'Squire Jones.

Ye clergy so wise,
Who myst'ries profound can demonstrate most clear,
How worthy to rise!
You preach once a week,
But your tithes never seek
Above once in a year:
Come here without failing,
And leave off your railing
'Gainst bishops providing for dull stupid drones;
Says the text so divine,
What is life without wine?
Then away with the claret, a bumper, 'Squire Jones.

Ye lawyers so just
Be the cause what it will, who so learnedly plead,
How worthy of trust!
You know black from white
Yet prefer wrong to right,
As you chance to be fee'd:
Leave musty reports,
And forsake the king's courts,
Where dulness and discord have set up their thrones;
Burn Salkeld and Ventris,[26]
With all your damn'd entries,
And away with the claret, a bumper, 'Squire Jones.

Ye physical tribe,
Whose knowledge consists in hard words and grimace,
Whene'er you prescribe
Have at your devotion,
Pills, bolus, or potion,
But what will the case:
Pray what is the need
To purge, blister, and bleed?
When ailing yourselves the whole faculty owns,
That the forms of old Galen[27]
Are not so prevailing
As mirth with good claret, and bumpers, 'Squire Jones.

Ye foxhunters eke,
That follow the call of the horn and the hound,
Who your ladies forsake,
Before they're awake
To beat up the brake
Where the vermin is found:
Leave Piper and Blueman,
Shrill Duchess and Trueman;
No music is found in such dissonant tones:
Would you ravish your ears
With the songs of the spheres,
Hark away to the claret, a bumper, 'Squire Jones.[28]

Original: from 'Teacht Conlaoich go hÉirinn'	Literal translation:
Mar chím airm an laoigh	Because I see the weapon of the warrior
Sgláth agus lann Chonlaoic	shield and blade of Conloch
is mar sin do bhímse ag caoi	it is because of that that I am mourning
mar fhear gan mhac gan mhnaoi.	as a man without a son, without a wife.
Is mé an tathair dho mharbh an mac	I am the father who killed the son
is nar chaitheadh mé crobh ná úrbhrat	and I did not throw out a hand or a new cloak
is mé an cnáimh nach fuil re forus	I am the bone that has no understanding
an dá láimh do bhí se lúath dhonus.	the two hands for which it was a frenzied misfortune.

Charlotte Brooke
(1740–1793)

The last of twenty-two children born to the prolific Anglo-Irish writer Henry Brooke, Charlotte Brooke first became interested in the Irish language, according to one account, when she heard a labourer in a field on the family estate in Co. Cavan read to an impromptu audience stories of Oisín and Cuchulain from some Irish-language manuscripts that he owned.[29] Inspired by the mid-eighteenth-century's fascination with things Celtic, a product in part of James Macpherson's popular but fraudulent translations of Oisín in the 1760s, Brooke published *Reliques of Irish Poetry* in 1789. Although the translations in this collection are very much the work of an English literary sensibility, the book constitutes a significant milestone in the history of verse translation from the Irish. For one thing, it was an extremely ambitious project, providing translations of a number of what Brooke called 'heroic poems', narrative poems from the Oisín tradition made popular by Macpherson, and various odes, elegies, and songs. Also, to give her work the scholarly authority neglected by Macpherson, she provided original Irish-language texts for her translations.

From 'Conloch'

(This poem tells the story of Cuchulain's killing of his son, Conloch. The selection here consists of Cuchulain's speech just after Conloch reveals his identity.)

> "Gone! – art thou gone? – O wretched eyes!
> See where my child! my murder'd Conloch lies!
> Lo! – in the dust his shield of conquest laid!
> And prostrate, now, his once victorious blade!
> O let me turn from the soul-torturing sight!
> O wretch! deserted and forlorn!
> With age's sharpest anguish torn! –
> Stript of each tender tie! each fond delight!
>
> "Cruel father! – cruel stroke! –
> See the heart of nature broke! –
> Yes, I have murder'd thee, my lovely child!
> Red with thy blood this fatal hand I view! –
> Oh, from the sight distraction will ensue,
> And grief will turn with tearless horror wild! –

19

Original: from 'Teacht Conlaoich
go hÉirinn' (cont.)

Literal translation (cont.):

Is mé an bárc ó thuinn go tuinn
is mé an long iar ndul da stiuir
is mé an tubhall a mbarr an chrainn
is beag do shaoilfeadh dhe do thuitim.[30]

I am the bark from wave to wave
I am the ship going back from its set direction
I am the apple in the top of the tree
it is little one would expect it to fall.

Original: from 'Thug me an
chuáirt 's bhaireach liom . . .

Literal translation

Thug me an chuáirt 's baireach liom,
  m'astar 's me air eis mo shúbhail,
air uáigh mo charad 's do mhearaigh
  sin radharc mo shúl
ni bhfuair me agum 's me falcadh na
  ndeor go húr,
ach cruadh leac dhaingean air leabaidh
  na créabh rochumhann.
Ní tréan mo labhairt 'se mheasom nach
  chúis náire,
aen bhocht sgaite me 's choilleas mo
  chúl báire,
nil pion, nil peanaid, nil galra co
  trom cráite,
le heug na ccarad, no sgaradh na
  ccompánach.
Mo leun! mo dheacair! mo mhilleadh!
  mo bhrón, 's mo chrádh!
mo cheol chrúit mhilis! mo bhinneas!
  mo shaidhbhrios dáin!
cia hoightheadh air dhuine bheith air
  buileadh, no bpein mar táim!
no déora fola do shileadh do dheigh
  gach lá.[31]

I visited, the morrow after going on my
  journey,
the grave of my friend and that view
  bewildered my eyes
I found nothing, and the tears washing me
  freely,
but a hard, strong rock on a bed of the clay of
  too much grief.
My speech is not strong, I think it is not a
  cause for shame,
one poor exposed person am I and I have lost
  my mainstay,
no pain, no torment, no disease as sad and
  agonizing
as the death of friends, or the separation of
  companions.
My woe, my hardship, my ruin, my sorrow,
  and my misery!
my sweet harp music, my sweetness, my
  riches of poetry!
what a tragedy is on a person to have on him
  madness or pain as I have!
or tears of blood dripping at the end of every
  day.

"Reason, – whither art thou fled? –
Art thou with my Conloch dead? –
Is this lost wretch no more thy care?
Not one kind ray to light my soul;
To free it from the black controul
    Of this deep, deep despair!

"As the lone skiff is toss'd from wave to wave,
    No pilot's hand to save!
Thus, thus my devious soul is borne!
Wild with my woes, I only live to mourn!

    "But all in death will shortly end,
And sorrow to the grave its victim send!
Yes, yes, I feel the near approach of peace,
    And misery soon will cease!
As the ripe fruit, at shady autumn's call,
Shakes to each blast, and trembles to its fall;
I wait the hour that shall afford me rest,
And lay, O earth! my sorrows in thy breast."[32]

'Elegy on the Death of Carolan'

(Brooke says the original was written by Charles McCabe, a friend of
the Irish poet and harper Turlough Carolan (1670–1738). McCabe had
not seen his friend for some time, and intending to pay him a visit,
passed by a churchyard on the way to Carolan's house, where he met
a peasant. When he asked after Carolan, the peasant pointed to
Carolan's grave and wept. In another version of the story, Carolan
wrote the poem after being tricked into believing that McCabe had
died during Carolan's absence.[33])

I came, with friendship's face, to glad my heart,
But sad, and sorrowful my steps depart!
In my friend's stead – a spot of earth was shown,
And on his grave my woe-struck eyes were thrown!
No more to their distracted sight remain'd,
But the cold clay that all they lov'd contained;
And there his last and narrow bed was made,
And the drear tomb-stone for its covering laid!

Alas! – for this my aged heart is wrung!
Grief choaks my voice, and trembles on my tongue.
Lonely and desolate, I mourn the dead,
The friend with whom my every comfort fled!
There is no anguish can with this compare!

Original: 'Duan Mharbhna a Mhna', by Toirdhealbhach Ó Cearbhalláin	Literal translation:
Inntleacht na Hereann, na Gréige 'sna Rómha,	The intellect of Ireland, of Greece, and of Rome,
Biodh uile a néinfheacht, a naen bheartin rómhamsa,	All being together in one small heap before me,
Ghlacfuinn mur fhéirin, tar an mhéidsin dona seoda,	I would take as a present, over and above that amount of jewels,
Máire on Eírne, as mé bheith dha pógadh.	Máire from the Erne, and me to be kissing her.
'Stursach tinn tréthlag, me féin gach tráth nóna	Tired, sick, weak I myself am every evening
'Sar maidin ag eirghe, mar d'ég uáim mo Nóchar	And in the morning rising, because my sweetheart died
Dha bhfaghainn anos tréda, 's gach saibhreas dár nósadh,	If I could have now herds and all the riches that will be told,
Ní ghlacfuinn do dhéidhse, aen bhean lé pósadh.	I would not take, on account of you, any woman for marrying.
Fúair mé seal in Erinn, go haerach, as go Sódhamhail,	I had a time in Ireland, lively and cheerful
Ag ól le gach trénfhear, bhí éfeachtach, ceolmhar,	Drinking with every strong man who was wise, musical,

No pains, diseases, suffering, or despair,
Like that I feel, while such a loss I mourn,
My heart's companion from its fondness torn!
Oh insupportable, distracting grief!
Woe, that through life, can never hope relief!
Sweet-singing harp! – thy melody is o'er!
Sweet friendship's voice! – I hear thy sound no more!
My bliss, – my wealth of poetry is fled.
And every joy, with him I lov'd, is dead!
Alas! what wonder, (while my heart drops blood
Upon the woes that drain its vital flood,)
If maddening grief no longer can be borne,
And frenzy fill the breast, with anguish torn![34]

'Carolan's Monody on the Death of Mary Mac Guire'

(This translation was not included in *Reliques of Irish Poetry*, but appeared three years earlier, in 1786, in an appendix on the life of Carolan in Joseph Walker's *Historical Memoirs of the Irish Bards*. Although Walker said he had been enjoined not to reveal the identity of the author, the translation has since been attributed to Brooke.[35] Walker said Carolan never recovered from the death of his wife, which occurred in 1733.)

Were mine the choice of intellectual fame,
        Of spelful song, and eloquence divine,
Painting's sweet power, Philosophy's pure flame,
        And Homer's lyre, and Ossian's harp were mine;
The splendid arts of Erin, Greece, and Rome,
        In MARY lost, would lose their wonted grace,
All wou'd I give to snatch her from the tomb,
        Again to fold her in my fond embrace.

Desponding, sick, exhausted with my grief,
        Awhile the founts of sorrow cease to flow,
In vain! – I rest not – sleep brings no relief; –
        Cheerless, companionless, I wake to woe.
Nor birth nor beauty shall again allure,
        Nor fortune win me to another Bride;
Alone I'll wander, and alone endure,
        Till death restore me to my dear-one's side.

Once every thought, and every scene was gay,
        Friends, mirth and music all my hours employ'd –
Now doom'd to mourn my last sad years away,
        My life a solitude! – my heart a void! –

Original: 'Duan Mharbhna a Mhna',   Literal translation (cont.):
by Toirdhealbhach Ó Cearbhalláin
(cont.)

Fágbhadh na dhéidhsin, leam féin me go   I was left after that by myself, sorrowful,
    brónach,
A ndeireadh mo shaeghail, 'sgan mo   At the end of my life, and my wife not being
    chéile bheth beo agom.   alive with me.

M'inntleacht mhaith aerach ní   My good lively intellect I am not
    fhedaim a cúmhdach,   able to keep,
M'intinn na dhéidhsin, is leir go bhfuil   My mind after that it is clear that it is
    smúiteach,   troubled,
Go deimhin ní fhedaim do dhéidh bheith   Indeed I am not able, on account of you, to be
    go súgach,   happy,
A Mhaire na cheille, an sa t'shaeghal bhí   Máire, wife, who in life was renowned.
    go cliúteach.[36]

Alas the change! – to change again no more!
       For every comfort is with MARY fled:
And ceaseless anguish shall her loss deplore,
       Till age and sorrow join me with the dead.

Adieu each gift of nature and of art,
       That erst adorn'd me in life's early prime! –
The cloudless temper, and the social heart,
       The soul ethereal and the flights sublime!
Thy loss, my MARY, chac'd them from my breast!
       Thy sweetness cheers, thy judgment aids no more: –
The muse deserts an heart with grief opprest –
       And lost is every joy that charm'd before.[37]

Original: from 'Cúirt an Mheán-Oíche', by Brian Merriman	Literal translation:
Is é chráigh mo chroí is do scaoil gan chéill me	It tormented my heart and left me without sense
Is d'fhág mo smaointe is m'intinn traochta,	And left my thoughts and my mind exhausted,
Tráite tinn mar taoim go tréithlag,	Dried up, sick as I am weakly feeble,
Cásmhar cloíte ag caoi is ag géarghol –	Pitiably subdued, lamenting and bitterly weeping –
An uair chím preabaire calma croíúil,	When I see a dashing, brave, cordial man
Fuadrach fearamhail baramhail bríomhar,	Bustling, manly, opinionated, vigorous,
Stuama feasamhach seasmhach saoithiúil,	Sensible, learned, steadfast, accomplished,
Gruadheas greannmhar geanamhail gnaíúil,	Pleasant-cheeked, humorous, loving, comely,
Nó buachaill bastalach beachanta bróigdheas,	Or a boy showy, vigorous, with a nicely shaped boot,
Cruacheart ceannasach ceapaithe córach –	Rightly hard, commanding, determined, shapely –
Buaite ceannaithe ceangailte pósta	Defeated, bought, bound, married
Ag fuaid, ag cailligh, ag aimid, nó ag óinmhid,	To a wretch, to a hag, to a witch, or to a simpleton,
Nó ag suairle[a] salach do chaile gan tionscal,	Or to a dirty churl of an old female without industry,
Stuacach stailiceach aithiseach stúncach,	Obstinate, starchy, shameful, prone to take offense,
Suaiteach sodalach foclach fáidhiúil,	Confusing, arrogant, verbose, prophetic,
Cuardach codlatach goirgeach gráiniúil.	Wandering, sleepy, irritable, hateful.
Mo chreach is mo lot, tá molt míb-héasach,	My ruin and my destruction, there is an impudent person,

Denis Woulfe
(fl.1789?)

Denis Woulfe was apparently a schoolmaster in the parish of Sixmilebridge, in Co. Clare. His vigorous translation of Brian Merriman's 'Cúirt an Mheán-Oíche' ('The Midnight Court'), was not published until 1880, when it appeared in an expurgated version, but Andrew Carpenter, relying on a manuscript note, has argued convincingly that the translation was done in 1789, within ten years of when the original was presumably composed.[38] Merriman's poem is a social satire constructed around a dream-vision in which a court is convened to entertain complaints of sexual frustration from Ireland's young women. For modern translations, see Percy Arland Ussher, pp. 237–241, and Frank O'Connor, pp. 277–285; for contemporary versions, see Seamus Heaney, pp. 347–351, and Ciaran Carson, pp. 387–393.)

From 'The Midnight Court'

(In this selection, a young woman makes her complaints to the court about the shortage of young Irish men willing to marry young Irish women.)

'My brain is racked my heart is torn
My mind relaxed and long forlorn
My wit decayed my fame declining
In sad extremes I am daily pining,
When prolific youth I view betrothed
To impotent fools profusily louthed
Frolicksome social jovial blades
All married to slothful moping maids.
A dashing sightly scion allured
Of handsome size and mind matured
Is often yoked in chains tis true
To wrinkled hag or cankered shrew
Or yet a greazy lazy load
Of fleshy frame or hateful toad
An overbearing beastly drone
To rash extremes from nature prone.
Oh galling news a stupid bride
Of legs obtuse and coarse grained hide
To night in state will married be
Oh hapless fate! not fancy me.

Original: from 'Cúirt an Mheán-Oíche', by Brian Merriman (cont.)	Literal translation (cont.):
Caile na gcos is folt gan réiteach,	An old female of feet and hair without tidiness,
Dá ceangal anocht 's é loisc go léir me	Being tied tonight and it scalding me entirely
Is ca bhfuil mo locht ná toifí réimpi?	And where is my fault that I would not be chosen before her?
Créad an t-abhar ná tabhairfí grá dhom	What is the reason that one would not give love to me
Is mé comh leabhair comh modhamhail, comh breá so?	And me so slender, so modest, so fine?
Is deas mo bhéal, mo dhéad 's mo gháire,	Nice is my mouth, my teeth and my laugh,
Is geal mo ghné is tá m'éadan tláith tais,	Bright is my appearance, and my forehead is mild, gentle,
Is glas mo shúil, tá m'urla scáinneach,	Green is my eye, my hair is in locks,
Bachallach búclach cúplach fáinneach,	Curled, ringleted, double-plaited, beautiful,
Mo leaca is mo ghnúis gan smúid gan smáchal,	My cheeks and my face without stain, without fault,
Tarringte cumtha lonrach scáfar,	Attractive, shapely, luminous, timid,
Mo phíob, mo bhráid, mo lámha 's mo mhéaraibh	My throat, my breast, my hands and my fingers
Ag síorbhreith barr na háille ó chéile.	Always competing for the height of beauty.
Féach mo chom, nach leabhair mo chnámha,	See my waist, are my bones not slender, I am not thin or stooped or stiff,
Níl me lom ná crom ná stágach,	
Seo toll is cosa agus colann nách nár liom	These buttocks and feet and body are not shameful to me
Is an togha go socair fá *cover* ná tráchtaim.	And the best at rest under cover I don't mention.
Ní suairle[b] caile ná sreangaire mná me,	I am not a churl of a hag or an ungainly woman
Acht stuaire cailce tá taitneamhach breá deas.	But a handsome, chalk-white woman who is pleasing, fine, nice,
Ní sraoill ná sluid ná luid gan fáscadh	Not a slattern, or a bad woman, or a slut without an embrace
Ná smíste duirc gan sult gan sásamh,	Or a boorish female without enjoyment, without satisfaction,
Lóiste lofa ná toice gan éifeacht	A decaying sluggard or a hussy without value,
Acht óigbhean scofa comh tofa is is féidir.[39]	But an eager young woman as choice as is possible.

---

[a] The literal translation assumes *samhairle*, as in Power.
[b] he literal translation assumes *samhairle*, as in Power.

Why not admire my size and gait
My skin so white, and smile so neat?
My teeth so fair of ivory hue
My smirking face compared by few
My hazel eye that brightly rolled
My neck designed in beauties mold
My symmetry in grand array
My dimpled cheek the rose display
My slender waist and graceful parts
No bent no bane no stain imparts.
My members all the laurels claim
With beauties still I will not name.
Count me not a cranky stake[40]
A drowsy gad[41] or rank old rake
A haughty hulk or humdrum hateful
Brawling butt or slut deceitful
Or sluggish ape devoid of glee
But the loveliest maid that eyes could see.[42]

Original: from 'Cúirt an Mheán-Oíche', by Brian Merriman	Literal translation:
Is feasach don taobh seo 'on tsaol mar bhí me	It is known to this side of the world how I was
Sealad dom réim 's dom laethaibh roimhe seo,	A period of my life and for my days before this,
Leitheadach láidir lán de shaibhreas,	Proud, strong, full of riches,
Eisteas le fáil is fáilte im theaghlach,	Accommodations available and a welcome in my household,
Caraid i gcúirt is cúnamh dlí agam	Friends in court and legal help for me
Ceannas is clú agus comhar na saoithe,	Authority and fame and the companionship of the learned,
Tathag im chaint is suim is éifeacht,	Substance in my speech and interest and importance,
Talamh is maoin ag suíomh mo chéille,	Land and wealth establishing my prudence,
M'aigne síoch is m'intinn sásta,	My spirit peaceful and my mind content,
Chailleas le mnaoi mo bhrí is mo shláinte.	I lost to a woman my strength and my health.
Ba taitneamhach leabhair an crobhaire mná í,	She was pleasing, slender, the strong, able woman
Bhí seasamh is com is cabhail is chámha aici,	She had poise and a waist and a body and bones,
Casadh 'na cúl go búclach trilseach,	A twist in her hair, ringleted, plaited
Lasadh 'na gnúis go lonrach soilseach,	A blush in her face, resplendent, luminous,
Cuma na hóighe uirthi is só ina gáire	The appearance of youth on her and joy in her laugh
Is cuireadh ina cló chum póige is fáilte.	And an invitation in her form for me of kisses and welcome.
Acht chreathas le fonn gan chonn gan chairde	But I shook with desire, without sense, without respite,
Ó bhaitheas go bonn go tabhartha i ngrá dhi.	From head to foot until taken in love by her.
Is dearbh gan dabhta ar domhan gur díoltas	It is certain without any doubt that it was vengeance,
Danartha donn, dom thabhairt ar m'aimhleas,	Extremely cruel, bringing me to my loss,
D'fhearthain go trom, ar bhonn mo ghníomhartha,	That rained heavily because of my deeds,
Ó fhlaitheas le fonn, do lom 'na líon me.	From heaven with zeal, that hauled me in its net.
Do snamanadh suíte snaidhm na cléire	Knotted, settled by the joining of the clergy
Is ceangladh sinn i gcuing re chéile.	And we were bound in a yoke together.
. . .	. . .
Mo dhíth gan easpa nár tachtadh le bia me	My loss without lack that I was not strangled with food
An oíche baisteadh nó as sin gur iarr me	The night I was baptized or from then till I tried

From 'The Midnight Court'

(In this selection, a man appears before the court, attacking the young woman who spoke earlier, and arguing that women, including his own wife, are deceitful.)

All around could now attest
The wealth and power I once possessed
My body straight and athletic
My acts proclaimed philanthropic
A friend in court my cause to plead
From Gentlefolks due honor paid
My words and wit with wisdom teemed
My land and store much more esteemed
My mind at ease in fair construction
Till woman sealed my souls destruction.
Her graceful form looked divine
Her waist so small and limbs so fine
Her golden hair in braids descending
Her comely face sun beams transcending
Her virgin bloom her courteous smile
Her looks demure ensured no guile.
My body shook from head to heel
Such ardent love I then did feel
Which hurried on so rapidly
That fate must plan my destiny
Such evils then did me beset
As made me rue blind Cupids net.
The nuptual knot was quickly tied
With mother church we soon complied

. . .

I wish I died in infancy
When daudled on my mothers knee
Before my bed had been defiled
And wit and wealth from me exiled.
From young and old I tidings got
Which proved my wife a drunken sot
Who tables rapped and draughts injected
And chastity esteemed rejected.
Her faults from proofs no longer doubted
But faults and proofs I scoffed and scouted,
It was feared by all in Evil hour
A naked elf unfelt I'd scour.
All in vain no tale I minded
My intellects so firmly blinded

Original: from 'Cúirt an Mheán-Oíche', by Brian Merriman (cont.)	Literal translation (cont.):
Síneadh ar leabain le ainnir do liath me	Stretching on a bed with a girl who turned me grey
Is scaoil le gealaigh gan charaid gan chiall me.	And let me go to madness without a friend, without sense.
Is é tásc do geobhainn ag óg 's ag aosta	It is a report that I would get from young and old
Gur breallán spóirt ag ól 's ag glaoch í	That she was a vessel for sport, drinking and shouting
I mbotháin ósta is boird dá bpléascadh,	In drinking shanties and banging their tables,
Ar lár 'na lóiste ag pósta is aonta.	On the floor a drone for married and single.
B'fhada dhá mheilt a teist 's a tuairisc,	It was long that her reputation and character were discussed,
B'fhada gur chreid me a bheag ná a mhuar dhe,	It was long before I believed little or much of it,
B'eaglach le gach beirt dá gcuala é	Fearful was every couple that heard it
Go rachainn im pheilt im gheilt gan tuairisc.	That I would go in my pelt in madness without a trace.
Fós ní ghéillfinn, caoch mar bhí me,	Still I would not yield, blind as I was,
Do ghlór gan éifeacht éinne mhaígh é,	To a voice without substance from anyone that declared it,
Acht magadh nó greim gan feidhm gan chéill	But a mockery or a morsel without use, without sense
Gur aithris a broinn dom deimhin gach scéil.	Until the example of her womb told me the truth of every story.
Níor chúrsaí leamhais ná durdam bréige é,	It was not matters of fun or chatter of falsehood,
Dúirt bean liom go ndúradh léithi é,	[Nor] a woman told me that it was told to her,
Acht labhair an bheart i gceart 's in éifeacht –	But the deed spoke truly and effectively
Bhronn sí mac i bhfad roimh ré orm.[43]	She presented a son to me long before time.

Until her size the truth revealed
No barefaced lie for me retailed.
No foolish whim or fib untrue
Or she told me as I told you
Before due time my wife so fair
To me consigned a son and heir.
Oh dire deceit when least expected
A fine young babe in haste ejected.[44]

Original: 'Pléaráca na Ruarcach', by Aodh Mac Gabhráin	Literal translation:
Pléaráca na Ruarcach	The revelry of O'Rourke
A ccuímhne auile dhuine,	In the memory of every person,
Da ttiucaidh da bhfaicfeadh	Of those who will come, of those who would see
'S da ccluinfeadh go fóill.	And of those who would hear for a while.
Seacht bhfithchead muc,	Seven score pigs,
Mart agus caora,	Bullocks and sheep,
Da ccascairt don ghasraidh,	Being slaughtered for the mob,
Gach aon, ló,	Every single day,
Na céada pál uisge-beatha,	Hundreds of pails of whiskey,
'S na meadra dha liónadh,	And the wooden cups being filled,
Ag éirghe air maidin,	Rising in the morning
Is againn a bhi an spóirt,	It is we who had the sport,

Charles Henry Wilson
(1757–1808)

Charles Henry Wilson's slender collection of five verse translations, *Select Irish Poems, Translated from the Irish*, may have been published as early as 1782, which would make Wilson the first translator of verse from the Irish to publish a collection.[45] Unlike Charlotte Brooke's *Reliques of Irish Poetry*, published in 1789, however, Wilson's book – and Wilson himself — seems to have received little notice. In 1786, Joseph Walker, the editor of *Historical Memoirs of the Irish Bards*, referred to him as 'a neglected genius, now struggling with adversity, in London',[46] and James Hardiman, writing in 1831, in his collection *Irish Minstrelsy*, referred to Wilson's translations as the work of 'a youth of promising genius, who afterwards repaired to the great theatre of Irish talent and Irish disappointment, London; where . . . he sunk, like most of his countrymen, unnoticed and unknown'.[47]

Wilson was born in Bailieborough, Co. Cavan, the son of a Church of Ireland clergyman, and studied law at Trinity College Dublin. At one point he seems to have been associated with the Brooke family, editing the papers, published in 1804, of Charlotte's father Henry. He left Ireland for London, possibly between 1782 and 1786, and seems to have lived the rest of his life there.

'The Feast of O'Rourke'

(The original of this translation, 'Pléaráca na Ruarcach', written by Aodh Mac Gabhráin [fl. 1715], was translated by Jonathan Swift in 1720 [see pp. 3–7]. Edward O'Reilly, in *A Chronological Account of Nearly Four Hundred Irish Writers*, published in 1820, said Wilson's version was a 'fuller and better translation' than Swift's.[48] For Austin Clarke's version, see pp. 255–257).

> O'Rourke's revel rout,
> Let no person forget;
> Who have been, who will be,
> Or never was yet.
> See seven score hogs
> In the morning we slay,
> With bullocks and sheep
> For the feasting each day:
> Hundred pails Usquebagh,[49]
> Drank in madders[50] like wort;
> In the morning we rise,
> And with us was the sport;

Original: 'Pléaráca na Ruarcach',
by Aodh Mac Gabhráin (cont.)

Literal translation (cont.):

Do briseadh mo phiopasa,	My pipe was broken,
Sladamh mo phócasa,	My pocket was robbed,
Guideadh mo bhrísdesi,	My breeches were stolen,
Loisgeadh mo chlócasa.	My cloak was burnt.
Caill me mo bhirréad,	I lost my cap,
Mfallainn is mfilleád;	My mantle and my fillet;
O dimigh na gairead,[a]	Since the friends left,
Ar sheacht mbeannacht leó,	Our seven blessings with them,
Spreag air ann cclairsigh sinn,	Urge on that harp,
Seinn an Pléaráca sin,	Play that Pléaráca,
Prap dhuinn sgáird don digh sin:	Quick for us a squirt of that drink:
A, sí so, an chuirm chóir.	Ah, this is the decent ale.
Lucht leanmhuna na Ruarcach	The refreshed people of O'Rourke
Ag crathadh a ccleitighe,	Shaking their coverings,
Tra chúala siad turman,	Once they heard a rumbling noise,
Is troipleásc a cheoil.	And the clatter of its music.
Gan aire air a ccoisreagadh,	Without heed to their acts of blessing,
Ag éirgha as a leapacha;	Rising out of their beds;
Is a bhean féin ar leathlaimh	And his own woman beside
Ag gach aon don choip.	Every one of the gang.
Budh láidir an seasamh,	Strong was the standing,
Don talamh, bhi fúthsa;	For the ground, which was under them;
Gan réabadh le sodar	Without shattering with trotting
Is glugar ann gach bróig.	And a squelching in it of every shoe.
Sláinte agus saoghal chugad	Health and life to you,
Mhaoileachluin uí Aonagáin,	Maoileachluin Ó Aonagáin,
Dar mo laimh is maith adhamhsas tu,	By my hand it is well you dance,
A Mhairsill ní Ghriodagain.	Mairsill ní Ghriodagain.
Súd ort a mhathair	Here's to you, mother
Go raibh maith agad, a Phadruig,	Thank you, Patrick,
Sgag thusa an sgála sin	Drain that bowl
Síos an do sgóig.	Down your throat.
Craith fúinn an tsráideóg sin,	Shake that pallet under us,
Leathnoigh oruinn an chátheóg sin,	Spread that rush mat on us,
An bugsa sin Áine is	That box, Áine, and
Graideóg[b] le na ól.	A bowl for the drinking.
Athair na ngrása cé be,	Father of grace, whoever
Chífeadh an ghasraidh,	Would see the mob,
Tar lionadh a ccroicne,	After filling their skins,
Is ar lasadh san ól,	And burning with the drink,
Bhí cnaimh-ruighead bachuird	A cubit of a carpenter's rule was
Ar far[c] ann gach sgín aca;	The length in every knife they had;
Ag stabadh 'sa gearradh	Stabbing and cutting
Go leor, go leoir.	In plenty, in plenty.

My breeches is stole,
My pipe it is broke;
My pocket is pick'd,
Where the devil's my cloak!
My kercher I've lost,
And my mantle's not on:
Sevn' blessings be with them,
My friends are all gone.
Come, strike up the harp,
Your music in haste;
A swill of your liquor,
How quiet the feast!
A shaking their feathers,
Just rous'd from their slumber;
By the noise of the harp,
And of feet without number:
The sons of O'Rourke,
Bounc'd up in a throng;
Each man with his woman,
And danc'd to the song;
'Till the ground shaking under,
Partook of their clogs,
Which as they quick trotted,
Glig'd, glug'd in their brogs.
Long life and good health
To you, Loughlin O'Enegan;
By my hand, you dance bravely,
Margery Grinigan.
Here's to you, dear mother,
I thank you dear Pat;
Pitch this down your throat,
I'm the better of that.
Come shake us down rushes,
An excellent bed;
And over us next
The winnow-cloth spread.
Dear Anna, more snuff
To keep me awake,
And a little to drink
As long as I speak.
Good heav'n! how strange,
What must people think;
After filling their skins
Thus to fight in their drink.
Such stabbing, such gashing,

Original: 'Pléaráca na Ruarcach',   Literal translation (cont.):
by Aodh Mac Gabhráin (cont.)

Céad aithshlisne darach air,	A hundred strong oak slats there,
Lasadh gabhail tríd na cheile;	Blazing, going confusedly
Ag cnagadh, ag leagadh,	Striking, knocking down,
A bhodaigh as é mathairse,	Lout, it is my father
Chuir mainistir na Búille suas,	Who founded the monastery of Boyle,
'Sligeach is Gailmhe is	Sligo and Galway and
Carruig Dhrum-Rúsga fós.	Carrick-on-Shannon also.
Se Iarla Chilldara,	It is the earl of Kildare,
Agus Biatach Mhuighnealta,	And Betagh of Moynalta,
Doil agus daltrom me	Who reared and fostered me
Fiosraidh do Mhóir.	Inquire of Mór.
Leagaidh an tamad sin,	Lower that timber,
Buailidh an stráméad sin,	Strike that heavy blow,
Cick an sa tárr is	A kick in the belly and
Cuff an sa tsróin.	A cuff on the nose.
Cia thoig an talarmsa?	Who raised this alarm?
Ar sa aon don eaglais,	Said one of the clergy,
Ag eirgidhe na sheasamh	Standing up
'Sa bagart go mór.	And threatening greatly.
Ni hi an spiredis choisriogtha,	It's not the consecrated aspergillum,
Bhi leis san racán;	That was with him in the riot;
Acht bata maith, cnapánach,	But a good, knobby stick,
Boglán dóirn.	Nearly the full of a fist.
Trath shaoil sé na caibhliorr[d]	For a time he let fly the bodies
A lasgadh 's do thiórail;	Lashing and knocking about,
Do faidgead an Sagart na mheall	Until they left the priest in a heap
Trasna faoi an mbórd.	Under the table.
Dirghe na braithre a thartail	The brothers rose up to defend
Na braoine sin;	Those misfortunes;
'S do faigead an tathar gardian,	And they left the guardian father
Ar athairr ansa graosacha.	On his belly in the ashes.
Nuair a bhi mise tall,	When I was overseas,
A glacadh na gradha,	Taking the orders
A bhfocair an phapa,	In the company of the pope,
Thall an sa Róimh.	Over there in Rome,
Se an *Seven Wise Masters*,	It is the *Seven Wise Masters*,
Bhi ar chluaisar a thar raige	That was heard above the noise
Is é[e] ag ithe bpotatuidh	While you were eating potatoes
Laimh le *Sheemór*.[51]	Close by *Sheemór*.

---

[a] The literal translation assumes *caraid*, based on a textual variant in Ó Máille.
[b] he literal translation assumes *scálóg*, a textual variant in Ó Máille.
[c] The literal translation assumes *fad*, as in Vallencey.
[d] The literal translation assumes *cabhail*, as in Harrison. It's also possible this is a phonetic rendering in Irish of cavaliers
[e] The literal translation assumes *is tú*, as in Harrison.

Such tugging and strife;
Half an arm at least
The length of each knife!
What whacking and cracking,
With cleftings of oak;
What sounding, rebounding,
A hundred heads broke!
My father he built
The mon'stry, you lusk;[52]
Of Boyle, Sligo, Galway,
With Carrickdrumrusk.[53]
Betagh of Moynalty,[54]
And the earl of Kildare,
I was nurs'd by their mother,
Ask that woman there.
Come down with that beam,
Defend that long whack;
A cuff in the nose,
Or a kick in the back.
Who rais'd this alarm?
Says one of the clergy;
A threatening severely,
Cease fight I charge ye.
A good knotted staff,
The full of his hand,
Instead of a spiradis[55]
Back'd his command;
So falling to thresh
Fast as he was able,
A trip and a box
Stretch'd him under the table;
Then rose a big fryar
To settle them straight,
But the back of the fire
Was quickly his fate;
From whence he cry'd out,
Do ye thus treat your pastors?
Ye, who scarcely were bred
To the *Seven Wise Masters*[56]:
That when with the Pope
I was getting my lore
Ye were roasting potatoes
Not far from *Sheemór*.[57]

Original: 'Aoimbo agus Umbo'	Literal translation:
Si mo chreach bean cheannaigh na féile,	She is my ruin, woman I bought at the festival,
Sa mhísge mhuírneach mo ghrad fein thu,	In cheerful drunkenness my love itself you are
Fada liom ataim dod éugmais;	It is a long time since I have been without you;
'S nach bhacaidh me ó namsa ne[a] thu,	And if I had not bothered with you since God's time,
Ni hiongnamh dhamsa bheadh go derach,	It would be no wonder if I were tearful,
Phós me gcion mo dha bliagn deug thu;	I married you at the end of my twelfth year;
'S nach deanna me riamh hartugear[b] chéile,	And I never changed, spouse,
Cionn mar beartha mo thoil fein damh:	Because you carried my will itself from me:
'S gus saol me nar sgarfainn go heg leat.	And I thought that I would not part from you until death.
Ni he so amháin maith da ndeanfa,	This is not the only good that you would do,
Trath gheabhadh clean[c] thu ar clár mur fheirin;	In every talkative time you are on the table like a present;
Shuibhalfain ana oidhche go haigean-teach éadrom,	I would walk in the evening cheerfully, lightly,
Is bhiadh steal chlabhar ár gach taebhd-hiomh;	And a quantity of mud was on every side of me;
An té bhios bocht ní tu sáidbhír;	Whoever was poor you made rich;
Is an té bhiadh bruideamhuil biadh se meinamhuil,	And whoever would be brutal, would be kind,
Sa té bhiadh cruáidh do ghluaisfeadh feile ann;	And whoever would be hard, generosity would move in him;
An té bhiadh fanntach an-amsgaith saeghalta;	Whoever would be miserly, very untidy, mundane;
Biadh sé greannmhuir fonnmhuir meadhrach.	He would be amiable, eager, merry.
'S maith amhuin tu dham, beadh tréigheach;	It is well you taught me to be talented;
Attengad mo mhathar 'san gach beárla;	My mother tongue is every language;
Anois fa raor ge taom gan énsmid;	Now alas although I am without a syllable,
Dinneósain far pairdad thredhibh;	I would tell about part of your accomplishments;
Is uaile thu no siol Ebha,	You are nobler than the seed of Ebha,
'S do bheartha buaidh air fhearibh éreand,	And you carried victory to the men of Ireland,
An té a bhios ciún do ní tu baeth dhe;	Whoever was quiet you made a fool of him;
Is óg arís an té is léithe	And young again the greyest person
Buaidh beag oile nach ennsighim fein ort;	Another small attribute I myself do not relate about you;
Ni fagn tu locht ar leabaidh no ar éadac,	You don't find fault with bed or clothing;
Ní fearr leat an doras no an gabhal eadain;	You don't prefer the door or the gable roof;
An trath deirgeadh amhac an dia an feusta,	When you came out the day of the feast
Luigh agus collin ba cuma ca ndéanamh,	Lying and sleeping it didn't matter what was being done;

'Aiombo and Umbo'

(The author of this paean to whiskey has not been identified. James
Hardiman said the poem was written in the latter part of the seven-
teenth century.[58])

A beauteous nymph distracts my brain,
The cause of all my joy and pain;
With breast transparent as the stream,
And dearest Whiskey is her name:
Ah! dearest Whiskey, still to me
The fairest nymph thou'lt ever be!
At twelve years old, I felt thy charms,
The very name my bosom warms;
Wed to thy sweets, I cannot rove,
And age thy beauties will improve.
Oh with thee blest beneath the shade,
In vain dull cares my breast invade;
When win'try storms would freeze my blood,
You add new vigour to the flood:
The purple flood that swells my veins,
Or else when summer cloathes the plains,
I seek the shelter of the shade,
Is blest with thee dear melting maid:
O never from my bosom part,
In thy soft durance hold my heart;
In vain without thee friends would smile,
And song the ling'ring hours beguile.
In vain the morn her sweets would shed,
And pleasure spread her downy bed;
In vain the rose her tints unfold,
Or lily spread her summer cold.
For thee what would I not endure?
Depriv'd of thee the rich are poor;
And who is poor of thee possest,
Thou dearest soother of the breast?
The covetous, once touch'd by thee,
Grow generous to the last degree;
The dumb thou cans't with words inspire,
The brave grow bolder from thy fire;
The song without thee now grows weak,
Transparent as the silver lake;
Oh quickly on the board appear,
And all my drooping spirits cheer.
Thy joys my ravish'd sense confound,
Soft leaping through thy christal mound;

Original: 'Aoimbo agus Umbo' (cont.)	Literal translation (cont.):
Bionann los feartainn is fas gan na néadan;	It was all the same to them the rain and it pressing on their faces;
Ni hiseoil aeréostar da ghaolta;	You are not low-born, deprived of relations;
Ni raibh mac deleacht[d] ó oechtar Éireann,	There was not a native son from the north of Ireland,
Nach raibh do ghaol leis trí na chéile;	That you were not related to thoroughly;
Siúr í Dhómnail agus siúr uí Néill thu,[59]	You are sister of the O'Donnell and sister of the O'Neill,
. . .	. . .
Is airde suas thu no cnoc na speire;	Higher up you are than a mountain of the sky;
'S mó go mo thu no cnoc greine,	And considerably greater you are than a mountain of the sun,
Is bhi tu isioll an lá na dheagh sin,	And you were low the day after that,
So fad thuarim is día dod réiteach,	In your opinion and God help you,
A lán sa chapan, is beidh me reidh leat.	A fullness in the cup, and I will make my peace with you.

An tabhráin	The Song
A mheisgeth reitheach,[e] bheasach, mhaiseach, shaimh,	Drunkenness accomplished, well-mannered, elegant, pleasant,
Is clisde thréinmhiur, mhaerdha measda a gcail;	And clever, strong, sprightly, esteemed in reputation;
Mise a cheile bheith maonar uasti lá	Myself, to be on my own away from her for a day
Is báos ceille is ceusugh buan andail.[60]	Is madness of mind, and the everlasting vexation of company.

---

^a The literal translation assumes *n-dé*, as in Hardiman.
^b The literal translation assumes *d'athrúghadh*, as in Hardiman.
^c The literal translation assumes *cách*, as in Hardiman.
^d The literal translation assumes *díleas*, as in Hardiman.
^e The literal translation assumes *thréigtheach*, as in Hardiman.

What nymph with thee say can compare?
Thy stream the ringlet of her hair;
Thy chrystal ray, what eye so bright?
Transparent azure ting'd with light;
The bed of stone you softly mould,
And shield the naked from the cold;
And lo, the generous race you boast!
How numerous! lo, a mighty host!
O'Domnaill, and the high *O'Neills*,
With all the great of Erin's vales;
Whether they boast the plume of war,
Or raise their voices at the bar;
By all endear'd, endear'd by all,
What millions at thy altar fall!

Versicle
How often on thy sweets I've hung,
Thy charms shall oft employ my tongue;
Still let thy sweets my verse employ,
Without thee, what is human joy![61]

Original: from 'Teagasc Flatha',
by Tadhg Mac Dáire Mac
Bruaideadha

Literal translation:

Mór a tá air thegasc flatha,
Aige tá techt degh-ratha;
Cuir ríghe an egar, mádh áil,
Legadh tíre no tógbháil.

Great is the instruction of a prince,
From him come good benefits;
To put the kingdom in order, if he desires,
To pull down or raise up the country.

Os do réir na neith do ní,
(Moíde is integaisc árdrí,)
Ticc lei no amhles an fhuinn,
Bés ní hanbhés a n-abruim.

Since it is according to the things he does,
(Solemn oath and fit doctrine of a high king,)
The misfortune of the end is possible;
Customs, not bad customs, I speak of.

Ticc do 'n rígh, rádh go ffiadhain,
Mádh é do ní nemhriaghail,
Cur cháich go léir tar a les,
N'í hé féin amháin mhilles.

The king is able – a saying with testimony –
If he misgoverns,
To put everyone beyond well-being,
It is not himself alone he ruins.

Teirce, daírse, díth ana,
Plágha, cogtha, conghala,
Dimbuaidh catha, gairbhshín, goid,
Tre anffír flatha fásoid.

Scarcity, slavery, deprivation there,
Plagues, wars, conflicts,
Defeat in battle, storm, plundering,
Through the falsehood of a ruined prince.

Theophilius O'Flanagan
(1764–1814)

Theophilis O'Flanagan was an important figure in the development of Irish antiquarianism at the end of the eighteenth century. He helped Joseph Walker and Charlotte Brooke with their work in translation, and in 1806, founded the Gaelic Society in Dublin. Two years later, *Transactions of the Gaelic Society of Dublin*, a compendium of a variety of Irish-language texts in prose and verse, with translations, was published. Although this book did not appear until 1808, most of the work in it was done during the last two decades of the eighteenth century. Only one of the verse translations in the collection was the work of O'Flanagan: a version of 'Teagasc Flatha' ('Advice to a Prince'), an ode composed in 1619 by Tadhg Mac Dáire Mac Bruaideadha, hereditary bard to Donough O'Brien, the fourth Earl of Thomond, to mark the earl's ascendancy. Mac Bruaideadha's ode counsels the earl, who took the English side in the Elizabethan wars, to adopt values associated with Gaelic kingship.

Born in Co. Clare, and a native Irish speaker, O'Flanagan was educated at Trinity College Dublin.

From 'Advice to a Prince'

How serious is the task, how vastly great,
To teach a prince his duty to the state!
'Tis his each blessing on the land to bring,
And, (what becomes a good and patriot king,)
To draw his glory from such order'd sway,
That all may love and chearfully obey: –
To raise his country to a prosp'rous height,
Or plunge it deep in dark, disastrous night!
Since by his deeds the state must rise or fall,
He should incline to hear th' advice of all; –
Nor wisdom's awful maxims dare to break,
Th' unerring rules of sacred truth I speak.
A king, as many a sage hath truly told,
If he his pow'r by tyranny uphold,
Must blast the public welfare and his own; –
He sacrifices not himself alone! –
Death, want, and famine, ghastly stalk around,
And rapine's voice is heard with horrid sound,
Plague, war and blood, disaster and defeat,

Original: from 'Teagasc Flatha', by Tadhg Mac Dáire Mac Bruaideadha (cont.)	Literal translation (cont.):
Ag lenmhuin rígh do 'n recht cháir,	A king following the law of honour
Ticc arís, (ríghdha an édáil,)	Makes possible again (a kingdom of riches)
Sgeith gach lántoraidh re a linn,	The overflowing of every full fruit in his time,
'S gach leith d' fántolaigh Fhéilim.	And everything more numerous in the sloping land of Féilim.

. . .

Molfaid grian laethe is glór én,	The sun of the days and the voice of birds will praise,
Molfaid úir, uisce is aiér,	Earth, water and air will praise,
Deghmholfa gach dúil fá nimh	Every part of nature under heaven will praise well,
Do shúil nemhdhocruidh, náraidh.	Your not-hateful, modest eye.
Biadh dord bech os bárraibh fedh,	There will be a drone of bees above the branches of the wood,
Biadh lúgh brec air fuid n-inbher,	There will be a movement of trout throughout the harbours,
Do chómholadh ag cur lem,	Making your praise with me
Is tromfhoghar n-damh n-dhílenn.	Are the heavy sounds of the reptiles of the sea.
Biadh an rí 'gá rádha ribh,	You will be the king by speaking,
Biadh an file 's an féinnidh,	You will be the poet and the hero,
Nach fuighthe, a rí, d'aen nech dh'ór,	One does not get, king, anyone of your gold,
Aen nech budh cuirthe ad chomhór.[62]	Anyone who would be set as your equal in gold.

The rage of elements, the crush of fate,
The bane of anarchy, – destructive train, –
Sprung from the monarch's crimes, assume th' imperial rein.
Not so the King, who rules with lawful sway,
No gloomy evil clouds his peaceful day! –
Abundance spreads her joys, with copious hand,
Throughout great Feilim's fair-inclining land.[63]

. . .

(The poem concludes with a prediction of what will happen 'if thou fulfil the purport of my lays'.)

The glorious sun shall spread thy praises round,
And feather'd songsters warble the sweet sound;
Each element beneath high Heav'n's expanse,
Earth, water, air, will in full choir advance,
To sing in strain sublime, that ne'er will die,
Thy beaming, sprightly, animated eye.
The hum of bees will murmur o'er the woods,
And sportive trouts will wanton thro' the floods,
And e'en the sea-calves their deep tones will raise,
At once with me to celebrate thy praise.
The king, the warrior, the poetic sage,
Who live to see the blessings of thine age,
Will praise thy name, thy great wise deeds avow,
And none thine equal, virtuous prince, allow.[64]

Original: from 'A Saerbhreathaigh Éachtaig', by Diarmaid Mac Seáin Bhuí Mac Cárthaigh

Literal translation:

A chladhaire an tarta 's a dhealbh mar ghósta,
Dá bhfionnadh na déithe baoghal dá shórt ort,
Is tréan do shéidfeadh réilteann cómet
Ag déanamh soluis i bhfochair gach cósta.

Rogue of drought and form like a ghost,
If the gods divined your kind of danger,
Most intensely star and comet would flame
Making light near every coast.

Do bheadh fraochnimh ar an spéir ag tóirnigh,
Is na réilte go léir as óirdin;
Do ghlaofadh go héigneach Tonn Tóime,
Is Tonn Chlíodhna do chaoifeadh go glórach.

A fury of piercing cold would be thundering in the sky,
And all the stars out of order;
Tonn Tóime would call violently,
And Tonn Clíodhna would lament clamourously.

Do bheadh an dá Mhuisire ag tuitim n-a óistibh,
Is Carraig an Truisc ag rith thar teórainn;

The two Musheras would be falling in coldness,
And Carraig an Truisc running over its border;

Loch Blárnann n-a thráigh gan deóir ann,
Nó, do bheadh in' fhuil go bhfios don chóige.

Loch Blarney a strand without a drop in it,
Or would be in blood as far as the province knows.

. . .

. . .

Do sceithfeadh Loch Léin tar Tóimibh,
Le méala do thaobh t'éaga 's nach beó sibh;
Is ann do glacadh chun tailimh ar dtóir sibh,
'S it bhéal binn an chéad chígh do deólais.

Loch Leane would overflow past Tóime,
With grief because of your death and you not alive;
It is there you were taken to ground in pursuit,
And in your sweet mouth the first pap that you sucked.

. . .

. . .

Micheál Óg Ó Longáin
(1667–1745)

Micheál Óg Ó Longáin was an Irish-language poet and scribe born into a learned family from Carrignavar, Co. Cork. Ó Longain is also the author of at least one translation from Irish verse into English, a version of an elegy on Lord Mount Cashel. The original is by Diarmaid mac Seáin Bhuí Mac Cárthaigh (1632-1705), the head of the school of Irish-language poets at Blarney, and the elegy is addressed to Justin Mac Carthy, Lord Mount Cashel, who died in 1694. The text of Ó Longáin's translation was said to have been found in a box in an unused chamber at the top of Carrignavar House, and was first published in 1882 in *The Journal of the Royal Historical and Archaeological Association of Ireland*. The first of the two selections below begins with an address to death, and the last, which concludes the translation, is addressed to Lord Mount Cashel himself.

From 'Mount Cashell's Elegy'

XVIII
Thou treacherous cur and bloodthirsty thief,
If the gods but knew your view for this chief,
Comets would blaze, enlightening every coast,
To avert the murder of old Erin's boast.

XIX
Rattling thunders roll and winds would blow,
Stars in disorder, rivers cease to flow,
Rocks would split, and waves would loudly roar,
And nature in confusion and uproar.

XX
Mushery Mountain[65] down in vallies brought,
And Kerry hills would sink themselves to nought,
The Lake of Blarney transformed into blood,
And the River Lee extend its awful flood.

XXI
Loch Lene[66] in woe o'erflow the county round,
And sweep the flocks from off the fertile ground.
'Twas there at first your vital breath you drew,
And there I first your manly presence knew.

. . .

Original: from 'A Saerbhreathaigh Éachtaig', by Diarmaid Mac Seáin Bhuí Mac Cárthaigh (cont.) | Literal translation (cont.):

Uaisle an chine do chuiris fá mhóircheart,

Nobles of the tribe that you put under great justice,

An fuigheall beag mhaireas den Charrathfhuil chródha;

The small remnant that survived of the brave Carrathfhuil;

Do bhráithre foirtille fola agus feóla,

Your brothers of strength of blood and of flesh,

Táid trét chumhadhsa brúidhte breoidhte.

They are through sorrow for you crushed, ailing.

Sé an treas truagh sin uaill na n-óigfear

That wretched file is group of young men

Do lean tú féin i gcéin tar bóchna,

That followed yourself far across the sea,

'S do lean go doimhin tú i bhfeidhm gach mórchath,

And indeed followed you in service in every great war,

Ní mhairfid tar th'éis táid créachtach crólag.

They will not live after you, they are wounded, disheartened.

. . .

Mo mhuclac laoch de tréanfhuil Eoghain,

My party of warriors of the warrior-blood of Eoghan,

Do cuiris i bhfolach is maide ar a ndoirsibh;

That you maintained, a bar is on their doors;

Dá gcaoi níos fuide ní furasa dhamhsa –

Mourning for them longer is not easy for me –

Is mithid dam codladh, do ghoileas mo dhóithin.[67]

It is time for me to sleep, I cried enough.

LII

Your loving friends and loving kinsmen dear,
The remnant still of them existing here,
Their trees are withered and their fruit grown old,
Since stript of you, their shield and Hector bold.

LIII

In pity, too, our countrymen abroad,
Their lives to them I think not worth a groat,
Who in following thee impending death despised,
And fought with valour the battles you prescribed.

LIV

My band of heroes, Heber's royal race,[68]
Tho' now laid up, they merit no disgrace.
I cry'd enough, of that I now shall cease,
Their souls may rest in sweet eternal peace.[69]

Mary Balfour
(1780–1819)

Although Mary Balfour's verse translations from the Irish were published at the beginning of the nineteenth century, her work in this vein is closer in form and style to eighteenth-century translation from the Irish than it is to the more romantic translations of poets like J.J. Callanan and James Clarence Mangan. Balfour contributed eight translations to the second edition of Edward Bunting's *A General Collection of the Ancient Music of Ireland*, published in 1809. They were written specifically for some of Bunting's airs, and each is accompanied by a note saying the poem was based on a literal translation from the Irish, presumably made by someone else.

Balfour was the daughter of a Church of Ireland rector in Derry, and worked as headmistress of a school in Belfast.

'Adieu! My Native Wilds, Adieu!'

(This translation, included in Bunting's collection, is accompanied by a musical score entitled 'Ulican Dubh Oh. – The Song of Sorrow'. No source for the translation has been found.)

>Adieu! my native wilds, adieu!
>>In Spring's green robe array'd,
>Where days of bliss like moments flew
>>Beneath the woodland shade.
>Now banish'd from sweet Erin's shore,
>>O'er trackless seas forlorn I go,
>In distant climates to deplore
>>My Ulican dubh, Oh![70]

>Our flame from every eye to hide
>>With anxious care we strove,
>For stately was her father's pride,
>>And I had nought but love.
>Oh! woe is me in evil hour
>>That secret love he came to know,
>And I must fly to shun his power,
>>My Ulican dubh, Oh!

Oh! how shall I resolve to part
  Our well known tree beneath!
Oh! how controul my bursting heart,
  A last farewell to breathe!
And oft, though far remote we dwell,
  And boundless floods between us flow,
I'll muse upon our last farewell,
  My Ulican dubh, Oh![71]

The Nineteenth Century

Original: 'Cuimhniughadh Mheic Liaig air Bhrian Boroimhe'	Literal translation:

Fada bheith gan aoíbhneas,
    Mar ná'r shaoíleas go bráth bheith; –
    Mar do bhádhus i g-Ceann-choradh chaoímh,
    Nior bh'uamhan liom aon do'm chreich.
	Long to be without pleasure,
	    As I never expected to be; –
	    When I sank deeply into lovely Kincora,
	    I did not fear any ruin for me.

Dá maireadh Brian Bheinne-builg!
    A's Murchadh a luirg na long!
    Ní bhéidhinn-si a n-Inse an Ghaíll-duibh,
    Mar a tt'ionnsaigh tuile a's tonn.
	If Brian of the courteous company were living!
	    And Murchadh who followed the ships!
	    I would not be in the Island of the dark Foreigner,
	    As flood and wave advanced.

Dá maireadh Conaing na g-cuan!
    Ormhuill sluagh, laoch ná'r lag!
    Fear mar é Eachtóir na sluagh,
    Ní léigfeadh mé uaidh a bh-fad.
	If Conaing of the harbours were living,
	    Great head of the host, warrior not weak!
	    He a man like Hector of the hosts,
	    I would not let myself be away from him for long.

Do bheir me duilbhir, doirbh,
    Nocha g-cluinim tairm na d-triath,
    Níor bh'ionann a's an siúbhal fuair,
    Dá ráinigh air cuairt go Cian.
	I am gloomy, depressed,
	    I do not hear the fame of the chiefs,
	    It was not the same and the going cold,
	    As coming on a visit to Cian.

Do chuadhas go Cian an Chairnn,
    Níor thriath gan tairm an tír theann,
 	
    Ní raibh, acht Brian na m-brat sróil,
 	
    Triath budh choir do chur 'n a cheann.[1]
	I went to Cian of the Cairn,
	    There was not a chief without fame in the strong land,
	    There was not, but Brian of the satin mantle,
	    The King that it was right to put as the head.

William Hamilton Drummond
(1778–1865)

William Hamilton Drummond was a Northern-born Protestant who gave his life to the study of Ireland's Gaelic culture. After being ordained a minister in 1800, Drummond settled in Dublin, where he became a prolific writer and translator. His extensive collection of verse translations from Oisín, *Ancient Irish Minstrelsy* (1852), is marred by the same kind of romantic artificiality that characterizes the more famous version of Oisín's lays published in the 1760s by the Scotsman James Macpherson, but in a few of the translations that he did for James Hardiman's *Irish Minstrelsy* (1831), Drummond occasionally found material appropriate to his sober poetic sensibility.

'Mac Liag, in Exile, Remembers Brian'

(Hardiman said the original of this lament for the defeat of Brian Ború at the Battle of Clontarf in 1014 was written by Brian Ború's chief poet Mac Liag, although modern scholarship suggests the poem may have been composed in the fourteenth century, and that Mac Liag may have been a literary creation rather than an actual person.)

> Tedious and sad lag on the joyous hours,
>> Ah! ne'er did fancy bode a change so dire!
> What time I dwelt in sweet Kincora's bowers,[2]
>> I little feared the barbarous spoiler's ire.
>
> Had Brian lived, munificent and good;
>> Or Morrogh,[3] in his stately mansions fair;
> Ne'er in the isle of strangers black and rude,[4]
>> Whelmed had I sunk beneath a flood of care.
>
> If Conaing[5] lived, the guardian of our coasts,
>> The chief of thousands, hero great in might
> As dauntless Hector, of the Trojan hosts;
>> Long had I ne'er been exiled from his sight.
>
> Grief and despair my anxious bosom fill,
>> To hear my prince's joyous voice no more;
> Oh! how unlike this journey drear and chill,
>> Was that to Cian,[6] in the days of yore!
>
> To Cian of the Cairn – to Cian, high
>> In wealth and power, I went with bounding speed:
> With him could none but royal Brian vie,
>> In every generous thought and glorious deed.[7]

Original: from 'A h-Uiscídhe Chroídhe na n-Anmann'	Literal translation:

A h-Uiscídhe chroídhe na n-anmann,
    Leagann tú air lár me,
Bídhim gan chéill gan aithne,
    'S é an t-eachrann do b'fheárr liom;
Bídheann mo chóta stracaidhthe,
    Agus cailim leat mo charabhat,
A's bíodh a n-deárnais maithmhe leat,
    Acht teangmhaidh liom a márach.

Whiskey, heart of the soul,
    You lay me on the ground,
I am without sense, without recognition,
    It is the confusion that I'd prefer;
My coat is torn,
    And I lose to you my cravat,
And I am forgiving you,
    Only meet me tomorrow.

An uiair éisdfidh tusa an t-aithfrionn,
    A's bheidh do shailm ráidhte,
Déin-si ionad-coinge liom,
    A's teangmhaidh liom a d-tigh an tábhairne;
Nar a bhfeicir cáirt a's cnagaire,
    A's coc a d-tóin an bharraile,
A's bíodh an iár anaice leat,
    A's rómhat-sa cuirfead fáilte.

When you will hear the mass,
    And your psalms will be said,
Make a rendezvous with me,
    And meet me in the public-house;
Where you will see a quart and a noggin,
    And a cock in the bottom of the barrel,
And the jar will be next to you,
    And I will put a welcome before you.

Och! mo stór agus mo chara tú,
    Mo shiúr agus mo bhráthair,
Mo chúirt, mo thigh, my thalamh tú,
    Mo chruach agus mo stáca,
Mo threabhadh, mo chéuchd, mo chapaill tú,
    Mo bha 's mo chaoíre geala tú,
A's thar gach nídh d'ár arimnígheas

    Do chongbhaidh me-si Páirt leat.

Oh, you are my treasure and my friend,
    My sister and my brother,
You are my court, my house, my land,
    My rick and my stack,
You are my husbandry, my plough, my horses,
    You are my cows and my white sheep,
And over and above everything which I counted
    I kept a portion for you.

John D'Alton
(1792–1867)

John D'Alton is arguably the most accomplished of the five transla-
tors who contributed to James Hardiman's *Irish Minstrelsy* (1831).
Born in Bessville, Co. Westmeath, and educated at Trinity College
Dublin, D'Alton was primarily known for his work as an historian.

'Why, Liquor of Life!'

(Such paeans to whiskey are fairly common in the Irish-language tra-
dition; see pp. 41–43 for Charles Wilson's eighteenth-century
translation of another one, and pp. 81–83 for one translated by
Matthew Graham in the nineteenth century.)

The Bard addresses Whiskey.
>   Why, liquor of life! do I love you so,
>   When in all our encounters you lay me low?
>   More stupid and senseless I every day grow,
>   What a hint – If I'd mend by the warning!
>   Tattered and torn you've left my coat,
>   I've not a cravat – to save my throat,
>   Yet I pardon you all, my sparkling doat!
>   If you'll cheer me again in the morning.

Whiskey replies.
>   When you've heard prayers on Sunday next,
>   With a sermon beside, or at least – the text,
>   Come down to the alehouse – however you're vexed,
>   And though thousands of cares assault you:
>   You'll find tippling there – till morals mend,
>   A cock shall be placed in the barrel's end,
>   The jar shall be near you, and I'll be your friend,
>   And give you a *"Kead mille faulte!"*[8]

The Bard resumes his address.
>   You're my soul, and my treasure, without and within,
>   My sister and cousin, and all my kin;
>   'Tis unlucky to wed such a prodigal sin, –
>   But all other enjoyment is vain, love!
>   My barley-ricks all turn to you, –
>   My tillage – my plough – and my horses too, –
>   My cows and my sheep they have – bid me adieu,
>   I care not while you remain, love!

Original: from 'A h-Uiscídhe Chroídhe na n-Anmann' (cont.)

Literal translation (cont.):

'S a mhurnín mhuinte, mhasgalaich,
  Is taithneamhach do Phóg liom,
Ná diúltuigh fós do'm charthannacht,
  A's gur de'n chineadh chóir me:
Leanán-ríghe leam Gin a's Rum,
  Bráthair gaoíl damh braén de'n t-sult,
Is cáirdeas-Críost damh boul of Punch,
  A's teangmhaidh liom d'á thóruíd hecht.

And well-mannered, vigorous darling,
  Your kiss pleases me,
Don't still refuse my friendship,
  And I being of the proper descent:
Royal lovers to me are Gin and Rum,
  A blood brother to me a drop of the pleasure,
And a godparent to me a bowl of Punch,
  And meet me to pursue them.

Is iomdha bruíghin a's eachrann
  Bhíd eadrainn le ráithe,
Acht ní fhanann brón am aigne,
  'N-uair líontar chúcam air clár tú:
Mo bhean agus mo leanbh tu,
  Mo mháthair agus m'athair tu,
Mo chóta-mór 's mo Napper tu,
  'S ní sgarrfaidh mé go bráth leat.

Many a strife and quarreling
  Were between us for a season,
But sorrow does not stay in my mind,
  When you are poured for me at table:
You are my wife and my child,
  You are my mother and my father,
You are my great-coat and my Napper,
  And I will never part from you.

Táid na gaolta is fearra agam
  Dá bh-fuil a d-talamh Eirean,
Leann a's brannda, a's uisce-beatha,
  Acht nach d-tagann an cláraéitt liom;
Bronnaim súd do'n n-Eagluis,
  Mar is mór mo dhúil 's a' m-bean-duightheacht,
'S gur mhaith leó braén do bhlaiseadh dhe,
  D' éis aithfrinn do léughadh dhúinn.[9]

I have the best relations
  Of those who are in the land of Ireland,
Ale and brandy, and whiskey,
  But the claret does not come with me;
I give that to the Church,
  As great is my desire for a blessing,
And they would like a drop of a taste of it,
  After saying masses for us.

Original: 'Cearbhall O'Dala agus an Macala', by Cearbhall Ó Dálaigh

Literal translation:

Cearbhall. – A Mhac-ala dheas,
  O's duit is feas a lán,
Cread, a glóraich ghrínn,
  Do bheir sinn d'ár g-crádh? –
  Macala – Grádh.

Cearbhall. – Kind echo,
  Since it is you [who] knows a lot,
What, perceptive voice,
  Brought us our torment?
  Echo – Love.

C. – Grádh! ní h-eadh d'ar n-dóich,
  Aithnidh dhamh-sa an gean,
Mo chéudfadh do chlódhaigh,
  Uch! d'ar n-dóich ní h-eadh! –
  M. – Ní h-eadh.

C. – Love! it is not that indeed,
  I am acquainted with love,
  My understanding of destruction,
  Ah, indeed it is not!
  E. – It is not.

Come, vein of my heart! then come in haste,
You're like Ambrosia, my liquor and feast,
My forefathers all had the very same taste –
      For the genuine dew of the mountain.
Oh, Usquebaugh![10] – I love its kiss! –
My guardian spirit I think it is,
Had my christening bowl been filled with this,
      I'd have swallowed it – were it a fountain.

Many's the quarrel and fight we've had,
And many a time you made me mad,
But while I've a heart – it can never be sad,
      When you smile at me full on the table:
Surely you are my wife and brother –
My only child – my father and mother –
My outside coat – I have no other!
      Oh, I'll stand by you – while I am able.

If family pride can aught avail,
I've the sprightliest kin of all the Gael –
Brandy and Usquebaugh, and ale!
      But claret untasted may pass us.
To clash with the clergy were sore amiss,
So for righteousness' sake I leave them this,
For claret the gownmen's comfort is,
      When they've saved us with matins and masses.[11]

'Carroll O'Daly and Echo'

(The original, believed to be one of the first echo poems in Irish writing, was composed by Cearbhall Ó Dálaigh [fl. 1620]. The form can be found in Irish poetry in English, in Yeats's 'Man and the Echo', for example, and Austin Clarke's 'The Echo at Coole', which contains a reference to Ó Dálaigh.)

Speak, playful echo, speak me well,
      For thou know'st all our care;
Thou sweet responding sybil, tell,
      Who works this strange affair? –
          Echo – A – fair!

A fair – no, no, I've felt the pain,
      That but from love can flow;
And never can my heart again
      That magic thraldom know. –
          Echo – No.

Original: 'Cearbhall O'Dala agus an Macala', by Cearbhall Ó Dálaigh (cont.)	Literal translation (cont.):

C. – Muna b'éad a tá,
    Do thuathaibh Dé rinne crádh,
    Liaigheas a n-dán damh,
    Innis damh ma tá? –
    M. – A tá.

C. – Unless it were envy,
    That made misery for the people of God,
    A remedy in store for me,
    Tell me if there is?
    E. – There is.

C. – A shíogaídhe ghlic, ghrínn,
    Friotal línn go réidh,
    Cread is liaigheas damh?
    Níor fhionnas ort bréag. –
    M. – Éag.

C. – Clever, perceptive fairy,
    A speech for us freely,
    What is a remedy for me?
    I did not discover a lie on you. –
    E. – Death.

C. – Má's é an t-éag, go deimhin,
    Is foirchionn tíre ár b-pian,
    Do dhruideamh liom,
    Do'b ait liom, dar fiadh! –
    M. – Dar fiadh!

C. – If it is death, indeed,
    It is the limit of the land of our pain,
    Approaching me,
    It would be strange for me, by heaven!
    E. – By heaven!

C. – Dar fiadh féin do'b ait!
    A ghlach ghlan gan ghó;
    Gidheadh, air do bhás!
    Ná cluineadh Cáit so. –
    M. – Cád so?

C. – By heaven itself, it would be strange!
    Pure hand without deceit;
    However, on your death!
    Let Kate not hear this.
    E. – What is this?

C. – Cad so, an diabhal ort!
    A thrúigh ná'r loc bréag!
    Fáth do mhagaidh ná can,
    Faoí Cháit is geal déad.
    M. – Éad.

C. – What is this, the devil on you!
    Wretch who did not refuse a lie!
    The reason for your mockery don't speak,
    About Kate of the whitest teeth.
    E. – Jealousy.

C. – Má's tré Narcissus tréan,
    A taoí ag éad reat olc,
    Beag an dith, dar Duach!
    A dhul uait 's an loch. –
    M. – Och!

C. – If it is on account of strong Narcissus
    That you are by jealousy accruing evil,
    Small the loss, by Jove,
    Going from you and the lake.
    E. – Oh!

C. – Míle och a's mairg,
    Do chluinim agaibh gach láoi; –
    Cread a tá libh 'g á luadh
    A thruagh chorrtha an chaoídh?
    M. – Caoídh!

C. – A thousand ohs and sorrows,
    I hear from you every day; –
    Why are you mentioning them,
    Peculiar wretch of the lament?
    E. – Lament!

Ah then, if envy's eye has ceased
    To mar my earthly bliss;
Speak consolation to my breast,
    If remedy there is. –
        Echo – There is.

Gay witty spirit of the air,
    If such relief be nigh;
At once the secret spell declare,
    To lull my wasted eye. –
        Echo – To die.

To die! and if it be my lot,
    It comes in hour of need;
Death wears no terror but in thought,
    'Tis innocent in deed. –
        Echo, (surprised) – Indeed!

Indeed, 'tis welcome to my woes,
    Thou airy voice of fate;
But ah! to none on earth disclose
    What you prognosticate. –
        Echo, (playfully) – To Kate.

To Kate, the devil's on your tongue,
    To scare me with such thoughts;
To her, oh could I hazard wrong,
    Who never knew her faults. –
        Echo – You are false.

If thy Narcissus could awake
    Such doubts, he were an ass,
If he did not prefer the lake,
    To humouring such a lass. –
        Echo – Alas!

A thousand sighs and rites of woe
    Attend thee in the air;
What mighty grief can feed thee so
    In weariless despair? –
        Echo – Despair.

Original: 'Cearbhall O'Dala agus an Macala', by Cearbhall Ó Dálaigh (cont.)	Literal translation (cont.):

C. – Do chaoídh Narcissus,
    Do rug bárr gach gnaoídh;
  Sguir a's go rug a áit,
    An bárr-so má's fíor. –
      M. – Is fíor.

C. – Narcissus wept,
    Who took the pinnacle of every beauty;
  Left and his place was taken,
    This pinnacle, if it is true. –
      E. – It is true.

C .– Beandacht air do bheal,
    Ná'r chan bréag a n-diúmh,
  O taoír ag dul a bh-fad,
    Cuirim leat adieú. –
      M. – Adieú.[12]

C. – A blessing on your mouth,
    That did not speak a lie today;
  Since you are going far,
    I send with you adieú.
      E. – Adieú!

Despair – not for Narcissus' lot,
   Who once was thy delight;
Another in his place you've got,
   If our report is right. –
      Echo – 'Tis right.

Dear little sorceress, farewell,
   I feel thou told'st me true;
But as thou'st many a tale to tell,
   I bid thee now adieu. –
      Echo – Adieu![13]

Original: 'Márghairiad Inghín Sheoirse Brún', by Toirdhealbhac Ó Cearbhalláin

Literal translation:

A Mhárghairiad Brún, is dúbhach do fhágbhais mé,
　Mo luíghe 's an n-uaigh 's gan cúmhdach mná orm féin,
Fuil 'g a scaoíleadh dhamh-sa a d-túis a's a n-deireadh gach laé,
　A's a Inghín Mheic Suíbhne, a rúin dhil, tárthaigh mé.

Margaret Brown, it is melancholy you left me,
　Lying in the grave and without a woman's cherishing for me,
Blood flowing from me at beginning and end of each day,
　And Daughter of Mac Sweeney, dear love, rescue me.

Ghluaiseas 'núnn dar liom fá'n tráth-so a n-dé,
　Fá'n g-coíll chroím, go cínnte b'árd mo léim;
Mo leabhrán grínn ag ínsinn fáth gach sgéil,
　Is eagal liom gur mhíll do ghrádh-sa me.

I went over, it seems to me, about this time yesterday,
　Under the drooping forest, certainly it was the height of my leap;
My accurate booklet giving a reason for every matter,
　I fear that your love ruined me.

'S í Már'iad an aindear shéimh is caoíne glór,
　Is binne a béul 'ná guth na d-téud a's 'ná na sígh-cheóil,
Is gile taobh ná an eala shéimh théidheann air linn gach ló,
　'Gus a mhaiseach, bhéusach, ghasta, thréidhtheach ná diúltaidh mé.

Margaret is the mild maiden of the sweetest voice,
　Sweeter her mouth than the voice of the strings or of the fairy-music,
Brighter her side than the gentle swan who moves in a pool every day,
　And, elegant, polite, clever, accomplished one, don't refuse me.

Dul eadar an dair 'sa croiceann, 'sé mheasaim gur cruadh an céim,
　Dul eadar mé agus rúin-shearc agus grádh mo chléibh,
Air chur mo lámh tháirsi ar maidin le bánúghadh an laé
　Fuair mé an staraídhe dubh ag ghleacaídheacht le grádh mo chuím.[14]

To go between the oak and its bark, [but] it is, I think, a harder step,
　To go between me and love, and the love of my bosom,
Putting my hand about her in the morning at the dawning of the day,
　I found the black boor wrestling with the love of my body.

Thomas Furlong
(1794–1827)

When James Hardiman first asked Thomas Furlong to contribute verse translations from the Irish to his collection *Irish Minstrelsy* (1831), Furlong reportedly replied, 'If they [the originals] possess any merit, I cannot conceive how they could have remained so long unknown.'[15] Whatever his view of the Irish-language tradition, Furlong's translations from it are heavily indebted to the anapestic rhythms and romantic-nationalist sentiments of Thomas Moore.

The son of a Co. Wexford farmer, Furlong wrote an elegy for a Dublin grocer to whom he was apprenticed as a young man; the elegy eventually came to the attention of the distiller John Jameson, and Furlong was given a job and support for his writing. But Furlong's life and career were, as one commentator put it, 'dodged by Bacchus and the shadow of death',[16] and his lonely existence came to an early end.

'Peggy Browne'

(The original was written by Turlough Carolan [1670–1738]. Hardiman identifies the woman in the poem as the daughter of one George Browne, from Co. Mayo. For Austin Clarke's twentieth-century version, see p. 253.)

Oh! dark! sweetest girl, are my days doom'd to be,
While my heart bleeds in silence and sorrow for thee:
In the green spring of life to the grave I go down,
Oh! shield me and save me, my lov'd Peggy Browne.

I dreamt, that at evening my footsteps were bound,
To yon deep spreading wood where the shades fall around;
I sought, 'midst new scenes, all my sorrows to drown,
But the cure of my sorrow rests with thee, Peggy Browne.

'Tis soothing, sweet maid, thy soft accents to hear,
For, like wild fairy music, they melt on the ear –
Thy breast is as fair as the swan's clothed in down;
Oh! peerless, and faultless, is my own Peggy Browne.

Dear! dear is the bark, to its own cherish'd tree,
But dearer, far dearer, is my lov'd one to me:
In my dreams I draw near her, uncheck'd by a frown,
But my arms, spread in vain to embrace Peggy Browne.[17]

J.J. Callanan
(1795–1829)

Writing at a time when the Irish language was disappearing at an alarming rate, J. J. Callanan sought in his verse translations to find a poetic language that would salvage literature written in Irish without betraying its authenticity, and Callanan stands at the head of a long line of verse translators in Ireland committed to representing in English verse the complex formal qualities and poetic textures of verse written in Irish.

Callanan was born in or near Cork City, and spent a considerable time in West Cork, collecting folk songs and poetry. A collection of his poems was published just weeks after his death in Lisbon.

'Dirge of O'Sullivan Beare'

(No specific source for this translation has been identified, although there are reportedly numerous poems in Irish about the death of Morty Óg Ó Sullivan, one of the O'Sullivans from Bearhaven, Co. Cork. Morty Óg, who lived in the eighteenth century, seems to have been connected with various smuggling enterprises, and according to some accounts, was betrayed first by his neighbour, a Mr. Puxley, and then, after he shot Puxley, by one of his own servants, a man named Scully, who wet the powder in the weapons that Ó Sullivan had assembled to defend himself against the soldiers sent to arrest him.)

> The sun upon Ivera
> > No longer shines brightly;
> The voice of her music
> > No longer is sprightly;
> No more to her maidens
> > The light dance is dear,
> Since the death of our darling
> > O'SULLIVAN Bear.
>
> SCULLY! thou false one,
> > You basely betrayed him;
> In his strong hour of need
> > When thy right hand should aid him;
> He fed thee; – he clad thee; –
> > You had all could delight thee;
> You left him; – you sold him; –
> > May Heaven requite thee!

SCULLY! may all kinds
        Of evil attend thee;
On thy dark road of life
        May no kind one befriend thee;
May fevers long burn thee,
        And agues long freeze thee;
May the strong hand of God
        In his red anger seize thee.

Had he died calmly,
        I would not deplore him,
Or if the wild strife
        Of the sea-war closed o'er him;
But with ropes round his white limbs
        Through ocean to trail him,
Like a fish after slaughter! –
        'Tis therefore I wail him.

Long may the curse
        Of his people pursue them;
SCULLY that sold him,
        And soldier that slew him,
One glimpse of Heaven's light
        May they see never;
May the hearth-stone of hell
        Be their best bed for ever!

In the hole which the vile hands
        Of soldiers had made thee,
Unhonoured, unshrouded
        And headless they laid thee;
No sigh to regret thee,
        No eye to rain o'er thee,
No dirge to lament thee,
        No friend to deplore thee.

Dear head of my darling
        How gory and pale,
These aged eyes see thee
        High spiked on their gaol;
That cheek in the summer sun
        Ne'er shall grow warm,
Nor that eye e'er catch light,
        But the flash of the storm.

A curse, blessed ocean,
    Is on thy green water,
From the haven of Cork
    To Ivera of slaughter,
Since the billows were dyed
    With the red wounds of fear,
Of Muiertach Oge,
    Our O'SULLIVAN BEAR.[18]

Original: 'Príosún Chluain Meala'	Literal translation:
Ó, bliain 's an lá amárach 'sea d'fhágas an baile, ag dul go hArd Pádraig 'cur lásaí lem hata: bhí Buachaillí Bána ann is rás acu ar eallaigh – is mé go dubhach uaigneach i bpríosún Chluain Meala.	Oh, a year it is tomorrow that I left home, going to Ard Pádraig, putting laces in my hat: Whiteboys were there and they having a run at cattle – and me sorrowfully, lonely in Cluan Meala prison.
Tá mo shrian is mo dhiallait, ar iasacht le fada, mo chamán ar fiaradh faoi iarthar mo leapa, mo liathróid á bualadh ag buachailli an ghleanna – is go mbualifinn poc báire chomh hard leis na fearaibh!	My bridle and saddle are on loan a long time, my hurley warping under the back of my bed, my ball being hit by the boys of the glen – and I would hit a goal-puck as high as the men!
A Chiarraígh, bídh ag guí liom, is bog binn liom bhur nglórtha, is beag a shíleas-sa choíche ná fillfinnse beo oraibh – 's go mbeidh ár dtrí cinn-ne ar thrí spící mar sheó acu, faoi shneachta na hoíche is gach síon eile á ngeobhaidh chughainn.	Kerrymen, be praying for me, soft, sweet to me are your voices, it is little I ever thought that I would not return alive to you – and that our three heads will be on three spikes as a show for them, under the snow of the evening and every other bad weather that will come to us.
Go hUíbh Ráthach má théann tú, beir scéala go dtí mo mhuintir go bhfuilim daor ar an bhfód seo is nach bhfuil beo agam ach go hAoine. Bailídh gléas tórraimh agus cónra bhreá im thimpeall – sin críoch ar Ó Dónaill is go deo deo bídh ag guí leis.[19]	If you go to Uíbh Ráthach, take news to my people that I am condemned on this ground and I have life only until Friday. Collect wake provisions and a fine coffin around me – that is the end of Ó Dónaill and always be praying for him.

'The Convict of Clonmel'

(This translation seems to be loosely based on an anonymous song associated with the agrarian troubles of the second half of the eighteenth century.)

How hard is my fortune
And vain my repining;
The strong rope of fate
For this young neck is twining;
My strength is departed,
My cheeks sunk and sallow;
While I languish in chains
In the gaol of Clonmala.

No boy of the village
Was ever yet milder;
I'd play with a child
And my sport would be wilder;
I'd dance without tiring
From morning 'till even,
And the goal-ball I'd strike
To the light'ning of Heaven.

At my bed foot decaying
My hurl-bat is lying;
Through the boys of the village
My goal-ball is flying;
My horse 'mong the neighbours
Neglected may fallow;
While I pine in my chains
In the gaol of Clonmala.

Next Sunday the patron[20]
At home will be keeping,
And the active young hurlers
The field will be sweeping;
With the dance of fair maidens
The evening they'll hallow,
While this heart once so gay
Shall be cold in Clonmala.[21]

Original A: 'Dhruimfhionn Donn Dílis'

	Literal translation:

A Dhruimfhionn donn dílis,
　　A shíoda na mbó,
Cá ngabhann tú san oidhche
　　'S cá mbíonn tú sa ló?
Bíonn mise ar na coillte
　　As mo bhuachaill im' chómhair,
Agus d'fhág sé siúd mise
　　Ag sileadh na ndeor.

Ní'l fearann, ní'l tigheas agam,
　　Ní'l fíonta ná ceol,
Ní'l flaithe im' choímhdeacht,
　　Ní'l saoithe ná slógh;
Acht ag síor-ól an uisce
　　Go minic sa ló,
Agus beath'-uisce 's fíon
　　Ag mo naímhdibh ar bord.

Dá bhfaighinn-se cead aighnis
　　Nó radharc ar an gcoróin,
Sasanaigh do leidhbfinn
　　Mar do leidhbfinn sean-bhróg,
Trí chnocaibh, trí ailltibh,
　　'S trí ghleanntaibh dubha ceoigh,
Agus siúd mar a bhréagfainn-se
　　An Droimeann donn óg.[22]

Loyal, brown white-backed cow,
　　Silk of the cows,
Where do you go in the evening
　　And where are you in the day?
I am in the woods
　　And my boy near me,
And he left me there
　　Shedding tears.

I have no land, no household,
　　No wines or music,
No prince in my company,
　　No wise men or armies,
But always drinking the water
　　Often in the day,
And whiskey and wine
　　Have my enemies at table.

If I could get leave for contention
　　Or a look at the crown,
Saxons I would thrash
　　As I would thrash an old shoe,
By hills, by cliffs,
　　And through dark glens of fog,
And that is how I would sooth
　　The young brown white-backed cow.

Original B: 'Dromin Dubh O!'

Literal translation:

'A dhroimeann dubh dílis, a scoith shíoda na mbó, cá bhfuil do mhuintir nó an maireann siad beo?'
'Loyal brown white-backed cow, choice silk of the cows, where are your people, or are they living?'

'Tá siad sna díogaibh sínte faoin bhfód, ag súil le Rí Séamus a théacht insa gcoróin.'
'They are in the ditches stretched under the sod, expecting King James coming into the crown.'

Dá bhfaighainnse cead aoibhnis nó radharc ar an gcoróin, thriallfainn go Sacsain d'oíche is de ló, ag siúl bogaigh is curraigh is sléibhte dubha ceo, nó go seinnfear ar dhromaibh 'An Droimeann Dubh Ó'!
If I could get permission for pleasure or a view of the crown, I would travel to England by night and by day, Walking boggy grounds and marshes and dark mountains of mist, Until one will be playing on drums 'The Brown White-Backed Cow, O!'

'Dia do bheatha don mbaile, a dhroimeann dubh ó! ba mhaith do chuid bainne is ba mhilis le hól, do chaoinfinn do leaca is do chom cailce mar rós, 's do mhalairt ní dhéanfad, a dhroimeann dubh ó![23]
'Welcome to the town, brown white-backed cow, o! Your milk would be good and would be sweet to drink, I would weep for your cheek and your chalk-white waist like a rose, and I will not exchange you, brown white-backed cow, o!'

'O Say My Brown Drimin!'

(This translation is one of three poems grouped under the heading
'Jacobite Songs' in the 1829 edition of Callanan's poems. 'Drimin', an
anglicisation of *droimeann*, meaning white-backed cow, is one of the
many allegorical names for Ireland. Two of the most common ver-
sions of the original are given here, but they are related to Callanan's
poem only in part.)

> O say, my brown Drimin, thou silk of the kine,
> Where, where are thy strong ones, last hope of thy line?
> Too deep and too long is the slumber they take,
> At the loud call of freedom why don't they awake?
>
> My strong ones have fallen – from the bright eye of day,
> All darkly they sleep in their dwelling of clay;
> The cold turf is o'er them; – they hear not my cries,
> And since Louis no aid gives I cannot arise.
>
> O! where art thou, Louis, our eyes are on thee?
> Are thy lofty ships walking in strength o'er the sea?
> In freedom's last strife if you linger or quail
> No morn e'er shall break on the night of the Gael.
>
> But should the King's son, now bereft of his right,
> Come proud in his strength for his Country to fight;
> Like leaves on the trees, will new people arise,
> And deep from their mountains shout back to my cries.
>
> When the Prince, now an exile, shall come for his own,
> The isles of his father, his rights and his throne;
> My people in battle the Saxons will meet,
> And kick them before, like old shoes from their feet.
>
> O'er mountains and valleys they'll press on their rout,
> The five ends of Erin shall ring to their shout;
> My sons all united shall bless the glad day,
> When the flint-hearted Saxons they've chased far away.[24]

'The Outlaw of Loch Lene'

(No original for this translation has been identified. Callanan may have been working either from the oral tradition or from several different poems in Irish.)

O many a day have I made good ale in the glen,
That came not of stream, or malt; – like the brewing of men.
My bed was the ground; my roof, the greenwood above,
And the wealth that I sought one far kind glance from my love.

Alas! on that night when the horses I drove from the field,
That I was not near from terror my angel to shield.
She stretched forth her arms, – her mantle she flung to the wind,
And swam o'er Loch Lene,[25] her outlawed lover to find.

O would that a freezing sleet-wing'd tempest did sweep,
And I and my love were alone, far off on the deep;
I'd ask not a ship, or a bark, or pinnace, to save, –
With her hand round my waist, I'd fear not the wind or the wave.

'Tis down by the lake where the wild tree fringes its sides,
The maid of my heart, my fair one of Heaven resides; –
I think as at eve she wanders its mazes along,
The birds go to sleep by the sweet wild twist of her song.[26]

Original: from 'Tuireadh air Bhás Mhná an Dara Ríghe Séumais', by Seán Ó Neachtain	Literal translation:
Fá theimhioll, fá cheóidh, tá an spéir ann sa ló,	Under darkness, under fog, the sky is during the day,
Mná-ríghe atá caoíneadh, gan sgíth ar a m-brón,	The Queen's women are keening, without rest from their sorrow,
Tá an t-aosda tá an t-óg, fá chlaoídhteacht a ngleóidh,	The old and the young are exhausted in their contention,
O d'íoc-súd an Rígh-bhean, a chíos leis an g-códh!	Since the Royal Lady paid the death tribute!
'S lag géimneach na m-bó, air léana ní'l feór,	Weak is the lowing of the cows, on the meadow there's no grass,
Na h-éin air na géugaibh, tá n-éugmais a g-ceóil,	The birds on the branches, their music is absent,
Ní'l éisg air an ló, ní'l léim ag an eó,	Fish are not in the water, no jumping by the salmon,
O d'íoc-súd an Rígh-bhean, a chíos leis an g-códh!	Since the Queen paid the death tribute!
Táid Gaodhlaibh gan treóir, do'n taobh-so de'n ghó,	Gaels are without direction, on this side of the sea,
Ann Síor-bhroid, a n-daoírsi, mo chnaoídhteacht, mo scleóidh!	In Eternal misery, in slavery, my powerlessness, my misery!
Tá traochadh air mo shógh, tá sgíos air mo sceódh,	A lessening is on my comfort, fatigue is on my understanding,
Ann sna ciantaibh mar a chídhthear, air díbirt an fó!	There in the distance where one looks, the banishment of the king!
Is tearc ádhbhar is mó, 'ná ádhbhar na n-gleóidh,	Few matters are greater than the matter of misery,
Sgéul cráidhte do thárlaigh, 's an áit-so go nuadh	An agonized story that happened in this place recently
Tá gártha ann gach ó, tá a g-cáirdeas do'n Róimh,	Cries are in every ear, their friendship for Rome,
Na Spáinne mar fágbhadh, léir-bháidhte, mo dhóith!	Of Spain as it was left, completely drowned, my hope!
Ní'l tádhbhacht ann mo bhlór, 's ní fháigfead mo dhóich,	There is no strength in my voice, and I will not leave my hope,
Na grása táid láidir, a's an t-árd-athair beóidh,	The graces are strong, and the high-father alive,
Léir-bháidhte ann sa n-gó, neart Pharaóh na m-bró,	Completely drowned in the sea, the strength of Pharoah of the masses,
'S rug Maoíse gan díth leis, 's a dhaoíne gan clódhadh!	And [the high-father] bore Moses without deprivation, and his people without defeat.
A ríogh-fhlaith cheirt, chóir, rug Maoíse as a' d-tóir,	Royal ruler of right and justice, who bore Moses out of their pursuit,
Na Gaodhail a tá taoíbh leat, tráth dídean a's fóir,	The Gaels who are on your side, give protection and succour,
Scuir díomas as spleóid, luchd chraoísach na m-bód,	Stop pride and boastfulness, the greedy people of the earth,
Do dhíbir go mí-cheart, ár n-daoíne 's ár nóith![27]	Who banished wrongly our people and our church!

Henry Grattan Curran
(1800–1876)

Henry Grattan Curran's translations appeared in James Hardiman's *Irish Minstrelsy* (1831). Curran was the son of the barrister and orator John Philpot Curran, and a barrister himself.

From 'Lament for the Queen of King James II'

(The original is an elegy written by Seán Ó Neachtain [1650?-1729], a leading member of an Irish-language literary circle in Dublin in the early decades of the eighteenth century. The second wife of James II, Mary D'Este [Mary of Modena], died 7 May 1718. The excerpt here consists of the final six stanzas of Curran's translation.)

> The mid-day is dark with unnatural gloom –
>   And a spectral lament wildly shrieked in the air,
> Tells all hearts that our princess lies cold in the tomb –
>   Bids the old and the young bend in agony there!
>
> Faint the lowing of kine o'er the seared yellow lawn!
>   And tuneless the warbler that droops on the spray!
> The bright tenants that flashed through the current are gone!
>   For the princess we honoured is laid in the clay. –
>
> Darkly brooding alone o'er his bondage and shame,
>   By the shore, in mute agony, wander the Gael –
> And sad is my spirit – and clouded my dream,
>   For my king – for the star my devotion would hail –
>
> What woe, beyond this, hath dark fortune to wreak?
>   What wrath o'er the land yet remains to be hurled?
> They turn them to Rome! but despairing they shriek,
>   For Spain's flag, in defeat, and defection is furled –
>
> Though our sorrows avail not – our hope is not lost –
>   For the Father is mighty! – the Highest remains! –
> The loosed waters rushed down upon Pharoah's wide host –
>   But the billows crouch back from the foot He sustains –
>
> Just power! that for Moses the wave didst divide,
>   Look down on the land where thy followers pine;
> Look down upon Erin! and crush the dark pride
>   Of the scourge of thy people – the foes of thy shrine.[28]

Original: 'Captain Fuiscí', by Peadar Ó Doirín	Literal translation
Níl cailleach i gclúid is a leaca ar a glún	There is not an old hag in a corner and her cheek on her knee
Dá mblaiseadh mo rún nach léim-feadh go hard,	[Who] if she tasted my dear one, would not leap up high,
Is a teangaidhse lúfar glic in gach cúrsa,	And her own tongue agile and clever in every matter,
Ag aithris a cliú is a maise ar na mná;	Narrating her renown and her beauty to the women;
Is é chuirfeadh úir isteach insa chnúidín,	It is he who would put freshness in the wizened person,
Chasfadh a chúla is a bhuiceoid le cách,	Who would spend his reserves and his buckets with everyone,
Is nár mhaire go Luan an fear a chuir smúid	And may he not live until Monday the man who put gloom
Ar mo charaid ba súgaí bhí in Inis Chrích' Fáil.	On the most mellow of my friends who were in Inis Chrích' Fáil.
Is é chuirfeadh beos is spracadh mar leon	It is he who would inspire life and energy like a lion
Sa ngliodaí gan treoir darbh ainm dhó an tráill,	In a wheedler without direction who has the name of the slave,
Bhíodh dhá thaobh an bhóthair leis, sin is a bhróga	He would take both sides of the road, that and his shoes
Ag tuiteam is a chóta folaithe i láib;	Falling off and his coat covered in mud;

Matthew Graham
(fl. 1833)

Matthew Graham, who was born near Dundalk, Co. Louth, belonged to a loosely connected group of writers and scholars in Belfast, Samuel Ferguson being the best-known of them, working to promote the Irish-language tradition in the early decades of the nineteenth century. Graham's one collection of poems and translations, *The Giantess, from the Irish of Oisin, and the War of Donomore*, was published in Belfast in 1833. Graham said that his translations were 'rendered as literal as I was able to do in verse', and that he preferred being called 'a servile translator, rather than strain my originals'.[29]

'Captain Whiskey: Translated from the Irish'

(The original was written by Peadar Ó Doirnín [d. 1768], an Ulster schoolmaster and writer. In a note to his translation, Graham says the poem came about when Ó Doirnín was dining with a respectable farmer in Co. Louth, and, in the midst of the festivities, a troop of soldiers raided the place where the farmer kept a private still, and carried it away. The news had scarcely reached the diners, Graham says, 'when the officer entered the dining-room; and, not satisfied with the plunder he made elsewhere, he carried away the decanters, glasses, etc. This insolent treatment provoked the poet to sing this song to Captain Whiskey'.[30])

> Can crippled housewives, doom'd to grief,
> E'er taste his joy without relief;
> Though poor and wretched be their state,
> By him they seem to change their fate.

> Although they're wrinkled, haggish, old,
> With babbling prate, they will unfold
> How much in beauty, and in fame,
> They now surpass each other dame.

> My friend's the vivifying he;
> Though lazy, loath the sluggard be,
> Though blunt, he feels his soul still fir'd
> By him, and fancies he's inspir'd.

Original: 'Captain Fuiscí',   Literal translation (cont.):
by Peadar Ó Doirín (cont.)

Níorbh eagal leis leonadh, tuirse nó brón   He would not fear injury, weariness or sorrow
   Dá dtagadh sin geosta is fiche ina   If a ghost and twenty came there in his
     dháil,   company,
Níorbh fhearr leisean fós ar leabaidh   He himself would still not prefer [to be] on a
   den tsról   bed of satin
   Nó ar leaca is gan róinne a bheith   Or on a flagstone and without a thread
     eadra sé is lár.   being between him and the ground.

Níorbh acmhainní cróga Hector i   He did not have the hardy resources of Hector
   ngleo   in combat
   Nó an leisíneach leonta is eisean a   Nor the person with a wounded game
     bheith dall,   leg and that fellow being blind,
Tráth shlugadh sé corn den fuiscí ina   The moment he would swallow a horn of
   scóig   whiskey in his throttle
   Do chumadh mar Ovid file gach   He would compose like Ovid the poet
     rann;   every verse;
Níl ceist insna leabhair nó ealaín arbh   Not a question in the books or art but he
   eol dho   knows
   A aithris gan ghó, gan chasadh, gan   How to recite without falsehood, without
     cham,   twisting, without crookedness,
An maireann neoch beo nach dtuitfeadh   Is there a person living who would not get
   i ngleo   into a fight
   Do thaithigh gach ló mo chaiptín   Who frequented every day my captain
     bhí teann?   who was strong?

Is ioma sin baol tháinig ar Ghaeil   It is many a danger came on the Gaels
   Ó thug Rí Laighean a choróin ar   Since the King of Leinster took his crown
     toinn,   on the waves,
Le ar chaill siad a gcéim, a bhfearanntaí   With it they lost their rank, their free hold-
   saora,   ings,
   A ngunnaí is a ngadhair is an breac   Their guns and their dogs and the trout
     insa linn;   in the lakes;
Is measa liom féin nó a dtáinig de léan   It is worse for myself than what came of grief
   Le Sibeoil ar Éirinn, caraid mo   With Sibeoil to Ireland, the friend of my
     choim   heart
A chailleadh, gan aon sáitheadh scine nó   To lose, without any thrust of a knife or a
   claímh,   sword,
   Mo chaiptín bhí tréan – an fuiscí   My captain who was strong – the bright,
     geal fionn.[31]   fair whiskey.

His homeward path thrice o'er he paces,
Brave as the brave, he danger faces;
Nor needs he clothes, nor shoes, nor hose,
Although it rains, it hails, or snows.

The costly couch of easy down,
With silken robes, well dress'd around,
He would not with more care desire,
Than heedless lie in mud and mire.

His courage ne'er can feel dismay,
Though ghosts and sprites meet in his way;
Though bugbears may his course impede,
Yet still, he never feels afraid.

Like Hector, bold and brave in fight,
Is every palsied gouty wight;
Though blind and worn, ne'er meets dismay,
When Captain Whiskey leads the way.

May every woe and curse attend
The Foe, who dar'd assail the Friend,[32]
That would cause joy, and mirth, and play,
To his frequenters every day.

Oh! many a dread defeat we bore,
And many a grievous loss before;
But worse, far worse for us than all
Is Captain Whiskey's great downfall![33]

Original: 'Bean na tTrí mBó'	Literal translation:
Go réidh a bhean na ttrí mbó	Be mild, Woman of the three cows
As to bhólacht ná bí teann	Because of your cattle don't be bold
Do chonairc meisi, gan gó,	I myself saw, without a lie,
Bean is ba dá mhó a beann.	A woman and twice greater was her portion.
Ní mhaireann saidhbhrios do gnáith	Riches do not survive as a rule
Do neach ná tabhair táir go mór	To anyone don't give contempt proudly
Chúghat an téag ar gach taobh	Around you is death on every side
Go réidh a bhean na ttrí mbó.	Be mild, woman of the three cows.

James Clarence Mangan
(1803–1849)

James Clarence Mangan's achievement as a verse translator in the dark years of the 1840s has much to do with his own melancholic romanticism. By all accounts, including his own, Mangan was a deeply, self-consciously unhappy man – 'A ruined soul in a wasted form' is how he described himself in a fragment of autobiography he left behind him[34] – and his translations often powerfully internalise the political and social deprivation that he saw around him. Although arguably more personal than political in motivation (Mangan came to nationalist politics late in his life), his translations were capable of inspiring strong cultural feeling, and, at times, quite revolutionary nationalist as well as romantic sentiment. The son of a Dublin grocer, Mangan found his way, in the 1830s, to the antiquarian circles of Eugene O'Curry and John O'Donovan. He also worked for the Ordinance Survey Office between 1833 and 1839, a position that brought him into contact with a number of other scholars and translators, including Samuel Ferguson. His verse translations were probably based on literal translations done by such scholars, as Mangan seems never to have mastered Irish himself. He contributed translations and original poems frequently to *The Nation* from 1846 on, and in 1849 his translations of the Jacobite poetry of Munster were published posthumously as *The Poets and Poetry of Munster*.

'The Woman of Three Cows'

(This is Mangan's earliest known translation from the Irish, first published in the *Irish Penny Journal* in August of 1840. He worked from a literal translation provided by Eugune O'Curry. The author of the original has not been identified.)

O, Woman of Three Cows, agragh![35] don't let your tongue thus rattle!
O, don't be saucy, don't be stiff, because you may have cattle.
I have seen – and, here's my hand to you, I only say what's true –
A many a one with twice your stock not half so proud as you.

Good luck to you, don't scorn the poor, and don't be their despiser,
For wordly wealth soon melts away, and cheats the very miser,
And Death soon strips the proudest wreath from haughty human brows;
Then don't be stiff, and don't be proud, good Woman of Three Cows!

Original: 'Bean na tTrí mBó' (cont.)	Literal translation (cont.):
Sliocht Eóghain Mhóir sa Múmhain	The descendants of Eoghan Mór in Munster
A nimtheacht do ní clú dóibh	Their going made renown for them
A seólta gur léigeadar síos	Their sails that they let down
Go réidh a bhean na ttrí mbó.	Be mild, woman of the three cows.
Clann ghaisce thighearna an Chláir	The warrior children of the lord of Clare
A nimtheacht sin ba lá leóin	Their going was a day of affliction
Sgan súil re na tteacht go bráth,	And without any expectation ever of their return,
Go réidh a bhean na ttrí mbó.	Be mild, woman of the three cows.
Dómhnall ó Dún-buídhe na long	Domhnall from Dún Baoi of the ships
Ó Súilleabháin nár thím glór	O'Sullivan whose speech was not faint
Féach gur thuit san Spáin re cloidheamh	See that he fell in Spain by a sword
Go réidh a bhean na ttrí mbó.	Be mild, woman of the three cows.
O'Ruairc is Maguidhir do bhí	O'Rourke and Maguire who were
Lá i n-Eirinn 'na lán beóil	Once in Ireland in the mouths of many
Féach féin gur imthigh an dís	See for yourself that the two are gone
Go réidh a bhean na ttrí mbó.	Be mild, woman of the three cows.
Síol gCearbhuill do bhí teann	The seed of O'Carroll that was bold
Le mbeirthí gach geall i ngleó	When every challenge in combat was borne
Ní mhaireann aon díobh mo dhíth	Not one of them survives, my deprivation,
Go réidh a bhean na ttrí mbó.	Be mild, woman of the three cows.
O aon bhoin amháin do bhreis	From your excess of only one cow
Ar mhnaoi eile is í a dó	Over another woman, and she having two
Do rinnisi iomorca aréir	You made too much last night
Go réidh a bhean na ttrí mbó.	Be mild, woman of the three cows.

An Ceangal	The Binding
Bíodh ar mfhallaing a ainnir as uaibhreach gnúis	By my cloak, young woman with the proud countenance
Do bhíos gan dearmad seasmhach buan sa' tnúith	I was without mistake, steadfast, long-lived in ambition,
Tríd an rachmus do ghlacais red bhuaibh ar túis	On account of the wealth you took with your cows at first,
Dá bhfaghainnsi seilbh a ceathair do bhuailfinn tú.[36]	If I could get possession of four, I would beat you.

See where Momonia's[37] heroes lie, proud Owen More's[38] descendants,
'Tis they that won the glorious name, and had the grand attendants!
If *they* were forced to bow to Fate, as every mortal bows,
Can *you* be proud, can *you* be stiff, my Woman of Three Cows!

The brave sons of the Lord of Clare,[39] they left the land to mourning;
Movrone![40] for they were banished, with no hope of their returning –
Who knows in what abodes of want those youths were driven to
    house?
Yet *you* can give yourself these airs, O, Woman of Three Cows!

O, think of Donnell of the Ships,[41] the Chief whom nothing daunted –
See how he fell in distant Spain, unchronicled, unchanted!
He sleeps, the great O'Sullivan, where thunder cannot rouse –
Then ask yourself, should *you* be proud, good Woman of Three Cows!

O'Ruark, Maguire,[42] those souls of fire, whose names are shrined in
    story –
Think how their high achievements once made Erin's highest glory –
Yet now their bones lie mouldering under weeds and cypress boughs,
And so, for all your pride, will yours, O, Woman of Three Cows!

The O'Carrolls[43] also, famed when Fame was only for the boldest,
Rest in forgotten sepulchres with Erin's best and oldest;
Yet who so great as they of yore in battle or carouse?
Just think of that, and hide your head, good Woman of Three Cows!

Your neighbor's poor, and you it seems are big with vain ideas,
Because, *inagh!*[44] you've got three cows – one more, I see, than *she* has.
That tongue of yours wags more at times than Charity allows,
But, if you are strong, be merciful, great Woman of Three Cows!

The Summing Up

Now, there you go! You still, of course, keep up your scornful bearing,
And I'm too poor to hinder you; but, by the cloak I'm wearing,
If I had but *four* cows myself, even though you were my spouse,
I'd thwack you well to cure your pride, my Woman of Three Cows![45]

Original: 'Róisín Dubh'	Literal translation:
A Róisín ná bíodh brón ort fár éirigh dhuit –	Róisín, do not be sorry about what has happened to you –
tá na bráithre ag dul ar sáile is iad ag triall ar muir,	the brothers are going on the sea and they journeying on the sea,
tiocfaidh do phardún ón bPápa is ón Róimh anoir	your pardon will come from the Pope and from Rome from the east
is ní spáráilfear fíon Spáinneach ar mo Róisín Dubh.	and Spanish wine will not be spared for my Róisín Dubh.
Is fada an réim a lig mé léi ó inné go dtí inniu,	Long is the course that I took with her from yesterday to today,
trasna sléibhte go ndeachas léi is mo sheólta ar muir;	across mountains I went with her and my sails on the sea;
an Éirne scoith sí de léim í cé gur mór é a sruth;	The Erne she left behind with a leap although it is a great stream;
is mar cheól téad ar gach taobh di a bhíonn mo Róisín Dubh.	and like music of strings on every side of her is my Róisín Dubh.
Mhearaigh tú mé, a bhradóg, is nár ba fearrde dhuit,	You bewildered me, roguish woman, and may it not be better for you,
's go bhfuil m'anam istigh i ngean ort is ní inné ná inniu.	and my soul is in love with you and not [only] yesterday or today.
D'fhág tú lag anbhann mé i ngné is i gcruth;	You left me very weak, feeble in form and in manner;
ná feall orm is mé i ngean ort, a Róisín Dubh.	don't betray me and I in love with you, Róisín Dubh.

'Dark Rosaleen'

(The original has occasionally been attributed to a Father Costello in
Co. Mayo.)

I

O, my Dark Rosaleen,
　　Do not sigh, do not weep!
The priests are on the ocean green,
　　They march along the Deep.
There's wine . . . from the royal Pope,
　　Upon the ocean green;
And Spanish ale shall give you hope,
　　My Dark Rosaleen!
　　My own Rosaleen!
Shall glad your heart, shall give you hope,
Shall give you health, and help, and hope,
　　My Dark Rosaleen!

II

Over hills, and through dales,
　　Have I roamed for your sake;
All yesterday I sailed with sails
　　On river and on lake.
The Erne, . . . at its highest flood,
　　I dashed across unseen,
For there was lightning in my blood,
　　My Dark Rosaleen!
　　My own Rosaleen!
Oh! there was lightning in my blood,
Red lightning lightened through my blood,
　　My Dark Rosaleen!

III

All day long, in unrest,
　　To and fro, do I move,
The very soul within my breast
　　Is wasted for you, love!
The heart . . . in my bosom faints
　　To think of you, my Queen,
My life of life, my saint of saints,
　　My Dark Rosaleen!
　　My own Rosaleen!
To hear your sweet and sad complaints,
My life, my love, my saint of saints,
　　My Dark Rosaleen!

Original: 'Róisín Dubh' (cont.)   Literal translation (cont.):

Shiúlfainn féin an drúcht leat is fásaigh goirt
mar shúil go bhfaighinn rún uait nó páirt ded thoil;
a chraoibhín chumhra, gheallais domsa go raibh grá agat dom,
is gurb í plúrscoth na Mumhan í mo Róisín Dubh.

I myself would walk the dew with you and the wild fields
in the hope that I would get love from you or part of your desire;
fragrant small branch, you promised me that you loved me,
and she is the choicest flower of Munster, my Róisín Dubh.

Dá mbeadh seisreach agam threabhfainn in aghaidh na gcnoc
is dhéanfainn soiscéal i lár an aifrinn de mo Róisín Dubh;
bhéarfainn póg don chailín óg a bhéarfadh a hóighe dhom
is dhéanfainn cleas ar chúl an leasa le mo Róisín Dubh.

If I had a team of horses I would plough against the hills
and I would make a sermon in the middle of mass for my Róisín Dubh;
I would bear a kiss to the young girl who would bring her virginity to me
and I would make sport behind the fairy mound with my Róisín Dubh.

Beidh an Éirne 'na tuilte tréana is réabfar cnoic,
beidh an fharraige 'na tonnta dearga is an spéir 'na fuil,
beidh gach gleann sléibhe ar fud Éireann is móinte ar crith,
lá éigin sul a n-éagfaidh mo Róisín Dubh.[46]

The Erne will be in strong flood and hills will be torn up,
the sea will be in red waves and the sky in blood,
every mountain glen throughout Ireland and the bogs will be trembling
some day before my Róisín Dubh will die.

IV

Woe and pain, pain and woe,
    Are my lot, night and noon,
To see your bright face clouded so,
    Like to the mournful moon.
But yet . . . will I rear your throne
    Again in golden sheen;
'Tis you shall reign, shall reign alone,
    My Dark Rosaleen!
    My own Rosaleen!
'Tis you shall have the golden throne,
'Tis you shall reign, and reign alone,
    My Dark Rosaleen!

V

Over dews, over sands,
    Will I fly, for your weal;
Your holy delicate white hands
    Shall girdle me with steel.
At home . . . in your emerald bowers,
    From morning's dawn till e'en,
You'll pray for me, my flower of flowers,
    My Dark Rosaleen!
    My fond Rosaleen!
You'll think of me through Daylight's hours,
My virgin flower, my flower of flowers,
    My Dark Rosaleen!

VI

I could scale the blue air,
    I could plough the high hills,
Oh, I could kneel all night in prayer,
    To heal your many ills!
And one . . . beamy smile from you
    Would float like light between
My toils and me, my own, my true,
    My Dark Rosaleen!
    My fond Rosaleen!
Would give me life and soul anew,
A second life, a soul anew,
    My Dark Rosaleen!

Original: 'Machtnamh an Duine Dhoilgheasaig, nó Caoineadh Thighe Molaga', by Seán Ó Coileáin

Literal translation:

Oidhche dham go doiligh, dubhach
  Cois fhairrge na dtonn dtréan
  Ag léir-smuaineadh as ag luadh
  Ar choraibh chruadha an tsaoghail.

An evening to me melancholy, dark
  By the sea of the fierce waves
  clearly thinking and speaking
  Of the hard twists of life.

Bhí an rae as na réalta suas,
  Níor clos fuaim toinne ná trágha,

  As ní raibh gal ann de'n ghaoith
  Do chroithfeadh barr crainn ná bláth.

The moon and the stars were up,
  The sound of the waves or the shore were not heard,
  And the fury of the wind was not there
  That would shake the tops of trees or blossoms.

Do ghluaiseas ag machtnamh 'm aon
  Gan aire ar raon mo shiubhail,
  Doras cille gur dhearc mé
  'San gconair réidh ar mo chionn.

I moved alone thinking
  Without noticing the direction of my walking,
  I saw a churchyard door
  In the smooth path in front of me.

Do stad mé 'san doras tsean
  'Nar ghnáth almsana as aoidhe,
  Dá ndáil do'n lobhar as do'n lag
  An tráth do mhair lucht an tighe.

I stopped in the old doorway
  In which alms and hospitality were usual,
  For dispensing to the lepers and the weak
  The time the people of the house lived.

VII

O! the Erne shall run red
   With redundance of blood,
The earth shall rock beneath our tread,
   And flames wrap hill and wood,
And gun-peal, and slogan cry,
   Wake many a glen serene,
Ere you shall fade, ere you shall die,
   My Dark Rosaleen!
   My own Rosaleen!
The Judgment Hour must first be nigh,
Ere you can fade, ere you can die,
   My Dark Rosaleen![47]

'Lament over the Ruins of the Abbey of Teach Molaga'

(The original was written, probably in 1813 or 1814, by Seán Ó Coileáin [1754–1817], who established a school in Myross, near Glandore, in West Cork. The abbey referred to is a Franciscan Friary built in the fourteenth century at Timoleague, Co. Cork, on the site of St. Molaga's seventh-century foundation.)

I

I wandered forth at night alone,
Along the dreary, shingly, billow-beaten shore.
Sadness that night was in my bosom's core.
   My soul and strength lay prone.

II

The thin wan moon, half overveiled
By clouds, shed her funereal beams upon the scene;
While in low tones, with many a pause between,
   The mournful night-wind wailed.

III

Musing of Life, and Death, and Fate,
I slowly paced along, heedless of aught around,
Till on the hill, now, alas! ruin-crowned,
   Lo! the old Abbey-gate!

IV

Dim in the pallid moonlight stood,
Crumbling to slow decay, the remnant of that pile
Within which dwelt so many saints erewhile
   In loving brotherhood!

Original: 'Machtnamh an Duine
Dhoilgheasaig, nó Caoineadh
Thighe Molaga', by Seán Ó Coileáin
(cont.)

Literal translation (cont.):

Bhí foradh fiar ar a thaoibh,
　Is cian ó cuireadh a chlódh –
　Ar a suidheadh saoithe as cliar
　As taistealaigh thriallta an róid.

A warped seat was on its side
　It is long since it was put in form –
　Sitting on it wise men and clergy
　And journeyed travellers of the road.

Shuidh mé síos le machtnamh lán,
　Do léigeas mo lámh fám' ghruadh,
　Gur thuit frasa diana déar
　Óm' dhearcaibh ar féar anuas.

I sat down full of thought,
　I placed my hand under my cheek,
　Until intense showers of tears fell
　From my eyes down onto the grass.

Adúbhairt mé annsin fá dhíth,
　Agus mé ag caoi go cumhach,
　Do bhí aimsear ann 'n-a raibh
　An teach so go soilbh subhach.

I said then alas,
　And I on a lonesome way,
　That there was a time in which
　This house was cheerful, merry.

Sonn do bhíodh cluig agus cliar,
　Dréachta as diadhacht d'á léigheadh,
　Córaidhe ceatal agus ceol
　Ag moladh mórdhachta Dé.

It is then there were bells and clergy,
　Tracts from divinity being read,
　Choir-singing and music
　Praising the greatness of God.

Fotharach folamh gan áird –
　Árus so is aosta túr –
　Is iomdha eascal agus gaoth
　Do bhuail fá mhaol do mhúr.

Empty ruin without dignity –
　This dwelling house and aged tower –
　It is much commotion and wind
　That struck around the top of your walls.

Is iomdha fearthainn agus fuacht
　As stoirm chuain do chuiris díot,
　Ó tiodhlaiceadh thú ar dtúis
　Do Rígh na nDúl mar thígheas.

It is much rain and cold
　From a harbour storm that you survived,
　Since you first were dedicated
　To the King of Creation as a household.

A mhúir naomhtha na mbeann nglas
　Dob' ornáid do'n tír so tráth,

Holy walls of the grey gables
　That were an ornament for this country once,

　Is díombádh dian liom do scrios
　Agus cur do naomh ar fán.

　Your ruin is an intense sorrow for me
　And the putting of your saints wandering.

Is uaigneach ataoi anois,
　Níl ionat córaidhe ná ceol
　Acht scréachach ghéar na gceann-
　　cait
　I n-ionad na salm sóghail!

It is lonely that you are now,
　There is no singing or music in you
　But the sharp screeching of the long-eared owls
　Instead of the satisfying psalms!

V

The memory of the men who slept
Under those desolate walls – the solitude – the hour –
Mine own lorn mood of mind – all joined to o'erpower
My spirit – and I wept!

VI

In yonder Goshen[48] once – I thought –
Reigned Piety and Peace: Virtue and Truth were there. –
With Charity and the blessed spirit of Prayer
Was each fleet moment fraught!

VII

There, unity of Walk and Will
Blent hundreds into one: no jealousies or jars
Troubled their placid lives: their fortunate stars
Had triumphed o'er all Ill!

VIII

There, knolled each morn and even
The bell for Matin and Vesper: Mass was said or sung. –
From the bright silver censer, as it swung,
Rose balsamy clouds to Heaven.

IX

Through the round cloistered corridors
A many a midnight hour, bareheaded and unshod,
Walked the Grey Friars, beseeching from their GOD
Peace for these western shores!

X

The weary pilgrim, bowed by Age,
Oft found asylum there – found welcome, and found wine.
Oft rested in its halls the Paladine,[49]
The Poet and the Sage!

XI

Alas! alas! how dark the change!
Now round its mouldering walls, over its pillars low,
The grass grows rank, the yellow gowans blow,
Looking so sad and strange!

XII

Unsightly stones choke up its wells;
The owl hoots all night long under the altar-stairs;
The fox and badger make their darksome lairs
In its deserted cells!

Original: 'Machtnamh an Duine Dhoilgheasaig, nó Caoineadh Thighe Molaga', by Seán Ó Coileáin (cont.)

Literal translation (cont.):

Eidhean ag eascar ós do stuadh,
Neanntóg ruadh id' urlár úr,
Tafann caol na seannach seang
As crónán na n-eas id' chlúid.

Ivy sprouting above your arch
Red nettle in your moist floor,
Shrill barking of the lean foxes
And the murmuring of the cataracts in your chimney corner.

Mar a nglaodhadh an fhuiseóg mhoch
Do chléir ag canadh a dtráth
Ní'l teanga ag corruighe anois
Acht teangtha gliogair na gcág.

Like the lark who cried
Your clergy [were] chanting their hours
No tongue is stirring now
But the rattling tongues of the jackdaws.

Atá do phroinnteach gan bhiadh,
Do shuain-lios gan leaba bhláith,
Do thearmoinn gan íodhbairt cliar
Ná aifrionn do Dhia d'á rádh.

Your refectory is without food,
Your sleeping house without a smooth bed,
Your sanctuary without offerings of the clergy
Nor God's mass being said by them.

D'imthigh do luam as do riaghail,
As do chuallacht fá chian cháidh,
Ní fhionnaim anois fá d'iadhadh
Acht carnán criadhta cnámh.

Your abbot and your authority have left,
And your longtime holy company,
I see nothing now within your enclosure
But earthen heaps of bones.

Och! anfhorlann as an-uaill,
Anbhroid an-uais as aindlighe,
Fóirneart námhad as creachadh cruaidh
D'fhúig uaigneach thú mar taoi.

Oh! Great oppression and great vanity,
Great bondage, great nuisance and lawlessness,
Strong troops of the enemy and hard losses
Left you lonely as you are.

Do bhíos-sa féin sona seal,
Faraoir! do chlaochluigh mo chlódh;
Tháinig tóir an tsaoghail im' aghaidh
Ní bhfuil feidhm orm acht brón.

I myself was happy a while,
Alas! my form changed;
The pursuit of the world came against me
Nothing is of use to me but sorrow.

D'imthigh mo luadhail as mo lúth,
Radharc mo shúl agus mo threoir,
Atáid mo cháirde 's mo chlann
'San gcill so go fann ag dreoghadh.

My motion and my vigour have left,
The vision of my eyes and my direction,
My friends and my children are
In this churchyard decomposing feebly.

Atá duairceas ar mo dhriuch,
Tá mo chroidhe 'n-a chrotal cnó;
Dá bhfóirfeadh orm an bás
Badh dhearbh m'fháilte fá n-a chomhair.[50]

Gloom is on my sickly appearance,
My heart is the shell of a nut;
If death would complete me
Certain would be my welcome for it.

XIII

Tempest and Time – the drifting sands –
The lightnings and the rains – the seas that sweep around
These hills in winter-nights, have awfully crowned
    The work of impious hands!

XIV

The sheltering, smooth-stoned, massive wall –
The noble figured roof – the glossy marble piers –
The monumental shapes of elder years –
    Where are they? Vanished all!

XV

Rite, incense, chant, prayer, mass, have ceased –
All, all have ceased! Only the whitening bones half sunk
In the earth now tell that ever here dwelt monk,
    Friar, acolyte, or priest.

XVI

Oh! woe, that Wrong should triumph thus!
Woe that the olden right, the rule and the renown
Of the Pure-souled and the Meek should thus go down
    Before the Tyrannous!

XVII

Where wert thou, Justice, in that hour?
Where was thy smiting sword? What had those good men done,
That thou shouldst tamely see them trampled on
    By brutal England's Power?

XVIII

Alas! I rave! . . . If Change is here,
Is it not o'er the land? – Is it not too in me?
Yes! I am changed even more than what I see.
    Now is my last goal near!

XIX

My worn limbs fail – my blood moves cold –
Dimness is on mine eyes – I have seen my children die.
They lie where I too in brief space shall lie –
    Under the grassy mould!

    . . .

I turned away, as toward my grave,
And, all my dark way homeward by the Atlantic's verge,
Resounded in mine ears like to a dirge
    The roaring of the wave.[51]

Original: 'Fuar Leam an Oidhche-se d'Aodh', by Eochaidh Ó hEódhasa

Literal translation:

Fuar leam an oidhche-se d'Aodh!
    Cúis toirse truime a ciothbhraon,

Mo thruaigh sein dar seise
Neimh fhuaire na hoidhcheise.

Anocht, is neimh rem chridhe,
    Fearthar frasa teintighe,
    I gcomhdháil na gclá seacdha
    Mar tá is orghráin aigeanta.

Do hosgladh ós ochtaibh néal
    Doirse uisgidhe an aiéar,
    Tug sé minlinnte 'n-a muir,
    Do sgé an fhirminnte a hurbhuidh.

Gémadh fiaidhmhíol i bhfiodhbhuidh,
    Gémadh éigne ar inbhiormhuir,

Gémadh ealta, is doiligh dhi

Soighidh ar eachtra an uairsi.

Saoth leamsa Aodh Mag Uidhir
    Anocht i gcrích comhuighidh,
    Fá ghrís ndeirg gcaorshoighnéan gceath
    Re feirg bhfaobhoirnéal bhfuigh-
    leach.

I gcóigeadh chloinne Dáire
    Dursan linn dar leannáinne
    Idir dorchladh bhfuairfhliuch bhfeóir
    Is confadh uaibhreach an aeóir.

Fuar leam dá leacain shubhaigh
    Fraoch na n-iodhlann n-earchumhail

Ag séideadh síonghaoth na reann
Fá ríoghlaoch ngéigeal nGaileang.

Saoth linn, do loit ar meanmain,
    Learg thais a thaoibh míndealbhaigh
    Dá mheilt i ngruamoidhche ghairbh
    I mbeirt fhuarfhoirfe iairn.

Bos tláith na dtachar neamhthláth
    Síon oighridh dá fuaighealtáth
    Re crann rionnfhuar gcaol gceise,
    Ionnfhuar d'Aodh san oidhcheise.

Narab aithreach leis ná leam
    A thuras timchioll Éireann,

Cold it seems to me this night for Hugh!
    A cause of weariness, heaviness its shower-drops,
    My long-standing pity for our companion
    The cold sting of this night.

Tonight, it is a sting to my heart,
    Lightning showers are poured out,
    His meeting with the spikes of frost
    As it is is a great, greedy terror.

From the mouth of a cloud opened
    A water-door of the air,
    It made small pools into seas,
    The firmament spewed its destruction.

Although it were a hare in a thicket,
    Although it were were a salmon in a sea-estuary,
    Although it were a flock of birds, it is difficult for them
    To seek an expedition at this time.

It is a regret to me Hugh Maguire to be
    Tonight in strange territory,
    Under the red fire of blazing lightning-showers
    With the anger of armed, savage clouds.

In the province of clan Dáire
    A calamity it seems to us that our favourite is
    Between a cold wet corridor of grass
    And the excited anger of the air.

Cold it seems to me for his cheerful cheeks
    The fierceness of the blasts of the great discharging
    A strong wind blowing the stars
    About the bright-limbed warrior-king of the Gaileanga.

A regret to us, it wounded our heart,
    The soft slope of his smooth, statuesque side
    Being crushed in a rough, gloomy night
    In a cold, complete suit of iron.

Gentle hand of ungentle attacks
    Icy weather binding it close
    With the narrow shaft of a cold-pointed spear,
    Bitterly cold it is for Hugh this night.

Let it not be a regret to him or me,
    His journey around Ireland,

'O'Hussey's Ode to the Maguire'

(The original was written in 1600 by Eochaidh Ó hEódhasa [1560?–
1612], head of the Ó hEódhasa poetic family, and chief bard to three
successive Maguire chieftans in Co. Fermanangh. The poem expresses
fear for the safety of Hugh Maguire, who was in Munster at the time
fighting with Hugh O'Neill's forces against the English.)

I

Where is my Chief, my Master, this bleak night, *movrone*?[52]
O, cold, cold, miserably cold is this bleak night for Hugh,
Its showery, arrowy, speary sleet pierceth one through and through,
Pierceth one to the very bone!

II

Rolls real thunder? Or, was that red livid light
Only a meteor? I scarce know; but through the midnight dim
The pitiless ice-wind streams. Except the hate that persecutes *him*,
Nothing hath crueller venomy might.

III

An awful, a tremendous night is this, meseems!
The floodgates of the rivers of heaven, I think, have been burst wide –
Down from the overcharged clouds, like unto headlong ocean's tide,
Descends grey rain in roaring streams.

IV

Though he were even a wolf ranging the round green woods,
Though he were even a pleasant salmon in the unchainable sea,
Though he were a wild mountain eagle, he could scarce bear he,
This sharp sore sleet, these howling floods.

V

O, mournful is my soul this night for Hugh Maguire!
Darkly, as in a dream, he strays! Before him and behind
Triumphs the tyrannous anger of the wounding wind,
The wounding wind, that burns as fire!

VI

It is my bitter grief – it cuts me to the heart –
That in the country of Clan Darry[53] this should be his fate!
O, woe is me, where is he? Wandering, houseless, desolate,
Alone, without or guide or chart!

VII

Medreams I see just now his face, the strawberry-bright,
Uplifted to the blackened heavens, while the tempestuous winds
Blow fiercely over and round him, and the smiting sleet-shower blinds
The hero of Galang[54] to-night!

Original: 'Fuar Leam an Oidhche-
se d'Aodh', by Eochaidh Ó
hEódhasa (cont.)

Literal translation (cont.):

Go ndeach tharuinn, ná tí m'olc,
An ní fá ngabhuim guasocht.

May it go over us, may my misfortune not come
The thing about which I feel dread.

Dá dtí ris an toisg do thrial
    Do chur chuarta chraoi
    Mhaicniadh –
Ní tháirtheamar séad mar soin –
Créad acht snáithghearradh
    saoghoil!

If he is able for the journey that he attempted,
    To visit the heart of Maicniadh –

We did not find a jewel like him –

What is it but a cutting of life's thread!

Líonaidh re hucht na n-ánroth
    Bruaigh ísle na n-uaránshroth,
Cluana sgor fá sgingbheirt reoidh
Dá gcor tar ingheilt d'aimhdheoin.

Rising against the bosoms of the warriors [are]
    The low banks of the river-pools,
Meadows of the horses under a frozen covering
Their turn for grazing past in spite of it.

Folchar a gciomhsa cheana,
    Nach léir do lucht foirgneamha
Bruaigh easgadh na ngrianshroth
    nglan –
Seasgadh fianbhoth ní féadtar.

Their borders gushing already,
    So that not clear to the people of the huts
[Are] the swampy banks of the clear sunny
    streams –
It is not possible for the warrior-hut to stand.

Eagail dó, díochra an anbhuain,
    Caill eachraidh is aradshluaigh,
Sul deachar tar síoth-Laoi siar
    Do chreachadh míonchraoi
    Mhaicniadh.

He fears, intense the unease,
    Loss of horses and high forces,
Before they went west over the peaceful Lee
Upon the roads of Maicniadh's smooth heart.

Ní hé budh uireasbhaidh linn
    A thuras an tráth smuainim,
Lór do chor chuarta ar gcridhe
Gomh fhuachta na haimsire.

It is not that it was a deficiency for us,
    His journey the time I'm thinking of,
Enough that his course moved our hearts
The cold sting of the weather.

Gidheadh is adhbhar téighthe
    Dá ghnúis shuaithnidh shoiléirthe
Slios gach múir ghorm-shaothraigh
    ghil
'Na dhlúimh thonn-ghaothmhair
    theintigh.

Nevertheless a reason to warm
    His clear, distinct countenance
Is the side of each bright, blue-worked castle

In a wind-waved fiery pall.

Téighfidh teannál an adhnaidh
    Sging reoidh an ruisg shochargh-
    lain;
Geimhle chuisne a chorrghlac ndonn
Donnbhrat luisne ros leaghonn.

Conflagration's firebrand will thaw
    The frozen covering of his beneficent, clear eye;
    The chains of frost on his brown tapering hands
The brown mantel of flames melts them.

Seachnóin Mhumhan na múr ngeal
    Iomdha ó airgtheoir fhuinn
    Ghaoidheal
Cúirte bruachnochta i mbeirt smóil
Ag ceilt fhuardhochta an aeóir.

Throughout Munster of the white castles
    Because of the plunderer of the lands of the
    Gaels, many
[Are the] courts of exposed borders in a cov-
    ering of smouldering fire
Concealing the stiff cold of the air.

Iomdha ó chuairt Aoidh Mhéig Uidhir,
    Feadh iarthair fhóid fhion-
    nfhuinidh,
Cúirt 'na doighir – ní díoth nuadh –
Críoch gan oighir gan iarmhua.[55]

Many, since the circuit of Hugh Maguire,
    Throughout the fair far lands of the west,
A court in flames – no new deprivation –
Territory without an heir, without a male
    descendant.

VIII

Large, large affliction unto me and mine it is,
That one of his majestic bearing, his fair, stately form,
Should thus be tortured and o'erborne – that this unsparing storm
Should wreak its wrath on head like his!

IX

That his great hand, so oft the avenger of the oppressed,
Should this chill, churlish night, perchance, be paralyzed by frost,
While through some icicle-hung thicket – as one lorn and lost –
He walks and wanders without rest.

X

The tempest-driven torrent deluges the mead,
It overflows the low banks of the rivulets and ponds –
The lawns and pasture-grounds lie locked in icy bonds,
So that the cattle cannot feed.

XI

The pale bright margins of the streams are seen by none.
Rushes and sweeps along the untamable flood on every side –
It penetrates and fills the cottagers' dwellings far and wide –
Water and land are blent in one.

XII

Through some dark woods, 'mid bones of monsters, Hugh now strays,
As he confronts the storm with anguished heart, but manly brow –
Oh! what a sword-wound to that tender heart of his were now
A backward glance at peaceful days!

XIII

But other thoughts are his – thoughts that can still inspire
With joy and an onward-bounding hope the bosom of Mac Nee[56] –
Thoughts of his warriors charging like bright billows of the sea,
Borne on the wind's wings, flashing fire!

XIV

And though frost glaze to-night the clear dew of his eyes,
And white ice-gauntlets glove his noble fine fair fingers o'er,
A warm dress is to him that lightning-garb he ever wore,
The lightning of the soul, not skies.

XV

Avran[57]

Hugh marched forth to the fight – I grieved to see him so depart;
And lo! to-night he wanders frozen, rain-drenched, sad, betrayed –
But the memory of the limewhite mansions his right hand hath laid
In ashes warms his hero's heart![58]

Original: from 'Gile na Gile', by Aodhagán Ó Rathaille	Literal translation:
Gile na gile do chonnarc ar slíghe a n-uaignios, Criosdal an chriosdail a gorm-rosg, rínn-uaithne; Binnios an bhinnis a friotal, nár chríon-ghruamadh, Deirge 's finne do fionnadh 'na gríos-ghruad'nadh.	The brightness of brightness I saw on a lonely way, The crystal of crystal her blue eye, green-tinged, The sweetness of sweetness her voice not despondent with age, Redness and whiteness discovered in her glowing cheeks.
Caise na caise ann gach ruibe dá buidhe-chuachaibh, Bhaineas an chruinne dá ruithne le rín-sguabaidh; Iorrad ba ghlaine ná glaine air a bruinn buacaidh, Do geineadh ar gheineamhain d'isi san tír uachtraigh.	The plaiting of plaiting in every rib of her yellow tresses, That deprived the earth of its radiance with its full sweeping; An ornament clearer than glass on her luxuriant bosom, That was created upon her creation in the land above.
Fios fiosach dam d'inis 's isi go fíor-uaignioch, Fios filleadh do'n duine do'n ionad ba rígh-dhualgas Fios milleadh na droinge chuir eision ar rín-ruagadh, 'S fios eile ná cuirfiod am luidhthibh le fíor-uamhan.	Knowledge of knowledge to me she told and she was truly lonely, Knowledge of the returning of the person to the place that was a king's due, Knowledge of the destruction of the people who expelled him, And other knowledge that I will not put in my lays because of great fear.
Leimhe na leimhe dam druidim 'na cruinn-thuairim, 'S mé am chuinge ag an chaime do shraidhmeadh go fíor-chruaidh mé; Ar ghoirm mhic Muire dham fhurtacht do bhíog uaimsi, 'S lingios an bhruingioll na luisne go Bruíghion Luachra.	The folly of folly to me that I approach near to her And I made prisoner by the prisoner who bound me very tightly; On summoning the son of Mary to aid me, she started from me, And the fair maiden started off in a flash for the fairy dwelling of Luachra.
Ruithim le mire am ruithibh go croidhe-luaimneach, Tré iomeallaibh churraig, tré mhong-taibh, tré shlímruaidhtibh; Do'n fhinne-bhrog tigim, ní thuigim cia 'n t-slíghe fuaras, Go h-ionad na n-ionad, do cumadh le draoigheacht Druagaibh.	I run with a quickness in my running, with leaping heart, Through edges of marshes, through fens, through bare moors.; To the mansion of strength I come, I don't know how I found the way, To the place of places, formed by the magic of Druids.
Brisid fá sgige go sgigeamhail, buidhin ghruagach, 'S fuireann de bhruingiollaibh siosgaid-hthe, dlaoichuachach; A n-geimheallaibh geimheal mé cuirid gan puinn suaimhnis, 'S mo bhruingioll ar bruinnibh ag bruin-nire bruinn-stuacach.	They broke into tittering scornfully, a band of wizards, And a band of fair maidens, trim, with plaited tresses; In shackles of shackles they put me without much peace And my fair maiden [taken] by her breasts by a lubberly, stout awkward fellow.

'The Brightest of the Bright'

(The original, by Aodhagán Ó Rathaille [c. 1675–1729], is one of the best-known of the *aisling* [vision] poems in the Irish-language tradition. Often promoting Jacobite ambitions, the form flourished particularly after the Williamite wars, and in Ó Rathaille's native Munster.)

The Brightest of the Bright met me on my path so lonely;
    The Crystal of all Crystals was her flashing dark-blue eye;
Melodious more than music was her spoken language only;
    And glories were her cheeks of a brilliant crimson dye.

With ringlets above ringlets her hair in many a cluster
    Descended to the earth, and swept the dewy flowers;
Her bosom shone as bright as a mirror in its lustre;
    She seemed like some fair daughter of the Celestial Powers.

She chanted me a chant, a beautiful and grand hymn,
    Of him who should be shortly Eire's reigning King –
She prophesied the fall of the wretches who had banned him;
    And somewhat else she told me which I dare not sing.

Trembling with many fears I called on Holy Mary,
    As I drew nigh this Fair, to shield me from all harm,
When, wonderful to tell! she fled far to the Fairy
    Green mansion of Sliabh Luachra[59] in terror and alarm.

O'er mountain, moor and marsh, by greenwood, lough and hollow,
    I tracked her distant footsteps with throbbing heart;
Through many an hour and day did I follow on and follow,
    Till I reached the magic palace reared of old by Druid art.

There a wild and wizard band with mocking fiendish laughter
    Pointed out me her I sought, who sat low beside a clown;
And I felt as though I never could dream of Pleasure after
    When I saw the maid so fallen whose charms deserved a crown.

Then with burning speech and soul, I looked at her and told her
    That to wed a churl like that was for her the shame of shames,
When a bridegroom such as I was longing to enfold her
    To a bosom that her beauty had kindled into flames.

Original: from 'Gile na Gile', by Aodhagán Ó Rathaille (cont.)	Literal translation (cont.):
D'innisios d'isi san bh-friotal ba fhíor uaim-si,	I spoke to her in the speech that was true for me,
Nár chuibhe dhi snaidhme le slibire slím-bhuartha;	That it was not fitting for her to join with a miserable, sorry slipshod churl;
'S an duine ba ghile air chine Scuit trí h-uaire,	And the brightest person of the Irish race three times over,
Ag feithiomh ar isi bheith aige mar chaoin-nuachar.	Waiting for her to be with him as a tender spouse.
Ar chluisdin mo ghutha dhi, goilean go fíor-uaibhreach,	On hearing my voice, she weeps very desolately,
Ruithean an fhliche go life as a gríos-ghru-adhaibh;	The wetness runs fluently from her glowing cheeks;
Cuirean liom giolladh mar choimirc ó'n m-bruíghin uaithe.	She gives me a guide as protection [in going] from the fairy dwelling away from her,
'S í Gile na Gile, do chonnarc ar slíghe a n-uaignios!	She is the brightness of brightness, I saw on the lonely way.

An Ceangal	The Binding
Mo thréighidh, mo thubhaíst, mo thur-rainn, mo bhrón, mo dhíth!	My pain, my calamity, my stroke of misfortune, my sorrow, my ruin!
Mo shoillseach mhuirneach mhiochair-gheal, bheól-tais, chaoin,	My fair maiden, tender, brightly kind, gentle-mouthed, delicate
Air adhairc fuireannuibh, miosgaiseach, crón-dubh, buidhe;	With a horned person, malicious, swarthy, yellow with a black troop
'S gan leíghios na goire go bh-fillfid na leóghain tar tuinn![60]	And without a cure of the wrong until the heroes will return over the wave!

Original: 'Bean na Cleithe Caoile', by Seán Ó Tuama	Literal translation:
Níor thagair liom ceart, beart 'ná briathar aoibhnis	I did not plea for justice, a promise or a word of sweetness
Leabhar ná ceacht, ná rann a dheilbh díreach;	A book or a lesson, or a verse in direct form;
Níor cáthag mé ar fad go teacht im sheirb-híseach,	I was not beaten at all until becoming a servant,
'S am reachtaire cearc ag Bean na cleithe caoile!	And becoming a steward of hens for the woman of the slender wattle!
Do chaithiosadh seal fá raith air leirg laoithe,	I spent a time prospering on the track of lays,
A g-caidriomh fear, 's flaith, 's creidiomh Iosa;	In the company of men, and lords, and faith in Jesus;
Airgiod geal am ghlaic gan doirbh nídh ar bith,	Bright money in my grasp without anything unfavourable at all,
Cia dealbh mo mheas ag Bean na cleithe caoile!	How bleak my esteem with the woman of the slender wattle!

But answer made she none; she wept with bitter weeping;
     Her tears ran down in rivers, but nothing could she say;
She gave me then a guide for my safe and better keeping, –
     The Brightest of the Bright, whom I met upon my way.

Summing Up

Oh, my misery, my woe, my sorrow and my anguish,
     My bitter source of dolor is evermore that she
The Loveliest of the Lovely should thus be left to languish
     Amid a ruffian horde till the Heroes cross the sea.[61]

'The Dame of the Slender Wattle'

(The original was written by Seán Ó Tuama [1706? –1775], one of the poets of the Maigue. Having run a school and an inn that was a meeting-place for poets in Croom, Co. Limerick, Ó Tuama apparently fell on hard times, and found himself, around 1740, working as a servant to a woman named Mrs. Quade in Adare, Co. Limerick.)

Ochone! I never in all my dealings met with a man to snub me,
Books I have studied, however muddied a person *you* may dub me,
I never was tossed or knocked about – I never was forced to battle
With the storms of life, till I herded your hens, O, Dame of the
    Slender Wattle!

I spent a season a-chanting poems, and free from toil and troubles,
The faith of Christ I ever upheld, though I mixed with the proudest
    nobles,
And gay was my heart, and open my hand, and I lacked not cash or
    cattle,
Though low my esteem to-day with you, O, Dame of the Slender
    Wattle!

Original: 'Bean na Cleithe Caoile',   Literal translation (cont.):
    by Seán Ó Tuama (cont.)

Is é lagaidh mo mheas, do mheath, do   What has weakened my esteem, decayed
    mheirbh m'inntinn,   and deadened my mind,
Nach mairion na flaith do lean an creid-   [Is] that the lords who followed the straight
    iomh díreach;   faith are not living;
Do channadh na rannadh a scannadh   Who chanted the verses that the tribes of
    treibh a sinnsear,   their ancestors composed,
'S do bhainfeadh an fhail de Bhean na   And who would take the place of the
    cleithe caoile!   woman of the slender wattle!

Is feasach nár chleachtas teacht a n-deire   It is known I wasn't used to arriving at the
    coímheasgair,   end of a battle,
Ag ceasacht 's ag caismirt caillídhe ceis-   From the complaining, and the commotion
    nídhe cínte;   of grumbling, stingy old women;
Ná'n acharan amh, a bh-fad ó bhreith an   Or from the raw quarrelling, far from the
    fhír-chirt,   judgment of the truly right,
Go ndeachadh fá smacht ag Bean na   Until going under the rule of the woman of
    cleithe caoile!   the slender wattle!

Cia fada mé 'g taisdiol treabh, 's tighthe   Although I am long travelling to tribes, and
    taoiseach,   the houses of chiefs,
'S go bh-feacadh gach reacht 's acht ar   And attending to every law and act
    feadh na ríoghachta;   throughout the kingdom;
Níor bh-feasach mé ar chleasadh frasadh   I did not know copious tricks, actively
    feill-ghníomhach,   treacherous,
Go "preabaire an Ghaid" atá ag Bean na   Until the "spring of willow rod" that the
    cleithe caoile!   woman of the slender wattle has!

Aitchim an Mac do cheap na ceithre   I beseech the Son who conceived the four
    soillse,   lights,
Flathas, Fearn, Feart, 's Dealbh daoine;   Heaven, Earth, Virtue, and the human Form;
Go ngabhadh m'anam feasda 'na fheilbh[a]   That my soul be taken henceforth into his
    dílis,   sweet possession,
'S mé sgaradh fá bhlas le Bean na cleithe   And that I be released from the taste of the
    caoile![62]   woman of the slender wattle!

---

[a] The literal translation assumes 'i seilbh' as in *Éigse na Máighe*.

My spirits are gone, my face is wan, my cheeks are yellow and hol-
lowed,
Because the nobles are dead by whom the true old Faith was fol-
lowed,
Who sang the glory of those that died for Eire's rights in battle,
And would soon bring down your paltry pride, my Dame of the
Slender Wattle!

'Tis very well known I always shunned contention, clamour, and
jawing,
And never much liked the chance of getting a barbarous clapper-
clawing;
I always passed on the other side when I heard a hag's tongue rattle,
Till I happened, *mo vrone!*[63] to stumble on you, O, Dame of the Slender
Wattle!

Though used to the ways of tribes and chiefs, and reading the deeds
that appear in
The chronicles and the ancient books that embody the lore of Erin,
I scarce ever knew what cruelty was, except through rumour or
prattle,
Till the dismal day that I felt your flail, O, Dame of the Slender Wattle!

O! I pray the Lord, whose powerful Word set the elements first in
motion,
And formed from nought the race of Man, with Heaven, and Earth,
and Ocean,
To lift my spirit above this world, and all its clangor and brattle,
And give me a speedy release from you, O, Dame of the Slender
Wattle![64]

Original: 'An Bonnaire Fiadha-
Phuic', by Seán Clárach Mac
Domhnaill

Literal translation:

A sé do leónaidh mo chumas;
    An bonnaire fiadha-phuic, fághain;
Do léim thar teóruinn do thurraic,
    Le'r milleadh le cian an mágha:
Faol-choin fóir-neirt le fuineamh,
    Chuir bris' air ó thriall a ghná'ais,
D'éimidh sé cómhrac gan mhisneach;
    'S d'imthigh ó rian a námhaid.

It is he who wounded my power;
    The wandering, wild 'deer';
He leapt over the border at a rush,
    And ruined the plain for a great time:
Wolfhounds of great violence with vigour
    Kept him from proceeding to his haunts,
He refused combat without courage;
    And departed from the track of his enemy.

Ata mo chóraid gan fuithin,
    'S mo chuingir gan féur, gan fás,
Ata an-shóigh air mo mhuirear,
    'S a n-uillinn gan éadach slán:
Atá an tóir air mo mhullach,
    Go minic ó thighearna 'n stáit;
'S 'tá mo bhróga-sa brisde,
    'S gan pingin da bh-fiach' am láimh.

My flocks are without shelter,
    And my herd without grass, without growth,
Hardship is on my family,
    And their elbows without sound clothing:
The pursuers are on top of me
    Often from the lord of the state;
And my shoes are broken,
    And not a penny of the debts in my hand.

Edward Walsh
(1805–1850)

Edward Walsh brought to verse translation from the Irish a strong commitment to nationalism and, like J. J. Callanan, a thorough grounding in Irish folk culture, especially of the southwest. He also brought with him the view that because Irish-language poetry is so successful in adapting 'the subject of the words to the song measure', as he put it, the verse translator must do all he can to insure that the original is not, in translation, forced out of its natural rhythms and phrasing, something that Walsh sees as a serious fault in the work of earlier translators like Charlotte Brooke and the contributors to James Hardiman's *Irish Minstrelsy*.[65]

Walsh grew up in Millstreet, Co. Cork, where he learned Irish and wandered the nearby mountainous countryside, collecting stories and songs. His outspoken nationalism cost him at least two posts as a schoolteacher, and he ended his days teaching in the Cork Union Workhouse.

'The Cruel Base-Born Tyrant'

(The original was written by Seán Clárach Mac Domhnaill [1691–1754], who lived near Charleville, Co. Cork, and was associated for a time with the poets of the Maigue in Croom, Co. Limerick. Mac Domhnaill's poem refers to the flight of James II after the Battle of the Boyne in 1690.)

> What withered the pride of my vigour?
>   The lowly-sprung tyrant train
> That rule all our border with rigour,
>   And ravage the fruitful plain –
> Yet once when the war-trumpet's rattle
>   Arous'd the wild clansman's wrath,
> They, heartless, abandon'd the battle,
>   And fled the fierce foeman's path!
>
> The loved ones my life would have nourish'd
>   Are foodless, and bare, and cold –
> My flocks by their fountain that flourish'd,
>   Decay on the mountain wold –
> Misfortune my temper is trying;
>   This raiment no shelter yields –
> And chief o'er my evils undying,
>   The tyrant who rules my fields!

Original: 'An Bonnaire Fiadha-Phuic', by Seán Clárach Mac Domhnaill (cont.)

Literal translation (cont.):

Is léir a ngleó-cnoic gur thuiteadar,
  Siollairídhe treun air lár;
'S gur thréig sinn mór-chuid deagh-chu-mainn,
  Misneach, is caomhna, is grádh:
B'fhéidir fós le Rígh Neimhe,
  Go d-tiocfadh an laoch thar sáil';
Do réighfeadh Fódla go h-uile,
  Ó Thurcachaibh daor an áirr.[66]

It is clear in the battle of the hill that they fell,
  Strong seed of kings laid low;
And that a great share of good companion-ship deserted us,
  Courage and protection and love:
Perhaps still, by the King of Heaven,
  The warrior would come over the sea;
Who would free *Fódhla* entirely
  From the severe Turks of the slaughter.

Original: 'An Raibh Tú ag an g-Carraig'

Literal translation:

I.

An raibh tú ag an g-Carraig, nó bh-faca tú féin mo ghrádh,
Nó a bh-faca tú gile, finne, agus sgéimh na mná,
Nó a bh-faca tú an t-ubhal ba chúbhartha is ba mhillse bláth,
Nó a bh-faca tú mo bhalantín nó a bh-fuil sí d'a claoidh mar táim?

I.

Were you at Carrick, did you yourself see my love,
Did you see the brightness, the fairness, and the beauty of the woman,
Did you see the apple of the creamiest and the sweetest blossom,
Did you see my valentine, is she destroyed as I am?

II.

Do bhíosa ag an g-Carraig, is do chonairc mé féin do ghrádh,
Do chonairc mé gile, finne, agus sgéimh na mná,
Do chonairc mé an t-ubhal ba cúbhartha is ba mhillse bláth,
Do chonairc mé do bhalantín agus ní'l sí da claoidh mar táir!

II.

I was at Carrick, and I myself saw your love,
I saw the brightness, the fairness, and the beauty of the woman,
I saw the creamiest and sweetest apple blossom,
I saw your valentine and she is not destroyed as you are!

III.

Is fiú cúig ghuinea gach ribhe da gruaigh mar ór,
Is fiú oiread eile a cuideachta úair raibh[a] ló;
A cúilín trom tripilich a tuitim léi síos go feóir
'Sa chuaichín na finne, ar mhiste do shlainte d'ól?

III.

Every rib of her hair like gold is worth five guineas,
Her company the hour before day is worth as much again;
Her heavy clustered tresses falling from her down to the grass
And pretty girl of fairness, would you mind drinking your health?

IV.

'N úair bhím-se am chodhla bían osnadh gan bhrígh am chliabh,
Is mé am lúidh eadar cnocaibh go d-tigidh an dúach[b] aníar;
A rúin dhil s'a chogair, ní'l fortacht mo chúis acht Dia,
Is go n-dearnadh loch fola do sholus mo shúl ad diaidh!

IV.

When I am asleep, a sighing with strength is in my bosom,
And I am lying between mountains until the sun comes back;
Dear love and sweetheart, there is no aid for my case but God,
And may a lake of blood be made of the light of my eyes pursuing you!

Alas! on the red hill where perish'd
    The offspring of heroes proud,
The virtues our forefathers cherish'd,
    Lie pall'd in their blood-stain'd shroud!
And O! for the one hero avenger,
    With aid o'er the heaving main,
To sweep from *Clar-Fodhla*[67] the stranger,
    And sever his bondage chain![68]

'Have You Been at Carrick?'

(Walsh identifies this as a song of the south, but says its location cannot be fixed precisely because Carrick appears so often in Irish place-names. John O'Daly, who included a version of the poem in *Poets and Poetry of Munster* [1849], along with Walsh's translation, says the original was the work of a Co. Tyrone poet named Dominic O'Mongan, and was written for a young woman who lived in Carrick, Co. Armagh.)

I.

Have you been at Carrick, and saw you my true-love there?
And saw you her features, all beautiful, bright, and fair?
Saw you the most fragrant, flowering, sweet apple-tree? –
O! saw you my lov'd one, and pines she in grief like me?

II.

I have been at Carrick, and saw thy own true-love there;
And saw, too, her features, all beautiful, bright, and fair;
And saw the most fragrant, flowering, sweet apple-tree –
I saw thy lov'd one – she pines not in grief, like thee!

III.

Five guineas would price every tress of her golden hair –
Then think what a treasure her pillow at night to share,
These tresses thick-clustering and curling around her brow –
O, Ringlet of Fairness! I'll drink to thy beauty now!

IV.

When seeking to slumber, my bosom is rent with sighs –
I toss on my pillow till morning's blest beams arise;
No aid, bright Beloved! can reach me save GOD above,
For a blood-lake is form'd of the light of my eyes with love!

Original: 'An Raibh Tú ag an g-Carraig' (cont.)

Literal translation (cont.):

V.

Is go d-tigidh an cháisc air lár an fhoghmhair bhuidhe,
Is lá fhéil Pátruig lá nó dhó na dhiaigh,
Go bh-fása an bláth bán tre lár mo chomhra chaol,
Páirt da grádh go brath ní thabharfad do mhnaoi!

And until Easter comes in the middle of yellow autumn,
And the feast day of Patrick a day or two after,
Until the white blossom grows through the middle of my narrow coffin,
A share of love I never will give to a woman!

VI.

Siúd í síos an Ríogh-bhean áluin óg,
A bhfuil a grúaig léi sgaoilte síos go béal a bróg,
'S í an eala í mar an lítis do shíolraigh ón t-sár-fhuil mhór,
Charaid gheal mo chroidhe, céad míle fáilte romhat![69]

There she comes down, the beautiful young queen,
Whose hair is released down to the edge of her shoe,
She is the swan like the whiteness that descended from the highest of great blood,
Bright friend of my heart, a hundred thousand welcomes to you

---

[a] The literal translation assumes *roimh*.
[b] The literal translation assumes *ghrian*, as in ND-I.

Original: 'Plúr na m-Ban Donn Óg'

Literal translation:

I.

Dá d-tiocfa-sa liomsa go Cúntae Liatroim;
A phlúr na m-ban donn óg,
Bhéarfainn-si mil bheach agus méad mar bhiadh dhuit,
A phlúr na m-ban donn óg,
Bhéarfad aer na long na seól 's na m-bád duit,
Faoi bharradhaibh na d-tom a's sinn ag filleadh ó'n d-tráigh,
'S ní léigfinn-si aen bhrón choidhche do'd dháil,
A phlúr na m-ban donn óg!

If you would come with me to County Leitrim;
O, flower of the young, dark-haired women,
I would bring bees' honey and mead as food to you,
O, flower of the young, dark-haired women,
I will bring the air of the ships of the sails and the boats to you,
Through the branches of thickets and we returning from the strand,
And I would never allow any sorrow near you,
Flower of the young, dark-haired women!

II.

Ní rachfaidh mise leat, a's ní'l maith duit do'm iarraidh,
Dubhairt plúr na m-ban donn óg;

Mar nach g-coinneóchadh do ghlórtha beó gan bhiadh mé,
Dubhairt plúr na m-ban donn óg;

Míle céad fearr liom bheith choidhche gan fhear,
Ná beith ag siubhal an druchta 's na bh-fásach leat,
Níor thug mo chroidhe dhuit grádh ná gean,
Dubhairt plúr na m-ban donn óg.

I will not go with you, and there's no good your asking me,
Said the flower of the young, dark-haired women,

As your speeches would not keep me alive without food,
Said the flower of the young, dark-haired women;

A thousand hundred times I would prefer ever to be without a man,
Than to be walking the dews and the wilderness with you,
My heart did not give you love or affection,
Said the flower of the young, dark-haired women

V

Until yellow Autumn shall usher the Paschal day,
And Patrick's gay festival come in its train alway –
Until through my coffin the blossoming boughs shall grow,
My love on another I'll never in life bestow!

VI

Lo! yonder the maiden illustrious, queen-like, high,
With long-flowing tresses adown to her sandal-tie –
Swan, fair as the lily, descended of high degree,
A myriad of welcomes, dear maid of my heart, to thee![70]

'Flower of Brown-Haired Maidens'

(Walsh says the original appears to have been written during a period
of famine.)

I.

Oh! if thou come to Leitrim, sure nought can us sever,
    A phlúr na m-ban donn óg![71]
Wild honey and the mead-cup shall feast us for ever,
    A phlúr na m-ban donn óg!
I'll show thee ships and sails, through the vistas grand,
As we seek our green retreat by the broad lake's strand,
And grief would never reach us within that happy land,
    A phlúr na m-ban donn óg!

II.

To Leitrim, to Leitrim, in vain thou would'st lead me,
    Duirt plúr na m-ban donn óg.
When pale hunger comes, can thy melodies feed me?
    Duirt plúr na m-ban donn óg.
Sooner would I live, and sooner die a maid,
Than wander with thee through the dewy forest glade,
That thou are my beloved, this bosom never said,
    Duirt plúr na m-ban donn óg.

III.

Over the mountain I once met the maiden,
    As a star through the mist might glow;
We reach'd, while I told her my tale sorrow-laden,
    The field of the kine below;
And there, in the hollow by the hedge-row tree,
I plighted her a promise, till life should flee,
To bear all the blame of her true love for me,
    Mo phlúr na m-ban donn óg.

Original: 'Plúr na m-Ban Donn
Óg' (cont.)

Literal translation (cont.):

III.

Chonairc mé ag teacht chugam í tré lár
an t-sléibhe,
Mar réiltion thríd an g-ceódh,
Bhí mé ag caint a's ag comhrádh léi
Go n-deachamar go páirc na m-bó.
Shuidhamairne síos i lúib an fháil,
Go d-tug mé dhi scríobhtha faoi mo
láimh,
Nach bh-fuil coir dá n-déanadh sí nach
n-íocfainn a cáin,
Do phlúr na m-ban donn óg.

III.

I saw her coming toward me through the
middle of the mountain,
Like a star through the fog,
I was talking and conversing with her
Until we went to the park of the cows.
We sat down in a recess of the hedge,
Until I brought to her a piece of writing under
my signature,
That there is no wrong that she would do that
I would not pay the penalty for,
For the flower of the young, dark-haired
women.

IV.

Mo chreach a's mo chrádh gan mé fáis-
gthe síos léi,
Mo phlúr na m-ban donn óg,
Air leaba chaol árd, no air chárn tuibhe,
Mo phlúr na m-ban donn óg,
Gan duine air bith a n-Eirinn bheith
láimh linn 'san oidhche
Acht ag súgradh agus ag gáireadh réir
mar budh mhiann linn,
A Dhia, nach cruadh an cás é muna
bhfaghidh mé mo mhiann,
Air phlúr na m-ban donn óg.[72]

IV.

My loss and my torment not [to be] squeezed
down with her,
My flower of the young, dark-haired women,
On a high narrow bed, or on a pile of straw,
My flower of the young, dark-haired women,
Without any person at all in Ireland to be near
to us in the evening
But playing and laughing according as we
desire,
Oh, God, won't it be a hard case if I will not get
my desire,
From the flower of the young, dark-haired
women.

Original: 'Atáim Sínte ar
do Thuamba'

Literal translation

I.

Atáim sínte air do thuamba,
A's do gheabhair ann do shíor mé;
Dá mbéidheadh bárr do dhá lámh 'gam,
Ní sgarfainn leat choidhche –
A úbhailín agus annsacht,
Is am damhsa luigh leat,
'Tá boladh fuar na criadh orm,
Dath na gréine 's na gaoithe!

I.

I am stretched on your tomb,
And you will possess me there forever;
If I could have the tip of your two hands,
I would not part from you ever –
Choice small thing and loved one,
It is time for me to lie with you,
The cold smell of the earth is on me,
The color of the sun and the wind!

II.

Atá cló air mo chroidhesi,
'Ta líonta le grádh dhuit,
Lionndubh air taobh shíos de,
Chómh cíar dubh le h-áirne.
Má bhainion aon nídh dham,
'S go cclaoidhfeadh an bás me,
Beidheadsa m' shíoth-gaoithe,
Rómhad shíos air na bánta!

II.

An impression is on my heart,
That is filled with love for you,
Melancholy on the lower side of it,
As swarthy black as a sloe.
If anything happens to me,
And death should subdue me,
I would be perpetual winds
Before you down on the grasslands!

IV.

Alas! my sad heart, that I kiss not thy blushes,
    A phlúr na m-ban donn óg.
On a rich, lofty couch, or a heap of green rushes,
    Mo phlúr na m-ban donn óg.
Alone, all alone, through the beautiful night,
Laughing in the fulness of our hearts' delight;
Alas, if thou be not mine, how woful is my plight,
    A phlúr na m-ban donn óg![73]

'From the Cold Sod That's O'er You'

(For a version by Thomas Kinsella, see pp. 317–319.)

I.

From the cold sod that's o'er you
    I never shall sever –
Were my hands twin'd in your's, love,
    I'd hold them for ever –
My fondest, my fairest,
    We may now sleep together,
I've the cold earth's damp odour,
    And I'm worn from the weather!

II.

This heart, fill'd with fondness,
    Is wounded and weary;
A dark gulf beneath it
    Yawns jet-black and dreary –
When death comes, a victor,
    In mercy to greet me,
On the wings of the whirlwind,
    In the wild wastes you'll meet me!

III.

When the folk of my household
    Suppose I am sleeping,
On your cold grave, 'till morning,
    The lone watch I'm keeping;
My grief to the night wind,
    For the mild maid to render,
Who was my betrothed
    Since infancy tender!

Original: 'Atáim Sínte ar
do Thuamba' (cont.)

Literal translation (cont.):

III.

Nuair is dóigh le mo mhuintir,
  Go mbímse air mo leaba;
Air do thuamba seadh bhídhim sínte
  O oidhche go maidion;
Ag cur síos mo chruadhtain,
  'S ag cruadh-ghol go daingion,
Tre mo chailín ciúin, stuamadh,
  Do luadhadh liom na leanbh!

III.

When it seems to my people
  That I am in my bed;
It is on your tomb I am stretched
  From night to morning;
Setting out my hardship,
  And severely weeping constantly,
For my quiet steady girl,
  Who as a child was spoken of as my future
  wife.

IV.

An cuimhin leatsa an oidhche,
  Do bhíosa 'gus tusa;
Fá bhun an chrainn draighnigh,
  'S an oidhche ag cur cuisne;
Céad moladh le h-Iosa,
  Nach dhéarnamar an milleadh,
'S go bhfuil do choróin mhaighdeanuis,
  Na crann soillse as do choinne!

IV.

Do you remember the evening
  That you and I were
Under the blackthorn tree,
  And the evening becoming cold;
A hundred praises to Jesus,
  We did not do the spoiling,
And that your crown of maidenhood is
  A tree of light in front of you.

V.

Tá na Sagairt 's na Bráithre,
  Gach lá liom a bhfearg;
Do choinn bheith a ngrádh leat,
  A óigbhean is tú marbh;
Dhéanfainn fosgadh air an ngaoith dhuit
  'S díon duit ó'n bhfearthainn;
Agus cúmhadh ghéar mo chroidhesi
  Thú bheith shíos annsa ttalamh!

V.

The Priests and the Brothers are
  Every day with me angry;
For being in love with you,
  Young woman, and you dead;
I would make a shelter from the wind for you
  And a roof for you from the rain;
And [it is] the bitter sorrow of my heart
  That you are down in the ground!

VI.

Tabhair do mhallacht dod mháthairín,
  'S áirmhidhsi t-athair;
'S a mairion dod cháirde,
  Go léireach na seasamh:
Nár léig dam thú phósadh
  'S tu beó 'gam ad bheatha,
Agus nach n-iarrfainn mar spréidh leat,
  Ach lúidhe liom air leaba![74]

VI.

Give your curse to your little mother,
  And include your father,
And to your friends who live,
  All in their standing:
Who did not permit me to marry you
  And you alive with me in your life,
And I would not ask as a dowry for you,
  But to lie with me on a bed!

IV.

Remember the lone night
   I last spent with you, love,
Beneath the dark sloe-tree,
   When the icy wind blew, love –
High praise to the Saviour
   No sin-stain had found you,
That your virginal glory
   Shines brightly around you!

V.

The priests and the friars
   Are ceaselessly chiding,
That I love a young maiden,
   In life not abiding –
O! I'd shelter and shield you,
   If wild storms were swelling,
And O! my wreck'd hope,
   That the cold earth's your dwelling!

VI.

Alas, for your father,
   And also your mother,
And all your relations,
   Your sister and brother,
Who gave you to sorrow,
   And the grave 'neath the willow,
While I crav'd, as your portion,
   But to share your chaste pillow![75]

Original: 'Condae Mhaigheo'	Literal translation:
Is ar an loingseo Phaidi Loingsigh do ghnimse an dubron	It is on this ship of Páidí Loingsigh's that I made great sorrow
Ag osnadh ann san oidhche is ag siorghol san ló	Sighing in the evening and always crying in the day
Muna mbeidh gur dalladh minntleacht is me a bhfad om mhuinntir	If it were not that my mind is confused and I'm far from my people
Dar a maireann! is maith a chaoinfinnsi Condae Mhaigheo.	By life! it is well I would lament County Mayo.
An uair a mhair mo chairde budh bhreagh mo chuid oir	The time that my friends lived, splendid was my share of gold
Dolainn lionn Spaineach i gcomhluadar ban og	I would drink Spanish ale in the company of young women
Muna mbeidh síor ol na gcárta, san dligh bheith ro láidir	If it were not for the constant drinking of the quarts, and the law being too strong
Ni a Santícrús a d'fhácfainn mo chnamha fán bhfod.	It's not in Santa Cruz that I would leave my bones under the sod.
Táid gadaidhnighe na háite seo eirgeadh go mhór[a]	The beguilers of these places are becoming too great
Fa chnotadha is fa hairbag gan tracht as bhúcladha brog	Under [top-] knots and hair-bags not to mention shoe-buckles
Da mairfheadh damsa an Iar-Umhall do dhéanfuinn díobh cianach	If I were living in Iar-Umhall I would make them sad
Muna mbeidh gur thagair Dia dham bheith a gciantaibh fa bhron.	Were it not that God desired me to be far away under sorrow.
Dá mbeidh Padruig Lochlainn ina iarla air Iar-Umhaill go foil	If Padruig Lochlainn were an earl in Iar-Umhall still
Brian dubh a chliamhain na thighearna ar Dhumhach-Mhoir	Dark Brian, his relation, a lord in Dumhach-Mór
Aodh dubh Mac Griada 'na choirnel a gCliara	Dark Hugh Mac Griada a colonel on Clare Island
Is ann niu bheidh mo thriallsa go Condae Mhaigheo.[76]	It is today that my journey would be to County Mayo.

---

[a] The literal translation assumes *ro mhór*, as in IM.

George Fox
(1809–1880?)

Born in Belfast and educated at Trinity College Dublin, George Fox worked with Samuel Ferguson in Belfast in the 1830s to advance the study and translation of Irish. The original of Fox's 'The County of Mayo' has sometimes been attributed to Thomas Flavell, a seventeenth-century poet possibly from Inishbofin, off the coast of Co. Galway.

'The County of Mayo'

I.

On the deck of Patrick Lynch's boat I sit in woeful plight,
Through my sighing all the weary day, and weeping all the night.
Were it not that full of sorrow from my people forth I go,
By the blessed sun, 'tis royally I'd sing thy praise, Mayo!

II.

When I dwelt at home in plenty, and gold did much abound,
In the company of fair young maids the Spanish ale went round –
'Tis a bitter change from those gay days that now I'm forced to go,
And must leave my bones in Santa Cruz, far from my own Mayo!

III.

They are altered girls in Irrul[77] now; 'tis proud they're grown and high,
With their hair-bags and their top-knots, for I pass their buckles by –
But it's little now I heed their airs, for God will have it so,
That I must depart for foreign lands, and leave my sweet Mayo!

IV.

'Tis my grief that Patrick Loughlin is not Earl in Irrul still;
And that Brian Duff no longer rules as Lord upon the hill;
And that Colonel Hugh Mac Grady should be lying dead and low,
And I sailing, sailing swiftly from the county of Mayo![78]

Original: 'Air Cheimsios
na n-Gaodhal', by Fear
Flatha Ó Gnímh

Literal translation:

Mo thruaigh! mar táid Gaoidhil!
   Annamh íntinn fhorbhfaoílidh,
   Air a'n-uair-si ag duine dhiobh; –
   A n-uaisle uile air neimhnídh!

My sorrow! How the Gaels are!
   Rarely a greatly joyful mind
   At this time has one of them; –
   All their nobles reduced to nothing.

Baramhail do bheirthear dóibh;
   Fuígheall tar éis a n-díoghbhoigh,
   Ag á sníomhadh ó 'croloíghe a g-
     cneadh;
   Nó is líon torraimhe air d-
     tilleadh: –

A likeness is borne by them;
   Survivors after their worst destruction,
   At their struggling since lying wounded in
     their groaning;
   Or they are the entire funeral cortege in
     their returning; –

Nó is luchd báirce fá'r bhrúcht muir;

Or they are people of a ship under an eruption
   of the sea;

Nó is drong fuair fios a saéghail;

Or they are a group who found knowledge
   of their life,

Nó is géill a n-géibheannaibh
   Gall,
Eireannaich fá fhéainn eachdrann!

Or they are hostages in the fetters of the
   Gall,
Irishmen under the yoke of foreigners!

Tugsad a d-tréine air thaise; –
   Tugsad maise air mhí-mhaise; –
   Tugsad meanma air mhaoith-
     mheirtne; –
   Laoích fheardha nach aitheantar!

They gave their strength for weakness; –
   They gave beauty for uncomeliness; –
   They gave spirit for faint-hearted weak-
     ness; –
   Manly warriors are not known!

Samuel Ferguson
(1810–1886)

Although Samuel Ferguson, a Belfast Protestant whose father belonged to the landed gentry, devoted most of his professional life to literary antiquarianism, his most important work as a verse translator from the Irish was done in his twenties. In 1834, when he was twenty-four, he published a scathing four-part review of James Hardiman's *Irish Minstrelsy* in the *Dublin University Magazine*, a periodical founded by a group of Trinity College Tories committed, as Ferguson himself was at the time, to anti-Catholicism. Ferguson attacked Hardiman himself for Catholic bias and his various translators for ineptitude, and attached to the final part of the review his own translations of nineteen poems that he saw as badly translated in Hardiman's collection; it is here that most of Ferguson's best work as a verse translator is to be found.

'The Downfall of the Gael'

(The original is attributed to Fear Flatha Ó Gnímh [1540?–1630?], head of the bardic family associated with the Ó Néills in Co. Antrim. Although Ferguson dates the poem to c. 1580, other scholars have argued that it was probably written after the plantation of Ulster early in the seventeenth century.)

My heart is in woe,
And my soul in deep trouble, –
For the mighty are low,
And abased are the noble:

The Sons of the Gael
Are in exile and mourning,
Worn, weary, and pale,
As spent pilgrims returning;

Or men who, in flight
From the field of disaster,
Beseech the black night
On their flight to fall faster;

Or seamen aghast
When their planks gape asunder,
And the waves fierce and fast
Tumble through in hoarse thunder;

121

Original: 'Air Cheimsios
na n-Gaodhal', by Fear
Flatha Ó Gnímh (cont.)

Literal translation (cont.):

Tá brat-chiaich ós a g-cionn,
   Múchas glóir Gaéidheal Eireann; –

   Mar néull g-ceath ghrian-bhaiteas
   goil,
   Do leath d'iarghnáitheas orrtha.

A cloak of gloom is over their heads,
   Which quenches the glory of the Gael of
   Ireland; –
   Like a cloud of weeping showers that
   eclipses the sunshine,
   Your anguish has spread over them.

Tárlaigh ó Bhóinn go bruach Léin,

   Dlígh is fiú andlígheadh; –
   Gur bhreath shaér le Fiannaibh
   Fáil,
   An riaghail chlaén do chongbháil.

It happened from the Boyne to the edge of
   Lighe,
   Law is worth no law; –
   So that it is a noble fate to the warriors of
   Fáil,
   To maintain the law of deceit.

Ní bhídh ag mac ríghe o'n riaghail,
   Aire air lúth eich óir-shrianaich,
   Nó air sheilg oíghe fá chíoch
   cnoic,
   Nó air ghníomh soíghe no seabhaic.

A king's son, by the law, did not have
   A noble on a swift gold-bridled horse,
   Nor of the hunting of the hind among the
   paps of the hill,
   Nor of the action of a bitch or a hawk.

D'fhearaibh Fódla is fáth orchra,

   Do threabhsad dáim danardha,
   A n-áit graifne a ngroídheadh seang,
   Gach faithche im oirear Eireann.

For the men of Fódla there is a reason for dejec-
   tion,
   They worked the brutal oxen,
   In place of racing their slender horses,
   Every green field around the region of
   Ireland.

Tréoid Gall a g-cluaintibh a g-ceann,
   Túir aélta ann áit a bh-foirgneadh;
   Margaídhe uadhtha ann gach
   oirear;
   Cruacha air árdaibh aénaígheadh.

Herds of the Gall in the meadows of their chiefs,
   Whitewashed towers in place of their build-
   ings;
   Markets taken from them in every region,
   Ricks on the assembly mounds.

Ní aithnígheann Inis Lógha;
   Nídh d'á faithchibh fonn mhóra;
   Cnoic dhlaoí-réidhe a n-diaigh an
   áir;
   Biaidh saér-Eire 'n a Sacsain!

The island of Lugh does not recognize
   Any of its pleasing green fields;
   Hills cut smooth after the slaughter;

   Free Ireland will be England!

Ní aithníd aicme Ghaéidheal,
   Banba, buime a macaomh;
   'S ní aithnídhenn Eire iad-sin
   Téidhid re chéile as a g-cruthaibh.

The Gaelic society does not recognise,
   Banba, nurse of her youth;
   And Ireland does not recognize them
   They go together out of their shapes.

Or men whom we see
That have got their death-omen –
Such wretches are we
In the chains of our foemen!

Our courage is fear,
Our nobility vileness,
Our hope is despair,
And our comeliness foulness.

There is mist on our heads,
And a cloud chill and hoary
Of black sorrow, sheds
An eclipse on our glory.

From Boyne to the Linn[79]
Has the mandate been given,
That the children of Finn
From their country be driven.

That the sons of the king –
Oh, the treason and malice! –
Shall no more ride the ring
In their own native valleys;

No more shall repair
Where the hill foxes tarry,
Nor forth to the air
Fling the hawk at her quarry:

For the plain shall be broke
By the share of the stranger,
And the stone-mason's stroke
Tell the woods of their danger;

The green hills and shore
Be with white keeps disfigured,
And the Mote of Rathmore
Be the Saxon churl's haggard!

The land of the lakes
Shall no more know the prospect
Of valleys and brakes –
So transform'd is her aspect!

Original: 'Air Cheimsios
na n-Gaodhal', by Fear
Flatha Ó Gnímh (cont.)

Literal translation (cont.):

Is sí an drong dhlígheas d'aithne,
   D' Inis Choínn is cómhtháth-
      uighthe;
   Ní Gaill is aoídheadha aca,

   Gaoídhil 'na n-droíng n-deórata!

It is the group that ought to be recognized
   By the island of Conn that are the for-
      eigners;
   It is not the Gall who are the strangers
      among them,
   The Gaels are the strange tribe!

Do léig Eire an tonn tríthi,
   D'iomchur fóirne coigcríche,
   Arthach Dháthí do tolladh,
   Is sí an-chruth d'fhéadamair!

Ireland allowed the wave through her,
   In tolerating a foreign crew,
   Dáthí's vessel is pierced,
   Deformity is what we are able to do!

Mar thímcheallas tonn anfaidh
   Le stoirm laoí luchd caoíl árthaich;
   Saithe Gall ar tí a a tímchill,
   Muna d-tí án d'Eireannchaibh.[80]

As a tempest wave surrounds
   With daily storm people of a narrow vessel,
   A swarm of foreigners is about to encircle,
   If noble Irishmen do not come.

Original: 'Máible Shéimh n-í
Cheallaich', by Toirdhealbhach Ó
Cearbhalláin

Literal translation:

Cia b'é bh-fuil sé a n-dán do,
   A lámh-dheas bheith faoí na ceann,
Is deimhin nach eagal bás do,
   Go bráth ná 'n a bheódh bheith tinn,
A chúil dheis na m-bachall bh-fáinneach,
   bh-fionn,
   A chuim mar an ealla ag snámhadh
      ar an d-tóinn,
Grádh 'gus spéis gasraidh, Máible
   Shéimh n-í Cheallaigh,
   Déud is deise leagadh ann arus a
      céinn.

Whoever is fated
   To have his right hand under her head,
It is certain that he does not fear death,
   Forever or in his life to be sick,
Pretty head of the beautiful, fair curls,

   Form like the swan swimming on the
      wave,
Love and interest of every youth, mild Mabel
   Ní Kelly,
   The prettiest teeth lying in the palace of
      her head.

Ní'l ceól d'á bhinne fós d'ar seinneadh,
   Ná'r bh' eólghach dhi-si thuigsin 's
      a rádh ann gach céim

There is no music however sweet yet played,
   That she would not know its sense and
      say every stage

The Gael cannot tell,
In the uprooted wild-wood
And red ridgy dell,
The old nurse of his childhood:

The nurse of his youth
Is in doubt as she views him,
If the wan wretch, in truth,
Be the child of her bosom.

We starve by the board,
And we thirst amid wassail –
For the guest is the lord,
And the host is the vassal!

Through the woods let us roam,
Through the wastes wild and barren;
We are strangers at home!
We are exiles in Erin!

And Erin's a bark
O'er the wide waters driven!
And the tempest howls dark,
And her side planks are riven!

And in billows of might
Swell the Saxon before her, –
Unite, oh, unite!
Or the billows burst o'er her![81]

'Mild Mabel Kelly'

(The original was written by the poet and harper Turlough Carolan [1670–1738]. Hardiman says the song was composed in Castle Kelly, Co. Galway, where Carolan was visiting, but Mabel Kelly has also been described as one of three daughters living near Tulsk, Co. Roscommon. For Austin Clarke's twentieth-century version of this poem, see pp. 251–253.)

Whoever the youth who by Heaven's decree
Has his happy right hand 'neath that bright head of thine,
'Tis certain that he
From all sorrow is free
Till the day of his death, if a life so divine
Should not raise him in bliss above mortal degree:
Mild Mabel-ni-Kelly, bright Coolun of curls,
All stately and pure as the swan on the lake;
Her mouth of white teeth is a palace of pearls,
And the youth of the land are love-sick for her sake!

Original: 'Máible Shéimh n-í Cheallaich', by Toirdhealbhach Ó Cearbhalláin (cont.)

Literal translation (cont.):

A gruadh mar rós ag drithleadh, is buan 'n a g-cómharsa an lile,
A rosg is míne, ghlaise 'ná bláith na g-craébh:
'S é deir olldhamh mollta chláir shíl Néill,
Go g-cuirfeadh na corradha a codla le sár-ghuith a béil,
Ní'l amhrus ann a súil bhreágh, lonnach,
Acht óltar línn go grínn do shláinte mhaith féin.[82]

Her cheek like a rose sparkling, the lily its enduring neighbour,
Her eyes finer, greener than the blossoms of the branches:
The praised master-poet of the plain of the race of Néill says,
That the herons would be put to sleep by the superior voice of her mouth,
There is no doubt in it, her eye fine and joyful,
But we drink steadfastly your own good health.

Original: 'Caisiol Múmhan'

Literal translation:

Phósfainn thú gan bha gan púint 's gan mórán spréidh,
A's phógfainn thú maidin drúchta le bánadh an lae;
Mo ghalar dúbhach gan mé a's tú, a dhian-ghrádh mo chléibh!
A g-Caisiol Múmhan, 's gan de leabaidh fúinn ann, acht clár bog deal.

I would marry you without cattle, without pounds, without much dowry,
And I would kiss you on a dewy morning at the dawning of the day;
My dismal disease that you and I are not, intense love of my bosom!
In Cashel of Munster, and without a bed under us there, but a soft-deal board.

A chaoin-bhean! An cuímhin leat-sa sliabh na m-ban fionn?
Nó an cuímheadh leat n'uair do bhíd-hinn-si 's mé fiadhach 'fá'n ngleann?
'Nois ó chaith an aoís mé a's gur liath mo cheann,
Ni chubhaidh dhuit mé dhíbirt, a's tá'n bhliadhain-so gann.

Mild woman! do you remember bright Slievenamon?
Or do you remember when you and I used to hunt around the glen?
Now since age has spent me and my head is grey,
It is not fitting for you to drive me away and this year meagre.

Ná saoíl-si gur b'ísioll a's nach uasal mé,
A's ná saoíl-si gur 'sa 'n-díg do fuaireadh mé;
Sín síos leam seal míosa agus cuartuigh mé,
Agus gheabhair sgriobhtha ann mo thaoíbh deas gur b'uasal mé.

Don't think that I'm lowly and not noble,
And don't think that it was in a ditch that I was got;
Lay down with me the spell of a month and seek me,
And you will take as written in my fine side that I am noble.

Ni'l ór buídhe ann mo phócaídhe ná airgiod geal,
Ná mo bólacht le seóladh tráthóna air fad,
Ní'l óig-bhean do thóigfeadh mé follamh gan bhóibh,
Nach d-tógfainn air mo sheólta go contaé-thíre-Eóghain.

Yellow gold is not in my pockets, nor bright silver,
Nor are my cattle for driving the long evening,
There is no young girl who would take me, empty-handed, without cows,
That I would not hoist my sails for, to Co. Tyrone.

A chailín, is maith-aithnímh go bh-fuil buaidhreadh ort,
Agus, a chailín, is maith aithním go bh-fuair tú guth;
Cailín mé fuair iomrádh faoí ghrádh fir,
A's fios me leath-troím, ná raibh ag mnáibh an t-saé-ghail uile.[83]

Girl, it is well I recognise that sorrow is on you,
And, girl, it is well I recognise that you got disgrace;
I am a girl that was talked about for the love of a man,
And knowledge of my injustice may the women of the whole world not have.

No strain of the sweetest e'er heard in the land
   That she knows not to sing, in a voice so enchanting,
    That the cranes on the strand
    Fall asleep where they stand;
   Oh, for her blooms the rose and the lily ne'er wanting
To shed its mild radiance o'er bosom or hand:
The dewy blue blossom that hangs on the spray,
   More blue than her eye, human eye never saw,
Deceit never lurk'd in its beautiful ray, –
Dear lady, I drink to you, *slainthe go bragh!*[84]

'Cashel of Munster'

I'd wed you without herds, without money, or rich array,
And I'd wed you on a dewy morning at day-dawn grey;
My bitter woe it is, love, that we are not far away
In Cashel town, though the bare deal board were our marriage-bed
 this day!

Oh, fair maid, remember the green hill side,
Remember how I hunted about the valleys wide;
Time now has worn me; my locks are turn'd to grey,
The year is scarce and I am poor, but send me not, love, away!

Oh, deem not my blood is of base strain, my girl,
Oh, deem not my birth was as the birth of the churl;
Marry me, and prove me, and say soon you will,
That noble blood is written on my right side still!

My purse holds no red gold, no coin of the silver white,
No herds are mine to drive through the long twilight!
But the pretty girl that would take me, all bare though I be and lone,
Oh, I'd take her with me kindly to the county Tyrone.

Oh, my girl, I can see 'tis in trouble you are,
And, oh, my girl, I see 'tis your people's reproach you bear:
'I am a girl in trouble for his sake with whom I fly,
And, oh, may no other maiden know such reproach as I!'[85]

Original: 'Ceann Dubh Díleas'	Literal translation:
A cheinn dhuibh dhílis, dhílis, dhílis!	Dear, dear, dear dark head!
Cuir do lámh mhín-gheal thorm a náll!	Put your smooth white arm round about me!
A bhéilín mheala, bh-fuil boladh na tíme air,	Little mouth of honey, which has the scent of thyme on it,
Is duine gan chroídhe nach d-tiubhradh duit grádh. –	It is a person without a heart who would not give you love.–
Tá cailíneadha air an m-baile-so air builleadh 's air buaidhreadh,	There are girls in this town mad and troubled,
Ag tarraing a n-gruaige 's dá léigeann le gaoíth,	Pulling their hair and releasing it to the wind,
Air my shon-sa, an scafaire is feárr ann san tuaithe,	On my behalf, the best strapping fellow in the country,
Acht do thréigfinn an méid sin air run dhil mo chroídhe.	But I would abandon all such for the dear love of my heart.
A's cuir do cheann díleas díleas díleas!	And put your dear, dear, dear head!
Cuir do cheann díleas tharm anall!	Put your dear head across me here!
A bhéilín mheala, a bh-fuil boladh na tíme air,	Little mouth of honey, which has the scent of thyme on it,
Is duine gan chroídhe nach d-tiubhradh duit grádh![86]	It is a heartless person who would not give you love!

Cean Dubh Deelish'

Put your head, darling, darling, darling,
      Your darling black head my heart above;
Oh, mouth of honey, with the thyme for fragrance,
      Who, with heart in breast, could deny you love?
Oh, many and many a young girl for me is pining,
      Letting her locks of gold to the cold wind free,
For me, the foremost of our gay young fellows;
      But I'd leave a hundred, pure love, for thee!
Then put your head, darling, darling, darling,
      Your darling black head my heart above;
Oh, mouth of honey, with the thyme for fragrance,
      Who, with heart in breast, could deny you love?[87]

Original: 'Rosc Catha na Mumhan'	Literal translation:
D'aithnídheas féin gan bhréig air fhuacht,	I myself recognised, without falsehood, by the cold,
'S air anfadh Thetis taobh re cuan;	And by the storm of Thetis beside the harbour;
Ar chana na n-éan go seanmhar, suairc,	By the contented, pleasant chanting of birds,
Go g-casfadh mo Shésar glé gan ghruaim.	That my bright Caesar would return without gloom.
Measaim gur súbhach do'n Mhúmhain an fhuaim,	I consider the sound is joyful for Munster,
Dá mairionn go dúbhach do chrú na m-buaidh;	Of those who live sorrowfully of the race of the victories,
Tarraing na d-tonn le sleasaibh na long,	The pull of the waves against the sides of the ships,
Tá tarraing go teann 'nár g-cionn air cuaird!	Which are moving forcefully toward us on a visit!

Tá lasadh san n-gréin gach lá go neoin,	A flaming is in the sun every day until noon,
Ní taise do'n rae, ní théighionn faoi neoil;	No shadow on the moon, it does not go under clouds;
Atá bárr na g-craobh ag déanadh sgeol,	The tops of the branches are telling a tale,
Nach fada bhiadh Gaoidheil go faon faoi cheó!	That it will not be long that the Gael will be limp under the fog!
Measaim gur súbhach do'n Mhúmhain an ceol,	I think the music is joyful for Munster,
Dá mairionn go dúbhach do chrú na d-treon,	Of those who live sorrowfully of the race of heroes,
Torann na d-tonn le sleasaibh na long,	The thunder of the waves against the sides of the ships,
Tarraing go teann, 'nár g-ceann faoi sheól!	Moving forcefully toward us under sail!

Tá Aoibhill ar mire 's Ainne óg,	Aoibheall is frenzied and young Aine,
Eana na m-bruingioll is áilne snódh;	Eana of the maidens of most beautiful complexion;
Táid míle 'gus tuile de'n táinseo fós,	There is a thousand and more of this multitude still
Dá suigheamh le buile gur d-táinidh an leoghan.	Bearing witness with frenzy that the lion will come.
Measaim gur súbhach do'n Mhúmhain an ceol,	I consider the music is joyful for Munster,
Dá mairionn go dúbhach do chrú na d-treon,	Of those who live sorrowfully of the race of heroes,
Torann na d-tonn le sleasaibh na long,	The thunder of the waves against the sides of the ships,
Tá tarruing anún 'nár g-cionn faoi sheól!	Which are moving hither toward us under sail!

Robert Dwyer Joyce
(1830–1883)

A native of Glenosheen, Co. Limerick, Robert Dwyer Joyce con-
tributed to *The Nation* and to the Fenian newspaper *The Irish People*
before going to America in 1866, where he became a successful physi-
cian in Boston. His brother, P. W. Joyce, became a well-known
collector of Irish music. Robert Dwyer Joyce's poems, including the
well-known 'The Boys of Wexford', were written under the penname
"Feardana" (bold man). What seems to be Joyce's one venture into
verse translation from the Irish is a version of a Jacobite poem enti-
tled 'Rosc Catha na Mumhan' ('Battle-Chant of Munster') written
around 1750 by Piaras Mac Gearailt (1702–1795), from Ballykinealy,
about fifteen kilometers east of Middleton, Co. Cork.

'Munster War Song'

I knew it well by storm and cold, –
The waves which lash'd the shore foretold –
The birds' sweet notes in forest tell,
Our Prince comes over ocean's swell –
> 'Tis time for Munster now to cheer,
> 'Twill glad our wasting clans to hear,
> The dash of the wave 'gainst the ships of the brave;
> And gallant hearts that are drawing near.

The sun's full splendour shines each day,
No cloud obscures the pale moon's ray,
The slender branches sigh the tale –
The mist shall soon rise from the Gael:
> 'Tis time for Munster now to cheer,
> 'Twill glad the sons of chiefs to hear
> The dash of the wave 'gainst the ships of the brave;
> And gallant hearts that are drawing near.

High triumph have Aoibheall and Aine at last,
Eana's fair virgins' gloom is past;
A thousand and more of this joyous train,
Now herald our hero with fairy strain:
> 'Tis time for Munster now to cheer,
> 'Twill glad our drooping tribes to hear,
> The dash of the wave 'gainst the ships of the brave;
> And gallant hearts now drawing near.

Original: 'Rosc Catha na Mumhan' (cont.)	Literal translation (cont.):

Ní h-anamh[a] maidin air amharc an Laoi,
Ná bainim chum ratha go fairge síos;
Mo dhearcadh dá leathadh ag faire do shíor,
Ar bharcaibh an fharruire ag tarraing na slíghe.

> Measaim gur súbhach do'n Mhúmhain, 'sgur binn,
> Dá mairionn go dúbhach do chrú na rígh,
> Torann na long a sgolta na d-tonn,
>
> Tá tarraing go teann 'nár g-cionn faoi sheól!

It's seldom in the morning on seeing the Lee,
That I don't take to my heels down to the sea;
My eyes wide open looking continually,

On ships of the soldiers cutting the course.

> I consider it is joyful for Munster, and that it is sweet,
> Of those who live sorrowfully of the race of the kings,
> The thunder of the ships splitting the waves,
> Which are moving forcefully toward us under sail!

Gach n-duine d'fhuil Mhíleadh bhán na g-créacht,
Curadha na Traoi mear láidir tréan
Do milleadh le dlígh is crádhagh le claon,
Cuirfid gan mhoill an báire séin.

> Measaim gur súbhach do'n Mhúmhain, 's aigéin
> Dá mairionn go dúbhach do chrú na d-tréin;
> Torann na d-tonn re sleasaibh na long,
> Tá tarraing go teann 'nár g-cionn le faobhar![88]

Every person of the fair blood of the Milesians of the wounds,
Champions of Troy, spirited, powerful, strong,
Who were destroyed with law and vexed with deceit,
They will win without delay the happy goal.

> I consider it is joyful for Munster, and in the distance,
> Of those who live sorrowfully of the race of warriors;
> The thunder of waves against the sides of the ships,
> Which are moving forcefully toward us with swords!

---

[a] The literal translation assumes *Is annamh*, as in *Amhráin Phiarais Mhic Gearailt*, FG, and DG.

In storm or calm at peep of day,
With eager steps I seek the bay;
And strain my eyes in hopes to greet,
The first glimpse of our Prince's fleet:
      Oh joyful in Munster the music rings,
      And joyful to all who mourn their kings;
      The dash of the wave 'gainst the ships of the brave
      And gallant band the future brings.

All ye whose hearts beat warm and fast
With gaelic blood, the die is cast –
Rise up, rise out, like chiefs of old,
And smite the foe whose doom is told:
      Oh sweet in Munster, sweet abroad
      To the sadden'd race of each proud lord,
      Is the dash of the wave 'gainst the ship of the brave,
      Who come to join us with the sword![89]

Original: from 'Eachtra Ghiolla an
Ammalláin', by Donnchadh
Ruadh Mac Conmara

Literal translation:

Ar theacht na maidne do phreabas go
   h-éadtrom
As mo leabaigh le taithneamh an sgéil sin;
Beirim ar mo bhata, 's ní stadfainn ar aon
   chor.
Bhí feirc ann mo hata 'san bh-faisean, a's
   faobhar air,
Do righneadh dham '*jackets*' beag', gearra,
   le sméideadh,
A's léinteacha breaca go barra mo mhéara.
Do chuireas slán rem' cháirde a n-
   éinfheacht,
'S le cuid níor fhágbhus slán le
   foiréigean;
Dá g-casfadh dham árthach d'fhághail a n-
   Eirinn,
Do rachfainn tar sáile a n-áit nár bhaoghal
   dam.
   Bíodh a fhios ag an d-talamh, 's ag
      maithibh geal' Paorach,
A liacht beathadh, mion-earra, a's
   gréithreadh,
Thug an pobal a bh-fochair a chéile,

Chum mo chothuighthe a g-cogadh nó a
   spéirlinn.
Stór ná caillfeadh suim do laethibh,
'S cófra doimhin 'na d-tollfainn féin ann;
Do bhí seacht bh-fithchid obh ceirce 's a n-
   annlann éisg ann,
Le h-aghaidh a n-ithte chómh minic 's budh
   mhéin liom:
Cróca ime do dingeadh le saothar,
'S spóla soille ba thruime do'n
   mhéithmhart;
Bhí seacht g-clocha mhin choirce ghloin
   créithre ann,
'S dríodair croidhte na loisde re chéile;

On the coming of morning I jumped
   nimbly
Out of my bed with the joy of that plan;
I carry my stick, and I wouldn't stop at all.
A peak was in my hat, in the fashion, and an
   edge on it,
Small, short 'jackets' were made for me in a
   wink,
And dappled shirts to the tips of my fingers.
I said farewell to my friends altogether,
And to some I did not leave a farewell with
   great speed;
If I could meet a vessel leaving Ireland,
I would go overseas to the place where there
   would not be danger for me.
   Let the country know, and the bright
      great ones of the Powers,
So much sustenance, small goods, and
   earthenware,
That the people brought along with them
   together,
For my nourishment in war or in strife.

A store that a sum of days would not spend,
And a deep chest in which I myself would fit;
There were seven score hens' eggs, and their
   complement of fish in it,
For eating as often as I would like:
A crock of butter that was packed with effort;
And a joint of the heaviest salted meat from
   the fat bullock;
There were seven stone of clean-sifted
   oatmeal in it,
And the remains of the entrails of the food
   trays together;

Standish Hayes O'Grady
(1832–1915)

Standish Hayes O'Grady, a cousin of the better-known Standish James O'Grady, was essentially a scholar, and most of his work as a translator – his prose translation of *Tóraigheacht Dhiarmada agus Ghráinne* and his translations of various medieval prose tales in *Silva Gaedelica* – is more scholarly than poetic. But his verse translation of Donnchadh Ruadh Mac Conmara's 'Eachtra Ghiolla an Ammalláin' ('The Adventures of the Simpleton'), published in 1853, marks O'Grady as a poetic translator as well.

O'Grady was born into an Anglo-Irish family in Castleconnell, Co. Limerick, and learned Irish in the Gaelic-speaking areas nearby. He was educated at Trinity College Dublin, and eventually worked with the leading antiquarians and scholars of his day, including John O'Donovan and Eugene O'Curry.

From 'The Adventures of Donnchadh Ruadh Mac Con-Mara, a Slave of Adversity'

(Donnchadh Ruadh Mac Conmara [1715–1810], a schoolteacher who lived and worked for much of his long life in Co. Waterford, seems to have written the original while on an uncompleted voyage to America, probably in 1745. For Tomás Ó Flannghaile's later translation of parts of the poem, see pp. 159–163. The poem opens with the narrator deciding that, like many of his poor countrymen at the time – the poem is dated 14 May 1745 – he will have to emigrate.)

> When morning broke I lightly left my bed,
> So pleas'd was I with all my plans, and sped
> To bid my friends farewell in such a haste,
> That to wish all goodbye seem'd quite a waste
> Of time; so with a knowing hat and band
> Of newest fashion, and my stick in hand,
> A jacket which a dandy would not scout,
> And clean check'd shirt with wristbands peeping out,
> Away I went determin'd if I found
> A single ship to distant regions bound,
> I'd seek my fortune where I might be sure
> That working manfully, I'd not die poor.

135

Original: from 'Eachtra Ghiolla an Ammalláin', by Donnchadh Ruadh Mac Conmara (cont.)	Literal translation (cont.):
Bhí lán barraille do b'fhearra bhí 'n-Eirinn	There was a full barrel of the best that was in Ireland
Do photátaidhe leathana ar eagla géarbhruid:	Of broad potatoes, for fear of extreme distress:
Do thugas caig leanna ann do lasfadh le sméideadh,	I received a keg of ale there that would kindle with a wink,
'S do chuirfeadh na mairbh 'na m-beatha, dá m'fhéidir.	And that would make the dead living, if it were possible.
Leaba a's clúda a g-ciumhais a chéile,	A bed and a blanket in a strip together,
Ceangailte ar dhrom mo thronnc le téada:	Tied on the back of my trunk with rope:
Bhí bróga astigh ann, 'wig' a's 'beaver,'	There were shoes inside it, a 'wig' and a 'beaver',
A's stór mar sin anois ná déarfad.	And a store like that now you would not suppose.
Go Portláirge de'n stáir sin téidhim-se,	To Waterford in that condition I go,
Chómh foránta re Conán na Féinne:	As boldly as Conan of the Fenians:
Ghlacas mo lóisdín, bórd bídh a's féasta,	I took my lodging, board and feast,
Farrais an óg-mhnaoi ba chóraidhe bhí 'n-Eirinn.	Beside the fairest young lady that was in Ireland.
Do bhí sí fáinneach, fáilteach, feasdach,	She was ringleted, welcoming, merry-making,
Ba chiuin, tais, náireach an 'drawer' le glaodhach í;	She was calm, gentle, modest when calling the 'drawer';
Gach sórt dá d-tagadh, a bhlaiseadh ní shéanfadh,	Every sort of those who came, his portion she would not refuse,
D'inneosadh eachtra, startha, a's sgéalta:	She would tell adventures, stories, and tales:
Ní ghlacfadh sí faladh ná fearg go h-éag leat,	She would never bear a grudge or anger for you,
An fhaid bhraithfeadh sí airgead agat gan traochadh.	As long as she could depend on money from you without exhaustion.
Do léigfeadh do lámh ar áit 'san t-saoghal di,	You could lay your hand in any place in the world of her,
O imeall a sál go barr a céibhe:	From the edge of her heel to the top of her hair:
'S a g-cúrsa mná ni thráchtaim féin air,	And about the matter of women I myself do not comment,
Acht cúis a gáire fáth mo sméideadh!	But the reason for her laughter is a reason for my winking!
Do rin sí mo chlú, dá m'fhiú mo shaothar,	She praised me, however worthy my effort,
'S do chuireadh sí am chúlsa púghdar gléigeal:	And she put on my hair pure white powder:
Bhíoch deoch ar maidin, 's mé am leabaigh, dá gléas dam,	There was a drink in the morning, and I in bed, dressing myself,
O bhonn go bathas 'sí bhearradh go léir mé,	From bottom to top it is she who shaved me entirely,
Ba mhór m'iongantus a soineandacht féile,	Great was my wonder at her innocence, generosity,
'S feabhas a buime chum pinghine d'éiliomh;	And the excellence of her mother for demanding pennies;
Ní maithfeadh a máthair cáirt ná braon dam,	Her mother would not forgive a quart or a drop from me,
Do chaithfeadh an táibhle d'fhágháil gan phléidh uaim.[90]	The tally would have to be left without disputation from me.

Let all the country know, and each proud chief
Of Power's blood,[91] what store for my relief
In battle's dangers, or in stormy weather,The people's
kindness freely brought together.
A store which many days would not expend –
A coffer which would hold me in one end;
Seven score of eggs, with their due share of fish,
To make me, when inclin'd, a sav'ry dish:
The choice of butter pack'd into a crock,
A lump of tallow, firm as any rock;
Seven stone of meal, the smoothest mill e'er made,
Such sausages as would supply a trade,
A heap of lumpers, that would put to shame
All other roots in Ireland of the name;
A keg of ale would make the mourner smile,
And, could aught do it, raise the dead awhile.
My bed and blankets on the trunk's outside,
With ropes together were securely tied;
While brogues within, and glossy beaver pack'd,
Made up a kit which nothing needful lack'd.
        Conan the Fenian had no bolder heart
Than I, when first I made my hopeful start
For Waterford, and there betook myself
To those snug quarters where a smiling elf,
Of graceful form, and face, and ringlets too,
With welcome beaming from her bright eyes, drew
The cheering draught; nor would refuse to sip
It with you, if you coax'd; and then her lip
You slyly might approach with yours, the while
She sang, or told the legend, and a smile
Would ever greet you; and whate'er you did,
Had you but money, you'd ne'er find she chid.
A woman's ways we'll not stop to discuss,
But what makes them laugh, gives a smile to us!
This lassie took a liking to me, I don't know
Wherefore, and ev'ry morning white as snow
She powder'd my peruke and brought me up,
'Ere I left bed, a fortifying cup.
And much I wondered at this kind display,
Till I considered how, from day to day,
Her mother scor'd the tally, nor would draw
For her fair child to treat me, as I saw,
A quart or single drop that was not laid
Straight to my charge, and worried me till paid.[92]

Original: from 'Eachtra Ghiolla an Ammalláin', by Donnchadh Ruadh Mac Conmara	Literal translation:
Bhí beatha gan roinn ag Tadhg O'Laoghaire,	Tadhg O'Laoghaire had food that was not divided,
'S ní bhlaiseadh sé greidhm le treighid, ná braon di;	And he did not taste a bite, with the colic, nor a drop of it;
Bhí Caoilte O'Caoimh ag caoineadh a chéile,	Caoilte O'Caoimh was keening his wife,
'S ní bh-fuigheadh sé a bhríste sgaoileadh ar aon chor;	And he didn't get his trousers to loosen in any case;
Bhí Peadair O'Dúbhda a g-cúinne an' aonar,	Peadar O'Dúbhda was in a corner alone,
A's é ag úirliocan ar shúsa Fhéidhlim;	And he vomiting on Féidhlim's blanket;
Bhí Cairbre, 's Tiobóid, 's Gearóid, ar saothar,	Cairbre, and Tiobóid, and Gearóid were at work,
Ag tarraing mo phlucóid a n-onóir na sgléipe;	Pulling on my stopper in honour of the sport;
Bhí buachaill Ui Leathlobhair ag altúghadh a mhéile,	A boy of O'Leathlobhair's was giving thanks for his meal,
'S cé bhuailfeadh é 'san leath-shúil acht Calbhach le sgéirde;	And who struck him in one eye but Calbhach of wild appearance;
Bhí Gearalt O'Dobhair a's Flann ag taosgadh,	Gearalt O'Dobhair and Flann were bailing,
Cathal a's Conn a n-gabhal a chéile;	Cathal and Conn were stuck together;
Bhí Seághan O'Troighthe 'san ruibe dá thraochadh,	Seághan O'Troighthe was in the fury of his exhaustion,
'S dhá cheann a ghoile ag cur air a-éinfheacht;	And each side of his stomach troubling him at the same time;
Do bhí sliocht Mhic Amhlaoibh a d-teanntaibh géar' ann,	The offspring of Mac Amhlaoibh were in keen difficulties there,
Ag aisiog 's ag brúchtghail ar shúsadhibh a chéile;	Vomiting and belching on blankets together;
Gur dhearbhaigh Diarmuid siar, a's faobhar air,	Diarmuid declared to the rear, and an edge to him,
Ná mairfeadh a d-trian dá d-triall ó Eirinn.[93]	That not a third of them journeying from Ireland would survive.

(The following passage describes the voyage during a storm. In the end, the ship fails to reach America, having been driven back to Ireland by bad weather.)

> Poor Teigue O'Leary's food unheeded lay,
> Strange qualms attacking took his taste away;
> Keelty O'Keeffe sat weeping for his bride,
> Nor had the strength to lay his breeks aside;
> Peter O'Dooda, in a quiet nook,
> Phelim's good blanket for a basin took,
> Carbry and Toby, with Garrett at their back,
> Dealt me for fun's sake many a sounding whack –
> A boy of Lawlor's race who tried to eat,
> Calvach capsiz'd by rolling from his seat;
> Gerald O'Dower was wasted to a thread,
> And Flann gave up all hope he'd quit his bed;
> While Shane O'Trihy by all nature's sluices
> His bursting sorrows in the scuppers looses;
> Cahal and Conn were, notwithstanding, fighting,
> And here, in one foul chorus all uniting,
> Of sighs, and groans, and many a doleful sound,
> Mac Auliffe's clan lay huddled in a mound.
> There Dermod lay, and as he lay he swore
> That not one third would e'er reach haven more.[94]

The Literary
Revival

Original: 'Scél Lemm Dúib'	Literal translation:
Scél lemm dúib:	I have tidings for you:
dordaid dam,	the stag bells,
snigid gaim,	winter drips,
ro-fáith sam;	summer is departed ;
gáeth ard úar,	wind high, cold,
ísel grían,	low the sun,
gair a rith,	short its course,
ruirthech rían;	the sea running swiftly;
rorúad rath,	very red the bracken,
ro-cleth cruth,	shape wholly hidden,
ro-gab gnáth	it has become customary,
giugrann guth;	the wild-goose call;
ro-gab úacht	cold has seized
etti én,	the wings of birds,
aigre ré:	season of ice:
é mo scél.[1]	these are my tidings.

George Sigerson
(1836–1925)

Starting with translations from the earliest days of Ireland's pre-Christian tradition, and proceeding chronologically to the eighteenth century, George Sigerson's ambitious collection of verse translation, *Bards of the Gael and Gall* (1897), constructs the Irish tradition in markedly pluralistic terms, while also calling into question the tendency of many poets working in the early days of the Irish literary revival to romanticise the Gaelic tradition. 'Those who want to associate Irish poetry with effusiveness of thought and luxuriance of language,' Sigerson says in his preface, 'will be surprised to find that bardic poetry was characterized by classic reserve in thought, form, and expression.'[2]

Sigerson was born in Co. Tyrone, and educated in France and at Queens College, Cork, where he took a degree in medicine. His first venture into verse translation from the Irish was the second series of *Poets and Poetry of Munster*, published in 1860. (The first consisted of translations by James Clarence Mangan). Sigerson later became president of the National Literary Society, the founding of which, in 1892, is often taken as a starting point for the literary revival.

'Winter's Approach'

(This translation is included in *Bards of the Gael and Gall* under 'The Fionn Period'. It has been dated to the ninth or tenth century. For Flann O'Brien's version, see p. 293.)

> List my lay: oxen roar,
> Winter chides, Summer's o'er,
> Sinks the sun, cold winds rise,
> Moans assail, ocean cries.
>
> Ferns flush red, change hides all,
> Clanging now, gray geese call,
> Wild wings cringe, cold with rime,
> Drear, most drear, ice-frost time.[3]

Original: 'Aobhinn anocht teaghlach Lir!'	Literal translation:

Aoibhinn anocht teaghlach Lir!
    Iomdha a miodh agus a bh-fíon;
    Gidh tá anocht a n-ádhbhadh fhuar,
    Dream do chuan róghlan an ríogh.

Pleasant tonight the household of Lir!
    Abundant their mead and their wine;
    Yet there is tonight in a cold abode,
    A company of the wholly innocent family of the king.

Is iad ár g-coilcibh gan locht,
    Folach ár g-corp do chlúmh chas,
    Gidh minic do deargthaoi sróll
    Iomainn ag ól mheadha mhas.

These are our quilts without fault,
    Covering our bodies with wreathed feathers,
    Although often were we dressed with satin
    About us drinking goodly mead.

Ag sin ár m-biadh agus ár bh-fíon,
    Gainimh fhionn is sáile searbh;
    Minic do ibhmís meadh cuill,
    Ó chuachán cruinn cheithre g-cearn.

There our food and our wine,
    White sand and sharp brine;
    Often we drank hazel mead,
    From round goblets with four corners.

Is iad ár leapacha, is iad lom,
    Carraig ós cionn na d-tonn d-tréan;
    Minic do deargthaoi dhúinn,
    Leaba do chlúmh ochta éan.

These are our beds, they are bare,
    A rock above the fierce waves;
    Often was dressed for us
    A bed of the breast-down of birds.

Gidh í ár n-obair snámh san sioc,
    Ar shruth na Maoile is trom toirm,
    Fá minic marcshluaigh mhac ríogh,
    Ag dul 'nár n-diaigh go Síoth Bhuidhbh.[4]

Although it is our work to swim in the frost,
    On the current of the Moyle that is a weight, a din,
    It was often a cavalcade of sons of kings,
    Were going after us to Síoth Bhuidhbh.

'On the Waters of the Moyle'

(Sigerson includes this translation in *Bards of the Gael and Gall* under the heading 'The Christian Dawn'. The original is part of *Oidhe Chloinne Lir: The Fate of the Children of Lir*, a mythological tale in which the children of Lir, a king of the legendary Dé Dannan, are transformed into swans by their foster-mother, jealous of Lir's affection for them. This song was composed by one of the children, Fionnuala, upon being told that her father and friends were celebrating a particular feast day. For a verse translation of another poem from *Oidhe Chloinne Lir*, see under John Todhunter, p.153.)

> Gay this night Lir's royal house,
> Chiefs carouse, mead flows amain:
> Cold this night his children roam,
> Their chill home the icy main.
>
> For our mantles fair are found
> Feathers curving round our breasts:
> Often silken robes we had,
> Purple-clad, we sat at feasts.
>
> For our viands here and wine –
> Bitter brine and pallid sands:
> Of the hazel mead they served
> In carved vessels to our hands.
>
> Now our beds are the bare rock
> Smit with shock of heavy seas:
> Often soft breast-down was spread
> For the bed of grateful ease.
>
> Though 'tis now, in frost, our toil
> To swim Moyle,[5] with drooping wings:
> Oft we rode as Royal Wards
> And our guards were sons of Kings.[6]

Original: 'Gormlaidh nic Fhlainn'	Literal translation:
Beir, a mhanaich, leat do chos, tog a nis de thaobh an Néill,	Take away, monk, your foot, take [it] now from Niall's side,
Is ro mhor a chuireas do chré air an ti le 'n luidhinn féin;	It is too much you put your clay on the person with whom I myself would lie;
Ro fhada ata a mhanaich shíar a' cur cré air Níall an áir,	Too long, monk, are you beyond, putting clay on Niall of the slaughter,
Go caoin uait a chara dhuinn, na buineadh do bhuinn ri lár;	Gently with you, friend of ours, don't touch your sole to the ground;
Na duin gu dion an uaigh och! a chleirich truagh do thoisg,	Don't firmly close the grave, oh! cleric, a pity your work,
Tog de Niall ghlundubh gheal, beir, a mhanaich, leat do chos;	Take away from bright Niall Glúndub, take away, monk, your foot;
Mac O'Neill an oir fhinn, ni de'm dheoin e bhi fo chrios,	Son of O'Neill of the fair gold, it is not my will that he was under a friar's belt,
Fágair a leachd 'us a fheart, beir a mhanaich leat do chos;	Leave his stone and his grave, take away, monk, your foot;
Is mi Gormlaidh chumas rainn, nic Fhlainn chruaidh o Dhún rois	I am Gormflaith who composes verses, daughter of hard Flann from Dún Rois;
Na bi ad sheasamh air a leachd, beir a mhanaich, leat do chos.	Don't be standing on his stone, take away, monk, your foot.
Beir a mhanaich.[7]	Take [it], monk.

'Niall's Dirge'

(The reputed author of the original is Queen Gormfhlaith. The daughter of one king and the wife first of the king of Cashel and then of the king of Leinster, Gormfhlaith married Niall Glúndub after the death of her second husband in 909. Ten years later, Niall, by then *ard-rí* of Leinster, was killed in a battle against the Vikings. Sigerson's translation is included under the heading 'Gael and Norse' in *Bards of the Gael and Gall*.)

> Move, O monk, thy foot away,
> Lift it now from Niall's side,
> Over-much thou'st cast the clay
> Where I would, with him, abide.
>
> Over-long thy task, this day,
> Strewing clay o'er Niall slain;
> Tread no further, friend, delay, –
> Raise it not to meet the plain.
>
> Ah, close not for aye the grave,
> Cleric sad, with solemn lay;
> From o'er Niall bright and brave
> Move, O monk, thy foot away.
>
> Golden King, not thus wert bound
> Had I power thy strength to stay,
> Leave his pillar, leave his mound,
> Move thy foot, O monk, away.
>
> I am Gormlai, who, in gloom,
> Sing for him the sorrowing lay;
> Stand not there upon his tomb,
> Move, O monk, thy foot away.[8]

Original: 'Aislingi domarfas-sa'

Aislingi domarfas-sa,
taidbsi ingnad indisimm
   i fhiadnaise cháich:
curchan gered gerthige
i purt locha lémnachta
   os lind betha blaith.

Lódmar isin lóechlestar,
laechda in chongaib chonaire
   dar bolclenna lir;
corbensom na sesbemend
dar muncind in murtráchta,
co tochrad a murthorud
   murgrian amal mil.

Coem in dúnad rancamár
cona rathaib robrechtán,
   resin loch anall:
ba himm úr a erdrochat,
a chaisel ba gelchruithnecht,
   a shondach ba sáll.

Ba suairc segda a shuidiugud
in tige treoin trebarda
   i n-dechad iartain:
a chomla do thirmcharnu,
a thairsech do thurarán,
   do maethluib a fraig.

Uaitne slemnai sencháise,
sailghe saille súgmaire
   serndais imasech;
sessa sena[a] senchrothi,
fairre finda fírgrotha
   foloingtís in tech.

Tipra d' fhín 'na fhíriarthar,
áibne beóri is brocóti,
   blasta cech lind lán;
lear do braichlis blaithlendai
os brú thopair thremantai
   doraí dar a lár.

Literal translation:

I had a vision,
a dream wonderful I tell
   in the presence of everyone:
a fatty, lardy coracle
in the port of a lake of milk
   over the nourishing sea of buttermilk.

We went in the small warrior-boat,
warriors in an expeditionary force
   over the swell of the sea;
we tore at the oar-strokes
in the straits of the sea-course,
summoning up the sea-harvest
   the sea-bottom like honey.

Protection of a fort we reached,
of a great bounty of custard,
   a measure beyond the lake;
fresh butter was its rear bridge,
its breastwork was bright wheat,
   its palisade was bacon.

Pleasant and substantial was its setting
the strong, secure house,
   behind to the west:
its door of dry meat,
its threshold of plain bread,
   of tender herbs its side-wall.

Smooth pillars of old cheese,
beams of juicy bacon
   ranged one by one;
ancient beams of ancient curds
white pillars of real curds
   they supported the house.

A well of wine exactly behind,
streams of beer and bragget,
   tasty every full pool;
a smoothly inclined sea of malt
over the brink of a spring of curds
   pouring through its centre.

'The Vision of Viands'

(This is based on a poem that appears in *Aislinge Meic Conglinne* [*Vision of Mac Conglinne*], a twelfth-century parody of the medieval vision and voyage tale. The protagonist is a young scholar who travels to a monastery in Cork seeking patronage for his poetic ambitions. He is persecuted by the monks and threatened with crucifixion until he saves himself by narrating a vision of a voyage on a lake of milk, which the abbot believes will cure Cathal, the king of Munster, of gluttony. Sigerson includes his translation in *Bards of the Gael and Gall* under the heading 'Gael and Norse'. For Austin Clarke's version of another poem connected with *Aislinge Meic Conglinne*, see p. 247.)

In a slumber visional,
Wonders apparitional
    Sudden shone on me:
Was it not a miracle?
Built of lard, a coracle
    Swam a sweet milk sea.

With high hearts heroical,
We stepped in it, stoical,
    Braving billow-bounds;
Then we rode so dashingly,
Smote the sea so splashingly,
That the surge sent, washingly,
    Honey up for grounds.

Ramparts rose of custard all
Where a castle muster'd all
    Forces o'er the lake;
Butter was the bridge of it,
Wheaten meal the ridge of it,
    Bacon every stake.

Strong it stood, and pleasantly
There I entered presently
    Hying to the hosts;
Dry beef was the door of it,
Bare bread was the floor of it,
    Whey-curds were the posts.

Old cheese-columns happily,
Pork that pillared sappily,
    Raised their heads aloof;
While curd-rafters mellowly
Crossing cream-beams yellowly,
    Held aloft the roof.

Original: 'Aislingi domarfas-sa' (cont.)	Literal translation (cont.):

Loch do braisig belaiche
fó barr úscai olordai
　　eturru ocus muir;
erbi imme oc imaire
fo chír blonci bratgile
　　imon múr amuig.

A lake of greasy porridge
under a top of swollen lard
　　between it and the sea;
arbours of butter in ridges
under a crest of a white-mantling lard
　　around the fortified wall outside.

Ecor d' áblaib fírchumra,
fid cona blath barrchorccra
　　eturra ocus sliab;
daire forard fírlossa,
do chainnind, do cherrbaccán,
　　for cúl tige tiar.

An arrangement of very fragrant apple-trees,
a wood of scarlet-topped blossoms
　　between it and the mountain;
a very high wood of real herbs,
of leeks, of carrots,
　　beyond the back of the house.

Muinnter enig inichin
d' ócaib dercaib tennsadchib
　　im thenid astig:
secht n-allsmaind, secht n-episle
do cháisib, do choelanaib,
　　fo bragait cech fhir.

An hospitable household within
of attractive, fully satiated watchmen
　　around a fire inside;
seven knots, seven necklaces
of cheese, of tripe,
　　around the neck of every man.

Atconnarc ni, in airchindech
cona broth raig boshaille
　　'má mnái miadaig maiss;
atconnarc in luchtaire
fó inbiur in ardchori,
　　'sa aehel ria ais.

I saw a champion, in authority
with a covering of beef-fat
　　beside his honourable wife of beauty;
I saw the cook
before a spit for a high cauldron,
　　and a glowing coal at his back.

Cathal maith mac Finguine,
fó fer dianad oirfited
　　airscéla bind braiss;
maith in menar oenuaire,
is aibind ria indisi,
immram luipe laechlestair

　　dar ler locha ais.[9]

Good Cathal Mac Finguine,
around him men eager for entertainment
　　from sweet, fine stories;
good in the household anytime
and pleasure with telling,
the meandering journey of the small warrior-
　　boat
　　to the sea-lake beyond.

---

[a] The literal translation assumes *segda*, a textual variant.

Wine in well rose sparklingly,
Beer was rolling darklingly,
    Bragget brimmed the pond.
Lard was oozing heavily,
Merry malt moved wavily,
    Through the floor beyond.

Lake of broth lay spicily,
Fat froze o'er it icily,
    'Tween the wall and shore;
Butter rose in hedges high,
Cloaking all its edges high
    White lard blossomed o'er.

Apple alleys bowering,
Pink-topped orchards flowering,
    Fenced off hill and wind;
Leek tree forests loftily,
Carrots branching tuftily,
    Guarded it behind.

Ruddy warders rosily
Welcomed us right cosily
    To the fire and rest;
Seven coils of sausages,
Twined in twisted passages,
    Round each brawny breast.

Their chief I discover him,
Suet mantle over him,
    By his lady bland;
Where the cauldron boiled away,
The Dispenser toiled away,
    With his fork in hand.

Good King Cathal, royally,
Surely will enjoy a lay,
    Fair and fine as silk;
From his heart his woe I call,
When I sing heroical,
How we rode, so stoical,
    O'er the Sea of Milk.[10]

Original: 'Éaccaointeach againn anocht'	Literal translation:
Éaccaointeach againn anocht,	Mournful are we tonight,
Gan clúmh ag tuighiodh ár g-corp,	Without feathers thatching our bodies,
'Sas fuar d'ár m-bonnaibh bláithe,	And it is cold for our gentle soles,
Ar chairrgibh andóbhráidhe.	On rocks of great wetness.
Dob olc ar leasmháthair ruinn,	It was evil our stepmother did,
D'ar imir draoídhiocht orruinn,	In inflicting a spell on us,
D'ar g-cur ar fad mara amach	In putting us far out to sea
A riocht ealadh n-iongantach.	In the shape of strange swans.
As é ar bh-folcadh ar dhruim cuain,	Our bathing is on wave-crests of the harbour,
Cúbhar an mhara mhong-ruaidh	Foam of the red-maned sea
As í ar g-cuid thall do'n chuirm,	Our share hereafter of the ale is
Sáile an mhara mhong-ghuirm.	Salt water of the blue-maned sea.
Aoin inghion, agus triar mac,	One daughter, and three sons,
Cleachtmaoid a g-cuasaibh carrach,	We are wont to be in rocky recesses,
Ar na cairrgibh cruaidh do neach,	On the rocks hard for anyone,
Ar m-beatha as éaccaointeach.[11]	Our lives are mournful.

John Todhunter
(1839–1915)

Like many writers associated with the early years of the literary revival, John Todhunter was drawn to the early sagas of the Irish-language tradition. With the encouragement of W. B. Yeats, Todhunter published in the 1880s and 1890s metrical versions of three tales, including the poems that appear within them, known collectively as 'The Three Stories of Story-Telling' – in Todhunter's versions, 'The Doom of the Children of Lir', 'The Fate of the Sons of Usna', and 'The Lamentation for the Three Sons of Turann'.

'Fianoula's Lamentation in the Cold'

(The original is a lyric from *Oidhe Chloinne Lir: The Fate of the Children of Lir*, a mythological tale in which the children of Lir, a king of the legendary Dé Dannan, are transformed into swans by their foster-mother, jealous of Lir's affection for them. This song was composed by one of the children. For a translation of a different lyric from this tale, see under George Sigerson, p. 145.)

1.

Ochone for the Swans left bare
Of the warm fleece of their feathers!
Ochone for the feet that bleed
On the rough teeth of the rocks!

2.

False, false was our mother,
When she drove us with Druid's craft
Adrift on the roaring waters,
In the outlawry of birds.

3.

For happy home she gave us
The fleeting surge of the sea,
For share of the lordly ale-feast
The loathing of bitter brine.

4.

One daughter, and three sons,
Behold us, Lir, on the rocks,
Featherless, comfortless, cold,
We print our steps in blood.[12]

Original: 'It é saigte gona súain'

It é saigte gona súain,
cech thrátha i n-aidchi adúair,
   serccoí, lia gnása, íar ndé,
   fir a tóeb thíre Roigne.

Rográd fir ala thíre
ro-shíacht sech a chomdíne
   ruc mo lí (ní lór do dath);
   ním-léci do thindabrad.

Binniu laídib a labrad
acht Ríg nime nóebadrad:
   án bréo cen bréthir mbraise,
   céle tana tóebthaise.

Literal translation:

These are the arrows that slay sleep,
every hour in the cold night,
   love-lamenting for the presence, after day,
   of a man from beside the land of Roigne.

Great love for a man from another land
who reached beyond his equals
   took my bloom (no sufficiency of colour [left]);
   it does not allow me rest.

Sweeter than songs his speech
save holy adoration of the King of heaven:
   noble flame without a word of boasting,
   slender, soft-sided mate.

Alfred Perceval Graves
(1846–1931)

Alfred Perceval Graves is best known as a prolific composer of popular songs and light verse in English. But Graves spent much of his youth in Parknasilla, Co. Kerry, and there developed a lifelong interest in the Gaelic tradition. No less an authority than Douglas Hyde has argued that there are passages in Graves's work of which it can be said that 'neither Callanan nor Mangan could have caught the Irish tone and conception more truly'.[13] In 1914, Graves published an anthology of Irish verse in English entitled *The Book of Irish Poetry* that included more than twenty of his own verse translations from the Irish, reaching as far back as the earliest known poems in the language and as far forward as the folk songs that Hyde had translated earlier in his *Love Songs of Connacht*.

Graves was born in Dublin, the son of a clergyman, and educated at Trinity College. He lived most of his adult life in England, and was the father of the poet and novelist Robert Graves.

'Song of Crede, Daughter of Guare'

(Although the background of the original is somewhat obscure, Créide was, according to some accounts, the daughter of Gúaire, king of Aidne, in southeast Co. Galway, in the seventh century. In 649, Gúaire was defeated in battle by Díarmait, king of Ireland, and Dínertach, one of Gúaire's allies from Munster, died from wounds suffered in the battle, but not before Créide fell in love with him.)

> These are the arrows that murder sleep
> At every hour in the night's black deep;
> Pangs of Love through the long day ache,
> All for the dead Dinertach's sake.
>
> Great love of a hero from Roiny's plain
> Has pierced me through with immortal pain,
> Blasted my beauty and left me to blanch,
> A riven bloom on a restless branch.
>
> Never was song like Dinertach's speech
> But holy strains that to Heaven's gate reach;
> A front of flame without boast or pride,
> Yet a firm, fond mate for a fair maid's side.

Original: 'It é saigte gona súain' (cont.)	Literal translation (cont.):

Imsa naídiu robsa náir:
ní bínn fri dúla dodáil;
   ó do-lod i n-inderb n-aís
   rom-gab mo théte togaís.

As a young girl I was modest:
I did not have an appetite for passionate desire;
   since I reached the uncertainty of age
   my wantonness has begun to beguile me.

Táthum cech maith la Gúaire,
la ríg nAidni adúaire;
   tocair mo menma óm thúathaib
   isin íath i nIrlúachair.

I have every good thing with Gúaire,
with the king of cold Aidne;
   but my mind strays from my people
   into the land in Irlúachair.

Canair i n-íath Aidni áin,
im thóebu Cille Colmáin,
   án bréo des Luimnech lechtach

   díanid comainm Dínertach.

They sing in the land of noble Aidne,
around the sides of Cill Colmáin,
   of the noble flame from the south of Limerick
   of the graves
   whose name is Dínertach.

Cráidid mo chride cainech,
a Chríst cáid, a fhoraided:
   it é saigte gona súain
   cech thrátha i n-aidchi adúair.[14]

It torments my tender heart,
chaste Christ, his extremely violent death:
   these are the arrows that slay sleep
   every hour in the cold night.

A growing girl – I was timid of tongue,
And never trysted with gallants young,
But since I have won into passionate age,
Fierce love-longings my heart engage.

I have every bounty that life could hold,
With Guare, arch-monarch of Aidne cold,
But, fallen away from my haughty folk,
In Irluachair's field my heart lies broke.

There is chanting in glorious Aidne's meadow,
Under St. Colman's Church's[15] shadow;
A hero flame sinks into the tomb –
Dinertach, alas! my love and my doom!

Chaste Christ! that now at my life's last breath
I should tryst with Sorrow and mate with Death!
At every hour of the night's black deep,
These are the arrows that murder sleep.[16]

Original: from 'Eachtra Ghiolla an
Amaráin', by Donnchadh Ruadh
Mac Conmara

Literal translation:

Buailimíd i ngeibheal a chéile	We proceed linked together
San uaimh sin síos ar shoillse an lae ghil,	Down into that cave by the light of the bright day,
Go bh-feachamar uainn ann cuanta as geur-mhuir	Until we saw in the distance there harbours and a bitter sea
As *Acheron* fuar ag gluasacht taobh linn.	And cold Acheron moving beside us.
Seo an t-anach 'na ngabhann an drong so d'eugann	This is the path in which goes this throng who die
Gach anam as samhailt i ngeall do daorthar,	Every soul and ghost condemned to enslavement,
Na mílte ceann bhí ann go deurach	The thousands who were there tearfully
Nach bh-fágadh dul anonn tar abhainn le réidhteach –	Were not let go across the river with clearance –
Ní h-ionann mar thuiteann ó *Virgil* san Aénéid	Not exactly as it happens in *Virgil* in the Aeneid
Gurb' le h-uireasba a g-cuirthe ar an saoghal so	That it is for a lack of their being buried in this world
Acht sloighte chathann le rabairne a saothar	But hosts who spend with extravagance their labour
Ag ól 's ag carbhus do bh-fanaid gan aon rud	Drinking and carousing until they remain without anything
Gan chobhachán aca ná an leath-phinginn deidheanach	Without a small coin among them or the last halfpenny
Le tabhairt don chaladh muna nglacaid mar dhéirc í!	For giving to the ferry unless they get it as charity!
'Sé chluinim d'á rádh ag lucht ráidhte as léiginn	I hear it said by those who recite and are learned
Gur bh'é duine bhí i mbád ann Cháron méirscreach,	That the person who was in the boat there was scarred Charon,
Acht deirim-se leó gur dóibh as breug sin,	But I say to them that that is a lie
'S gur cleithire mór de phóir na h-Eireann	And that it was a large rascal of the seed of Ireland
Do chímís i sean-bhád d'á thiomáin go saothrach –	That we saw in the old boat guiding it labouriously –
An díthreabhach galánta, Conán na Féinne!	The gallant recluse, Conán of the Fenians!
Bhí croiceann dubh fóisce ar a thóin mar eudach	The dark fleece of a yearling ewe was on his bottom as clothing
'S nír bheag linn go deo mar chomhartha an mhéid sin –	And that was no small [thing] indeed for us as a sign –
Ní thabharfadh se Sacsanach tar caladh gan réal geal	He would not take a Saxon over by ferry without a bright sixpence
'S ní labharfadh dadamh acht Laidin nó Gaedhilig!	And would not speak anything but Latin or Gaelic!

. . .   . . .

Tomás Ó Flannghaile
(1846–1916)

Tomás Ó Flannghaile was one of the writers working during the early years of the literary revival to save the Irish language. Having learned Irish in his youth (he was born near Ballinrobe, Co. Mayo), he taught classes in the language at the Southwark Literary Society and, later, the Irish Literary Society in London, where he lived much of his adult life. Ó Flannghaile's principal work as a translator was his version of Donnchadh Ruadh Mac Conmara's 'Eachtra Ghiolla an Amaráin', published in 1897 under the title of 'The Adventures of a Luckless Fellow'.

From 'The Adventures of a Luckless Fellow'

(Donnchadh Mac Conmara [1715–1810], a schoolteacher who lived and worked for much of his life in Co. Waterford, seems to have written the original while on an uncompleted voyage to America, probably in 1745. This passage, which occurs in the second half of the poem, describes a dream-vision that comes to the narrator while he is on board a ship for America. In the vision, the legendary Aoibheall leads the narrator to the underworld. For a selection from Standish Hayes O'Grady's earlier translation of Mac Conmara's poem, see pp. 135–139.)

> Down through the cave, the daylight leaving
> We hastened together, my breast quick heaving,
> And soon we reached the shores infernal
> Where Acheron flows with wail eternal.
> All men who die must face this river
> And some pass o'er, nor seem to shiver,
> Yet thousands are here, all tearful, wailing
> Their prayer for a passage across unavailing
> Not as the Roman poet[17] pretendeth
> The spirits of men unburied Jove sendeth –
> But the shades of those who revell'd and feasted
> And in this world their wealth e'er wasted,
> Who sported and spent without cessation
> And brought not a penny to pay portation!
>   I've heard it said by poets and sages
> That Charon was ferryman there these ages,
> But I can give them some new information –
> 'Twas a slasher renown'd of the Irish Nation

159

Original: from 'Eachtra Ghiolla an Amaráin', by Donnchadh Ruadh Mac Conmara (cont.)

Literal translation (cont.):

Téidheam tar sruthán 'san g-curachán caol dubh
As déanam an t-aithgheárr g'nuig cnocán beag aereach
Go rángamar anaighe 'raibh geataidhe gan aon ghlas
Áit a raibh maistín ag glamaoíl gan traochadh.
Ní bhréag do *Virgil* adeir in a bhéarsa
Gur bh'é seo *Cerberus* theibeadh an réidhteach,
'Na chodladh bhí ar cheart-lár an chosáin 's gan fae sin
Acht soparnach piseán 's é ag srannán 's a' séideadh.
        Do rug an fear fóirneirt de phóir ghil na h-Éireann
Go dubh ar a scórnach le fórsa a gheuga,
'S nír léig don mhadra feacadh ná staonadh
Gur ritheamar thairis faoi eagla ár ndaothhin.
Nír fanadh linn go barra an chnoic don réim sin
Mar ar stadadh linn a' machtnamh 's a' feuchain
Go bhfeacamar uainn an sluagh ar gach taobh dhínn
Ag tarraing 'má g-cuaird 'sa ruagadh a chéile –
Adubhairt linn suidhe go n-innseóch' éifeacht
As contas díreach buidhne as beusa.

· · ·

"A g-cloisir an glór so ag slógh na n-éigeas
Ag seinm a g-ceolta as spórt as plé aca?

Tá *Horace* ann ag mealladh a shuilt *Maecenas*
'S d'a ngearradh sin gan laga ar bith le géire –
Ovid 'na shuidhe ar bhínse féir ghlais
As nóta aige d'á scríobh' go faoidheach chum Caesar
Juvenal's a phionn-san idir a mheuraibh
As domblas mar dhubh aige as géar-nimh –
Aodh Buidhe Mac Cruitín as Éirinn
As é 'filidheacht go guith-bhínn i nGaedhilig –
A b-prionnsa suilt go ceannsa, glic, d'a mbreugadh
As fonn a ghuib go d'tabharfadh duine ón eug leis!

· · ·

We went across the stream in the old narrow dark curragh
And we took the shortcut as far as a small airy hillock
Until we arrived before [a place] where there were gates without any lock
A place where a mastiff was howling without exhaustion.
It is not a lie that Virgil says in his verses
That this was Cerberus who prohibited the clearing of a passage,
He was asleep in the very centre of the path and nothing under him
But a litter of tares and he snoring and blowing.
        The man of strength of the bright seed of Ireland caught
Severely his throat with the force of his limbs,
And he didn't allow the dog to move or flinch
Until we ran past him in our fill of fear.
We did not stop on that course until the top of the hill
Where we stopped to think and look around
Until we saw in the distance the crowd on every side of us
Drawing around and chasing each other –
He told us to sit until he would relate the significance
And a true account of the company and customs.

· · ·

"Do you hear this noise from the host of the learned
Playing their music and having sport and disputation?

Horace is there beguiling his delight, *Maecenus*
And cutting those, without any moderation, and with sharpness –
Ovid sitting on a bank of green grass
Writing a note plaintively to Caesar
Juvenal and his pen between his fingers
And having gall as ink and bitter poison –
Aodh Buidhe Mac Cruitín from Ireland
And he versifying elegantly in Gaelic –
Their prince of delight, mildly and cleverly cajoling them
And the delight of his mouth that would bring a person from death with it!

· · ·

We saw in the old boat, pulling right lustily,
Conán the Fenian, calling quite crustily –
A sheepskin woolly his rear protected
Sufficient to sign, though ne'er expected –
For no tongue but Irish or Latin he'd bearing
And a Saxon sixpence should pay for his faring!

·   ·   ·

Over the stream we passed together
And landed beyond with brighter weather –
A path we reached with a gateway gaping
Where a mastiff lay, all grim, mis-shapen,
The same that Vergil describes in his verses,
That Cerberus savage that man still curses –
But now he was sleeping, snoring, snorting,
His foul straw lair not ill assorting.
At once Conán ran up to seize him,
His throat he grasped and never did ease him,
Never allowed him twisting or turning
Till we were sure of our safety earning.
And soon we reached a hillock more airy
Whereon we rested our feet now weary,
And here we saw far off hosts moving,
Chasing each other their prowess proving –
Then Conán at length bade us both be seated
Whilst of these hosts and their ways he treated.

·   ·   ·

"Hark the voices tuneful-sounding
Of bards rejoicing, mirth-abounding!
Horace is there his patron lauding
Assailing some and some applauding –
There Ovid is seen on bank reclining
To Caesar writing, with heart repining –
Juvenal wields his pen censorious –
For venom and gall to all notorious –
And Hugh MacCurtin,[18] bard from Erin,
Sweetest of poets that e'er lived therein –
Prince of them all, and all spell-holden
With songs of the Gael in Gaelic golden!

·   ·   ·

"See Luther there, and spare thy loathing,
And Calvin crusted, with fatness frothing,
Henry the Eighth and queen beside him,
All hanging in chains, with nought to hide them –
Each Protestant passing those gibbets in sadness –
Strikes the vile four with a vengeful madness –

Original: from 'Eachtra Ghiolla an Amaráin', by Donnchadh Ruadh Mac Conmara (cont.)

Literal translation (cont.):

"Machtnuigh-se Lútar d'iompuidh an téarma,

"Contemplate Luther who perverted the text,

As Cailbhín 'na chrústa ag cubhar le méithreas,

And close-fisted Calvin frothing with fat,

An t-Ochtmhadh Hannraí 's a bhainríoghan taobh leis

The Eighth Henry and his queen beside him

Crochta le slabhraidhibh as bhrannraidhibh daora –

Hung from chains and gibbets of the condemned

Gach Sacsanach ghabhann an ball so pleuscann

Every Saxon who passes this place thumps

An ceathrar cam so d'iompuidh an chléir uainn –

These crooked four who turned the clergy from us –

Iad so tá scaoilte 's do chidhir gan aon ghlas

These who are released and whom you see without any fetters

Béarfar arís go ríoghacht Mhic Dé 'steach!

Will be brought again into the kingdom of the Son of God!

"Imthigh-se a bhaile" ar an faraire treunmhar

"Go home," said the valiant warrior

"A dhuine so thagann mar theachtaire as Éirinn,

"Oh person who comes as a messenger from Ireland,

Ní fada bhéidh síolradh mín, tais Shéamuis

Not long will the gentle, compassionate progeny of James be

Fá cheannas an rígh tá 'díbirt Gaedhil-fhear,

Under the authority of the king who is banishing the Gaelic man,

Go n-éireóchaibh plannda de shean-tshliocht Éibhir

Until will rise a scion of the old progeny of Heber

Do dhéanfadh concas mar gheall ar éigeart,

Who will make a conquest as payment for injustice,

Do bhainfidh an choróin den chóip 'na éiric

Who will take the crown from the gang in compensation

'S do leanfaidh go deo de phóir Mhilésius!

And will continue forever with the seed of Milesius!

Seachain an t-olc do loit síol Éabha air fad,

Avoid the evil that spoiled all the seed of Eve,

Gabh paidir as troscadh as cros Mhic De ort,

Take prayer and fasting and the cross of the Son of God on you,

Bí déirceach, carthanach, ar lasadh le daonnacht

Be charitable, kind, on fire with humanity

As réim na bh-flathas do gheobhair más féidir!

And the glory of heaven you will get if it is possible!

Rachad-sa ar siubhal, tá liú agus glaodh orm

I will go away, there is a shout and a call for me

Ag an aicme so Lúthair do bhrúidh na h-aedhe 'nam –

From this tribe of Luther that bruised the liver in me –

Do mharbh an Francach an domhan san saoghal díobh

The Frenchman killed a vast number of them in the world

As caithfead-sa a d-tabhairt anall don taobh so!"[21]

And I have to take them over from this side!"

But those thou see'st unfettered, in freedom,
An angel hereafter to heaven shall lead them!
     "And now return from this fearsome faring
And take this message from me to Erin –
Not long the Gael, e'er famed for bravery
Shall crouch to a foreigner king in slavery,
Till a prince of Heber's race[19] most royal,
Shall right dear Erin as son most loyal,
He'll snatch the crown from the clown doth bear it
And Erin e'ermore on her brow shall wear it!
Shun all wrong-doing, the ruin of nations,
Give them to fasting and pray with patience,
Forget not alms to the poor and lowly
And at length ye'll gain God's kingdom holy!
But I must away – my name they're calling,
Those sons of Luther my spirits are galling –
The French have just sent a word of them hither,
And I must convey them over the river!"[20]

Original: 'Cáthír Chíarain Cluain mic Nóis', by Enoch O'Gillan	Literal translation:
Cáthír Chíarain Cluain mic Nóis, Baile druchtsholus, deargrois, Da shíl ríghráighi as buan blagh, Sluaigh fan sithbaile sruthghlan.	City of Ciaran of Clonmacnoise, Town of dew-light, red-rose, Of the seed of kings and lasting fame, Hosts under the clear-streamed, peaceful town.
Ataid fhuaisli cloindi Cuind Fan reilig leacaid leargdhuind, Snaidim no craebh os gach cholaind Agus ainm chaemh cheart oghaim.	Nobles of the clan of Conn are Under the flag-stoned, brown-sloped burial ground, A knot or a branch above each body And a noble, correct Ogham name.
Cland Chairbri fa tuathibh toir, Na seacht tromlaithi a Teamraidh, Imdha dosmeirg ar gort gaidh Ag locht crosleirg Chiaran.	The clan of Cairbre from the territories of the east, The seven great warriors from Tara, Many a protecting standard on a field of battle With the people of the plain of crosses of Ciaran.
Fir Theafai is tuatha Breag, Fa uir Cluana docuireadh; Brigh eis feile tall fo tuinn, Sil Creide is clann Conaill.	The men of Teffia and the tribes of Breagh, Under the ground of Cluain were buried; The troop of virtue and hospitality under the earth- surface, The seed of Creide and the clan of Conaill.
Is imdo clainn Cuinn na cath Gu tus deirg is fod fa falach, Imdha suil úaine is ball ban Fa úir uaidhe chland Golman.[22]	Many are the children of Conn of the battles With the red tuft and sod covering them, Many the green eye and white limb Under the soil of the tomb of Clan Colman.

T.W. Rolleston
(1857–1920)

With W. B. Yeats and others, T. W. Rolleston edited *Poems and Ballads of Young Ireland* (1888), the first important literary-revival anthology. He published just one collection of his own, *Sea Spray: Verses and Translations* (1909).

Rolleston was born in Co. Offaly, and educated at Trinity College Dublin, where he studied German as well as Irish literature.

'The Dead at Clonmacnois'

(The original is attributed to Enoch O'Gillan, a fourteenth-century poet who lived in Co. Galway. Clonmacnoise, in Co. Offaly, was one of the centres of European Christianity in the seventh and eighth centuries, but as this poem makes clear, it also has ties to Ireland's pagan past.)

> In a quiet-water'd land, a land of roses,
>   Stands Saint Kieran's city fair,[23]
> And the warriors of Erinn in their famous generations
>   Slumber there.
>
> There beneath the dewy hillside sleep the noblest
>   Of the Clan of Conn,[24]
> Each below his stone: his name in branching Ogham
>   And the sacred knot thereon.
>
> There they laid to rest the Seven Kings of Tara,
>   There the sons of Cairbrè[25] sleep –
> Battle-banners of the Gael, that in Kieran's plain of crosses
>   Now their final hosting keep.
>
> And in Clonmacnois they laid the men of Teffia,[26]
>   And right many a lord of Breagh;[27]
> Deep the sod above Clan Creidè and Clan Connall,
>   Kind in hall and fierce in fray.
>
> Many and many a son of Conn the Hundred-Fighter
>   In the red earth lies at rest;
> Many a blue eye of Clan Colman the turf covers,
>   Many a swan-white breast.[28]

Original: 'Fuitt co bráth'	Literal translation:
Fuitt co bráth!	Cold forever!
Is mó in donenn ar cách,	The storm is greater than everything,
is ob cach etrice án,	every ditch there is a river,
ocus is loch lán cach áth.	and a full lake is every ford.
Is méit muir mór cech loch lonn,	The size of a great sea is every angry lake,
is dronng cech cuiri gúr gann,	a multitude is every sharp, thin company,
mét taul scéith banna dond linn,	the size also of the company's shield is a splash of water,
mét moltchrocann find cech slamm.	the size of a white wether's skin every flake.
Méit cuithi cach lattrach léig,	The size of a pit every puddle
coirthe cach réid, caill cach móin,	A standing-stone every level plain, a forest every peat-bog;
na helta ní costá dín,	The flocks of birds enjoy no shelter,
snechta finn fír doroich tóin.	Bright, white snow to the back door.

Eleanor Hull
(1860–1935)

Eleanor Hull played an important part in the campaign during the years of the literary revival to improve the visibility of the Irish-language tradition. In addition to producing a two-volume *Textbook of Irish Literature* in 1906, she helped establish the Irish Texts Society, and, with the encouragement of Standish Hayes O'Grady and Douglas Hyde, also published a significant anthology of verse translation from the Irish, *The Poem-Book of the Gael*, in 1913. In the introduction to that collection, she argues against romanticising the Irish-language tradition: 'The reader who does not know Ireland or know Gaelic is ready to accept softness . . . what he is not prepared for is the sudden break into matter-of-fact, the curt tone that cuts across much Irish poetry.'[29]

Hull was born in Manchester. Her family moved to Dublin when her father became director of the Geological Survey of Ireland, and she was educated in Ireland.

'Second Winter-Song'

(The original has been dated to the ninth or early tenth century. According to one account, the poem was recited by a member of Fionn's household one night when he and Fionn were separated from their band of warriors at a place known as Colt's standing stone on Slieve Gullion, west of Kells, in Co. Meath. Fionn had asked the young man to seek water for them, and the poem is the boy's response.)

> Cold till Doom!
> Glowers more fearfully the gloom!
> Each gleaming furrow is a river,
> A loch in each ford's room.
>
> Each pool is deepened to a perilous pit,
> A standing-stone each plain, a wood each moor;
> The clamouring flight of birds no shelter finds,
> White snow winds towards the door.
>
> Like to a spectral host each sharp slim shape,
> Each leaping lake swelled to a mighty main;
> Wide as a wether's skin each falling flake,
> Shield-broad, each drop of rain.

Original: 'Fuitt co bráth' (cont.)

Literal translation (cont.):

Ro-íad réod róta gribb
íar ngléo glicc im Choirthi Cuilt,

congab donenn dar cach leth,
co ná abair nech acht fuit!³⁰

Frost has clenched the swift roads
After a struggle of contention around Colt's
standing-stone,
The storm has spread on every side,
Until no one says anything but cold!

Original: 'Do bádussa úair'

Literal translation:

Do bádussa úair
   fa fholt buide chas,
is nách fuil trem chenn
   acht finnfad gear glas.

I was once
   covered with yellow, ringleted hair,
and [now] there is nothing on my head
   but short grey hair.

Robad luinne lem
   folt ar dath in fhíaich
do thoidhecht trem chenn
   ná finnfad gerr líath.

I would prefer
   hair of the colour of a raven
coming from my head
   to short grey hair.

Suirge ní dluig dam,
   óir ní mellaim mná;
m'fholt in-nocht is líath;
   ní bía mar do bá.³¹

Courting is not a fitting thing for me
   for I do not beguile women;
my hair tonight is grey;
   I am not as I was.

Original: 'Sí bláth geal na
smér í'

Literal translation:

Sí bláth geal na smér í
Is bláth deas na subh craebh í
Sí planda bfhearr meín mhaith
Le hamharc a súl.

She is the bright blossom of the blackberry,
And she is the fine blossom of the raspberry,
She is the best plant of good character
By the look of her eyes.

Sí mo chuisle sí mo rún í
'As í bláth na nubhall cúmhra í
Is samhradh ansan fhuácht í
Eidir Nodluig 's Caisg.³²

She is my pulse, she is my sweetheart,
And she is the blossom of the fragrant apples,
And she is summer in the cold,
Between Christmas and Easter.

Swift frost again hath fastened all the ways,
It strove and struggled upwards o'er the wold,
About Colt's standing-stone the tempest sways,
Shuddering, men cry, "'Tis cold!"[33]

'Youth and Age'

(The original is ascribed to Oisín. It has been dated to around 1200 AD.)

Once I was yellow-haired, and ringlets fell,
    In clusters round my brow;
Grizzled and sparse tonight my short grey crop,
    No lustre in it now.

Better to me the shining locks of youth,
    Or raven's dusky hue,
Than drear old age, which chilly wisdom brings,
    If what they say be true.

I only know that as I pass the road,
    No woman looks my way;
They think my head and heart alike are cold –
    Yet I have had my day.[34]

'She'

The white bloom of the blackthorn, she,
    The small sweet raspberry-blossom, she;
More fair the shy, rare glance of her eye,
    Than the wealth of the world to me.

My heart's pulse, my secret, she,
    The flower of the fragrant apple, she;
A summer glow o'er the winter's snow,
    'Twixt Christmas and Easter, she.[35]

Original: 'Mala Néifin'	Literal translation:
Dá mbéidhinn-se air Mhala Néifin	If I were on the Brow of Nephin
'S mo cheud-ghrádh le mo thaoibh,	And my hundred-times love by my side,
Is lághach choideólamaois i n-éinfheacht	It is pleasantly we would sleep together
Mar an t-éinín air an g-craoibh.	Like the small bird on the branch.
'Sé do bhéilín binn briathrach	It is your melodious, wordy small mouth
Do mheudaigh air mo phian,	That increased my pain
Agus codladh ciúin ní fhéudaim,	And a quiet sleep I cannot have
Go n-eugfad, faraor!	Until I will die, alas!
Dá mbéidhinn-se air na cuantaibh	If I were on the harbours
Mar budh dual dam, gheobhainn spórt,	As would be natural for me, I would get sport,
Mo cháirde uile faoi bhuaidhreadh	All my friends in trouble
Agus gruaim orra gach ló.	And gloom on them every day.
Fíor-sgaith na ngruagach	True blossom of the champions

Douglas Hyde
(1860–1949)

Although Douglas Hyde claimed to be less interested in verse translation as an art form than in salvaging Ireland's rapidly disappearing Irish-language folk culture, his translations into verse of the folk songs and poetry of Connacht, in insisting implicitly on the poetic merit of the colloquial, provided a powerful – and decidedly poetic – counter to the literary revival's early dependence on *fin-de-siècle* aesthetics. Hyde's verse translations, published in the 1890s and the first decade of the twentieth century, also worked against many of the stereotypes of rural Ireland that were in place at the time by calling attention to the theme of melancholy that pervaded the remote, vulnerable world of Irish-speaking Ireland, and by recognizing the strong presence of sexuality and violence in that world.

Hyde was born at Frenchpark, Co. Roscommon. His father was a Church of Ireland rector, and Hyde learned Irish from the country people near his home. His advocacy of the Irish language as the only medium for authentic Irish writing – most famously in his address in 1892 entitled 'On the Necessity for De-Anglicizing Ireland' – alienated him from many of the leading figures of the revival. He founded the Gaelic League in 1893, and was elected President of Ireland in 1938.

'The Brow of Nefin'

(Hyde says he heard part of this song from a woman in Co. Roscommon. Nephin is a mountain in Co. Mayo.)

> Did I stand on the bald top of Néfin
> And my hundred-times loved one with me,
> We should nestle together as safe in
> Its shade as the birds on a tree.
> From your lips such a music is shaken,
> When you speak it awakens my pain,
> And my eyelids by sleep are forsaken,
> And I seek for my slumber in vain.
>
> But were I on the fields of the ocean,
> I should sport on its infinite room,
> I should plough through the billow's commotion
> Though my friends should look dark at my doom.
> For the flower of all maidens of magic

Original: 'Mala Néifin' (cont.)	Literal translation (cont.):

Fuair buaidh a's clú anns gach gleó,
'S gur b'é mo chroidhe-stigh tá 'nna
    ghual dubh,
Agus bean mo thruaige ní'l beó.

Who got victory and fame in every battle,
It is my inner heart that is a dark coal,

And a woman to pity me is not alive.

Nach aoibhinn do na h-éiníníbh
    A éirigheas go h-árd,
'S a chodluigheas i n-éinfheacht
    Air aon chraoibhín amháin.
Ní mar sin dam féin
    A's do m' cheud míle grádh
Is fada o na chéile orrainn
    Éirigheas gach lá.

Is it not delightful for the small birds
    Who rise up high,
And who sleep together
    On one small branch.
It is not like that for myself
    And for my hundred-thousand-times love
It is far from each other that on us
    Every day rises.

Cad é do bhreathnughadh air na
    spéarthaibh
Tráth teas air an lá,
Na air an lán-mara ag éirighe
    Le h-eudan an chloidhe áird?
Mar súd bhíos an té úd
    A bheir an-toil do 'n ghrádh
Mar chrann air mhala sléibhe
    Do thréigfeadh a bhláth.[36]

What is your judgment on the skies

    When heat is on the day,
Or on the full tide rising
    Against the high ditch?
Like that is that person
    Who bears a great desire for love
Like a tree on the brow of a mountain
    That its flowers would forsake.

Original: 'Mo Bhrón ar an bhFairrge'	Literal translation:

Mo bhrón air an bhfairrge
    Is é tá mór,
Is é gabhail idir mé
    'S mo mhíle stór.

My grief on the sea
    It is it that is great,
It is going between me
    And my thousand-times treasure.

D'fhágadh 'san mbaile mé
    Deunamh bróin,
Gan aon tsúil tar sáile liom
    Choidhche na go deó.

I was left at home
    Making sorrow,
Without any hope to be over the sea
    Ever or forever.

Mo léun nach bhfuil mise
    'Gus mo mhúirnín bhán
I g-cúige Laighean
    No i g-condaé an Chláir.

My sorrow that I am not
    And my fair sweetheart
In the province of Leinster
    Or in the county of Clare.

Mo bhrón nach bhfuil mise
    'Gus mo mhíle grádh
Air bord loinge
    Triall go 'Mericá.

My sorrow that I am not
    And my thousand-times love
On board a ship
    Voyaging to America.

Is beside me where'er I may be,
And my heart like a coal is extinguished,
   Not a woman takes pity on me.

How well for the birds in all weather,
   They rise up on high in the air
And then sleep upon one bough together
   Without sorrow or trouble or care;
But so it is not in this world
   For myself and my thousand-times fair,
For away, far apart from each other,
   Each day rises barren and bare.

Say, what dost thou think of the heavens
   When the heat overmasters the day,
Or what when the steam of the tide
   Rises up in the face of the bay?
Even so is the man who has given
   An inordinate love-gift away,
Like a tree on a mountain all riven
   Without blossom or leaflet or spray.[37]

'My Grief on the Sea'

(Hyde says he had this poem from an old woman named Brighid Ní Chosruaidh, living in a hut in Co. Roscommon.)

My grief on the sea,
   How the waves of it roll!
For they heave between me
   And the love of my soul!

Abandoned, forsaken,
   To grief and to care,
Will the sea ever waken
   Relief from despair?

My grief, and my trouble!
   Would he and I were
In the province of Leinster,
   Or county of Clare.

Were I and my darling –
   Oh, heart-bitter wound! –
On board of the ship
   For America bound.

Original: 'Mo Bhrón ar an bhFairrge' (cont.)	Literal translation (cont.):

Leabuidh luachra
    Bhí fúm aréir,
Agus chaith mé amach é
    Le teas an laé.
	A bed of rushes
	    Was under me last night,
	And I threw it off
	    With the heat of the day.

Táinig mo ghrádh-sa
    Le mo thaébh
Guala air ghualain
    Agus beul air bheul.[38]
	My love came
	    To my side
	Shoulder on shoulder
	    And mouth on mouth.

Original: 'A Ógánaigh an Chúil Cheangailte'	Literal translation :

A ógánaigh an chúil cheangailte
    Le a raibh mé seal i n-éinfheacht
Chuaidh tu 'réir, an bealach so
    'S ní tháinig tu do m'fheuchaint.
Shaoil mé nach ndeanfaidhe dochar duit
    Dá dtiucfá, a's mé d' iarraidh,
'S gur b'í do phóigín thabhairfeadh sólás
	Youth of the tied back hair
	    With whom I was once together
	You went last night this way
	    And you did not come to see me.
	I thought no harm will be done to you
	    If you would come, and ask for me,
	And that it would be your little kiss that
	    would give comfort

Dá mbeidhinn i lár an fhiabhrais.	If I were in the midst of the fever.

Dá mbeidheadh maoin agam-sa
    Agus airgead ann mo phóca
Dhéanfainn bóithrín aith-giorrach
    Go doras tighe mo stóirín,
Mar shúil le Dia go g-cluinnfinn-se
    Torann binn a bhróige,
'S is fad an lá ann ar chodail mé
    Acht ag súil le blas do phóige.
	If I had wealth
	    And money in my pocket
	I would make a handy small road
	    To the door of the house of my sweetheart,
	As I hoped to God that I would hear
	    The melodious sound of his shoe,
	And long ago is the day in it that I slept
	    But hoping for a taste of his kiss.

A's shaoil mé a stóirín
    Go mbudh gealach agus grian thu,
A's shaoil mé 'nna dhiaigh sin
    Go mbudh sneachta ar an tsliabh thu,
A's shaoil mé 'nna dhiaigh sin
    Go mbudh lóchrann o Dhia thu,
No gur ab tu an reult-eólais
    Ag dul rómham a's mo dhiaigh thu.
	And I thought, sweetheart,
	    That you were the moon and the sun,
	And I thought after that
	    That you were snow on the mountain
	And I thought after that
	    That you were a light from God,
	Or that you were the star of knowledge
	    You going before me and after me.

Gheall tu síoda 's saitin dam
    Callaidhe 's bróga árda,
A's gheall tu tar éis sin
    Go leanfá tríd an tsnámh mé.
Ni mar sin atá mé
    Acht mo sgeach i mbeul bearna,
Gach nóin a's gach maidin
    Ag feuchaint tighe m' athar.[39]
	You promised me silk and satin
	    Cloaks and tall shoes,
	And you promised after that
	    That you would follow me through the sea.
	I am not like that
	    But I am a thornbush in the mouth of a gap,
	Every noon and every morning
	    Watching the house of my father.

On a green bed of rushes
All last night I lay,
And I flung it abroad
With the heat of the day.

And my love came behind me –
He came from the South;
His breast to my bosom,
His mouth to my mouth.[40]

'Ringleted Youth of My Love'

Ringleted youth of my love,
With thy locks bound loosely behind thee,
You passed by the road above,
But you never came in to find me;
Where were the harm for you
If you came for a little to see me,
Your kiss is a wakening dew
Were I ever so ill or so dreamy.

If I had golden store
I would make a nice little boreen
To lead straight up to his door,
The door of the house of my storeen;[41]
Hoping to God not to miss
The sound of his footfall in it,
I have waited so long for his kiss
That for days I have not slept a minute.

I thought, O my love! you were so –
As the moon is, or sun on a fountain,
And I thought after that you were snow,
The cold snow on top of the mountain;
And I thought after that, you were more
Like God's lamp shining to find me,
Or the bright star of knowledge before,
And the star of knowledge behind me.

You promised me high-heeled shoes,
And satin and silk, my storeen,
And to follow me, never to lose,
Though the ocean were round us roaring;
Like a bush in a gap in a wall
I am now left lonely without thee,
And this house I grow dead of, is all
That I see around or about me.[42]

Original: 'An Searc 'Gá Dhiúltughadh'	Literal translation:
Mo ghrádh, ón 'sí mo ghrádh An bhean is mó bhíos 'g am' chrádh, Is annsa í ó m' dhéanamh tinn Ná an bhean do m' dhéanamh slán.	She is my love, oh she is my love The woman who is most tormenting me, She is dearer since making me ill Than the woman making me well.
'Si mo stór, ón 'sí mo stór, Bean an roisg uaithne mar an rós, Bean nach g-cuirfeadh lámh fá m' cheann Bean nach luidhfeadh liom ar ór.	She is my treasure, oh she is my treasure, The woman of the green eye, [she] like the rose, A woman who would not put a hand under my head A woman who would not lie with me for gold.
Sí mo shearc, ón 'sí mo shearc An bhean nár fhág ionnam neart, Bean nach leigfeadh mo dhiaidh och Bean nach g-cuirfeadh liag am' leacht.	She is my love, oh she is my love The woman who left no strength in me, A woman who would not utter for me an 'alas' A woman who would not put a headstone at my grave.
'Sí my rún, ón 'sí mo rún Bean nach n-innseann aon nidh dhúinn, Bean nach leigfeadh am' dhiaidh och, Bean nach ndeunfadh sile súl.	She is my secret love, oh she is my secret love A woman who tells us nothing, A woman who would not utter for me an 'alas', A woman who would not cry.
'Sí mo chruth, ón 'sí mo chruth, Bean nach g-cuimhnuigheann mé bheith amuigh, Bean nach ngoilfeadh uair mo bháis 'Sí chrádhaigh mo chroide go lár.	She is my form, oh she is my form, A woman who does not remember my being out, A woman who would not cry at the hour of my death It is she who tormented my heart to the core.
Mór mo chás, ón mór mo chás Is iongnadh fhad go bhfághaim bás, Bean nach dtiúbhradh taobh liom Dar mo mhionn is í mo ghrádh.	Great my case, oh great my case It is a wonder the length of time until I die, A woman who will not rely on me By my oath, she is my love.
'Si mo roghan, ón 'sí mo roghan Bean nach ndearcfadh siar orm, An bhean nach ndeunfadh liom-sa sith A's tá de shíor lán de ghráin.	She is my choice, oh she is my choice A woman who would not look back on me, The woman who would not make peace with me And who is always full of hatred.
Is mór mo bhrón, ón 's mór mo bhrón Fá an droch-mheas mór Ag an mnaoi do mo chlaoidh' Is í shlad mé ó mo bheó.	Great is my sorrow, oh great is my sorrow About the great contempt The woman has in destroying me It is she who robbed me of my life.
'Si mo mhian, ón 'sí mo mhian, Bean is annsa liom faoi 'n ngréin, An bhean nach g-cuirfeadh orm binn Dá suidhfinn le na taébh.	She is my desire, oh she is my desire, The dearest woman to me under the sun, The woman who would not take heed of me If I would sit by her side.
'Sí do chrádhaigh mo chroide A's d'fhágbhuigh osna am' lár, Muna dtógthar an t-olc so óm' chroide Ní bhéidh mé go deó slán.[43]	It is she who tormented my heart And left a sigh in my breast, If this evil is not raised from my heart I will never be healthy.

'My Love, Oh, She Is My Love'

She casts a spell, oh, casts a spell,
    Which haunts me more than I can tell,
    Dearer, because she makes me ill,
    Than who would will to make me well.

She is my store, oh, she my store,
    Whose grey eye wounded me so sore,
    Who will not place in mine her palm,
    Who will not calm me any more.

She is my pet, oh, she my pet,
    Whom I can never more forget;
    Who would not lose by me one moan,
    Nor stone upon my cairn set.

She is my roon, oh, she my roon,[44]
    Who tells me nothing, leaves me soon;
    Who would not lose by me one sigh,
    Were death and I within one room.

She is my dear, oh, she my dear,
    Who cares not whether I be here.
    Who would not weep when I am dead,
    Who makes me shed the silent tear.

Hard my case, oh, hard my case,
    How have I lived so long a space,
    She does not trust me any more,
    But I adore her silent face.

She is my choice, oh, she my choice,
    Who never made me to rejoice;
    Who caused my heart to ache so oft,
    Who put no softness in her voice.

Great my grief, oh, great my grief,
    Neglected, scorned beyond belief,
    By her who looks at me askance,
    By her who grants me no relief.

She's my desire, oh, my desire,
    More glorious than the bright sun's fire;
    Who were than wind-blown ice more cold,
    Had I the boldness to sit by her.

She it is who stole my heart,
    But left a void and aching smart,
    And if she soften not her eye
    Then life and I shall shortly part.[45]

Original: 'Bruadar Smiot a's Glin
(Mallacht)'

Literal translation:

Bruadair, Smiot a's Glin,
    Amén, a Mhic, – an triúr –
Nára cian go rabhaid fé leacaibh,
    Go marbh, lag, fuar 'san úir.
                Amén!

Bruadar, Smith and Glinn,
    Amen, Son, – the three –
May it not be long until they are under stones,
    Until dead, weak, cold in the earth.
                Amen!

Bruadair, Smiot a's Glin,
    Go fánach, singil, fuar,
Amén, a Righ na n-aingeal,
    A's go tréith-lag truithill truagh.
                Amén!

Bruadar, Smith and Glinn,
    Straying, single, cold,
Amen, King of the angels,
    And weakly feeble, miserable, pitiful.
                Amen!

Bruadair, Smiot a's Glin,
    Fa glas, ar lic na bpian,
Cúis caoi agus sileadh deór
    Go raibh gach ló ag an dtriar.
                Amén!

Bruadar, Smith and Glinn,
    Under lock, on the slab of the pains,
A cause of lament and dropping of tears
    May the three have every day.
                Amen!

Dálladh ar Smiot go grod,
    Lagughadh ar gheugaibh Bhruadair,
Amén, a Righ na Gile,
    A's Glin ar easbaidh luadair.
                Amén!

Blindness on Smith soon,
    A weakening on Bruadar's limbs,
Amen, King of the Brightness,
    And Glinn in want of movement.
                Amen!

Smiot i gcarcair pian,
    Bruadair gan rian gan rath,

Amén! a Righ na ndúl,
    A's Glin gan lúth i meath.
                Amén!

Smith in a prison of pain,
    Bruadar without a course, without prosperity
Amen! King of the elements,
    And Glinn without vigour in decline.
                Amen!

Bruadair go grod san uaigh,
    Glin go fuar 'n chriaidh,
Amén, a Righ an Dómhnaigh,
    A's Smiot fá shlabhraibh an diabhail.
                Amén!

Bruadar suddenly in the grave,
    Glinn coldly in the clay,
Amen, King of Sunday,
    And Smith under the chains of the Devil.
                Amen!

Dith-chéille ar Bhruadair chlaon,
    Pian ar muin péine ar Ghlin,
Amén, a Righ na Reanna
    An Diabhal ag cabhair ar Smiot.
                Amén!

A loss of sense on crooked Bruadar,
    Pain on top of pain on Glinn,
Amen, King of the Stars
    The Devil helping Smith.
                Amen!

'Bruadar and Smith and Glinn: A Curse'

(Hyde says the spirit of this extended curse poem is thoroughly
pagan, despite the fervent appeals to the God of Christianity, identi-
fied by many of the names that Gaelic culture has given Him.)

Bruadar and Smith and Glinn,
    Amen, dear God, I pray,
May they lie low in waves of woe,
    And tortures slow each day!
                Amen!

Bruadar and Smith and Glinn
    Helpless and cold, I pray,
Amen! I pray, O King,
    To see them pine away.
                Amen!

Bruadar and Smith and Glinn
    May flails of sorrow flay!
Cause for lamenting, snares and cares
    Be theirs by night and day!
                Amen!

Blindness come down on Smith,
    Palsy on Bruadar come,
Amen, O King of Brightness! Smite
    Glinn in his members numb.
                Amen!

Smith in the pangs of pain,
    Stumbling on Bruadar's path,
King of the Elements, Oh, Amen!
    Let loose on Glinn Thy Wrath.
                Amen!

For Bruadar gape the grave,
    Up-shovel for Smith the mould,
Amen, O King of the Sunday! Leave
    Glinn in the devil's hold.
                Amen!

Terrors on Bruadar rain,
    And pain upon pain on Glinn,
Amen, O King of the Stars! And Smith
    May the devil be linking him.
                Amen!

<table>
<tr><td>

Original: 'Bruadar Smiot a's Glin (Mallacht)' (cont.)

Glin i bhfiabhras creatha,
   Cancar i dteangain Bhruadair,
Amén! a Righ na bhFlaitheas,
   A's Smiot a measc na gcruadhtan.
                 Amén!

Glin fé thart gan deoch,
   Smiot go docht fé bhrón,
Amén! a Righ na Naomh,
   A's Bruadair go faon ag dreógh'.
                 Amén!

Smiot gan neach ar a shliocht,
   Bruadair gan bun gan stór,

Amén! a Righ na h-Aoine,
   A's Glin gan bhrigh 'na ghlór.
                 Amén!

Bruadair gan bhrigh 'na bhallaibh,
   Glin d'á thachtadh i gcnáib,
Amén! A Righ an tsoluis;
   A's Smiot i nglothar báis.
                 Amén!

Glin go fuar 'na stalca,
   Smiot go creathach truaill,
Amén! A Righ na bhFeart,
   A's Bruadair go beacht 'na thruagh.
                 Amén!

Smiot 'na chriathar poll,
   Bruadair ag lobhadh 'na ghoile,
Amén! A Righ na n-órd,
   A's Glin 'na bhoc-seó ar buile.
                 Amén!

Creach-ruathar gan mhoill ar Smiot,
   Glin fá chóir a chrochta,
Amén! a Righ an Luain,
   A's Bruadair san uaigh go lobhtha.
                 Amén!

Mo mhallacht go buan do Ghlin,
   Mallughadh a's meath ar Bhruadair,
Amén! a Righ na bhFlaitheas,
   Agus Smiot i gcarcair truagh lag.
                 Amén!

</td><td>

Literal translation (cont.):

Glinn in a shaking fever,
   A canker on Bruadar's tongue,
Amen, King of the Heavens,
   And Smith in the midst of hardships.
   Amen!

Glinn in thirst without a drink,
   Smith strictly under sorrow,
Amen! King of the Saints
   And Bruadar limply decaying.
                 Amen!

Smith without a person in his descendants,
   Bruadar without a foundation, without treasure,
Amen! King of Friday,
   And Glinn without substance in his voice.
                 Amen!

Bruadar without power in his limbs,
   Glinn strangling in hemp,
Amen! King of the light,
   And Smith in his death-rattle.
                 Amen!

Glinn coldly stiff,
   Smith shiveringly miserable,
Amen, King of the Miracles,
   And Bruadar perfectly pitiful.
                 Amen!

Smith a sieve of holes,
   Bruadar rotting in his belly,
Amen! King of the orders
   And Glinn a mad he-goat.
                 Amen!

A rush of ruin without delay on Smith,
   Glinn near his hanging,
Amen! King of Monday,
   And Bruadar in the grave rottenly.
                 Amen!

My curse forever on Glinn,
   Cursing and wasting on Bruadar,
Amen! King of the Heavens,
   And Smith in prison, pitiful and weak.
                 Amen!

</td></tr>
</table>

Glinn in a shaking ague,
      Cancer on Bruadar's tongue,
Amen, O King of the Heavens! and Smith
      For ever stricken dumb.
                              Amen!

Thirst but no drink for Glinn,
      Smith in a cloud of grief,
Amen! O King of the Saints; and rout
      Bruadar without relief.
                              Amen!

Smith without child or heir,
      And Bruadar bare of store,
Amen, O King of the Friday! Tear
      For Glinn his black heart's core.
                              Amen!

Bruadar with nerveless limbs,
      Hemp strangling Glinn's last breath,
Amen, O King of the World's Light!
      And Smith in grips with death.
                              Amen!

Glinn stiffening for the tomb,
      Smith wasting to decay,
Amen, O King of the Thunder's gloom,
      And Bruadar sick alway.
                              Amen!

Smith like a sieve of holes,
      Bruadar with throat decay,
Amen, O King of the Orders! Glinn
      A buck-show every day.
                              Amen!

Hell-hounds to hunt for Smith,
      Glinn led to hang on high,
Amen, O King of the Judgment Day!
      And Bruadar rotting by.
                              Amen!

Curses on Glinn, I cry,
      My curse on Bruadar be,
Amen, O King of the Heaven's high!
      Let Smith in bondage be.
                              Amen!

Original: 'Bruadar Smiot a's Glin (Mallacht)' (cont.)	Literal translation (cont.):

Mí-ádh ar an dtriúr, 'na cheathaibh,
   Masladh, mí-rath, a's máchail,
Náire shaoghalta dhearbh,
   Amén! a Righ na ngrás ngeal.
      Amén!

Bad luck on the three, in showers,
   Insult, misfortune, and injury,
Certain earthly shame,
   Amen! King of the bright graces.
      Amen!

Léirsgrios a's leaghadh go h-obann
   I ndáil an triair adubhart,
Bruadair Smiot a's Glin,
   Gan rath gan rith gan lúth.
      Amén!

Complete destruction and dissipating suddenly
   For the three I spoke of,
Bruadar, Smith and Glinn
   Without prosperity, without surviving,
   without power.
      Amen!

Greim nimhe tríot-sa, a Smiot!
   A's nár imthighidh mo ghuth le gaoith,
Fuil do chroidhe fé bhliadhain ó 'ndiú
   Go raibh 'na sruth le d' thaoibh.
      Amén!

The bite of poison through you, Smith!
   And may my voice not be gone with a wind,
The blood of your heart within a year of today
   May it be in a stream by your side.
      Amen

Gan tigh gan áit do Smiot!
   Fán fada ar Bhruadair!
An Diabhal ar dheas-láimh Ghlin
   Gach maidin ag ceangail suas de.
      Amén!

No house, no place for Smith!
   A long wandering on Bruadar!
The devil on the right hand of Glinn
   Every morning tying him up.
      Amen!

Olc a's ár-ghoin ós gach áird
   Go bhfeicead-sa i ndáil an triair,
A's sin fé bhliadhain ó indiú,
   I gcarcair dhuibh gan rian.
      Amén!

Evil and a plague of wounding from every direction
   May I see being distributed for the three,
And within a year of today,
   In a dark prison without a trace.
      Amen!

Briseadh a's brúghadh ar Ghlin!
   Fuil a's inchinn le Bruadair claon!
Amén! a Íosa! éist le m' ghuth,
   A's Smiot gach lá go féig.
      Amén!

Breaking and bruising on Glinn!
   Blood and brains decline with Bruadar!
Amen! Jesus! listen to my voice,
   And Smith every day weak.
      Amen!

Gearánaim Glin a's Bruadair,
   A's Smiot, go cruaidh le Dia,
Basgadh a's bearnadh ar an dtriúr,
   A's mo mhallacht go dlúth 'na ndiaidh.
      Amén!

I complain of Glinn and Bruadar,
   And Smith, severely to God,
Destruction and a biting on the three,
   And my curse closely after them.
      Amen!

Gach n-aon do chuir ionnainn lámh,
   Ar bhearna a n-aimhlis dóibh!
Creach-ruathar anuas ó neamh
   Go dtugaidh sgrios 'na measg aon-lá.
      Amén!

Every one who put a hand against us,
   To the chasm of their loss with them!
A rush of ruin down from heaven
   May bring destruction in their midst one day.
      Amen!

Showers of want and blame,
    Reproach, and shame of face,
Smite them all three, and smite again,
    Amen, O King of Grace!
                Amen!

Melt, may the three, away,
    Bruadar and Smith and Glinn,
Fall in a swift and sure decay
    And lose, but never win.
                Amen!

May pangs pass through thee Smith,
    (Let the wind not take my prayer),
May I see before the year is out
    Thy heart's blood flowing there.
                Amen!

Leave Smith no place nor land,
    Let Bruadar wander wide,
May the Devil stand at Glinn's right hand,
    And Glinn to him be tied.
                Amen!

All ill from every airt
    Come down upon the three,
And blast them ere the year be out
    In rout and misery.
                Amen!

Glinn let misfortune bruise,
    Bruadar lose blood and brains,
Amen, O Jesus! hear my voice,
    Let Smith be bent in chains.
                Amen!

I accuse both Glinn and Bruadar,
    And Smith I accuse to God,
May a breach and a gap be upon the three,
    And the Lord's avenging rod.
                Amen!

Each one of the wicked three
    Who raised against me their hand,
May fire from heaven come down and slay
    This day their perjured band,
                Amen!

Original: 'Bruadar Smiot a's Glin (Mallacht)' (cont.)

Literal translation (cont.):

Gan sliocht os cionn a mbáis,
    Cé b' obann a dtásg 'san tslógh,
Gach easgaine i Sailm na bhFáidh
    Go bhfeicead 'na ndáil ar sógh.
        Amén!

Without descendants after their deaths,
    Although sudden was their fame in the crowd,
Every curse in the Psalms of the Prophets
    May I in joy see being distributed to them.
        Amen!

Gan cluas, gan croiceann a bplaesg,
    Gan éisteacht, gan radharc, gan glór,
Sul a mbéidh an bhliadhain seo astigh,
    Agus amén! a Mich na h-Óighe.
        Amén!

Without an ear, without skin on their skulls,
    Without hearing, without sight, without a voice,
Before this year will be in,
    And Amen! Son of the Virgin.
        Amen!

Ní deireadh do'n díogras, trick of the loop,
    Nimh gach a ndubhart, maille le cách,
Go dtuitidh ar an 'bpeeler' ciar,
    A's amén! a Dhia, gach lá.
        Amén![46]

No end to the passion, trick of the loop,
    The poison of all that I said, along with everything,
May it fall on the swarthy 'peeler',
    And Amen! God, every day.
        Amen!

May none of their race survive,
　　May God destroy them all,
Each curse of the psalms in the holy books
　　Of the prophets upon them fall.
　　　　　　　Amen!

Blight skull, and ear, and skin,
　　And hearing, and voice, and sight,
Amen! before the year be out,
　　Blight, Son of the Virgin, blight.
　　　　　　　Amen!

May my curses be hot and red
　　And all I have said this day,
Strike the Black Peeler too,
　　Amen, dear God, I pray!
　　　　　　　Amen![47]

Original: 'Slán leat a shiúr'   Literal translation:

Slán leat a shiúr,   Farewell, dear,
Ni fuláir dham 'bheith ar siubhal,   I must be going,
Le h-eagla do mhasladh, 's go g-   For fear of your disgrace, and that you would
    caillfeá do chlú;   lose your reputation;
'S go n-déarfaidhe go h-árd   And that it would be said loudly
Gur liúm 'bhí do pháirt,   That with me was your love,
A mhodhail-bhean, do gheall dam, 's   Gracious woman, who promised me, and who
    do mheall mé mar chách.   charmed me like everyone.

Ar mo luighe dham' aréir,   On my lying down last night,
Do smaoineas trém' néal   I thought in my sleep
Gur síobhra 'chaith saighead leam, 's   That it was a fairy-child who shot an arrow
    do mhill mé go h-aéibh;   through me, and spoiled me to the heart;
Cé gheóbhainn sínte rem' thaobh,   Who would I find stretched by my side,
Go caoin is go faon,   Gently and quietly,
Acht Bríghdeac na rinn rosg, ó thaoibh   But Bridget of the star-eyes, from the side of
    Locha Léin.   Loch Leane.

Do sgríobhasa chúghat,   I wrote to you,
Go caoin is go ciúin,   Gently and calmly,
Leitir faoi shéala, chum éalaighthe liúm;   A letter under seal, about eloping with me;
A phéarla na lúb,   Pearl of the curl,
Mana n-déanair-si súd,   Unless you do that,
Béad am' shíobhra 'n-gleannta, nó a d-   I will be a fairy-child of the glens, or in a
    teampall fá'n úir.   churchyard under the ground.

Patrick Joseph McCall
(1861–1919)

Patrick Joseph McCall's verse translations from the Irish exemplify the literary revival's roots in Ireland's folk tradition. Moreover, like J. J. Callanan and Edward Walsh before him, McCall sought to reproduce in his translations the patterns of assonance found in Irish-language poetry.

Born in Dublin, McCall was a founding member of the National Literary Society in Dublin, and edited collections of music for the Gaelic League. He is perhaps best known for his ballad 'Boulavogue', celebrating a parish priest in Co. Wexford who led his parishioners against the British militia in the 1798 insurrection.

'Richard Cantillon's Lament'

(George Petrie, in whose *Ancient Music of Ireland* McCall found the source of this translation, says the original was written around 1750 by Richard Cantillon of Co. Kerry.)

> To thee, dear, adieu!
> I must flee from thy view,
> Lest people who see me believe thee untrue!
> And knowing my case,
> The woes of disgrace
> Would flow o'er the rose and the snows of thy face!
>
> This day, dreaming dole,
> The fairy queen stole,
> Who named me and claimed me and chained up my soul;
> Till, calling in pain,
> I saw thee again –
> My one little, fond little swan from Loch Léine![48]
>
> I wrote then and sealed
> A note, that revealed
> My hope thou wouldst roam to my home, far afield;
> Else, dying to men,
> I'd fly to some fen,
> And sigh through the night with the Sprites of the Glen!

Original: 'Slán leat a shiúr' (cont.)　　　　Literal translation (cont.):

Mo chreadh is mo dhíth,
Nach í Máire 'tá 'na luíghe,
Agus Bríghid an chúil chraobhaigh
　　'beith taobh liúm na suídhe;
Gur le guth binn a cinn
Thig na róinte dho'n linn,
An fiadh-phoc ó'n g-ceó-chnoc, 's an
　　smólach do'n chraoibh.

My loss and my ruin,
That it is not Máire who is lying down,
And Bridget of the flowing hair to be sitting
　　beside me;
That with the melodious voice from her head
The seals came from the sea,
The male deer from the misty hill, and the
　　thrush from the branch.

Nach dúbach bocht an cás,
'Bheith ag tuitim a n-grádh
Le gile, le finne, 's le buige na mná;

Is the case not melancholy, poor,
To be falling in love
With brightness, with fairness, and with the
　　softness of the woman;

A chraobh úr gan cháim,
Ná'r thréig riamh a bláth,
'S gur as Gaoidhilge do léighfinn do
　　thréighibh, a bháb.

Fresh branch without blemish,
Whose blossom never deserted it,
It is in Gaelic that I would declare your traits,
　　maiden.

'Seo beannacht dhuit uaim,
Gan stad, siar ó thuaigh,
Ó fhágann sí Ráith Fraoigh, go d-téidh
　　do'n Chill Mhuair;
A laegh ghil, 's a uain,
Léad' théacht chúgham go luath
'S gheóbhair lán an tighe d'fháiltíbh, is
　　lán mhí chum suain.

This blessing for you from me,
Without stopping, to the northwest,
From when it leaves Rathfree, until it comes to
　　Cillmore;
Oh bright calf, and lamb,
With your coming to me soon
And you will get a houseful of welcomes, and a
　　full month for rest.

Croidhe cráidhte ar gach aon
'Thabharfadh náire dhúinn araon,
Is déarfadh gur bheárnasa bán-chnis
　　na g-craobh;
'S gur lán-fhíor dho'n t-saoghal
Ná deárnas riamh lé
Acht súgradh gan tábhacht, no gáire
　　gan chlaon.[49]

A heart torn with anguish for everyone
Who would give shame to us both,
And would say that I breached the fair bark of
　　the branches;
It is completely true for the world
That I never did with her
But jesting without importance, or laughing
　　without deceit.

If Maureen lay cold
This morn in the mould,
With honour I'd call thee my claursach[50] of gold!
Birds hearing its glee
Would steal from the tree,
The sheep from the fields and the seals from the sea!

Oh, why was I born
To sigh thus forlorn?
O Lightness and Brightness and Whiteness of Morn!
O maid without blame,
Unshaded by shame –
'Tis daily I praise in my Gaelic thy name!

What greetings I'll pour,
To meet thee, astore,[51]
When leaving Rathfree until reaching Cillmore,
The day thou wilt roam
O'er wave and o'er loam,
To grace with thy face the wild waste of my home!

Sad grief on the throng
Who see hidden wrong;
And speak of the weak 'neath the shield of the strong!
God sees all the while
No sin in our smile –
Our bliss without guilt and lips without guile![52]

Original: 'Caillech Bérri'	Literal translation:

Aithbe damsa bés mora;
    sentu fom-dera croan;
toirsi oca cía do-gnéo
    sona do-tét a loan.

Ebb-tide to me as to the sea;
    old age makes me yellow;
although I may grieve at it,
    it approaches its provisions joyfully.

Is mé Caillech Bérri, Buí;
no meilinn léini mbithnuí;
    in-díu táthum dom shéimi,

    ná melainn cid aithléini.

I am the Old Woman of Beare, Baoi;
I used to wear an ever-new smock;
    today, it has befallen me, because of my
        mean estate,
    I could not even wear a cast-off smock.

It moíni
cartar lib, nídat doíni;
    sinni, ind inbaid marsaimme
    batar doíni carsaimme.

It is riches
that you love, not people;
    as for us, when we lived
    it was people that we loved.

Batar inmaini doíni
    ata maige 'ma-ríadam;
ba maith no-mmeilmis leo,
    ba becc no-mmoítis íaram.
       .   .   .

Beloved were the people
    whose plains we ride over;
it was well that we fared with them,
    it was little that they boasted afterwards.
       .   .   .

Stephen Gwynn
(1864–1950)

Stephen Gwynn was a Nationalist MP for more than ten years, and wrote much political propaganda on behalf of Home Rule. (His mother was the daughter of William Smith O'Brien, one of the leaders of the Young Ireland movement of the 1840s.) He also wrote several novels having to do with Irish issues, and biographies of a number of Irish writers, including Thomas Moore and Oliver Goldsmith. Gwynn's experience of Irish culture was informed by the years he spent as a young boy in Co. Donegal.

'The Woman of Beare'

(The original poem on which this is based, 'Caillech Bérri', is believed to have been composed as early as the ninth century. The old woman of Beare, a pagan goddess who finds herself in a community of nuns at the end of her long life, is often associated with the Beare peninsula in Cos. Cork and Kerry.)

> *Ebbing, the wave of the sea*
> *Leaves, where it wantoned before,*
> *Wan and naked the shore,*
> *Heavy the clotted weed:*
> *And in my heart, woe is me!*
> *Ebbs a wave of the sea.*

> I am the Woman of Beare,
> Foul am I that was fair:
> Gold-embroidered smocks I had,
> Now in rags am hardly clad.

> Arms, now so poor and thin,
> Staring bone and shrunken skin,
> Once were lustrous, once caressed
> Chiefs and warriors to their rest.

> Not the sage's power, nor lone
> Splendour of an agèd throne,
> Wealth I envy not, nor state:
> Only women folk I hate.

Original: 'Caillech Bérri' (cont.)	Literal translation (cont.):

Ot é cnámacha cáela
  ó do-éctar mo láma; –
ba inmain dán do-gnítis:
  bítis im ríga rána.

. . .

t is bony and slender
  my arms are seen; –
it was worthy craft they used to practise;
  they used to be around glorious kings.

. . .

It fáilti na ingena
  ó thic dóib co Beltaine;
is deithbiriu damsa brón:
  sech am tróg, am sentainne.

. . .

It is joyful the maidens are
  once they come to May-day;
more fitting to me is grief:
  not only am I miserable, I am an old woman.

. . .

Lia na Ríg hi Femun,
Caithir Rónáin hi mBregun,
  cían ó ro-síachtar sína
  a lleicne; nít senchrína.

The Stone of the Kings in Femen,
the Chair of Rónán in Bregon,
  it is long since storms reached
    their cheeks; but they are not old and
    withered.

Is labar tonn mora máir;
ros-gab in gaim cumgabáil:
  fer maith, mac moga, in-díu
  ní freiscim do chéilidiu.

Noisy is the wave of the great sea;
winter has begun to raise it;
  a noble man, a son of a slave, today
  I do not expect on a visit.

Is éol dam a ndo-gniat,
  rait ocus do-raat;
curchasa Átha Alma,
  is úar in adba i faat.

. . .

I know what they are doing,
  rowing and rowing;
the reeds of Áth Alma,
  cold is the dwelling in which they sleep.

. . .

A-minecán! mórúar dam;
  cach dercu is erchraide.
Íar feis fri caindlib sorchuib
  bith i ndorchuib derthaige!

Indeed! a great cold is on me;
  every acorn is apt to decay.
After feasting by bright candles
  to be in the darkness of an oratory!

Rom-boí denus la ríga
oc ól meda ocus fhína;
  in-díu ibim medcuisce
eter sentainni crína.

I have had my day with kings
drinking mead and wine;
  today I drink whey-water
among shriveled old hags.

Rop ed mo choirm cóidén midc;
  ropo toil Dé cecham-theirb;
oc do guidisiu, a Dé bí,
  do-rata . . . fri feirg.[a]

. . .

Let my ale be a small cup of whey;
  let it be God's will whatever vexes me;
praying to you, O God,
  may my body's blood turn from anger.

. . .

On your heads, while I am cold,
Shines the sun of living gold;
Flowers shall wreathe your necks in May;
For me every month is gray.

Yours the bloom: but ours the fire,
Even out of dead desire.
Wealth, not men, ye love; but when
Life was in us, we loved men.

Fair the men, and wild the manes
Of their coursers on the plains;
Wild the chariots rocked, when we
Raced by them for mastery.

Lone is Femen, vacant, bare,
Stands in Bregon Ronan's Chair.[53]
And the slow tooth of the sky
Frets the stones where my dead lie.

The wave of the great sea talks:
Through the forest winter walks.
Not to-day by wood and sea
Comes King Diarmuid here to me.

I know what my king does.
Through the shivering reeds, across
Fords no mortal strength may breast,
He rows – to how chill a rest!

Amen! Time ends all.
Every acorn has to fall.
Bright at feasts the candles were,
Dark is here the house of prayer.

I, that when the hour was mine,
Drank with kings the mead and wine,
Drink whey-water now, in rags
Praying among shrivelled hags.

Amen! Let my drink be whey!
Let me do God's will all day –
And, as upon God I call,
Turn my blood to angry gall.

Original: 'Caillech Bérri' (cont.)	Literal translation (cont.):

Tri thuile
do-ascnat dún Aird Ruide:
  tuile n-oac, tuile n-ech,
  tuile mílchon mac Luigdech.
· · ·
	Three floods
	approach the fort of Ard Ruide:
	  a flood of warriors, a flood of steeds,
	  a flood of the greyhounds of Lugaid's sons.
	· · ·

Tonn tuili
  ocus ind aile aithbi:
dom-áncatarsa uili
  conda éolach a n-aithgni.
	The flood wave
	  and that other that is ebb:
	all have come to me
	  so that I know how to recognize them.

Tonn tuili
nícos-tair socht mo chuile!
  cid mór mo dám fo deimi
fo-cress lám forru uili.
· · ·
	The flood wave,
	it does not come to the silence of my pantry!
	  although great is my company in darkness
	a hand was laid on them all.
	· · ·

Céin mair insi mora máir;
dosn-ic tuile íarna tráig;
  os mé, ní frescu dom-í
  tuile tar éisi n-aithbi.
	It is well for an island of the great sea:
	flood comes to it after the ebb;
	  as for me, I do not expect for me
	  a flood after the ebb.

Is súaill mennatán in-díu
  ara taibrinnse aithgne;
a n-í ro boí for tuile
  atá uile for aithbe.[54]
	Wretched is my dwelling-place today
	  to which I would give recognition;
	what was in flood
	  is all on ebb.

---

[a] The literal translation assumes 'do-rata cró clí fri feirg', as in Greene and O'Connor.

Ebb, flood, and ebb: I know
Well the ebb, and well the flow,
And the second ebb, all three –
Have they not come home to me?

Came the flood that had for waves
Monarchs, mad to be my slaves,
Crested as by foam with bounds
Of wild steeds and leaping hounds.

Comes no more that flooding tide
To my silent dark fireside.
Guests are many in my hall,
But a hand has touched them all.

Well is with the isle that feels
How the ocean backward steals:
But to me my ebbing blood
Brings again no forward flood.

Ebbing, the wave of the sea
Leaves, where it wantoned before,
Changed past knowing the shore,
Lean and lonely and gray;
And far and farther from me
Ebbs the wave of the sea.[55]

Original: 'Dá dtéidhinn-se siar'   Literal translation:

Dá dtéidhinn-se siar is aniar ni thiucfainn,	If I went west, it is from the west I would not come,
Air an g-cnoc do b'áirde is air a sheasfainn,	It is on the highest hill I would stand,
'S í an chraobh chúmartha is túisge bhain-finn	It is the fragrant branch I would take first,
'Gus is é mo ghrádh féin as luaithe lean-fainn.	And it is my own love I would follow soonest.
Tá mo chroidhe chomh dubh le áirne,	My heart is as black as a sloe
Ná le gual dubh a dhóighfidhe i g-ceartaidh,	Or as a black coal that would be burnt in a forge,
Le bonn bróige air hállaidhibh bána,	Or as the sole of a shoe on white halls,
'S tá lionndubh mór os cionn mo gháire.	And a great melancholy is over my laugh.
Tá mo chroidhe-se brúighte briste	My heart is crushed, broken
Mar leac-oidhre air uachtar uisge,	Like ice on top of water,

Thomas Boyd
(1867–1927)

Thomas Boyd's one volume of poetry, published in 1906, was praised
by Thomas MacDonagh in his influential study *Literature in Ireland* as
being in the Irish mode, and Boyd's poems clearly reflect the interest
in Gaelic folklore and mythology that inspired many writers of the lit-
erary revival. He is perhaps best remembered for his poem 'To the
Leanan Sidhe'. He was born in Carlingford, Co. Louth, and worked
as a solicitor in London and Manchester.

'I Would Go into the West'

(The anonymous original, included in Douglas Hyde's *Love Songs of
Connacht*, is often associated with the folk song 'Dónall Óg', possibly
dating to the sixteenth or seventeenth century.)

> I would go into the West,
> Lonely here I cannot rest;
> > Were I only in the West
> > I would never more return.
> I would climb to my delight,
> I would climb the highest height,
> And yet higher still above
> Would I follow mine own love,
> > And would pluck the scented branch
> > Of the blossom and the thorn.
>
> Dark the heart within me borne,
> Dark as wild-sloe of the thorn;
> > As the stone of darkness dire
> > Thrown into the smith's red fire,
> As the shadowed foot that falls
> Black within white gleaming halls,
> It is heavy, it is dark,
> And my laughter none may mark;
> > It is dead with sorrow dark
> > And the weight of my desire.
>
> Ah, my heart is overborne,
> Broken, broken, bruised and torn,
> > As the ice that melts and breaks
> > In black waters of the lakes,

197

Original: 'Dá dtéidhinn-se siar'   Literal translation (cont.):
(cont.)

Mar bheidh' cnuasach cnó léis a mbriste,   As a collection of nuts will be after being
Ná maighdean óg léis a pósta.   broken,
                                               Or a young maiden after her marriage.

Tá mo ghrádh-sa air dhath na sméara,   My lover is the colour of the blackberries,
'S air dhath na súgh-craobh, lá breágh   And the colour of the raspberries, a fine
   gréine,   sunny day,
Air dhath na bhfraochóg budh duibhe   The colour of the blackest bilberries of the
   an tsléibhe,   mountain,
'Gus is minic bhí ceann dubh air   And it is often a dark head was on a white
   cholainn ghlégil.   body.

Is mithid damh-sa an baile seó a fhágb-   It is time for me to leave this town,
   háil,
Is geur an chloch 'gus is fuar an láib   The stone is sharp and the mud is cold in it,
   ann,   It is there I got blame without profit,
Is ann a fuaireas guth gan éadáil,   And a heavy word from the people of
Agus focal trom ó lucht an bhiodáín.   calumny.

Fuagraim an grádh, is mairg do thug é   I denounce love, it is a pity I gave it
Do mhac na mná úd, ariamh nár thuig é,   To the son of that woman who never under-
Mo chroidhe ann mo lár gur fhágbhuidh   stood it,
   sé dubh é,   My heart in my breast that he left it black,
'S ní fheicim air an tsráid ná i n-áit air   And I do not see him on the street or in any
   bith é.[56]   place at all.

As the fruit of broken rind,
Withered in the bitter wind,
As the maiden of the poor
Torn from out her father's door
  When the lighted feast is o'er
  And the lover love forsakes.

Oh, my love is dark and bright –
Dark as berries of the night,
  Bright as berries all aglow
  That in sunny gardens grow.
Sweet for lip and sweet for eye,
Dewy-bright the living dye.
Dark as, on the mountain track,
Wild heath-berries, azure-black.
  Oh, his head, black-curled, has lain
  Often on a breast of snow.

It is time that I should go
From this place of joy and woe,
  Where I hear the heavy sound
  Of the name that I have found;
Where they take in cruel theft
All the little, love has left.
I will leave this bitter town,
Where the dark words drag me down,
  Where the very ground is cold,
  And the very stones – they wound.

Bitter blame on love I lay;
I with love am cast away.
  Little knew that woman's son
  Of the riches he had won,
Or he would not leave my heart
Aching, breaking with the smart.
Yet I look that we may meet,
Yet I seek in field and street;
  But no more beneath the sun
  Shall I meet him – he is gone![57]

Original: 'A bhean lán do stuaim',   Literal translation:
          by Seathrún Céitinn

A bhean lán do stuaim,   Woman full of ingenuity,
    Congbhuigh uaim do lámh   Keep from me your hand
Ní fear gníomha sinn,   I am not a man of action,
    Gé taoi tinn d'ár ngrádh.   Although you are sick for our love
              . . .   . . .

Ná síl mé go saobh,   Don't think me perverse,
    A-rís ná claon ceann,   Again, don't bend your head,
Bíodh ár ngrádh gan ghníomh,   Let our love be without action,
    Go bráth, a shíodh sheang.[58]   Forever, graceful fairy.

J.M. Synge
(1871–1909)

Although he was fluent in Irish, J. M. Synge did little work in verse translation from the language: parts of two poems by the seventeenth-century historian and poet Seathrún Céitinn (Geoffrey Keating), published in book reviews, and a translation, more prosaic than poetic, of a lengthy folk song that he heard when visiting the Aran Islands, and that he included in *The Aran Islands*. Synge did, however have strong views about the verse translation from the Irish done in the nineteenth century, describing it as a 'mass of tawdry commonplace jingle'.[59]

'Oh woman full of wiles'

(For James Stephens's fuller translation of this poem by Céitinn, see pp. 219–221.)

> Oh woman full of wiles,
> Keep away from me thy hand.
> I am not a man for these things,
> Though thou art sick for my love.
>
> Do not think me perverse,
> Do not bend thy head,
> Let our love be inactive
> Forever, oh slender fairy.[60]

Original: 'Stuairín na mBachall   Literal translation:
      mBreagh Réidh'

Táid na reulta 'na seasadh ar an aer,   The stars are standing in the air,
  An ghrian a's an ghealach 'na luídhe;   The sun and the moon are lying down;
Tá an fhairge tráighte gan braon   The sea is dried up without a drop
  'S ní'l réim ag an eala mar bhíodh;   And the swan has no sway as it did;
Tá an chuaichín i mbarraibh na ngeug,   The small cuckoo is in the tops of the branches
  'Gá shíor-rádh gur éaluigh sí uainn,   Continually saying that she slipped away
      from us,

A stuairín na mbachall mbreagh réidh   Young handsome girl of the smooth, fine curls
  D'fhág Éire faoi fhadtuirse cruaidh!   Who left Ireland under hard, long afflic-
      tion!

Trí nídh do chím trés an ngrádh,   Three things I see on account of love,
  An peacadh, an bás, a's an pian,   Sin, death, and pain,
Agus m'íntinn d'á ínsin, gach lá dhom,   And my mind is saying every day to me,
  M'aigne gur chrádh sí le ciach.   My spirit she tormented with grief.
A mhaighdean, do mhill tú am' lár mé   Maiden, you ruined me in my heart
  Agus m' impídhe ó'm láimh   And my prayer from my hand to you
    chúghatsa n'iar,   after,
Mo leigheas ó na saigheadaibh-si am' lár,   My remedy for those arrows in my heart,
  'S go bhfaghaidh tú na grása ó   And that you will get graces from God!
    Dhia!

Is binne í 'ná an bhéidhlínn 's ná an liút,   She is sweeter than the violin and than the lute,
  'S 'ná ceileabhar na gcéirseach 'tá   And than the melody of the thrush that
    ciar;   is dark brown;
Is dealraíghe í ná an feur trés an ndrúcht,   She is more shining than the grass after dew,
  'S is fíor-dheas gach alt ann a cliabh;   And truly nice is every joint in her body;
Tá a píob mar an eala ar an dtráigh,   Her throat is like the swan on the strand,
  'S is dóigh liom gur breaghta í ná 'n   And it seems to me that she is finer than
    ghrian;   the sun;
'S é mo chumha gheur mar thugas dí   It is my bitter sorrow that I gave her love,
    grádh,
    'S go mb'fhearr liom nach bhfe-   And I would prefer that I had never seen
    icfinn í riamh![61]   her!

Thomas MacDonagh
(1878–1916)

Thomas MacDonagh put into practice his theory that Irish poets ought to replace the cultural stereotypes engendered by the Celtic-Twilight aesthetics of the early years of the literary revival with what he referred to as the 'Irish mode' – poetry in English that was 'from, by, of, to and for the Irish people'[62] – in his handful of verse translations, which reflect the patterns of ordinary speech and folksong in Irish.

Born in Cloughjordan, Co. Tipperary, into a family of school-teachers, MacDonagh was teaching at University College Dublin at the time of his execution for his part in the Easter Rising.

'The stars stand up in the air'

The stars stand up in the air,
    The sun and the moon are gone,
The strand of its waters is bare,
    And her sway is swept from the swan.

The cuckoo was calling all day,
    Hid in the branches above,
How my stóirín[63] is fled far away –
    'Tis my grief that I give her my love!

Three things through love I see,
    Sorrow and sin and death –
And my mind reminding me
    That this doom I breathe with my breath.

But sweeter than violin or lute
    Is my love, and she left me behind –
I wish that all music were mute,
    And I to all beauty were blind.

She's more shapely than swan by the strand,
    She's more radiant than grass after dew,
She's more fair than the stars where they stand –
    'Tis my grief that her ever I knew![64]

Original: 'An Bonnán Buí', by
Cathal Buí Mac Giolla Ghunna

Literal translation:

A bhonnáin bhuí, is é mo chrá do luí
   is do chnámha críon tar éis a gcreim,
is chan díobháil bídh ach easpa dí
   d'fhág tú do luí ar chúl do chinn;
is measa liom féin nó scrios na Traí
   thú bheith sínte ar leacaibh lom,
is nach ndearna tú díth ná dolaidh is
      tír,[a]
   is nárbh fhearr leat fíon nó uisce
      poill.

Yellow bittern, it is my misery your lying
   and your withered bones past their erosion,
it is not a want of food but a lack of drink
   that left you lying stretched out on your back;
worse for myself than the ruin of Troy
   you to be stretched on bare, flat stones,
and you didn't do harm or destruction in the
      country,
   and you didn't prefer wine or bog-hole
      water.

. . .

A bhonnáin óig, is é mo mhíle brón
   thú bheith romham i measc na dtom,
is na lucha móra ag triall chun do thór-
      raimh
   ag déanamh spóirt is pléisiúir ann;
dá gcuirfeá scéal go luath mo dhéinse
   go raibh tú i bpéin, do bheinn mo rith
nó go mbrisfinn béim as Loch Mac nÉan
   a fhliuchfadh do bhéal is do chorp
      istigh.

Young bittern, it is my thousand sorrows
   you to be before me among the shrubs,
and the large mice coming to your wake
   making sport and pleasure there;
if you had sent news early to me
   that you were in pain, I would be running
until I would break a slice from the Lake of the
      Son of the Birds
   that would wet your mouth and your body
      inside.

. . .

Dúirt mo stór liom ligean den ól
   nó nach mbeinnse beo ach seal beag
      gearr,
ach dúirt mé léi go dtug sí bréag
   is gurbh fhaide mo shaolsa an deoch
      'ud a fháil;
nach bhfaca sibh éan an phíobáin réidh
   a chuaidh a dh-éag den tart ar ball? –
a chomharsain chléibh, fluichaidh bhur
      mbéal,
   óir chan fhaigheann sibh braon i
      ndiaidh bhur mbáis.

My sweetheart told me to give up the drink
   or I would not be alive but a little, short
      time,
but I told her that she lied,
   and that my life was longer getting that
      drink;
did you not see the bird of the smooth throat
   that died of the thirst a while ago? –
bosom neighbors, wet your mouths,

   for you don't get a drop after your deaths.

Ní hé bhur n-éanlaith atá mise ag éagnach
   an lon, an smaolach, ná an chorr ghlas;
ach mo bhonnán buí a bhí lán den chroí,
   is gur cosúil liom féin é ina ghné is a
      dhath;
bhíodh sé choíche ag síoról na dí,
   agus deir na daoine go mbím mar sin
      seal,
is níl deor dá bhfaighead nach ligfead
      síos
   ar eagla go bhfaighinnse bás den tart.

It is not your birds that I am lamenting
   the blackbird, the thrush, or the grey heron;
but my yellow bittern who was full of heart,
   and who is like myself in his appearance
      and his colour;
he was always taking a drink,
   and people say that I am like that a while,

and there is not a drop of what I will find that I
      will not let down
   for fear that I would die of the thirst.

'The Yellow Bittern'

(The original was written by Cathal Buí Mac Giolla Ghunna [c. 1680-1756], born in Co. Fermanagh but reportedly spending much of his life in Co. Cavan. For a contemporary translation of this poem, see under Gabriel Fitzmaurice, pp. 409–411.)

The yellow bittern that never broke out
    In a drinking bout, might as well have drunk;
His bones are thrown on a naked stone
    Where he lived alone like a hermit monk.
O yellow bittern! I pity your lot,
    Though they say that a sot like myself is curst –
I was sober a while, but I'll drink and be wise
    For fear I should die in the end of thirst.

It's not for the common birds that I'd mourn,
    The black-bird, the corn-crake or the crane,
But for the bittern that's shy and apart
    And drinks in the marsh from the lone bog-drain.
Oh! if I had known you were near your death,
    While my breath held out I'd have run to you,
Till a splash from the Lake of the Son of the Bird[65]
    Your soul would have stirred and waked anew.

My darling told me to drink no more
    Or my life would be o'er in a little short while;
But I told her 'tis drink gives me health and strength
    And will lengthen my road by many a mile.
You see how the bird of the long smooth neck
    Could get his death from the thirst at last –
Come, son of my soul, and drain your cup,
    You'll get no sup when your life is past.

In a wintering island by Constantine's halls
    A bittern calls from a wineless place,
And tells me that hither he cannot come
    Till the summer is here and the sunny days.
When he crosses the stream there and wings o'er the sea
    Then a fear comes to me he may fail in his flight –
Well, the milk and the ale are drunk every drop,
    And a dram won't stop our thirst this night.[66]

Original: 'An Bonnán Buí', by
Cathal Buí Mac Giolla Ghunna
(cont.)

Literal translation (cont.):

Tá an bonnán donn ar Hallaí Choinn
    ar cheathrú gheimhridh is is olc a
    dhóigh,
is é deir sé liom nach dtig sé anall
    go dtara an samhradh fada
    róidh;
tá 'an Rós is an Rí' in imeall na slí,
    is an iomadaí dí ann ag Gael is ag
    Gall,
is ag bord mo shuí bím ag ól na dí,
    is cé gur dorcha an oích' ní
    dhéanaim stad.[67]

     . . .

The brown bittern is at Conn's Halls
    in the winter quarter and poor is his condi-
    tion,
and what he tells me is that he is not coming over
    until the long summer of mildness comes;

'The Rose and the King' is on the side of the road,
    and plenty of drink is there for Gael and for
    Gall,
and sitting at a table I am taking a drink,
    and though the night is dark I am not stop-
    ping.

---

[a] The literal translation assumes *sa tír*, as in Ó-C.

Original: 'Mé Eba ben Adaimh
uill'

Literal translation:

Mé Eba ben Adaimh uill,
Mé rosháirigh Iosa thall,
Mé róthall nemh ar mo chloinn,
Cóir is me dochóidh 's a crand.

I am Eve, wife of mighty Adam,
It is I who profaned Jesus long ago,
It is I who stole heaven from my clann,
[More] right for me to go on the tree.

Roba lem rightegh dom réir,
Olc in mithoga romthár,
Olc in cosc cinad romchrín,

Forír! ní hiodan mo lamh.

I had a kingly house at my service,
Evil in the bad choice that shamed me,
Evil in the hindering of offspring that withered
me,
Alas! my hand is not undefiled.

Ní biadh eighredh in gach dú,
Ní biadh geimreadh gaothmar glé,
Ní biadh iffern, ní biadh brón,
Ní biadh omun, minbadh mé.[68]

Ice would not be in every place,
Windy, clear winter would not be,
There would be no hell, there would be no sorrow,
There would be no terror had I not been.

'Eve'

(The original is dated to the ninth or tenth century.)

I am Eve, great Adam's wife,
I that wrought my children's loss,
I that wronged Jesus of life,
Mine by right had been the cross.

I a kingly house forsook,
Ill my choice and my disgrace,
Ill the counsel that I took
Withering me and all my race.

I that brought winter in
And the windy glistening sky,
I that brought sorrow and sin,
Hell and pain and terror, I.[69]

Original: 'Eamonn an Chnoic'

Cia h-é sin amuich,
  'Na bh-fuil faobhar ar a ghuith,
Ag raobadh mo dhoruis dúnta?
  Mise Eamonn an Chnoic,
  'Tá báidhte fuar, fluich,
Ó shíor-shiúbhal sléibhte 's gleannta!
  A laogh dhil 's a chuid,
  Cread a dhéanfainn-si dhuit,
Muna a g-cuirfinn ort beinn da m'
    ghúna.
  'S go bh-fuil púghdar go tiugh,
  Dá shíor-shéide riot,
'S go m-beadhmaois araon múchda!

Is fada mise amuich,
  Faoi shneachta 'gus faoi shioc
'S gan dánacht agam ar aon neach;
  Mo sheisreach gan sgur,
  Mo bhranar gan cur,
A's gan iad agam ar aon chor!
  Ní'l caraid agam,
  Is dainídh liom san,
Do ghlacfadh mé moch ná déanach,
  'S go g-caithfeadh mé dul,
  Tar fairge soir,
Os ann nach bh-fuil mo ghaodhalta.[70]

Who is that outside,
  Who has an edge in his voice,
Beating on my shut door?
  I am Edmund of the Hill,
  Who is drowned, cold, wet,
From long walking mountains and glens!
  Beloved and dear darling,
  What would I do for you,
Unless I would put on you the skirt of my
    gown.
  And gunpowder is thick
  In its continual blasting at you,
And we both would be obliterated!

It is long I am outside,
  Under snow and under frost
And without familiarity with any person;
  My plough without horses,
  My fallow field without sowing,
And I not having them any way!
  I have no friends,
  Grief is with me in that,
That would accept me early or late,
  And I would have to go,
  Over the sea to the east,
Since my kindred are not there.

Patrick Pearse
(1879–1916)

Patrick Pearse translated a wide variety of poems from the Irish, ranging from the politically motivated work of seventeenth-century poets, with whom he obviously felt much affinity, to love songs in the folk tradition, to versions of his own poems in Irish. Born in Dublin, Pearse served as editor of *An Claidheamh Soluis*, the journal of the Gaelic League, and founded a school in Dublin to promote Irish-lan-gauge education. He was executed for his part in the Easter Rising.

'Eamonn an Chnuic'

(The original describes a famous seventeenth-century rapparee from Co. Tipperary named Edmund O'Ryan and known as 'Edmund of the Hill'.)

"Who is that without
With voice like a sword,
That batters my bolted door?"
"I am Eamonn an Chnuic,
Cold, weary, and wet
From long walking mountains and glens."
"O dear and bright love,
What would I do for you
But cover you with a skirt of my dress.
For shots full thick
Are raining on you,
And together we may be slaughtered!"

"Long am I out
Under snow, under frost,
Without comradeship with any;
My team unyoked,
My fallow unsown,
And they lost to me entirely;
Friend I have none
(I am heavy for that)
That would harbour me late or early;
And so I must go
East over the sea,
Since 'tis there I have no kindred!"[71]

Original: 'Do threasgair an saoghal is do shéid an ghaoth mar smál'

Literal translation:

Do threasgair an saoghal is do shéid an ghaoth mar smál

The world has annihilated and the wind has blown like ashes

Alastram, Caesar, 's an méid do bhí 'na bpáirt,

Alexander, Caesar, and those who were of their part,

Tá an Teamhair 'na féar, is féach an Traoi mar tá, –

Tara is grass, and look at Troy as it is, –

'S na Sasanaigh féin do b'fhéidir go bhfuighidís bás![72]

And the English themselves, it is possible that they may die!

'The world hath conquered, the wind hath scattered like dust'

(The original was probably composed in the seventeenth or eighteenth century.)

> The world hath conquered, the wind hath scattered like dust
> Alexander, Caesar, and all that shared their sway,
> Tara is grass, and behold how Troy lieth low,
> And even the English, perchance their hour will come![73]

Original: 'An Droighneán Donn'	Literal translation:

Saoileann ceud fear gur leó féin mé nuair ólaim lionn,
'S téidheann dá dtrian síos díom nuair smaoinighim air do chómhrádh liom.
Do chum is míne 'ná an síoda air Shliabh uí Fhloinn,
'S go bhfuil mo ghrádh-sa mar bhláth an áirne air an droighneán donn.

Agus slán feasta do'n bhaile údaigh, shiar ameasg na g-crann
Is ann sin atá mo tharraingt go luath 'gus go mall,
'S iomdha anach fliuch salach agus bóithrín cam,
Gabhail idir mé 's an baile bhfuil mo stóirín ann.

Tá ribín ó mo cheud-searc ann mo phóca shíos,
Agus fir Éireann ní leigheasfadaois mo bhrón, faraor!
Tá mé réidh leat go ndeuntar dam cómhra chaol
'S go bhfásfaidh an feur 'nn dhiadgh sin tríd mo lár aníos.

'S a Phaididh an misde leat mé bheith tinn
No a Phaididh an misde leat mé dul 'sa 'g cill?
A Phaididh an chúil cheangailte 's é do bheul atá binn,
'S go dtéidhim 'san dtalamh béidh mo ghean ort faoi do chómhrádh liom.

Is fear gan chéill a rachfadh a' dréim leis an gcloidhe bheidh' árd
'S cloidhe ísioll le na thaoibh air a leagfadh sé a lámh.
Cidh gur árd é an crann caorthainn bíonn sé searbh as a bhárr
'S fásann sméartha 'gus sugh-craebha air an g-crann is ísle bláth.

A hundred men think that I am theirs when I drink ale,
And two-thirds sink from me when I think on your conversation with me.
Your shape smoother than the silk on the Mountain of Flynn,
And my love is like a blossom of the sloe on the blackthorn.

And farewell henceforth to the town beyond, to the west among the trees
It is there I am drawn early and late,
And many the wet dirty marsh and crooked small road
Going between me and the town that my treasure is in.

A ribbon from my first love is down in my pocket,
And the men of Ireland, they would not cure my sorrow, alas!
I am ready for you until a narrow coffin is made for me
And until the grass will grow, after that, up through my heart.

Paddy, do you care about my being sick
Or Paddy, do you care about my going into the churchyard?
Paddy of the tied-back hair, it is your mouth that is sweet,
And until I go in the ground my love will be for you for your conversation with me.

It is a man without sense who would go climbing the ditch that is high
And a low ditch by his side that he could lay his hand on.
Although the rowan tree is tall, it is bitter at its top
And blackberries and raspberries grow on the tree of the lowest blossom.

Padraic Colum
(1881–1972)

Born in a Co. Longford workhouse, and brought up by his grand-mother in Co. Cavan, Colum brought to his writing a keen sense of the reality of Irish peasant life, and of the folklore and traditions that nourished it. 'You might say,' Colum once said, 'that I had the advantage of the disadvantages that Yeats and the others didn't have.'[74] The relatively few verse translations that Colum produced, almost all of them early in his career, reflect that 'advantage', expressing, like the translations of Douglas Hyde, a decidedly melancholic post-famine rural consciousness.

'An Drinaun Donn'

(This translation is based on a well-known Irish song that occurs in a number of different versions. It has been argued that the song originated in Co. Roscommon, in the area around Ballinlough, and some versions, including the one below, include the place-name Sliabh uí Fhloinn, probably a reference to a hill between Ballinlough and Castlerea to the east. For Donagh MacDonagh's version, see pp. 299–301.)

A hundred men think I am theirs when with them I drink ale,
But their presence fades away from me, and their high spirits fail,
When I think upon your converse kind by the meadow and the linn,[75]
And your form smoother than the silk on the Mountain of O'Flynn.

Oh, Paddy, is it pain to you that I'm wasting night and day,
And, Paddy, is it grief to you that I'll soon be in the clay?
My first love with the winning mouth, my treasure you'll abide,
Till the narrow coffin closes me, and the grass grows through my side.

The man who strains to leap the wall, we think him foolish still
When to his hand is the easy ditch to vault across at will:
The rowan tree is fine and high, but bitter its berries grow,
While blackberries and raspberries are on shrubs that blossom low.

Farewell, farewell, forever, to yon town amongst the trees,
Farewell, the town that draws me, on mornings and on eves,
Oh, many's the ugly morass now, and many's the crooked road,
That lie henceforth between me and where my heart's bestowed.

Original: 'An Droighneán Donn' (cont.)

Literal translation (cont.):

'S a Mhuire dhílis créad deunfas mé má imthigheann tu uaim,
Ní'l eólas chum do thighe agam, chum d'agaird ná do chruach,
Comhairle dhíleas do thug mo mhuinntir dham gan eulógh leat,
'S go raibh ceud cor ann do chroidhe-stigh 'gus na mílte cleas.[76]

And dear Mary, what will I do if you depart from me,
I don't know the way to your house, to your haggard or your stacks,
Reliable advice my people gave me not to elope with you,
And that a hundred twists were inside your heart and thousands of tricks.

Original: 'Ní bhFágh Mise Bás Duit'

Literal translation:

Ní bhfágh mise bás duit
    A bhean úd an chuirp mar ghéis,
Daoine leamha do mharbhais riamh
    Ni ionann iad a's mé féin.

I shall not die for you
    Woman there of the body like a swan,
Weak people that you killed before this
    They and myself are not the same.

Créad fáth rachfainn d'eug
    D'on ghob dearg, do'n deud mar bhláth?
An cruth mhíonla, an t-ucht mar ghéis,
    An dóibh súd gheabhainn féin bás?

Why would I go to die
    For the red mouth, for the teeth like a blossom?
The gentle form, the breast like a swan,
    Would I die for those?

Na cíocha corra, an chneas úr,
    Na gruadha corcra, an cúl fiar,
Go deimhin ní bhfuighfead-sa bás
    Dóibh súd, go mbudh áill le Dia.

The pointed breasts, the fresh skin,
    The scarlet cheeks, the ruffled head of hair,
Indeed I will not die
    For those, may it be God's wish.

Do mhalaibh caola, d'fholt mar ór,
    Do rún geanmaidhe, do ghlór leisg,
Do shál chruinn, do cholpa réidh,
    Ní mharbhfaid siad acht duine leamh.

Your narrow brows, your hair like gold,
    Your chaste secret, your measured voice,
Your round heel, your smooth calf,
    They will not kill but a weak person.

Do mhéin aoibh, d'aigne saor,
    Do bhos tana, do thaobh mar chuip,
Do rosg gorm, do bhrághad bhán,
    Ní bhfágh mise bás duit.

Your cheerful disposition, your free spirit,
    Your slender palm, your side like foam,
Your blue eye, your white throat,
    I shall not die for you.

A bhean úd, an chuirp mar ghéis,
    Do h-oileadh mé ag duine glic,
A bhos thana, a bhráighe bháin
    Ní bhfágh mise bás duit.[77]

Woman there of the body like a swan,
    I was reared by a clever man,
Slender palm, white throat,
    I shall not die for you.

And Mary, Ever Virgin, where will I turn my head!
I know not where his house is built, nor where his fields are spread.
Ah, kindly was the counsel that my kinsfolk gave to me,
'The hundred twists are in his heart, and the thousand tricks has he.'[78]

'I Shall Not Die for Thee'

(The original has been dated to the seventeenth century.)

O woman, shapely as the swan,
On your account I shall not die:
The men you've slain – a trivial clan –
Were less than I.

I ask me shall I die for these –
For blossom-teeth and scarlet lips?
And shall that delicate swan shape
Bring me eclipse?

Well-shaped the breasts and smooth the skin,
The cheeks are fair, the tresses free –
And yet I shall not suffer death –
God over me!

Those even brows, that hair like gold,
Those languorous tones, that virgin way –
The flowing limbs, the rounded heel
Slight men betray!

Thy spirit keen through radiant mien,
Thy shining throat and smiling eye,
Thy little palm, thy side like foam –
I cannot die!

O woman, shapely as the swan,
In a cunning house hard-reared was I:
O bosom white, O well-shaped palm,
I shall not die![79]

Original: 'Mala an tSléibhe Ruaidh'	Literal translation:

Tá mé ann mo shuidhe
    O d'éirigh an ghealach aréir,
Ag cur teineadh síos
    Agus go síor 'gá fadóghadh go geur,
Tá muinntir an tighe
    'Nna luidhe agus mise liom féin,
Tá na coillighe ag ghlaodhach
    Agus an tír 'nna codladh acht mé.

I have been up
    Since the moon rose last night,
Putting down a fire,
    And ever kindling it fiercely,
The people of the house are
    Lying down and I by myself,
The cocks are crowing
    And the land is asleep except for me.

Ná'r fhágbhuigh mé an saoghal so
    Go sgaoilfidh mé díom an mí-ádh,
Go raibh bath agam agus caoirighe
    A's mo mhian de bhuachaill amháin,
Níor bhfada liom an oidhche
    Bhedhinn sínte le na bhrollach mín
      bán
'S go dtiúbhrainn cead do shíol Éabha
    'Nna dhiaigh sin a rogha rud a rádh.

May I not leave this world
    Until I will loose from me the bad luck,
Until I have cows and sheep
    And my desire of one boy,
May it be not long for me the evening
    I would be stretched by his smooth
      white breast
And I would give permission to the race of
      Eve
    After that to say the thing of their choice.

Foluigheann grádh gráin
    Ann gach áit a mbíonn maise 'san
      mnaoi
Air leabaidh caol árd
    Le ráithche níos bhfada mo luidhe,
Nuair chuimhnigh mé air mo ghrádh
    D'fhág mé air mhala an tsléibhe
      ruaidh
Goilim mo sháith
    'Gus is fánach thiormuigheas mo
      ghruaidh.
      . . .

Love covers hate
    In every place where there is beauty in
      a woman
On a narrow high bed
    For longer than three months my lying
When I remembered my love
    Whom I left on the brow of the red
      mountain
I weep my fill
    And it is rare that I dried my cheek.
      . . .

'S a bhuachaillín óig
    Ní ádhbhar air bith magaidh dhuit mé,
Ní'l agad le rádh
    Acht amháin go bhfuil mé gan spré,
Ní tusa mo ghrádh
    Agus mo chrádh má's misde liom é,
'S má tá mé gan bholacht
    Is leor dham laidhe liom féin.[80]

And young boy,
    I am not any object of mockery for you,
You have nothing to say
    Except that I am without a dowry,
You are not my love
    And my misery if I mind it,
And if I am without a stock of kine
    It is enough for me to lie by myself.

'The Poor Girl's Meditation'

I am sitting here,
Since the moon rose in the night;
Kindling a fire,
And striving to keep it alight:
The folk of the house are lying
In slumber deep;
The cocks will be crowing soon:
The whole of the land is asleep.

May I never leave this world
Until my ill-luck is gone;
Till I have cows and sheep,
And the lad that I love for my own:
I would not think it long,
The night I would lie at his breast,
And the daughters of spite, after that,
Might say the thing they liked best.

Love covers up hate,
If a girl have beauty at all:
On a bed that was narrow and high,
A three-month I lie by the wall:
When I bethought on the lad
That I left on the brow of the hill,
I wept from dark until dark,
And my cheeks have their tear-tracks still.

And, O, young lad that I love,
I am no mark for your scorn:
All you can say of me
Is undowered I was born:
And if I've not fortune in hand,
Nor cattle nor sheep of my own,
This I can say, O lad,
I am fitted to lie my lone![81]

Original: 'A bhean lán do
stuaim', by Seathrún Céitinn

A bhean lán do stuaim,
   Congbhuigh uaim do lámh
Ní fear gníomha sinn,
   Gé taoi tinn d'ár ngrádh.

Féach ar liath dom fholt!
   Féach mo chorp gan lúth!
Féach ar thraoch dom fhuil!
   Créad re a bhfuil do thnúth?

Ná síl mé go saobh,
   A-rís ná claon ceann,
Bíodh ár ngrádh gan ghníomh,
   Go bráth, a shíodh sheang.

Druid do bhéal óm bhéal,
   Doilghe an scéal do chor,
Ná bíom cneas re cneas,
   Tig ón dteas an tol.

Literal translation:

Woman full of ingenuity,
   Keep from me your hand
I am not a man of action,
   Although you are sick for our love.

Look at the grey of my hair!
   Look at my body without vigour!
Look at the weariness of my blood!
   What is your desire for?

Don't think me perverse,
   Again, don't bend your head,
Let our love be without action,
   Forever, graceful fairy.

Move your mouth from my mouth,
   Distressing the matter of your wiles;
Let us not be skin with skin,
   The will comes from heat.

James Stephens
(1882–1950)

James Stephens saw the Irish-language tradition, especially from the seventeenth century on, as remarkably modern, both in its understanding of loss and exile, and in its sceptical attitudes toward established authority. Stephens's verse translations from the Irish clearly reflect this view. They also are far less concerned with scholarly accuracy than are those of many other revival translators; in the preface to *Reincarnations* (1918), his one collection of translations, Stephens said the book 'ought to be called Loot or Plunder or Pieces of Eight of Treasure-Trove . . . for although everything in it can be referred to the Irish of from one hundred to three hundred years ago the word translation would be a misdescription'.[82]

Stephens was born in Dublin. He is perhaps best known for two novels, both published in 1912, *The Charwoman's Daughter* and *The Crock of God*.

'O woman full of wiliness!'

(The original is by Seathrún Céitinn [Geoffrey Keating] [1580?–1644?]. For J. M. Synge's translation of the first and third stanzas, see p. 201.)

For J. M. Synge's translation of the first and third stanzas, see p. 201.

O woman full of wiliness!
      Although for love of me you pine,
Withhold your hand adventurous,
      It holdeth nothing holding mine.

Look on my head, how it is grey!
      My body's weakness doth appear;
My blood is chill and thin; my day
      Is done, and there is nothing here.

Do not call me a foolish man,
      Nor lean your lovely cheek to mine:
O slender witch, our bodies can
      Not mingle now, nor any time.

So take your mouth from mine, your hand
      From mine, ah, take your lips away!
Lest heat to will should ripen, and
      All this be grave that had been gay.

Original: 'A bhean lán do stuaim', by Seathrún Céitinn (cont.)	Literal translation (cont.):

Do chúl craobhach cas,
    Do rosc glas mar dhrúcht,
Do chíoch chruinn gheal bhláith,
    Tharraingeas mian súl.
	Your clustering, plaited locks,
	    Your grey eye like dew,
	Your round, white, smooth breast,
	    Attract desire of the eyes.

Gach gníomh acht gníomh cuirp,
    Is luighe id chuilt shuain,
Do-ghéanainn dod ghrádh,
    A bhean lán do stuaim.[83]
	Every act but the act of the body,
	    And lying in your quilt of sleep,
	I would do for your love,
	    Woman full of ingenuity.

Original: from 'Anach Cuain', by Antoine Raiftearaí	Literal translation:

Bhí Máire Nic Ruadháin ann, buinneán glégeal,
    An cailín spéireamhail bhí againn san áit,
Ghléas sí í féin go moch Dia Céadaoin
    Le dul chum aonaigh ó Chnoc Dealáin.
Bhí cóta uirri de thogha an éadaigh,
    Cáipín lace a's ribíní bán',
Agus d'fhág sí a máithrín brónach cráidhte
    Ag seilt na ndeór arís go bráth.[84]
	Máire Nic Ruadháin was there, a beautiful sapling,
	    The most attractive girl we had in the place,
	She dressed herself early Wednesday
	    To go to the fair from Cnoc Dealáin.
	A coat was on her of choice cloth,
	    A lace cap and white ribbons,
	And she left her darling mother sorrowful, tormented
	    Shedding tears forever and ever.

It is this curl, a silken nest,
    And this grey eye bright as the dew,
And this round, lovely, snow-white breast
    That draws desire in search of you.

I would do all for you, meseems,
    But this, tho' this were happiness!
I shall not mingle in your dreams,
    O woman full of wiliness![85]

'Mary Ruane'

(The original of this translation is one stanza from 'Anach Cuain' ['Annaghdown'], a poem written by the Co. Mayo poet Antoine Raiftearaí [Antony Raftery] describing an accident that occurred on Lough Corrib, Co. Galway, in 1828. According to Raiftearaí's account, nineteen of thirty-one people on their way to the Galway fair from Annaghdown, on the eastern shore of Lough Corrib, drowned when one of the sheep they were taking with them put its foot through the bottom of their boat. One body was never recovered, that of Máire Nic Ruadháin.)

The sky-like girl whom we knew!
    She dressed herself to go to the fair
In a dress of white and blue;
A white lace cap, and ribbons white
    She wore in her hair;
She does not hear in the night
Her mother crying for her,
    Where,
        Deep down in the sea,
She rolls and lingers to and fro
    Unweariedly.[86]

Original: 'An Tan D'Aistrigh go
Duibhneachaibh Láimh le Tonn Tóime
i g-Ciarraighe', by Aodhagán Ó
Rathaille

Literal translation:

. . .

An Carrathach groidhe fíochmhar ler
fuadhadh an meang,
Is Carrathach Laoi i ndaoirse gan fuas-
cladh fann,
Carrathach rí Chinn Tuirc i n-uaig 's a
chlann
'S is atuirse trím chroidhe gan a dtuairisc
ann.

The strong fierce MacCarthy to whom guile
was hateful,
And MacCarthy Lee in bondage without
deliverance, weak,
MacCarthy king of Kanturk in the grave
and his children,
And sorrow is through my heart without
tidings of them there.

Do shearg mo chroidhe im chlíteach do
bhuaidhir mo leann;
Na seabhaic nár fríth cinnte, ag ar dhual an
eang
Ó Chaiseal go Tuinn Chlíodhna 's go
Tuamhuin tall,
A mbailte 's a maoin díth-chreachta ag slu-
aightibh Gall.

My heart withered in my breast, the
humours of my body grieved;
The warriors who were not found stingy,
who had the land by inheritance
From Cashel to Tonn Chlíodhna and to
Thomond beyond,
Their towns and their property destructively
plundered by hosts of foreigners.

A thonn so thíos is aoirde céim go h-árd,
Meabhair mo chínn claoidhte ót bhéiceach
tá;
Cabhair dá dtigeadh arís go hÉirinn bháin
Do ghlam nach binn do dhingfinn féin it
bhrághaid.[87]

Wave there below, of the highest rank up,
The sense of my head is harrowed by your
shouting;
If help would come again to fair Ireland,
Your howl that is not melodious I myself
would stuff in your throat.

'Clann Cartie'

(The original is by Aodhagán Ó Rathaille [1670?–1729]. For Eavan Boland's version, see pp. 379–381.)

My heart is withered and my health is gone,
For they who were not easy put upon,
Masters of mirth and of fair clemency,
Masters of wealth and gentle charity,
They are all gone. Mac Caura Mór[88] is dead,
Mac Caura of the Lee[89] is finishéd,
Mac Caura of Kanturk[90] joined clay to clay
And gat him gone, and bides as deep as they.

Their years, their gentle deeds, their flags are furled,
And deeply down, under the stiffened world,
In chests of oaken wood are princes thrust,
To crumble day by day into the dust
A mouth might puff at; nor is left a trace
Of those who did of grace all that was grace.

O Wave of Cliona,[91] cease thy bellowing!
And let mine ears forget a while to ring
At thy long, lamentable misery:
The great are dead indeed, the great are dead;
And I, in little time, will stoop my head
And put it under, and will be forgot
With them, and be with them, and thus be not:
Ease thee, cease thy long keening, cry no more:
End is, and here is end, and end is sore,
And to all lamentation be there end:
If I might come on thee, O howling friend!
Knowing that sails were drumming on the sea
Westward to Eiré, and that help would be
Trampling for her upon a Spanish deck,
I'd ram thy lamentation down thy neck.[92]

Original: 'Seirbhíseach Seirgthe',
by Dáibhí Ó Bruadar

Literal translation:

I

Seirbhíseach seirgthe íogair srónach seasc
d'eitigh sinn is eibior íota im scórnaigh
feacht
beireadh síobhra d'eitill í gan lón tar
lear
an deilbhín gan deirglí nár fhóir mo
thart.

A shriveled, touchy, nosy, barren servant
refused us once and the apex of thirst in my
throat
may a fairy-child of flight bear her without
provisions over the sea
the miserable figure without a ruddy com-
plexion who did not relieve my thirst.

II

Dá reicinn í san bhfeileghníomh do
gheobhadh ceacht
is beirt an tighe go leigfidís im scórsa
casc
ó cheisnimh sí go bhfeirg linn is beoir na
gar
don steiling í nár leige rí na glóire i
bhfad.

If I could proclaim her in the treacherous act,
she would get a lesson
it is the couple of the house who would allow
on my tally a cask
since she grumbled angrily at us and beer
near her
at the bench for barrels may the king of glory
not let her be long.

III

Meirgíneach bheirbhthe í gan ceol na
cab
do theilg sinn le greidimín san bpóirse
amach
gé cheilim ríomh a peidigraoi mar
fhógras reacht
ba bheag an díth dá mbeireadh sí do
ghósta cat.[93]

A crabby, boiled woman she, without music in
her mouth
who cast us with a gesture of hostile contempt
out through the porch
although I conceal an account of her pedigree
as law proclaims
little would be the harm if she would bear a
cat to a ghost.

Original: from 'Mithigh Soicheim',
by Dáibhí Ó Bruadar

Literal translation:

. . .

VI

Blogh   dom   branndán   bheith   fá
mhoghaibh
    cá measa dhom bheith fa bhróin
tugsad liosta a lúb sa leadán
    mo scúg scriosta ar beagán lóin.

. . .

A fragment of my trouble to be among
slaves
    how worse for me to be under sorrow
a list of their deceits and their abuses gave
    my throat ruined from little food.

. . .

XIV

Gé madh leabhrán níor an agam
    iomdha braitheoir bhíos im cheann
a los íoca an bhainne bhearrtha
    líonta ár laidne is gearrtha.

Although of booklets I had not one
    there are many spies attending to me
for the sake of payment for the skimmed milk
    lines of our Latin are cut.

'Righteous Anger'

(The original is by Dáibhí Ó Bruadair [1625?–1698], nine of whose poems are represented in *Reincarnations*. See pp. 359–361 for a version by Michael Hartnett.)

The lanky hank of a she in the inn over there
Nearly killed me for asking the loan of a glass of beer:
May the devil grip the whey-faced slut by the hair,
And beat bad manners out of her skin for a year.

That parboiled imp, with the hardest jaw you will see
On virtue's path, and a voice that would rasp the dead,
Came roaring and raging the minute she looked at me,
And threw me out of the house on the back of my head!

If I asked her master he'd give me a cask a day;
But she, with the beer at hand, not a gill would arrange!
May she marry a ghost and bear him a kitten, and may
The High King of Glory permit her to get the mange.[94]

'Skim-Milk'

(This is based on four stanzas taken from a lengthy panegryic by Dáibhí Ó Bruadair [1625?–1698] to Cormac Mac Donagh MacCarthy, chief of Duhallow, Co. Cork, near the end of the seventeenth century.)

A small part only of my grief I write;
        And if I do not give you all the tale
It is because my gloom gets some respite
        By just a small bewailing; I bewail
That I with sly and stupid folk must bide
Who steal my food and ruin my inside.

Once I had books, and each book beyond compare,
        But now no book at all is left to me,
And I am spied and peeped on everywhere,
        And my old head, stuffed with latinity,
And with the poet's load of grave and gay
Will not get me skim-milk for half a day.

Original: from 'Mithigh Soicheim',
  by Dáibhí Ó Bruadar (cont.)

Literal translation (cont.):

XV

D'easbuidh gan m'each caoin ná cean-
  ntréan
    fán gcoill seolaim gacha se
roghnáth ár muin ó an gcuail
  cnapach
    suail nach muidh mo mharcach e.

· · ·

XV

Owing to my want of a horse gentle or head-
  strong
    around the wood I walk at every turn
too accustomed our back to the lumpy
  faggot-bundles
    my rider all but broke it.

· · ·

XVIII

Amhail Oisín d'éis na Féinne
  fuaras Pádraig irseach óg
caidhe is dile dúil dá n-aithle
  bile búidh gan raifne i ród.[95]

XVIII

Like Oisín after the Fenians
  I found a young, faithful Patrick
What is more beloved of desire after them
  a gentle scion without roughness in
  his way.

Wild horse or quiet, not a horse have I,
      But to the forest every day I go
Bending beneath a load of wood, that high!
      Which raises on my back a sorry row
Of raw, red blisters; so I cry, alack,
The rider that rides me will break my back.

Ossian, when he was old and near his end,
      Met Patrick by good luck, and he was stayed;
I am a poet too and seek a friend,
      A prop, a staff, a comforter, an aid,
A Patrick who will lift me from despair
In Cormac Uasal Mac Donagh of the golden hair.[96]

Modern
Ireland

Original: 'Cridhe so dá ghoid uainne', by Maghnus Ó Domhnaill

Literal translation:

Cridhe so dá ghoid uainne, –
   cá ní is truaighe for talmhain
ná duine i mbí dá anam
   do bheith tamall gan anmain?

This heart that is stolen from us, –
   where is a thing more pitiful on earth
than a living person whose soul
   is to be for a while not remaining?

Uaimse ag inghin an iarla
   truagh gan iasacht mo chroidhe,
go dtuigeadh féin nach bhféadar
   bréagadh croidhe i mbí toirse.

From me to the daughter of the earl
   a pity not to loan my heart,
until she herself understood that it is not possible
   to sooth a heart in affliction.

Cuirfead iomchar mo chroidhe
   ar dhuine oile i-mbliadhna;
gidh eadh, dá gcleachta a iomchar,
   biaidh sí diomdhach don iasacht.

I will put the load of my heart
   on another person this year;
although, if accustomed to its load,
   she will be vexed with the loan.

Biaidh sí tinn, biaidh sí corrach,
   biaidh sí gan chodladh choidhche,
biaidh sí ciamhair cumhach,
   biaidh sí dubhach gach n-oidhche.

She will be sick, she will be unsteady,
   she will be without sleep ever,
she will be melancholy, mournful,
   she will be grieved every evening.

Ní iarrfa adhbhar gáire,
   badh sáimhe lé bheith dubhach,

go sgara sí rem chroidhe
   go bráth ní bhfoighe furtacht.

You would not look for a cause of laughter,
   it would be a pleasure for her to be melancholy,
until she relinquished my heart
   for ever she would not get comfort.

Uch! ní cothrom an roinn-se
   do-ní an toirrse, dar linne, –
croidhe nó dhó ag duine
   's duine oile gan chridhe![1]

Oh! it is not fair play the sharing
   of a thing of affliction, it seems to us, –
a heart or two for a person
   and another person without a heart!

Robin Flower
(1881–1946)

Robin Flower is perhaps best known as the translator of Tomás Ó Criomhthain's writings about life on the Blasket Islands. But Flower also published, in the 1920s and 1930s, several substantial collections of verse translations, representing a wide variety of Irish-language poetry. He also wrote a survey of Irish-language literature, *The Irish Tradition* (1947), which includes verse translations not in his earlier collections. In his introduction to one of these, Flower, an Englishman educated at Oxford, argues that Irish-language love poetry of the sixteenth and seventeenth centuries can be read profitably in the context of Elizabethan, Jacobean and Caroline poetry in English, a connection that is evident in many of Flower's verse translations of Irish love poetry.

'Manus O'Donnell and the Earl's Daughter'

(The original was written by Maghnus Ó Domhnaill [d. 1563], best known for his biography of Colum Cille. Ó Domhnaill had a castle at Lifford, on the Donegal-Tyrone border.)

> Lacking the heart she stole, what shall I do?
> Most pitiful of all things born I live,
> Reft of my soul though all men else have two.
> Ah! could I but for one swift moment give
> To the Earl's daughter, she that wrought my woe,
> This heart and its immedicable grief,
> Then in her secret bosom would she know
> Love's sorrow; and how barren of relief
> Drags the long year; and with what fell disease
> The sick soul tosses, day and night the same,
> Feeding on grief since laughter cannot please
> Until she give the heart back whence it came
> Unjust exchange! whereby my life's undone,
> My true love hath two hearts and I not one.[2]

Original: 'Neimhthinn an galar é an grádh', by Cúchonnacht Ó Cléirigh

Literal translation:

Neimhthinn an galar é an grádh,
    bréag a ráidhid cách dá thaoibh;
éinneach riamh ní raibhe slán
    ag nách raibhe grádh do mhnaoi.

The disease of love is not sickness,
    everyone tells a lie about it;
anyone ever who was not healthy
    did not have the love for a woman.

Grádh mná 'gá bhfuilim i láimh,
    ní bhaim tríd ag dáil na ndeór;
is fada ó do-ghéabhainn bás,
    acht an grádh dom chongbháil beó.

Love of a woman whichI have in hand,
    I am not because of it pouring out the drops;
it is long since I would have died,
    but for love keeping me alive.

Do chongaibh mé m'fheóil is m'fhuil
    do ghrádh ainnre an chuirp mar ghéis;
ithim mórán, do-ním suan,
    in gach ceól is buan mo spéis.

I kept my flesh and my blood
    for the love of a girl with a body like a swan;
I eat a lot, I sleep,
    in all music my interest is steadfast.

Moille mé ná crann re sruth;
    atá mo ghuth ar mo bhreith;
dá mbeidís bruit Leithe Cuinn
    fá mo dhruim, do bheith sé te.

I am more languid than a tree by a stream;
    my voice is of my choosing;
if they were burning Leith Cuinn
    under my back, it would be warm.

Is teó an teine ná mo chneas,
    dá mbeinn fá eas do bheinn fuar;
dá ndeacha duine seang slán,
    do-ghéabha mé bás go luath.

The fire is warmer than my skin,
    if I were under a waterfall I would be cold;
if a slender healthy person went,
    I would die soon.

Toramsa do thiocfadh téad,
    is fliche mo bhéal ná an sponc,
dar fia! ní íobhainn an loch,
    is cruaidhe cloch ná mo bholg.

Around me a rope would come,
    wetter is my mouth than the sponge,
by heaven! I would not drink the lake,
    a stone is harder than my belly.

Aithnim nách oidhche an lá,
    aithnim an bád tar an luing,
aithnim an dubh tar an mbán,
    tar a bhfuil do ghrádh fám thuinn.

I recognize that night is not day,
    I distinguish the boat from the ship,
I distinguish the black from the white,
    notwithstanding that love is under my skin.

Aithnim nách capall an fiadh,
    aithnim nách é an sliabh an mhuir,
aithnim an beag tar an mór,
    aithnim nách é an rón an chuil.

I recognize that a horse is not a deer,
    I recognize the mountain is not the sea,
I distinguish the small from the big,
    I recognize the seal is not the fly.

. . .   . . .

'The Free Lover'

(The original has been attributed to Cúchonnacht Ó Cléirigh, a member of the learned Ó Cléirigh family of Co. Donegal. He is thought to have lived in the latter half of the sixteenth century.)

They lie who say that love must be
A sickness and a misery;
He that ne'er loved woman knows
Never anything but woes.

I too love a woman; yet
My clear eyes are never wet;
Death has claimed me for his own,
Yet I live by love alone.

Clad in flesh and blood I move,
Though a swanwhite maid I love;
Though I love I eat and sleep,
Music's service still I keep.

I'm no reed in water swaying,
My free thought goes lightly playing;
I'm no lover chill through all
The piled cloaks of Donegal.

I'm a man like others still,
Fires burn me, waters chill;
If the young and strong must die,
Ne'er so doomed a man as I.

Rope will bind me, this know I,
Like a sponge my mouth's ne'er dry,
Softer is my flesh than stone,
I can't drink the sea alone.

Though love within my bones doth play,
I know the night is not the day,
Black's black, white's white, a boat's a boat
And not a stately ship afloat.

I never call a horse a crow,
The sea's no hill, that much I know,
Small is less than great I feel
And a fly smaller than a seal.

Original: 'Neimhthinn an galar é an grádh', by Cúchonnacht Ó Cléirigh (cont.)

Literal translation (cont.):

Aoinbhean is annsa fán ghréin, –
   ní bhia mé níos sia dá cheilt –
ní rug a grádh uaim mo chonn;
   dar an Rígh, ní holl mo neimh![3]

One woman is more dear under the sun,–
   I will no longer conceal it –
her love does not carry my reason from me;
   by the King, not great my grief!

Original: 'M'airiuclán hi Túaim Inbir'

Literal translation:

M'airiuclán hi Túaim Inbir
ni lántechdais bes sestu
cona retglannaib a réir
cona gréin cona escu.

My little oratory in Túaim Inbir
   a full house is not more delightful
with its stars in attendance
   with its sun, with its moon.

Gobbán durigni insin
conecestar duib astoir
mu chridecan dia du nim
is hé tugatoir rodtoig.

It is Gobbán who made it
   that its story may be told to you
my beloved, God from heaven,
   he is the thatcher who built it.

Tech inna fera flechod
maigen na áigder rindi
soilsidir bid hi lugburt
ose cen udnucht nimbi.[4]

A house in which rain does not fall,
   a place in which spear-points are not feared;
bright as being in a garden
   and without a palisade around it.

Original: 'Clocán binn'

Literal translation:

Clocán binn
benar i n-aidchi gaíthe:
   ba ferr lim dola ina dáil
indás i ndáil mná baíthe.[5]

Melodious bell
ringing on a windy night:
   I would prefer to go in its company
than in the company of a wanton woman.

Though I love her more than all
The sun-riped maids of Donegal,
Yet, by all the gods above!,
I'm no sufferer for her love.[6]

'The Ivy Crest'

(The original is one of the many poems attributed to Suibhne Geilt [Mad Sweeney], a seventh-century Ulster king who, driven mad by battle, attacked a cleric named St. Rónán, and flung his psalter into a lake. St. Rónán put a curse on Suibhne, praying that he would wander companionless through the world, and Suibhne spent years living alone in the wilderness and composing poems. For Brendan Kennelly's translation of another of Sweeney's poems, see pp. 339–341; for Seamus Heaney's version of still another, see pp. 343–345.)

In Tuaim Invir[7] here I find
No great house such as mortals build:
A hermitage that fits my mind
With sun and moon and starlight filled.

'Twas Gobbán[8] shaped it cunningly
– This is a tale that lacks not proof –
And my heart's darling in the sky
Christ was the thatcher of its roof.

Over my house rain never falls,
There comes no terror of the spear;
It is a garden without walls
And everlasting light shines here.[9]

'The clear-voiced bell'

(The original is one of numerous fragments and poems composed by religious hermits during the early Christian period. It probably dates to the ninth century. For another version, see under Brendan Kennelly, pp. 339.)

The clear-voiced bell
On chill wild night God's hours doth tell;
Rather in it I'll put my trust
Than in a wanton woman's lust.[10]

Original: from 'Cúirt an
Mheán-Oíche', by Brian
Merriman

Literal translation:

Ar maidin inné bhí an spéir gan cheo,
Bhí Cancer ón ngréin 'na caortha teo,

Is í gafa chun saothair tar éis na h-oíche
Agus obair an lae sin roimpi sínte.
Bhí duilliúr craobh ar ghéaga im thim-
    peall,
Fiorthann is féar 'ina slaoda taobh liom,
Bhí glasra fáis ann, bláth 'is luibheanna,
Scaipfeadh chun fáin dá chráiteacht
    smaointe.
Bhí mé cortha 'san codladh im thraochadh,
Shín mé tharm ar chothrom an fhéir ghlais
In aice na gcrann i dteannta trínse,
Taca lem cheann 'smo hannlaí sínte.
Ar gceangal mo shúl go dlúth le chéile,
Greamaithe dúnta i ndubhghlas néalta,
'Is m'aghaidh agam folaithe ó chuilibh go
    sásta,
I dtaidhreamh d'fhulaing mé an chuilithe
    cráite,

Yesterday morning the sky was without fog,
Cancer from the sun was a warm glowing
    mass,
And it harnessed for work after the night
And the work of that day stretched before it.
The leaves of the branches were on limbs
    around me,
Wheat grass and grass in swaths beside me,
Luxuriant greens there, blossoms and herbs,
That would scatter astray thoughts however
    troubled.
I was exhausted and sleepy in my weariness,
I stretched out on the level of green grass
Next to the trees near a trench,
A prop for my head and my limbs stretched.
On fastening my eyes tightly together,
Fixed shut in the firm lock of sleep,
And my face hidden from flies satisfactorily,

In a dream I suffered the tormented
    whirlpool

Percy Arland Ussher
(1899–1980)

Born in London and educated at Cambridge, Percy Arland Ussher settled in Co. Waterford, where his family had a farm, and there edited a collection of folklore from the Waterford Gaeltacht. Ussher's translation of Brian Merriman's eighteenth-century satire on sexual behaviour, 'Cúirt an Mheán-Oíche' ('The Midnight Court'), was published early in his career, in 1926. It relies heavily on internal rhyme, assonance and consonance in an attempt to reproduce in English the effect of the rich and lively sound patterns of the original. Ussher was perhaps best known for his literary criticism, much of which was written after he moved to Dublin in 1953.

From 'The Midnight Court'

(This selection represents part of the opening of Merriman's poem, in which the narrator, wandering through the countryside, falls into a dream-vision, as in the traditional *aisling* (vision) poem, but sees not the conventional beautiful young woman, but an ugly hag. For selections from Denis Woulf's eighteenth-century translation of 'Cúirt an Mheán-Oíche', see pp. 27–33; for selections from Frank O'Connor's twentieth-century version, see pp. 277–285; for selections from two contemporary translations, see under Seamus Heaney, pp. 347–351, and Ciaran Carson, pp. 387–393.)

> Yesterday morn the sky was clear
> In the dog-days' heat of the mad mid-year,
> And the sun was scouring the slumb'rous air
> With his burning beams and gleaming glare,
> And the leaves lay dense on the bending trees
> And the lush grass waved in the scented breeze.
> Blossom and spray and spreading leaf
> Lightened my load and laid my grief,
> Weary and spent with aching brain
> I sank and lay on the murmuring plain,
> In the shade of a tree with feet outspread
> With my hot brow bared and shoe-gear shed.
> When I closed the lids on my languid eyes
> And covered my face from teasing flies
> In slumber deep and in sleep's delusion
> The scene was changed in strange confusion,

237

Original: from 'Cúirt an Mheán-Oíche', by Brian Merriman (cont.)	Literal translation (cont.):
A chorraigh go lom, a pholl go h-ae mé,	Moving me to distress, piercing me to the heart,
'S mé im chodladh go trom gan mheab-hair, gan éirim.	And I was sleeping heavily without conscious-ness, without intelligence.
Ba ghairid mo shuan nuair chualas, shíleas,	My rest was not long when I heard, I thought,
An talamh máguaird ag luascadh im thimpeall,	The surrounding ground rocking around me,
Anfa aduaidh agus fuadach fíochmhar,	A storm from the north and a fierce squall,
Agus caladh an chuain ag tuargan tinte.	And the harbour of the bay pounding fusillades.
Siolla dem shúil dar shamhlaíos uaim,	A glance from my eye in which I imagined
Chonaic mé chugam le ciumhais an chuain	I saw coming toward me at the edge of the harbour,
An mhásach bholgach tholgach thaibh-seach	The big-thighed person, big-bellied, violent, flamboyant,
Chnámhach cholgach ghoirgeach ghaib-hdeach.	Big-boned, bristling, surly, stout-calved.
A h-airde i gceart, mar a mheasaim, díreach,	Her height correctly, as I judge, exactly,
A sé nó seacht de shlata 's fuíollach.	Six or seven yards and more.
Péirse beacht dá brat léi scaoilte	Her cloak spread an exact perch
Ina diaidh san tslab le drab is raoibeal.	Behind her in the mud with mire and moisture.
Ba mhór, ba mhiar, ba fhiain le féachaint	It was great, it was absurd, it was wild to be looking
Suas ina h-éadan créachtach créimeach;	Up into her gashed, corroded face;
Ba anfa a cealltair, 's ba scanradh saolta	A tempest was her visage, and an utter terror were
A draid is a drandal mantach méis-creach.	Her mouth and her fissured, gap-toothed gums.
A Rí gach má! ba láidir líofa	King of every fate! strong and smooth was
A bíoma láimhe agus lánstaf inti,	Her beam of a hand and a great staff in it,
Comhartha práis inairde ar spíce	An emblem of brass at the top of the spike
Agus cumhachta báille ina bharr air scríofa.	And the authority of a bailiff written on top of it.
Agus dúirt go goirceach d'fhoclaibh dána:	And she spoke harshly in bold words:
Múscail! corraigh! a chodlataigh ghránna![11]	Awake! move! ugly sleeper!

Original:	Literal translation:
'Sé chráigh mo chroí 'is scaoil gan chéill mé,	It tormented my heart and left me without sense,
'Is d'fhág mo smaointe 'is m'intinn traochta,	And left my thoughts and my mind exhausted,
Cráite tinn mar táim go tréithlag,	Tormented and sick as I am weak,
Go cásmhar cloíte ag caoi 'is ag géarghol,	Pitiable, subdued, lamenting and keenly weeping
An uair do chínn preabaire calma croíúil	When I would see a dashing, brave, cordial man
Fuadrach fearúil seasmach saoithiúil	Bustling, manly, steadfast, accomplished
Stuama starrúil barrúil bríomhar	Sensible, vigorous, funny, lively
Gruadheas greannmhar geanúil gnaoiúil;	Pleasant-cheeked, humorous, loving, comely;
Nó buachaill beachanta bastalach bíogach	Or a boy vigorous, showy, sprightly

My frame was heaved and my head turned round
Without sense or sight in sleep profound.
I fancied there as I dare avouch
That the land was quaking beneath my couch,
And a hurricane blew with fury o'er me
And tongues of fire flared forth before me.
I threw a glance with beglamoured eyes
And beheld a hag of hideous guise,
Her shape with age and ague shook,
The plain she scoured with glowering look,
Her girth was huge, her height was quite
Seven yards or more if I reckoned it right,
Her cloak's tail trailed a perch's length,
She gripped a staff with manful strength,
Her aspect stark with angry stare,
Her features tanned by wind and air,
Her rheumy eyes were red and blear,
Her mouth was stretched from ear to ear,
A plate of brass held fast her bonnet
With bailiff's powers inscribed upon it.
She grimly gazed and gruffly spake: –
'You lazy laggard, arise! awake!'[12]

(In his vision, the narrator is taken by the hag to a court presided over by a fairy-queen and entertaining complaints of sexual frustration from Ireland's young women. The following selection is spoken by a young woman testifying before the court.)

My heart is torn and worn with grieving,
And my breast distressed with restless heaving,
With torture dull and with desperation
At the thought of my dismal situation,
When I see a bonny and bold young blade
With comely features and frame displayed,
A sturdy swearer or spanking buck,
A sprightly strapper with spunk and pluck,
A goodly wopper well made and planned,
A gamey walloper gay and grand,
Nimble and brave and bland and blithe,
Eager and active and brisk and lithe,

Original: from 'Cúirt an Mheán-
Oíche', by Brian Merriman (cont.)

Literal translation (cont.):

Cruacheart ceannasach ceaptha córach,
– Buaite ceannaithe ceangailte pósta
Ag fuaid, ag cailligh, ag amaid nó ag
    óinsigh;
Nó ag samhairle salach de chaile gan tion-
    scal,
Stuacach stailceach aithiseach stúncach
Suaite sotalach foclach fáidhiúil
Cuairdeach codlatach goirgeach gráiniúil.
Mo chreach! mo lot! atá molt míb-
    héasach,
Caile na gcos 'is folt gan réiteach,
Á ceangal anocht; Is é loisc go h-ae mé.
Agus cá bhfuil mo locht ná toghfaí
    roimpi?[13]

Rightly hardy, commanding, determined, shapely,
– Defeated, bought, bound, married
To a wretch, to a hag, to a witch, or to a foolish
    woman;
Or to a dirty whelp of a girl without industry,

Sulky, starchy, shameful, peevish
Confusing, arrogant, verbose, gossiping
Acquisitive, sleepy, irritable, hateful.
My ruin! my destruction! there is an ill-mannered
    sulky person,
A girl of legs and hair untidy
Being tied tonight; it is burning me to the heart.
And where is my fault that I would not be chosen
    before her?

Original:

Literal translation:

Bhí sí lag, gan bha, gan phúnta,
Bhí sí i bhfaid gan teas, gan chlúdach,
Cortha dá saol, ar strae á seoladh,
Ó phosta go piléar, gan gaol, gan chóngas,
Gan scíth, gan spás, de lá ná oíche,
Ach ag sracach an aráin ó mhná nár chuí
    léi.
Gheall an fear so greas socúil di,
Gheall an spreas so teas 'is clúdach,
Cothram glan agus ba le crú di,
Codladh fada ar leaba chlúimh di,
Teallaí teo 'is móin a dóthain,
Ballaí fód gan leoithne gaoithe,
Fothain 'is díon ón síon, ón spéir di,

Olann 'is líon le sníomh chun éadaigh.
Dob fheasach don saol agus don méid so
    láithreach
Nach taitneamh, ná téamh, ná aon phioc
    grá dó
A cheangail an péarla maorga mná so,
Ach easnamh an tsaoil 'is ba dhéirc léi an
    tsástacht.
Ba dhubhach an fuadar suairceas oíche,
Smúit 'is ualach, duais 'is líonadh,
Lúithní luaidhe agus guaille caola
Agus glúine crua chomh fuar le h-oighre –
Casta, feoite, dóite ón ngríosach –
Agus colann dreoite breoite críonna.
An bhfuil stuaire beo ná feofadh liath

Ag cuail dá short a bheith pósta riamh?
Nár chuardaigh fós faoi dhó le bliain
Cé buachaill óg í, feoil nó iasc,
'San feofach fuar so suas léi sínte,

Dreoite, duairc, gan bhua, gan bhíogadh.
Och! cár mhór di bualadh bríomhar
Ar nós ba dhual dhá uair san oíche?[14]

She was poor, without cows, without pounds,
She was long without heat, without covering,
Wearied of her life, being blown astray,
From post to pillar, without kin, without a relative,
Without rest, without space, by day or night,
But tearing the bread from women who scorned
    her.
This man promised a spell of comfort to her,
This dry twig promised heat and covering,
Complete fair play and cows for milking to her,
Long sleeping on a feather bed to her,
Warm hearths and turf in plenty,
Walls of sod without a breath of wind,
Shelter and a roof from the weather, from the sky,
    to her,
Wool and flax for spinning into clothes.
It was known to the world and to those present

That it was not pleasure, nor warming, nor any
    bit of love for him
That bound this stately pearl of a woman,
But a worldly deficiency and sufficiency seemed
    to her a charity.
Gloomy was the business of a night's jollity,
Gloom and a burden, sorrow and agitation,
Sinews of lead and narrow shoulders
And hard knees as cold as ice –
Gnarled, withered, burnt from the embers –
And a body decayed, ailing, old.
Is there a handsome girl alive who would not
    wither to grey
To be always married to a heap of bones of his sort?
Who moreover did not examine twice a year
Whether she was a young boy, meat or fish,
And this cold withered old man stretched out by
    her,
Putrefied, surly, without virtue, without vigour.
O! how great for her a strong seizing
As would be natural twice in the night?

Of noted parts and of proved precocity,
Sold to a scold or old hidiosity,
Withered and worn and blear and brown,
A mumbling, grumbling, garrulous clown,
A surly, sluttish and graceless gawk
Knotted and gnarled like a cabbage's stalk,
A sleepy, sluggish decayed old stump,
A useless, juiceless and faded frump.
Ah, woe is me! there's a crumpled crone
Being buckled to-night while I'm left lone,
She's a surly scold and a bold-faced jade
And this moment she's merry – and me a maid![15]

(In the following selection, the woman who testified in the above passage returns to the court to defend a young woman of her acquaintance charged with having betrayed her aged husband.)

She was poor and in sad plight
Without shelter from wind and rain at night,
Homeless and driven for no sin
From fence to ditch without friends or kin.
The old stick offered her silver and gold,
A roof and turf from the rain and cold,
Flax and wool to weave and wear,
And cattle and sheep and goods and gear.
The world and this worm himself well knew
She cared not for him nor ever could do,
But worn by want and her abject state
Chose the lesser ill of an unloved mate.
Woeful work was his weak embrace
And the old goat's rough mouth on her face,
His limbs of lead and his legs of ice
And his lifeless load on her breast and thighs,
His blue-blotched shins so bleak and cold
And the bleached skin hanging in fold on fold.
Was there ever a fine girl fresh and fair
Who would not grow gray with grief and care
To bed with a bundle of stick and bone
As cold and stiff as a stick or stone,
Who would scarcely lift the lid from the dish
To know was it flesh or fowl or fish?
Ah say, I pray, had she not the right
To one caress in the course of a night?[16]

Original: 'Seanduine Chill Chocáin'

Is teinn dúch an pósa so, fó-ríor, a gealladh dom,
  Go h-óg mé ceangailthe 'g críon-donán!
Nuair a cuireadh le fórsa 'n-a chomhair go tigh an tsagairt me
  Im chroí bhí m'atuirse ar linn é rá.

Ní thaitneann a shiúl, a lúth ná a sheasamh liom,
A mhala throm chlúmach ná a shúile dearaga,
Go mb'fhearr liom óigfhear a phógfadh mo leaca,
  Mo chroí gur cheangail san óg-bhuinneán!

'S a chailíní óga, mo chomhairle má dheineann sibh,
  'S is teinn dúch atuirseach bhím dá bharr,
'S mé 'luí le seanduine caite gan luadar,

  'S ná fuil dá bharr agam ach uail bheag cnámha!
A' machtnamh a bhím san oíche ar mo leabaidh
Ar a' seanduine gcríonna, len' aois go gcrapann sé,
Seochas a' groí-fhear a shínfeadh ar leabaidh liom,
  'S go mb'fhiú é ar maidin a phóg úd 'fháil!

Thúrfainn sé phíosa, 's é 'dhíol ar a' dtairrnge,
  D'éinne beó ghlacfadh mo sgéal 'n-a láimh,
Do luífeadh ar shúil mo sgrúile seanduine,

  Má thiocfadh a gan fhios i gcomhair é 'lámhach:
Chuirfeadh 'á bhátha é i lár na fairrge,

Shínfeadh sa' díg é 's a' claí do leaga air,

Nú cár bh'fhearr é mar ní ná an píop a chnaga dhe,
  'S mo sgrúile 'fháil marbh leath-uair roim lá?

Literal translation:

It is woeful, sorrowful this wedding, alas, that I was promised,
  That I am tied young to a withered wretch!
When I was taken by force with him to the priest's house
  In my heart was dejection while it was being said.

Neither his eyes, his agility nor his standing pleases me,
His heavy, furry eyebrows nor his red eyes,
I would prefer a young man who would kiss my cheek,
  My heart tied to the young sapling.

And young girls, if you take my advice,

  And I am woeful, sorrowful, weary because of it,
And I lying with a spent old man without vigour,

  And I have nothing as a result of it but a small heap of bones!
I am thinking in the evening in my bed
On the withered old man, with the age that shrinks him,
Instead of the vigorous man who would stretch on the bed with me,
  And whose kiss it would be worth getting in the morning!

I would give a piece, and pay it on the nail,

  To anyone alive would take my cause in his hand,
Who would close the eyes of my wretched old man,

  If he would come without his knowledge to shoot him:
Would put him to drown in the middle of the sea,

Would stretch him in a ditch and knock the wall down on him,

Or what would be better than anything than to crack the neck of him,
  And leave my wretch dead half an hour before day?

Donal O'Sullivan
(1893–1973)

In the introduction to his collection *Songs of the Irish*, Donal O'Sullivan describes his verse translations as intended 'to exhibit the metrical structure in each case' and 'to convey something of the spirit'.[17] Born in Liverpool of Kerry parentage, O'Sullivan became the director of studies in Irish folk music at University College Dublin, and wrote a life of the eighteenth-century poet and harpist Turlough Carolan.

'The Old Man of Kilcockan'

(The original probably comes from Co. Waterford; Kilcockan [Cill Chocáin] is a parish in Co. Waterford about ten miles north of Youghal, on the River Blackwater.)

By prayer and entreaty and threat they did worry me
    To be wed to the gaffer my youth denied,
On leaden feet to the priest they did hurry me,
    With a heart stone dead while the knot was tied.
I like not his gait nor the rheumy red eyes of him,
His furry grey brows, the groans and the sighs of him,
I long for a young man, to lie and to rise with him,
    Who would kiss and caress me at morning-tide!

All maids yet unwed, whether wealthy or dowerless,
    Be warned by my fortune against old drones;
For I lie by a dotard both shrivelled and powerless,
    As good to possess as a heap of bones.
Wide-eyed each night, with a heart that's like lead in me,
I think of the withered old creature that's wed to me,
Compared to the stalwart that might lie abed with me,
    Clasping me to him with love's sweet tones!

Six guineas I'd give, and I'd pay it right readily,
    If someone would put my old man away,
Come on him by stealth and take aim at him steadily,
    Make sure of the target and earn his pay:
Or if in the sea he could be set about drowning him,
Lay him flat in the ditch and knock the wall down on him,
Or perhaps better still just to throttle the jowl of him
    And leave him for dead just before the day!

243

Original: 'Seanduine Chill
Chocáin' (cont.)

Literal translation (cont.):

Araoir ar mo leabaidh 's mé a' macht-
namh trím néaltaibh,
  'Sea d'airíos gur cailleadh mo sheann-
donán;
D'éiríos im sheasamh 's do ghabhas míle
baochas
  Leis a' té úd a mhairbh sa' díg é ar lár.
'Sé airím 'á bhuachtaint gur shuathadar
eatorrtha é
Gurbh í an láir rua do bhuail is do
mhairbh é,
Beir sgéal leat uaim go dtí an buachaillín
meacanta
  Gur chuireas mo sheanduine i gCill
Chocáin![18]

Last night in my bed and while I was thinking
in my sleep,
  I heard that my old wretch was dead;
I rose up and I gave a thousand thanks

  To whoever killed him in the ditch on the
ground.
I hear it being decided, that they discussed it
between them
That it was the red mare that struck and killed
him,
Take news from me to the honest young boy
  That I buried my old man in Kilcockan!

Last night as I lay between waking and sleeping
      I heard that my wretched old man was dead;
I leapt from the pillow, my gratitude heaping
      On the man in the ditch who had done the deed.
They made up their story while still there was breath in him,
'Twas the bay mare that kicked him – and that was the death
  of him,
Go, take to the young man this news that is best for him –
      In the grave at Kilcockan my wretch is laid![19]

Original: 'Beatha an Scoláire'	Literal translation:

Aoibhinn beatha an scoláire
    bhíos ag déanamh a léighinn;
is follas díbh, a dhaoine,
    gurab dó is aoibhne in Éirinn.
	Delightful the life of the scholar
	    who is doing his studies;
	it is clear to you, people,
	    that his is the most delightful in Ireland.

Gan smacht ríogh ná rófhlatha
    ná tighearna dá threise,
gan chuid cíosa ag caibidil,
    gan moichéirghe, gan meirse.
	Without the discipline of a king or a prince
	    or a lord however strong,
	without a share of rent to a chapterhouse,
	    without early rising, without bondage.

Moichéirghe ná aodhaireacht
    ní thabhair uadha choidhche,
's ní mó do-bheir dá aire
    fear na faire san oidhche.
	Early rising or herding
	    he does not attempt them ever,
	and no more does he take notice of
	    the watchman in the evening.

Austin Clarke
(1896–1974)

Insisting on the realistic and often sexually uninhibited nature of writing in Irish, Austin Clarke turned to the Gaelic tradition in part as a way of undermining efforts to forge links between Gaelicism and puritanical Catholicism in mid-century Ireland. Clarke also brought to the tradition of verse translation from the Irish a commitment to reshaping the forms of English verse to accommodate the formal qualities of verse in Irish, especially the various patterns of assonance common to much Irish-language poetry.

Born in Dublin and educated in the same Jesuitical tradition that inspired James Joyce's critiques of Irish Catholicism, Clarke was a prominent literary figure in Dublin throughout the middle decades of the twentieth century.

'The Scholar'

(This poetic translation first appeared in Clarke's play *The Son of Learning* [1927], based on the twelfth-century work *Aislinge Meic Conglinne* [*Vision of Mac Conglinne*], a parody of the medieval vision and voyage tale in which the protagonist is a young scholar who travels to a monastery in Cork seeking patronage for his poetic ambitions. In a note to the play, Clarke described 'The Scholar' as a 'free paraphrase' that in assonantal patterns 'is more or less equivalent with the classical metre of the original'.[20] For George Sigerson's translation of another poem connected with *Aislinge Meic Conglinne*, see pp. 149–151.)

> Summer delights the scholar
> With knowledge and reason.
> Who is happy in hedgerow
> Or meadow as he is?
>
> Paying no dues to the parish,
> He argues in logic
> And has no care of cattle
> But a satchel and stick.
>
> The showery airs grow softer,
> He profits from his ploughland
> For the share of the schoolmen
> Is a pen in hand.

Original: 'Beatha an Scoláire' (cont.)

Literal translation (cont.):

Maith biseach a sheisrighe
    ag teacht tosaigh an earraigh;
is é is crannghail dá sheisrigh
    lán a ghlaice de pheannaibh.

The good health of his plough-team
    coming at the beginning of spring;
the plough for his plough-team is
    his fist full of pens.

Do-bheir sé greas ar tháiplis,
    is ar chláirsigh go mbinne,
nó fós greas eile ar shuirghe
    is ar chumann mná finne.[21]

He spends time at draughts,
    and on a harp sweetly,
or still another time on wooing
    and on the love of a woman of beauty.

Original: 'Lon Doire an Chairn'

Literal translation:

Binn sin, a luin Doire an Chairn,
    Ní chuala mé i n-aird san mbith
Ceol badh bhinne ná do ghuth
    Agus tú fá bhun do nid.

That is sweet, blackbird of Doire an Chairn,
    I never heard anywhere in the world
Music sweeter than your voice
    And you about your nest.

Aoin-cheol is binne fán mbith,
    Mairg nach éisteann ris go fóil,
A mhic Alphruin na gclog mbinn,
    'S go mbéarthá a-rís ar do nóin.

The most melodious music in the world,
    A pity you are not listening to it yet,
Mac Alphruin of the melodious bells,
    And that you were taking again your nones.

Agat, mar tá agam féin,
    Dá mbeith deimhin sgéil an eóin,
Do dhéantá déara go dian,
    'S ní bhiadh th'aire ar Dhia go fóil.

If you had, as I myself have,
    The real story of the bird,
You would make tears fiercely,
    And your attention would not be on God for
    a while.

I gcrích Lochlann na sreabh ngorm,
    Fuair mac Cumhaill na gcorn ndearg
An t-éan do-chíthí a-nois,
    Ag sin a sgéal duit go dearbh.

In a region of Norway of the blue streams,
    Mac Cumhaill of the red goblets got
The bird that is seen now,
    That is his story for you truly.

Doire an Chairn an choill úd thiar,
    Mar a ndéindís an Fhiann fos,
Ar áille 's ar chaoimhe a crann
    Is eadh do cuireadh ann an lon.

Doire an Chairn, that wood over there,
    Where the Fianna would take a rest,
For the beauty and for the grace of its trees
    It is there the blackbird was put.

Sgolghaire luin Doire an Chairn,
    Búithre an daimh ó Aill na gCaor,
Ceol le 'gcodladh Fionn go moch,
    Lachain ó Loch na dTrí gCaol.

The cry of the blackbird of Doire an Chairn,
    The bellowing of the stag from Aill na gCaor,
Music with which Fionn slept early,
    Ducks from Loch na dTrí gCaol.

Cearca fraoich um Chruachain Chuinn,
    Feadghail dobhráin Druim Dhá Loch,
Gotha fiolair Ghlinn na bhFuath,
    Longhaire cuach Chnuic na Sgoth.

Grouse around Cruachan Chuinn,
    Whistling of the otters of Druim Dhá Loch,
Voices of the eagles of Gleann na bhFuath,
    Birdsong of the cuckoos of Cnoc na Sgoth.

Gotha gadhair Ghleanna Caoin
    Is gáir fhiolair chaoich na sealg,
Tairm na gcon ag triall go moch,
    Isteach ó Thráigh na gCloch nDearg.

Voices of the dogs of Gleann Caoin
    And cry of the dim-eyed eagles of the hunting,
Clamour of the hounds moving early
    In from Tráigh na gCloch nDearg.

An tráth do mhair Fionn 's an Fhiann
    Dob' annsa leo sliabh ná cill;
Fá binn leo-san fuighle lon,
    Gotha na gclog leo níor bhinn.[22]

The time that Fionn and the Fianna lived,
    Dearer to them was mountain than cell;
Melodious to them the speech of blackbirds,
    Voices of the bells to them were not melo-
    dious.

When midday hides the reaping,
He sleeps by a river
Or comes to the stone plain
Where the saints live.

But in winter by the big fires,
The ignorant hear his fiddle,
And he battles on the chessboard,
As the land lords bid him.[23]

'The Blackbird of Derrycairn'

(This poetic translation was included in Clarke's play *As the Crow Flies* [1942]. The original is one of the lyrics attributed to Oisín, the son of the legendary pre-Christian warrior Fionn Mac Cumhaill. Oisín returns to Ireland after spending three hundred years in the Land of Youth to find St. Patrick and Christianity driving out the pagan culture that he knew.)

Stop, stop and listen for the bough top
Is whistling and the sun is brighter
Than God's own shadow in the cup now!
Forget the hour-bell. Mournful matins
Will sound, Patric, as well at nightfall.

Faintly through mist of broken water
Fionn heard my melody in Norway.
He found the forest track, he brought back
This beak to gild the branch and tell, there,
Why men must welcome in the daylight.

He loved the breeze that warns the black grouse,
The shouts of gillies in the morning
When packs are counted and the swans cloud
Loch Erne, but more than all those voices
My throat rejoicing from the hawthorn.

In little cells behind a cashel,
Patric, no handbell gives a glad sound.
But knowledge is found among the branches.
Listen! That song that shakes my feathers
Will thong the leather of your satchels.[24]

Original: 'Máible Shéimh n-í
Cheallaich', by Toirdhealbhach
Ó Cearbhalláin

Literal translation:

Cia b'é bh-fuil sé a n-dán do,
　A lámh-dheas bheith faoí na ceann,
Is deimhin nach eagal bás do,
　Go bráth ná 'n a bheódh bheith tinn,
A chúil dheis na m-bachall bh-fáinneach,
　　bh-fionn,
　　A chuim mar an ealla ag snámhadh
　　ar an d-tóinn,
Grádh 'gus spéis gasraidh, Máible
Shéimh n-í Cheallaigh,
　　Déud is deise leagadh ann arus a
　　céinn.

Whoever is fated
　To have his right hand under her head,
It is certain that he does not fear death,
　Forever or in his life to be sick,
Pretty head of the beautiful, fair curls,

　　Form like the swan swimming on the
　　wave,
Love and interest of every youth, mild Mabel Ní
Kelly,
　　The prettiest teeth lying in the palace of her
　　head.

Ní'l ceól d'á bhinne fós d'ar seinneadh,
　Ná'r bh' eólghach dhi-si thuigsin 's
　a rádh ann gach céim
A gruadh mar rós ag drithleadh, is buan
　'n a g-cómharsa an lile,
　　A rosg is míne, ghlaise 'ná bláith na
　　g-craébh:
'S é deir olldhamh mollta chláir shíl
Néill,
　　Go g-cuirfeadh na corradha a codla
　　le sár-ghuith a béil,
Ní'l amhrus ann a súil bhreágh, lonnach,
　　Acht óltar línn go grínn do shláinte
　　mhaith féin

There is no music however sweet yet played,
　　That she would not know its sense and say
　　every stage
Her cheek like a rose sparkling, the lily its
　　enduring neighbour,
　　Her eyes finer, greener than the blossoms
　　of the branches:
The praised master-poet of the plain of the race
of Néill says,
　　That the herons would be put to sleep by
　　the superior voice of her mouth,
There is no doubt in it, her eye fine and joyful,
　　But we drink steadfastly your own good
　　health.

O d'éagadar na mná mánla
　Air a d-tráchdadaoís an domhain go
　léir,
Measaim nach bh-fuil 'n a n-áit aguinn
　Acht Máible le clú ann gach céim.
Annsacht gach duine a g-cáilígheachd 's
　a g-céill; –
　　Is ághmhar do'n bh-filidh a fághail
　　d'á n-déis,
Cúl na g-craébh is finne, lúb na d-téud is
　binne,
　　Snuadh na géise gile, a brághaid a's
　　a taébh.

Since the stately women died
　About whom the whole world spoke,
I think we have no one in their place
　　But Mabel with a reputation in every
　　degree.
Beloved of every person their qualities and their
　　wisdom; –
　　And fortunate for the poets to have in their
　　territory,
Hair of the fairest branches, plait of the most
　　beautiful strands,
　　The complexion of the white swan, her
　　bosom and her side.

'Mabel Kelly'

(This is one of a number of what Clarke referred to as 'free variations' based on poems by the poet and harper Turlough Carolan [1670–1738]. For Samuel Ferguson's version, see pp. 125–127.)

Lucky the husband
Who puts his hand beneath her head.
They kiss without scandal
Happiest two near feather-bed.
He sees the tumble of brown hair
Unplait, the breasts, pointed and bare
When nightdress shows
From dimple to toe-nail,
All Mabel glowing in it, here, there, everywhere.

Music might listen
To her least whisper,
Learn every note, for all are true.
While she is speaking,
Her voice goes sweetly
To charm the herons in their musing.
Her eyes are modest, blue, their darkness
Small rooms of thought, but when they sparkle
Upon a feast-day,
Glasses are meeting,
Each raised to Mabel Kelly, our toast and darling.

Gone now are many Irish ladies
Who kissed and fondled, their very pet-names
Forgotten, their tibia degraded.
She takes their sky. Her smile is famed.
Her praise is scored by quill and pencil.
Harp and spinet
Are in her debt
And when she plays or sings, melody is content.

Original: 'Máible Shéimh n-í Cheallaich', by Toirdhealbhach Ó Cearbhalláin (cont.)

Ní'l aén dá bh-feiceann an t-saoí-bhean mhaiseach,
Nach éirghídheann mar na geiltibh, a m-barradhaibh na g-craébh,
A's an t-é nach léur do an choingeal, lán de sbéis an leinbh,
Is fearr tréighthe a's tuigsi dhe náisiún Gaédheal: –
Is sí is deise cos, bas, lámh, agus béul,
Péighre rosg, a's folt ag fás léi go féur,
Tá an bháire-si línn ag sárúghadh luchd greínn,
Fá rádh go bh-fuair mé an fháill, is ághmhar liom é.[25]

There is no-one who sees the graceful, cultured woman,
Who does not rise like the madmen in the tops of the branches,
And [she is] the one for whom the candle is not enough, full of the interest of a child,
Of best accomplishments and wisdom of the Gaelic nation: –
She has the prettiest foot, palm, hand, and mouth,
Pair of eyes, and hair growing down to the grass,
This is our goal, surpassing the lovers,
Since I got the opportunity, it is lucky for me.

Original: 'Márghairiad Inghín Sheoirse Brún', by Toirdhealbhac Ó Cearbhalláin

Literal translation:

A Mhárghairiad Brún, is dúbhach do fhágbhais mé,
Mo luíghe 'san n-uaigh 's gan cúmhdach mná orm féin,
Fuil 'g a sgaoíleadh dhamh-sa a d-túis a's a ndeireadh gach laé,
A's a Inghín Mheic Suíbhne, a rúin dhil, tárthaigh mé.

Margaret Brown, it is melancholy you left me,
Lying in the grave and without a woman's cherishing for me,
Blood flowing from me at beginning and end of each day,
And daughter of Mac Sweeney, dear love, rescue me.

Ghluaiseas 'núnn dar liom fá 'n tráth-so a n-dé,
Fá'n g-coíll chroím, go cínnte b' árd mo léim;
Mo leabhrán grínn ag innsin fáth gach sgéil,
Is eagal liom gur mhíll do ghrádh-sa me.

I went over, it seems to me, about this time yesterday,
Under the drooping forest, certainly it was the height of my leap;
My accurate booklet giving a reason for every matter,
I fear that your love ruined me.

'S í Már'iad an aindear shéimh is caoíne glór,
Is binne a béul 'ná guth na d-téud a's 'ná na sígh-cheóil,
Is gile taobh ná an eala shéimh théidhean air linn gach ló,
'Gus a mhaiseach, bhéusach, ghasta, thréidhtheach, ná diúltaidh mé.

Margaret is the mild maiden of the sweetest voice,
Sweeter her mouth than the voice of the strings or of fairy music,
Brighter her side than the gentle swan who moves in a pool every day,
And elegant, polite, clever, accomplished one, don't refuse me.

Dul eadar an dair 'sa croiceann, 'sé mheasaim gur cruadh an céim,
Dul eadar mé agus rúin-shearc agus grádh mo chléibh,
Air chur mo lámh thairsí air maidin le bánúghadh an lae
Fuair mé an staraídhe dubh ag gleacaídheacht le grádh mo chuím.[26]

To go between the oak and its bark, [but] it is, I think, a harder step,
To go between me and love, and the love of my bosom,
Putting my hand about her in the morning at the dawning of the day,
I found the black boor wrestling with the love of my body.

No man who sees her
Will feel uneasy.
He goes his way, head high, however tired.
Lamp loses light
When placed beside her.
She is the pearl and being of all Ireland
Foot, hand, eye, mouth, breast, thigh and instep, all
that we desire.
Tresses that pass small curls as if to touch the ground;
So many prizes
Are not divided
Her beauty is her own and she is not proud.[27]

'Peggy Browne'

(This is another of Clarke's free translations from Turlough Carolan.
For Thomas Furlong's version, see p. 67.)

The dark-haired girl, who holds my thought entirely
Yet keeps me from her arms and what I desire,
Will never take my word for she is proud
And none may have his way with Peggy Browne.

Often I dream that I am in the woods
At Westport House. She strays alone, blue-hooded,
Then lifts her flounces, hurries from a shower,
But sunlight stays all day with Peggy Browne.

Her voice is music, every little echo
My pleasure and O her shapely breasts, I know,
Are white as her own milk, when taffeta gown
Is let out, inch by inch, for Peggy Browne.

A lawless dream comes to me in the night-time,
That we are stretching together side by side,
Nothing I want to do can make her frown.
I wake alone, sighing for Peggy Browne.[28]

Original: 'Pléaráca na Ruarcach', by Aodh Mac Gabhrán	Literal translation:
Pléaráca na Ruarcach i gcuimhne gach uile dhuine 　Dá dtiocfaidh, dá dtáinic, 's dá maireann go fóill: Seacht bhfichid muc, mart agus caora 　Dhá gcascairt don ghasraí gach aon ló. Céad páil uisge bheatha 's na meadra dhá líona, 　Ar éirighe ar maidin is againn bhí an spóirt. Briseadh do phíopa-sa, sladadh mo phóca-sa, Goideadh do bhríste-sa, loisgeadh mo chlóca-sa, Chaill mé mo bhairéad, m'fhallaing is m'fhiléad, 　Ó d'imigh na gairead,[a] ar seacht mbeannacht leó! Cuir spraic ar a' gcláirsigh, seinn suas a' pléaráca, 　An busca sin, 'Áine, 'gus greadóg le n-ól!	O'Rourke's revelry is in the memory of every person 　Of those who will come, of those who came, and of those living still: Seven score pigs, cows and sheep 　Being cut up for the company every single day. A hundred pails of whiskey and the wooden cups being filled, 　Rising in the morning it is we who had the sport. Your pipe was broken, my pocket was plundered, Your breeches were stolen, my cloak was burnt, I lost my cap, my mantle, and my kerchief, 　Since the friends left, our seven blessings with them! Put a lively tune on the harp, play up the revelry, 　That box, Áine, and an appetizer for drinking!
Lucht leanamhna na Ruarcach a' cratha a gcleití, 　Tráth chuala siad tormán nó troimpléasg an cheóil; D'éirigh gach aon aca gan coisreaca 'n-a leabaidh, 　Is a bhean leis ar strachailt in gach aon chórn. Nár láidir an seasamh don talamh bhí fútha, 　Gan réaba le sodar agus glug ins gach bróig! Saol agus sláinte dhuit, 'Mh'leachlainn Uí Fhionnagáin! Dar mo láimh is maith a dhamhsuíos tu, 'Mhársail Ní Ghriodagáin! *Here's to you, 'mháthair, I pledge you, God save you!* 　Beir ar a' sgála seo, sgag é in do sgóig. Craith fúinn an tsráideóg, sín tharuinn an bhán-phluid, 　Tugthar ar sáith dhúinn de lionn-choirm chóir!	The followers of O'Rourke shaking their feathers, 　The time they heard the noise or heavy explosion of the music; Every one of them arose without a blessing from his bed 　And his woman with him, being dragged along with every cup. Was not the standing of the ground under them strong 　Not to shatter with the trotting and plop in every shoe! Life and health to you, Maoileachlainn Ó Fionnagáin! By my hand it is well you dance, Mársail Ní Griodagáin! Here's to you, mother, I pledge you, God save you! 　Grab this bowl, drain it off in your throat. Shake that pallet under us, stretch over us the white blanket, 　Give us our fill of proper ale!

'O'Rourke's Feast'

(The original was written by Aodh Mac Gabhráin] [fl. 1715], a poet born in Co. Cavan who frequented the circle of Irish-language scholars in Dublin centered around Tadhg Ó Neachtain in the eighteenth century. The original may describe a feast to mark the departure of the powerful Ulster chieftain O'Rourke for a visit to Queen Elizabeth. For two eighteenth-century verse translations of the poem, see under Jonathan Swift, pp. 3–7, and Charles Henry Wilson, pp. 35–39.)

Let O'Rourke's great feast be remembered by those
Who were at it, are gone, or not yet begotten.
A hundred and forty hogs, heifers and ewes
Were basting each plentiful day and gallons of pot-still
Poured folderols into the mugs. Unmarried
And married were gathering early for pleasure and sport.
'Your clay pipe is broken.' 'My pocket picked.' 'Your hat
Has been stolen.' 'My breeches lost.' 'Look at my skirt torn.'
'And where are those fellows who went half under my mantle
And burst my two garters?' 'Sure, no one's the wiser.'
'Strike up the strings again.' 'Play us a planxty.'
'My snuff-box, Annie, and now a double sizer.'

Men, women, unmugged upon the featherbeds,
Snored until they heard the round clap, the step-dance,
Again, jumped up, forgot to bless their foreheads,
And jigging, cross-reeling from partner to partner, they
    trampled
With nail in brogue that cut the floor to shavings.
'A health, long life to you, Loughlin O'Hennigan.'
'Come, by my hand, I'll say it in your favour,
You're dancing well, Marcella Gridigan.'
'A bowl, Mother, and drink it to the last drop.'
Then came a big hole in the day. Light failed.
'Shake rushes for Annie and me, a blanket on top
And let us have a slap-and-nap of decent ale.'

Original: 'Pléaráca na Ruarcach',
by Aodh Mac Gabhrán (cont.)

Literal translation (cont.):

A Árd-Rí na gcarad, cébi 'tchifeadh an ghasraí
Ar líona a gcraicní nó ar lasa san ól!
Cnáimh righe bacaird ar fad in gach sgín aca,
A' gearra 's a' cosgairt go mór, mór, mór;
A slisneacha darach ar lasa a' gabháil fríd a chéile,
A' buala, a' greada, a' losga 's a' dódh.
A bhodaigh, 'sé m'athair-se chuir Mainistir na Búille suas,
Sligeach is Gaillimh is Caraidh Dhroma Rúisgthe fós.
Iarla Chill' Dara agus Biadhtach Mhuí-n-Ealta,
Siad d'oil agus d'altruim mé, fiosraigh so de Mhór.
Tóig suas a' t'adhmad agus buail an t-alárm air,
Preab ionsa táirr agus cic ionsa tóin!

Beloved High King, whoever would see the company
Their skins filled or inflamed with the drink!
A cubit of a rule in length in each of their knives,
Cutting and rending greatly, greatly, greatly;
Their sticks of oak inflamed going through each other,
Hitting, beating, searing, and burning.
Churl, it is my father who founded Boyle Abbey,
Sligo and Galway and Carrick-on-Shannon in addition.
The Earl of Kildare and Betagh of Moynalty,
It is they who reared and fostered me, ask this of Mór.
Lift up the board and strike the alarm on it,
A blow in the belly and a kick on the backside!

'Cé thóig an t-alárm so?' ar aon den Eaglais,
Ar éirighe 'n-a sheasamh 's a' bagairt go mór;
Ní h-é spairgeas uisge coisreactha ghlac sé sa gcíora
Ach bata maith darach, bog-lán dóirn!
Tráth shíl sé na caithmhílidh a chasairt 's a chíora,
Do fágadh an sagart 'n-a mheall chasta fán mbórd.
D'éirigh na bráithre a' tárrtháil na bruíne,
Is fágadh an t-Athair Gáirdian ar a thárr 'n-áirde sa ngríosaí.
'Trath bhínn-se ag an bPápa ar stuidéar na ngrásta,
'S a' glaca na ngrádhamh tháll ins a' Róimh,
'Sé an *Seven Wise Masters* bhí agad ar do tháirr,
Is tú a' rósta na bprátaí láimh leis a' tSídh Mhór!'[29]

'Who raised that alarm,' said one of the clergy,
Rising up and threatening greatly;
It was not a blessed water aspergillum that he took to their rows
But a good stick of oak, easily the full of a fist!
The time he thought to slaughter and harass the heroes,
The priest was left in a twisted heap under the table.
The brothers rose to mediate the quarrel,
And the Father Guardian was left on his belly on top of the embers.
'The time I was with the Pope at the studying of the graces,
And taking the orders over in Rome,
It was the *Seven Wise Masters* that you had on your belly,
And you roasting potatoes beside Sígh Mór!'

---

[a] The literal translation assumes *caraid*, based on a textual variant in Ó Máille. O'Sullivan, in a literal translation appended to the text of the original, translates the word as 'garters', and this word appears in Clarke's poetic translation. The Irish for garters is *gairtéir*.

Merciful Heaven, whoever saw such a big crowd
So drunk, the men with belt-knives at slashing, stabbing,
The women screaming, trying to hold up trousers
And others upon the table, twirling an oak-plant?
The Sons of O'Rourke came rolling from the doorway
In somersaults of glory. Bachelor boys
Were boasting, cudgelling more, more, more.
'My father built the monastery at Boyle . . .'
'The Earl of Kildare and Major Bellingham were
My . . .' 'Sligo harbour, Galway, Carrick-drum-rusk,
And I was fostered . . .' 'Pull the alarum bell.'
'A blow for your elbow grease.' 'A kick in the tump.'

'Who gave the alarm?' demanded one of the clergy
And swung his big oak stick – not as a censer.
Right, left, he plied it soundly to asperge them
In blood-drops, gave a dozen three more senses.
The friars got up with their cowhorn beads to haul him
Back, dust his habit. Three Reverences tumbled
Into the ashes; Father Superior bawling
Until that congregation went deaf and dumb:
'While I was studying with His Holiness
And taking Roman Orders by the score,
Yiz sat on a settle with an old story-book,
All chawing roast potatoes at Sheemore.'[30]

Original: 'M'ænurán im airiclán'

M'ænurán im airiclán   cen duinén im gnáis,
      robo inmuin ailithre   ría ndul i ndáil mbáis.

· · ·

Nóibad cuirp co sobésaib,   slatrad ferda foir,
      súilib tláithib todéraib   do dílgud mo thoil.

· · ·

Dérgud adúar áigthide,   ba sé telgun troch,
      cotlud gairit gáibthide,   díucra minic moch.

· · ·

Arán toimse tírmaide,   maith donairnem gnúis,
      uisce lerga lígmaise,   ba sí deog no lúis.

· · ·

Literal translation:

All alone in my little cell   without a person in my company,
      the pilgrimage has been desirable   before going to meet death.

· · ·

Sanctifying the body with good habits,   trampling like a man upon it,
      eyes weak, tearful   for forgiveness of my desire.

· · ·

A couch cold, fearsome,   as it were the lying down of a doomed man,
      a short, distressed sleep   frequent early outcries.

· · ·

Dry, measured bread,   good the lowering of our faces,
      water from a many-coloured slope,   it is the draught I would drink.

· · ·

Sean O'Faolain
(1900–1991)

Sean O'Faolain studied Irish at University College Cork, where he came under the influence, later repudiated, of the writer and scholar Daniel Corkery, who also inspired much of Frank O'Connor's interest in the Irish-language tradition. O'Faolain belonged to the Gaelic League, and he and O'Connor frequently visited the West Cork Gaeltacht. O'Faolain especially admired the poetry of the Old and Middle Irish periods, which he described as 'objective and dramatically impersonal'.[31] In 1938, he published *The Silver Branch*, a collection of translations, including some of his own.

'The Desire for Hermitage'
(The original is dated to the eighth or ninth century.)

Ah! To be all alone in a little cell
with nobody near me;
beloved that pilgrimage
before the last pilgrimage to Death.

To be cleansing my flesh with good habits,
trampling it down like a man;
to be weeping wearily,
paying for my passions.

A cold bed of fear –
the lying down of a doomed man;
a short sleep, waking to danger;
tears from early morning.

Dry bread portioned out
a good thing to hollow the face;
an end to gossip; no more fables;
the knees constantly bent.

Original: 'M'ænurán im airiclán' (cont.)

Robo inmain araide   anim nechta nóib,
    leicne tírma tanaide,   tonn crocnaide cóil.

Céim íar sétaib soscéla,   salmchetal cach tráth,
    crích fri rád, fri roscéla,   filliud glúine gnáth.

.   .   .

Ba sí in chrích fri dúailchiu   itir lisu lann:
    locán álaind iladlán,   as mé m'ænur and.

M'ænurán im airiclán,   m'ænurán imne,
    m'ænur dolod forsin mbith,   m'ænur ragad de.[32]

Literal translation (cont.):

It was a desirable token,   pure blemishes of saints,
    cheeks withered, thin,   skin shrivelled, emaciated.

Stepping along the ridges of the gospel,   psalm-singing every hour,
    An end to speaking, to tales,   bending of the knees customary.

.   .   .

This would be an end for vices   among the forts of the lands:
    a delightful little spot full of tombs   and I alone there.

All alone in my little cell,   all alone with my spirit,
    alone I came into the world,   alone I will go from it.

Original: 'Emer is lat in fer'

A Emer is lat in fer   ocus romela a deig ben,
aní ná roich lam cid acht   is écen dam a dútracht.

Mor fer ro bói com iarraid   eter chlitar is diamair,
no co dernad ríu mo dál,   dáig is misi rop irán.

Mairg dobeir seirc do duni   menestarda dia airi,
is ferr do neoch a chor ass,   mene chartar mar charas.[33]

Literal translation:

Emer, the man is yours   and may he be palatable, good woman,
yet, the thing the hand does not reach   its desire is necessary for me.

Many men were asking me   both protective and mysterious
if I would share myself with them   since it is I who am faithful.

A pity to bear love to a person   unless one gives her a sign,
it is better to turn a person out   unless one is loved as she loves.

Original: 'A ben fhuil isin chuiliu'

A ben fhuil isin chuiliu,   in tabrai bíad do duiniu?
in tabrai dam, a ben bán,   saill, loimm, imm ocus arán?
Atá form   meni tuca bíad im dorn:
bér-sa th' enech, a ben bán,   is indisfet dom deán.[34]

Literal translation:

Woman who is in the pantry,   will you give food to a person?
will you give me, fair woman,   bacon, milk, butter, and bread?
It is my intention that   unless you put food in my fist:
I will bear away your honour, fair woman,   and I will inform my foster-father.

That will be an end to evil
when I am alone
in a lovely little corner among tombs
far from the houses of the great.

Ah! To be all alone in a little cell,
to be alone, all alone,
alone as I came into the world –
and as I shall go from it.[35]

'Fand Yields Cuchulain to Emer'
(The original is associated with the Ulster cycle of
pre-Christian Irish legends.)

Emer, he is your man, now,
and well may you wear him,
when I can no longer hold him,
I must yield him.

Many a man has wanted me,
but I have kept my vows.
I have been an honest woman,
under the roofs and boughs.

Pity the woman loves a man,
when no love invites her.
Better for her to fly from love
if unloved, love bites her.[36]

'The Cad'

O woman in the pantry,
unless you feed me good and plenty,
unless you let me gather
bread and butter from the larder,
I'll squeeze you in a corner,
and when I've ruined your honour,
I'll go and tell my master![37]

Original: 'Féach féin an obair-se,   Literal translation:
                a Aodh'

Féach féin an obair-se, a Aodh,   Look, yourself, on this work, Hugh,
a mhic Bhriain, a bhláth fionnchraobh,   Son of Brian, flower of the fair branch,
    a ghéag amhra is uaisle d'fhás,   greatest and noblest branch that grew,
    san uair-se tharla ar Thomás.   in this time that Thomas came.

Luathaigh ort, ainic mise,   Hurry, protect me,
má tá tú ler dtairise;   if you are faithful to us;
    ag so síodhruire bruaigh Bhreagh   from this fairy-lord of the bank of the Breagh,
    uaibh dom fhíorghuidhe ós íseal.   from his constantly beseeching me in a low voice.

A mhic Bhriain, a bhrath mh'éigse,   Son of Brian, who perceived my learning,
más díth leat mo leithéid-se,   if you need such as I,
    dom   chabhair,   a   chaomhshlat   for my help, gentle prince of love,
        ghráidh,   speak to the free son of Siúrtán.
    labhair le saormhac Siúrtáin.

Innis dó, re gcur 'na cheann,   Tell him, by putting it in his head,
nách mór dhaoibh, d'éigsibh Éireann,   it is not great for you, for the poets of Ireland,
    mar ghné sheise ó chraoibh   as a kind of companion from the branch of
        Charadh   Caradh,
    meise daoibh do dheónaghadh.   for you to bestow me.

Ar mo thí an tan-sa ó tharla   On my track this time since he came
mealltóir an uird ealadhna,   a seducer of the artful practice,
    bíodh go ngeallfadh sé mar soin,   although he would promise nonetheless,
    nách meallfadh mé ná measaidh.   [that he] would not beguile me or worse.

Da meastá, ní meastar liom,   If you thought, it was not thought by me,
gadaighe fhileadh Éireann,   thief of an Irish poet,
    béidleómhan do thuair mo thoil,   to signify my will,
    nách éigneóbhadh uaim mh'aon-   you would not force my consent from me.
        taidh.

Dá mealltaoi ar aoi n-annsa   If one were beguiled because of affection,
na háith, a Aodh, oramsa   the fords, Hugh, were forced on me
    le brath soibheart cuaine Cuinn,   with expectation of the blessing of the family of
    toidheacht uaidhe ní fhéadaim.   Conn,
                                             I would not be able to come away from him.

Earl of Longford
(Edward Arthur Henry Pakenham)
(1902–1961)

The Earl of Longford published three collections of verse translations from the Irish in the 1940s, all based on poems written in the bardic tradition between the thirteenth and seventeenth centuries. A fluent Irish speaker, Longford said his translations were designed chiefly 'for the sake of those who do not read Irish with any ease or pleasure, and who are apt to assume that there is nothing worth reading in Irish'.[38] The sixth Earl of Longford devoted much of his life and private fortune to keeping the Gate Theatre afloat in the middle decades of the twentieth century. He also wrote a number of plays, the best-known of which is *Yahoo*, based on the life of Swift.

'O Rourke's Wife and Thomas Costello'

(The subject of this seventeenth-century poem was a well-known figure in folklore in the west of Ireland.)

> O son of Brian, noble Hugh,
> O fairest flower that ever blew,
> Behold, O branch of the grandest tree,
> What Thomas now would do with me!
> If still my love is dear to you,
> Come quickly, help me, keep me true.
> The fairies of the mounds of Breagh
> Keep gently whispering 'Come away!'
> If ever, subject of my art,
> The like of me could keep your heart,
> Sweet husband, lest you find me gone,
> I'd have you speak with Siurtan's son.
> Go now to Thomas Costello,
> And tell him – for he may not know –
> You cannot give me out of hand
> To one of Ireland's poet band.
> Since from that learned order came
> A coaxing thief to steal my fame,
> Let him not think my spoils to take,
> Whatever promises he make.
> I swear the thing is past belief,
> That he, this ravening poet-thief,

Original: 'Féach féin an obair-se, a Aodh' (cont.)   Literal translation (cont.):

Minic tig ar thí mbréagtha
Tomás i dtlacht uaithbhéalta,
do cheilt ar saoireactra sunn,
i mbeirt dhraoidheachta im dhóchum.

Often on the track of cajolery comes
Thomas in dreadful garb,
in concealment, in freedom, here,
in magical covering, to me.

Minic tig athaidh oile
rem ais d'eitill sheabhcaidhe,
i measg cáigh d'fuadach mh'annsa
'na gruagach cháidh chugamsa.

Often another creature comes
beside me, in hawklike flight,
among jackdaws, to carry off my affection,
an enchanter of chastity for me.

Mar mhnaoi tháidhe i dtuighin fir
minic tig sé dár soighin
le briocht druadh, le diamhair ndán,
dom iarraidh uam ar éaládh.

Like a woman of fornication in the cloak of a man
often he comes to attack us
with spell of druid, with darkness of verse,
beseeching me to elope.

Tig i ndeilbh dhaonna dhuine,
tig fós i bhfoirm síodhaighe,
tig uair i n-ionnas taidhbhse;
cionnas uaidh do anfainn-se?

He comes in the shape of a human being,
comes again in the form of a fairy,
comes one time in the manner of a ghost;
how could I stay away from him?

I gcéin ar chogadh clann Néill
gluaistear leis, cuid dom chaithréim;
sínidh ar óigh dhearbhtha dhe
i ndóigh go meallfa mise.

Far to the war of the clan of Néill
with him goes, part of my triumph;
stretching with a certain maiden
in a way that would deceive me.

It éagosg-sa, a Aodh Uí Ruairc,
minic tig sunn ar saorchuairt,
draig ciúntláith ór doilghe dol,
oighre Siúrtáin dár siabhradh.

In your aspect, Hugh O'Rourke,
often he comes here on a free visit,
a quiet, gentle, troublesome dragon of snares,
Siúrtán's inheritor, for our deception.

Tig dá theacht 'na Thomás féin
mo chur seocham ar saoibhchéill,
nó gur sguch mh'annsa dhá halt;
damhsa ní guth a ghluasacht.

He can come as Thomas himself
putting me beside myself with false meaning,
until my affection went out of joint;
not a reproach moving me.

Muna bhfuil intleacht éigin
agaibh d'fhurtacht mh'fhoiréigin,
a sheise, a sheangadh ar ngráidh,
do mealladh meise, a mhacáimh.

Unless there is some understanding
from you of help for my oppression,
companion, slender person of our love,
I would be enticed, young warrior.

M'iomlat eadraibh níor fhéad sinn:
do shearc-sa, a Aodh, im intinn
ar aoi gur hiarnadh 'na shás,
dom shiabhradh a-taoi, a Thomás.

My moving between you was not possible:
your love, Hugh, in my mind
because it is as hard as iron in its means,
for me, you are sorcery, Thomas.

Da mbeith sochar ruibh a rádh,
coisg dhínn, a dheighmhic Siúrtáin,
a rún cháigh gan chlaon n-irse,
ná cráidh Aodh fám aithghin-se.

If there is relief to speak with you,
cease from us, good son of Siúrtán,
sweetheart and jackdaw without an inclination of engagement,
don't torment Hugh about knowing me.

This beast of prey, should force consent,
And I to his desire be bent.
But blame me not for grievous wrong,
If treacherous art be yet too strong,
And love assume some flattering shape
Too soft and wily to escape.
He often comes to work me harm
In magic form of dire alarm,
He comes with tricks of druidry
To vanquish thoughts of chastity.
And oft beside me he'll appear
A swooping hawk in full career,
My love by dreadful wizardry
In view of all to snatch from me.
Or privately in man's attire
He cometh often to conspire
With secret spell and rhyme obscure
My flight and ruin to assure.
As mortal man he visits me,
In fairy shape as readily.
And then he cometh like a ghost,
And I must flee from him or be lost.
Now see him ride to battles far,
And I'm the booty of his war:
And now he woos some provéd maid,
That I may be the more betrayed.
And Hugh O Rourke, he comes to me
In your own shape, as bold and free,
And like a stealthy dragon charms
The wife into the lover's arms:
And then like Thomas Costello
With passion doth my wits o'erthrow.
And then so far in love am I
That I've no strength to move or cry.
Unless you swiftly plan aright
To save me from my desperate plight,
My husband, comrade, love of old,
By Thomas' arts am I cajoled.
My struggling heart is lost between
My love that hath so constant been
For Hugh, and that which now I know,
O crafty wizard Costello!
If I could say what best would be,
Good son of Siurtan, go from me!
To treason you did ne'er incline:

Original: 'Féach féin an obair-se, a
Aodh' (cont.)

Literal translation (cont.):

A Thomáis, a thocht meanmnach,
a bhráighe ghill Choisdealbhach,
  sguir dhín, ní fheallabh ar mh'fhior,
  sín ar mhealladh na maighdean.

Thomas, spirited oppression,
bright hostage Costello,
  release us, don't betray my ordeal,
  arrange for the deception of the maidens.

Ní hionnan mé is mná málla
mhealltaoi, a óig andána;
  mo shiabhradh ní dáigh dhuibhse,
  a ghrianghal sháimh shamhraidh-se.

I am not like the affable women
that you need to beguile, extremely bold youth;
  my deception is not a hope for you,
  sun-haze of tranquility of summer.

Ná creid cách, ní meirdreach mé;
óg fuaras fios mo chéile;
  fada ó tharla Aodh ormsa;
  th'fhabhra ná claon chugamsa.

Don't believe everyone, I am not a harlot;
I knew my husband young;
  it is long since Hugh came to me;
  don't incline your eye to me.

Bhar bhfé fia ní feirrde dhuit,
aithnim thú d'aimhdheóin h'iomlait;
  a bhradaire, ná mill mé;
  fill, a ghadaighe an gháire.

Your wild lust is not best for you,
I know you despite your changing;
  Thief, don't ruin me;
  turn back, laughing thief.

Cosg th'álghais uaim ní bhfuighe,
a bhraidín, a bhréagaire;
  let uaisle ná mearaigh mé;
  buail-se um cheanaibh gach críche.

The slaking of your desire you will not get from me,
plunderer, liar;
  with your nobility don't distract me;
  strike up passions in every territory.

A shaoirmhic Shiúrtáin bhuidhe,
a bhláth coilleadh cumhraidhe,
  ar ghaol, ar chrodh ná ar choimse
  dol ó Aodh ní fhéadaim-se.

Free son of tawny Siúrtán,
blossom of perfumed woods,
  for kinship, for wealth, or for moderation
  I am not able to go from Hugh.

.   .   .

.   .   .

A theanchair ghríosaighe an ghráidh,
a ghlór le mbréagthar bandáil,
  a phost gáidh cagaidh d'íbh Cuinn,
  má táim agaibh, ní admhaim.

Tongs stirring up love,
voice with which a company of women are deceived,
  prop against the danger of war, grandson of Conn,
  if I am yours, I do not admit it.

A Thomáis, d'aithle mh'ionnlaigh,
a chuingidh chrú Choisdealbhaigh,
  atá ar gcridhe dhá rádh rinn,
  do ghrádh d'ibhe, dhá n-ibhinn.

Thomas, after my washing,
champion of the blood of Costello,
  our heart is telling us,
  to drink your love, if I would drink.

Mo bheannacht leat óm lántoil,
a dheaghua dil Dubháltaigh;
  a bhúidh bharrghloin, ná bréag mé,
  ná damnaigh d'éad ar nAoidhne.

My blessing with you, with my full will,
beloved, excellent grandson of Dubháltach;
  gentle, excellent warrior, don't deceive me,
  don't condemn to jealousy our Hugh.

Sgarthain libh gidh tuar tuirse,
ag so Aodh dom fhéachain-se;
  luathaigh thoram (truagh an airc!),
  mo-nuar, oram ná hamhairc.[39]

Our separation, although a cause of affliction,
  at this, Hugh sees me;
  move past me (a pity the hardship!)
  my grief, do not look on me.

Pierce not Hugh's heart in winning mine.
My glorious captive, Costello,
That did your captor's wits o'erthrow,
Use not O Rourke so treacherously,
Make free with girls and not with me.
Some women love to be cajoled,
Not I. You're young and overbold:
Tho' all the summer's in your face,
Don't hope to charm me to disgrace.
I am no whore, believe not so, –
I met my husband long ago:
When I was young my love was he:
So do not bend those eyes on me.
For all your tricks, your name I'll tell.
Your changes shall not serve you well.
You smiling cheat, you thief, begone,
Or she you courted is undone.
Of me you ne'er shall have your will,
You lying rogue, I know you still:
I'd have you seek another's arms,
Nor try to inflame me with your charms.
Sweet son of yellow Siurtan's race,
With flowering forests in your face,
For love or wealth, in gold or kind,
I cannot leave O Rourke behind.[40]

. . .

O tongs that stir love's sleeping fire,
O traitor's voice that lures desire,
O prop of all in stress of war:
If I am yours, I say no more.
When I in water dip my face,
O Thomas, champion of your race,
My heart is whispering, I think:
'Oh, drink his love, if you would drink'.
So take my blessing and begone,
Dear offspring of Dubháltach's son,
My gentle friend, delude not me,
Lest Hugh be damned thro' jealousy.
To part with you doth presage grief –
My husband sees me, so be brief! –
Ah, woe! the hunger and the pain! –
And never look at me again.[41]

Original: 'An t-Im', by Tadhg Dall Ó Huiginn	Literal translation:

Fuarus féin im maith ó mhnaoi:
    an t-im maith – mása maith é –
dóigh linn nách fa bhoin do bhí,
    an ní dá bhfoil do mhill mé.
	I myself got good butter from a woman:
	    the good butter – if it is good –
	it seems to us that it was not from a cow,
	    the thing that it is ruined me.

Do bhí féasóg ar bhfás air –
    ná rab slán d'fhéasóig an fhir;
súgh as nách neimhnighe neimh,
    geir go mblas seirbhdhighe sin.
	A beard was growing on it –
	    it was not the health of a man's beard;
	juice out of it that poison did not nullify,
	    lard with the taste of that bitter drink.

Do ba bhreac, fa hodhar é;
    ní fa ghobhar bhleacht do bhaoi;
fada ó im i n-aisgidh é,
    'sa ghné d'fhaicsin linn gach laoi.
	It was speckled, it was greyish-brown;
	    it is not from a milch goat that it was;
	it was far from butter as a gift,
	    in the form seen by us every day.

A ghíomh leabhar mar fholt eich,
    uch ní fríoth sgeana ro-sgoith;
fada is tinn an tí ro-s-caith,
    an t-im maith ro bhí 'nar mboith.
	Its long lock of hair like horsehair,
	    alas, knives were not found to cut it;
	long is the sickness of whoever consumed it;
	    the good butter that was in our cottage.

Brat eisréide fan ngréis ngoirt
    mar eisléine d'éis a chuirp;
dob airdhe déisdin le deirc
    an cheirt d'fhéiscin d'aidhbhle a huilc.
	A covering spread around the sour grease
	    like a shroud in the absence of its corpse;
	it was a characteristic of disgust to the eye
	    seeing the rag in the immensity of its evil.

Do bhí ar an fearsoin túth trom
    do mhúch is do mhearuigh ionn;[b]
tarfás dúinn gach aondath ann,
    barr craobhach clúimh ós a chionn.
	A heavy stench was on that piece
	    that suffocated and confused us;
	every single colour in it was revealed to us,
	    a branching crop of feathers over its head.

Ní fhaca sé an salann riamh,
    ní fhaca an salann é acht uadh;
ní léigfe a chuimhne sinn slán,
    im bán is guirme iná an gual.
	It never saw salt,
	    salt never saw it, except away from it;
	its memory would not leave us healthy,
	    white butter bluer than the coal.

Do bhí an ghréis ann, 'sní hí amháin,
    do bhí gach re mball don chéir;
beag d'im do-uadhus 'na dheóigh –
    an t-im 'na fheóil fuarus féin.[42]
	Grease was in it, and not only that,
	    every part of it was of wax;
	little of butter I ate after that –
	    the butter that was flesh that I myself got.

---

[a] The literal translation assumes *sinn*, a textual variant.

'A Present of Butter'

(The original is attributed to Tadhg Dall Ó hUiginn [1550-1591], a member of a prominent bardic family living chiefly in Co. Sligo.)

A woman gave me butter now,
  Good butter too it claimed to be.
I don't think it was from a cow,
  And if it was it finished me.

A beard was growing on the stuff,
  A beastly beard without a doubt,
The taste was sickly, sour and rough,
  With poison juices seeping out.

The stuff had spots, the stuff was grey,
  I doubt if any goat produced it.
I had to face it every day,
  And how I wish I had refused it!

This splendid butter had a mane,
  The glory of my humble home.
No knife could cut it down again,
  It made me sick for weeks to come.

This nasty grease a wrapping had
  Like a discarded winding sheet.
Its very aspect was so bad,
  I scarcely had the nerve to eat.

This horror had a heavy stink
  That left one fuddled, stunned and dead.
'Twas rainbow-hued, with what you'd think
  A crest of plumes above its head.

The salt's a thing it hardly knew,
  In fact I think they'd barely met.
It was not white, but rather blue.
  I am not quite recovered yet.

'Twas made of grease and wax and fat,
  O thoughts too horrible to utter!
You may be sure that after that,
  I rather lost my taste for butter.[43]

Original: from 'Caoineadh Airt
Uí Laoghaire', by Eibhlín
Dhubh Ní Chonaill

Literal translation:

(i)

Mo ghrá go daingean tu!
Lá dá bhfaca thu
Ag ceann tí an mhargaidh,
Thug mo shúil aire dhuit,
Thug mo chroí taitneamh duit,
D'éalaíos óm charaid leat
I bhfad ó bhaile leat.

(i)

You are my love forever!
The day I saw you
At the gable-end of the house,
My eyes took notice of you,
My heart gave pleasure to you,
I ran away from my friends with you
Far from home with you.

(ii)

Is domhsa nárbh aithreach:
Chuiris parlús á ghealadh dhom
Rúmanna á mbreacadh dhom,
Bácús á dheargadh dhom,
Brící á gceapadh dhom,
Rósta ar bhearaibh dom,
Mairt á leagadh dhom;
Codladh i gclúmh lachan dom
Go dtíodh an t-eadartha
Nó thairis dá dtaitneadh liom.

(ii)

And I did not regret:
You caused a parlour to be brightened for me
Rooms to be decorated for me,
A bakery to be reddened for me,
Brick-shaped loaves to be made for me,
Roasts on spits for me,
Oxen slaughtered for me;
Sleeping on duck down for me
Until noon came
Or past it if it pleased me.

Frank O'Connor
(1903–1966)

Inspired in part by the Cork writer and scholar Daniel Corkery, Frank O'Connor published a considerable body of verse translation from the Irish throughout his career; his first collection of translations was published in 1932, and the last in 1959, seven years before his death. Like Austin Clarke, O'Connor was fiercely opposed to the conservative and puritanical values of mainstream Irish culture in the post-Free State decades, and many of his translations call into question the sanitised versions of Gaelic culture used to underpin those values. In turn, much of O'Connor's work, including his provocative translation of Brian Merriman's 'Cúirt an Mheán-Oíche' ('The Midnight Court'), was banned under the Censorship Act of 1929.

From 'The Lament for Art O'Leary'

(The original is considered one of the great laments in the Irish-language tradition. It is attributed to Eibhlín Dhubh Ní Chonaill, of Derrynane, Co. Kerry [an aunt of Daniel O'Connell] whose husband, Art Ó Laoghaire, a young captain in the Hungarian Hussars, was killed in 1773 in Carriganimmy, Co. Cork, by the bodyguard of Abraham Morris, the high sheriff of the district.[44] According to some versions of the story, the quarrel between Morris and Ó Laoghaire had to do with Ó Laoghaire's refusal to sell Morris a brown mare. The selection here is taken from the opening of O'Connor's translation.)

My love and my delight,
The day I saw you first
Beside the markethouse
I had eyes for nothing else
And love for none but you.

I left my father's house
And ran away with you.
And that was no bad choice;
You gave me everything.
There were parlours whitened for me
Bedrooms painted for me,
Ovens reddened for me,
Loaves baked for me,
Joints spitted for me,
Beds made for me

271

Original: from 'Caoineadh Airt Uí Laoghaire', by Eibhlín Dhubh Ní Chonaill (cont.)	Literal translation (cont.):
(iii)	**(iii)**
Mo chara go daingean tu!	You are my friend forever!
Is cuimhin lem aigne	I remember in my mind
An lá breá earraigh úd,	That fine spring day,
Gur bhreá thíodh hata dhuit	How well a hat became you
Faoi bhanda óir tarraingthe,	Under a band of stretched gold,
Claíomh cinn airgid –	A sword with a hilt of silver –
Lámh dheas chalma –	A fine brave hand –
Rompsáil bhagarthach –	A threatening prancing –
Fír-chritheagla	A real trembling fear
Ar námhaid chealgach –	On deceitful enemies –
Tú i gcóir chun falaracht,	You ready for trotting,
Is each caol ceannann fút.	And a slim, white-faced horse under you.
D'umhlaídis Sasanaigh	The English used to bow
Síos go talamh duit,	Down to the ground for you,
Is ní ar mhaithe leat	And not for your good
Ach le haon-chorp eagla,	But with sheer fear,
Cé gur leo a cailleadh tu,	Although by them you were killed,
A mhuirnín mh'anama.	Sweetheart of my soul.

. . .   . . .

(vii)	**(vii)**
Mo chara thu go daingean!	You are my friend forever!
Is níor chreideas riamh dod mharbh	And I never believed in your death
Gur tháinig chugham do chapall	Until your horse came to me
Is a srianta léi go talamh,	And her reins to the ground,
Is fuil do chroí ar a leacain	And the blood of your heart on her cheek
Siar go t'iallait ghreanta	[Going] back to your beautiful saddle
Mar a mbítheá id shuí 's id sheasamh.	Where you used to sit and stand.
Thugas léim go tairsigh,	I gave a leap to the threshold,
An dara léim go geata,	The second leap to the gate,
An tríú léim ar do chapall.	The third leap on your horse.

(viii)	**(viii)**
Do bhuaileas go luath mo bhasa	I clapped my hands quickly
Is do bhaineas as na reathaibh	And I took up the running
Chomh maith is bhí sé agam,	As well as I could,
Go bhfuaras romham tu marbh	Until I found you dead before me
Cois toirín ísil aitinn,	Beside a small, low furze-bush,
Gan Pápa gan easpag,	Without Pope, without bishop,
Gan cléireach gan sagart	Without clergy, without priest
Do léifeadh ort an tsailm,	Who would read over you the psalm,
Ach seanbhean chríonna chaite	But a spent old woman
Do leath ort binn dá fallaing –	Who spread on you part of her cloak –
Do chuid fola leat 'na sraithibh;	Your blood from you in streams;
Is níor fhanas le hí ghlanadh	And I didn't stay to clean it
Ach í ól suas lem basaibh.	But drank it up with my palms.

To take my ease on flock
Until the milking time
And later if I pleased.

My mind remembers
That bright spring day,
How your hat with its band
Of gold became you,
Your silver-hilted sword,
Your manly right hand,
Your horse on her mettle
And foes around you
Cowed by your air;
For when you rode by
On your white-nosed mare
The English lowered their head before you
Not out of love for you
But hate and fear,
For, sweetheart of my soul,
The English killed you.

           .   .   .

My love and my mate
That I never thought dead
Till your horse came to me
With bridle trailing,
All blood from forehead
To polished saddle
Where you should be,
Either sitting or standing;
I gave one leap to the threshold,
A second to the gate,
A third upon its back.

I clapped my hands,
And off at a gallop;
I never lingered
Till I found you lying
By a little furze-bush
Without pope or bishop
Or priest or cleric
One prayer to whisper
But an old, old woman,
And her cloak about you,
And your blood in torrents –
Art O'Leary –
I did not wipe it off,
I drank it from my palms.

Original: from 'Caoineadh Airt
Uí Laoghaire', by Eibhlín
Dhubh Ní Chonaill (cont.)

Literal translation (cont.):

(ix)

Mo ghrá thu go daingean!
Is éirigh suas id sheasamh
Is tar liom féin abhaile,
Go gcuirfeam mairt á leagadh,
Go nglaofam ar chóisir fhairsing,
Go mbeidh againn ceol á spreagadh,
Go gcóireod duitse leaba
Faoi bhairlíní geala,
Faoi chuilteanna breátha breaca,
A bhainfidh asat allas
In ionad an fhuachta a ghlacais.[45]

(ix)

You are my love forever!
And get up
And come home with me,
So that I could cause oxen to be slaughtered,
So that I could call for a generous feast,
So that we will have music to rouse us,
So that I will make a bed for you
Under bright sheets,
Under fine speckled quilts,
That will bring the sweat out of you
Instead of the cold that you took.

Originals: 'Goradh an mhic i
dtigh an athar' and 'Féach leat,
ón féach leat'

Literal translation:

I.

Goradh an mhic i dtigh an athar,
        goradh fairsing fial;
goradh an athar i dtigh an mhic
        is a dhá ghlúin 'na chliabh.

I.

The son warming in the house of the father,
        warming, generous, lavish;
The father warming in the house of the son,
        and his two knees in his chest.

II.

Féach leat, ón féach leat
dála na cloinne nách ceart:
        gach ní bhus leat is leó,
is gach ní is leó ní leat.[46]

II.

Look, indeed look
the distributions of the children are not right:
        everything that is yours is theirs,
and everything that is theirs is not yours.

My love and my delight
Stand up now beside me,
And let me lead you home
Until I make a feast,
And I will roast the meat
And send for company
And call the harpers in,
And I shall make your bed
Of soft and snowy sheets
And blankets dark and rough
To warm the beloved limbs
An autumn blast has chilled.[47]

'Fathers and Sons'

1.

Young at his father's fire
    He lords it and takes the best;
Old, at the fire of his son,
    He covers his knees with his breast.

2.

Father and son take shares?
    The son the father devours!
All that is ours is theirs,
    Nothing of theirs is ours.[48]

Original: from 'Cúirt an Mheán-Oíche', by Brian Merriman

Literal translation:

Original	Literal translation
Mo dhochar! mo dhíth! mo bhrón mar bhím	My harm! my destruction! my sorrow as I am
Gan sochar gan seoid gan só gan síoth	Without profit, without jewels, without comfort, without rest
Go doilbhir duaiseach duamhar dítheach	Gloomy, cheerless, toilsome, destitute
Gan chodladh gan suan gan suaimhneas oíche	Without sleep, without rest, without peace at night
Ar leaba leamhfhuar im shuathadh ag smaointe.	On a tepic bed disturbed by thoughts.
A Cháigh na Carraige! breathnaigh go díreach	Cáigh of Carraig! examine directly
Mná na Banba in anacrain sínte	The women of Ireland in affliction stretched
Ar nós má leanaid na fearaibh dá bhfuadar,	In such a way that if the men follow their inclination,
Och! mo lagar! go gcaithfeam a bhfuadach!	Oh! my weakness! we will have to abduct them!
An t-am inar mhéinn leo céile a phósadh,	The time when they desire to marry a wife,
An t-am nar mhéinn le h-éinne gabháil leo.	[Is] the time no one desires to go with them.
An t-am nárbh fhiú bheith fúthu sínte –	The time it would not be worth it to be stretched under them –
An tseandacht thamhanda suite chloíte.	The lethargic, fixed, exhausted antiquity.
Dá dtagadh amach le teas na h-óige,	If one were to emerge with the heat of youth,
Duine a phósfadh ar theact féasóige,	To marry a person, just when the beard comes,
Ceangail le mnaoi, ní míntais thógfadh,	To tie up with a woman, it is not a delicate wraith he would take,
Thaitneamhach, suite de shíol ná d'fhoghlaim,	Pleasing, proved of race or of learning,
Cló dheas chaoin nó míonla mhánla,	A pleasant, refined or gentle, gracious form,
Dá mb'eol di suí nó tíocht i láthair,	Who would know whether to sit or come in,
Ach doineantach odhar nó donn doilíosach,	But a cheerless dull person, or a melancholy brown-coloured person,
A chruinnigh le doghraing cabhair nár chuí dí.	Who gathered with difficulty help that was not proper to her.
'Sé chráigh mo chroí 'is scaoil gan chéill mé,	It tormented my heart and left me without sense,
'Is d'fhág mo smaointe 'is m'intinn traochta,	And left my thoughts and my mind exhausted,
Cráite tinn mar táim go tréithlag,	Tormented and sick as I am weak,
Go cásmhar cloíte ag caoi 'is ag géarghol,	Pitiable, subdued, lamenting and keenly weeping,
An uair do chínn preabaire calma croíúil	When I would see a dashing, brave, cordial man
Fuadrach fearúil seasmhach saoithiúil	Bustling, manly, steadfast, accomplished
Stuama starrúil barrúil bríomhar	Sensible, vigorous, funny, lively
Gruadheas greannmhar geanúil gnaoiúil;	Pleasant-cheeked, humorous, loving, comely;
Nó buachaill beachanta bastalach bíogach	Or a boy vigorous, showy, sprightly
Cruacheart ceannasach ceaptha córach,	Rightly hardy, commanding, determined, shapely,

From 'The Midnight Court'

(In Brian Merriman's eighteenth-century social satire 'Cúirt an Mheán-Oíche' ['The Midnight Court'], the narrator, while wandering the countryside, falls into a dream-vision, and is taken to a court presided over by a fairy-queen and entertaining complaints from Ireland's young women of sexual frustration. For an eighteenth-century version of Merriman's poem, see under Denis Woulf, pp. 27–33; for Percy Arland Ussher's translation, roughly contemporary with O'Connor's, see pp. 237–241; for two more recent versions, see under Seamus Heaney, pp. 347–351, and Ciaran Carson, pp. 387–393. The following selection is spoken by one of the young women testifying before the court.)

> Wouldn't you think I must be a fright,
> To be shelved before I get started right;
> Heartsick, bitter, dour and wan,
> Unable to sleep for the want of a man?
> But how can I lie in a lukewarm bed
> With all the thoughts that come into my head?
> Indeed, 'tis time that somebody stated
> The way that the women are situated,
> For if men go on their path to destruction
> There will nothing be left to us but abduction.
> Their appetite wakes with age and blindness
> When you'd let them cover you only from kindness,
> And offer it up for the wrongs you'd done
> In hopes of reward in the life to come:
> And if one of them weds in the heat of youth
> When the first down is on his mouth
> It isn't some woman of his own sort,
> Well-shaped, well-mannered or well-taught;
> Some mettlesome girl who studied behaviour,
> To sit and stand and amuse a neighbour,
> But some pious old prude or dour defamer
> Who sweated the couple of pounds that shame her.
> There you have it! It has me melted,
> And makes me feel that the world's demented:
> A country's choice for brains and muscle,
> Fond of a lark and not scared of a tussle,
> Decent and merry and sober and steady,
> Good-looking, gamesome, rakish and ready;

Original: from 'Cúirt an Mheán-Oíche', by Brian Merriman (cont.)

Literal translation (cont.):

– Buaite ceannaithe ceangailte pósta
Ag fuaid, ag cailligh, ag amaid nó ag óinsigh;
Nó ag samhairle salach de chaile gan tionscal,
Stuacach stailceach aithiseach stúncach
Suaite sotalach foclach fáidhiúil
Cuairdeach codlatach goirgeach gráiniúil.
Mo chreach! mo lot! atá molt míb-héasach,
Caile na gcos 'is folt gan réiteach,
Á ceangal anocht; Is é loisc go h-ae mé.

– Defeated, bought, bound, married
To a wretch, to a hag, to a witch, or to a foolish woman;
Or to a dirty whelp of a girl without industry,
Sulky, starchy, shameful, peevish
Confusing, arrogant, verbose, gossiping
Acquisitive, sleepy, irritable, hateful.
My ruin! my destruction! there is an ill-man-nered sulky person,
A girl of legs and hair untidy
Being tied tonight; it is burning me to the heart.

Agus cá bhfuil mo locht ná toghfaí roimpi?
Céard é an t-abhar ná tabharfaí grá dom
'Is mé chomh leabhair, chomh modhúil, chomh breá so?
Is deas mo bhéal, mo dhéad, mo gháire;
Is geal mo ghné 'is tá m'éadan tláth tais;
Is glas mo shúil agas tá m'úrla scáinneach
Bachallach búclach cúplach fáinneach;
Mo leaca, mo ghnúis gan smúit, gan mháchail,
Tarringteach cumtha lonrach scáfar;
Mo phíob, mo bhráid, mo lámha, mo mhéara,
Ag síorbhreith barr na h-áille ó chéile.

And where is my fault that I would not be chosen before her?
Why would someone not love me
And I as slender, as modest, as fine as this?
Nice is my mouth, my teeth, my laugh;
And bright my appearance, and my forehead is mild and gentle;
Grey are my eyes and my hair in locks
Curled, ringleted, double-plaited, beautiful;
My cheeks, my face without defect, without blemish,
Attractive, shapely, luminous, timid;
My throat, my bosom, my hands, my fingers,
Forever vying with one another for the height of beauty.

Féach mo chom; nach leabhair mo chnámha?
An bhfuil mé lom ná cam ná stágach?
Ag sin toll 'is cosa agus colainn nach náir' dom
Agus togha an ghiorta chun fireannaigh a shásamh.
Ní samhairle caile ná spangarra mná mé,
Ach stuaire cailce atá taitneamhach breá deas;
Ní sraoil ná sluid ná luid gan fáscadh,

Smíste duirc gan sult gan sásamh,

Lóiste liosta ná toice gan éifeacht,
Ach ógbhean scofa chomh tofa 'sis féidir.[49]

Look on my waist; are my bones not slender?
Am I bald or bent or stiff?
Of that posterior and legs and body I am not ashamed
And the choice girth for satisfying the male kind.
I am not a whelp of a wench or a barren cow of a woman
But a handsome, chalk-white woman who is pleasing, fine, nice;
Not a slattern, nor a stooped beldam, nor a slut without tidiness,
A lazy person without enjoyment, without satisfaction,
A tiresome idler nor a hussy without effort,
But an eager young woman as choice as is possible.

With a gracious flush and a passable figure
Finds a fortune the best attraction
And sires himself off on some bitter extraction;
Some fretful old maid with her heels in the dung,
Pious airs and venomous tongue,
Vicious and envious, nagging and whining,
Snoozing and snivelling, plotting, contriving –
Hell to her soul, an unmannerly sow
With a pair of bow legs and hair like a tow
Went off this morning to the altar
And here am I still without hope of the halter!
Couldn't some man love me as well?
Amn't I plump and sound as a bell?
Lips for kissing and teeth for smiling,
Blossomy skin and forehead shining?
My eyes are blue and my hair is thick
And coils in streams about my neck –
A man who's looking for a wife,
Here's a face that will keep for life!
Hand and arm and neck and breast,
Each is better than the rest.
Look at that waist! My legs are long,
Limber as willows and light and strong.
There's bottom and belly that claim attention,
And the best concealed that I needn't mention.
I'm the sort a natural man desires,
Not a freak or a death-on-wires,
A sloven that comes to life in flashes,
A creature of moods with her heels in the ashes,
Or a sluggard stewing in her own grease,
But a good-looking girl that's bound to please.[50]

Original: from 'Cúirt an Mheán-
Oíche', by Brian Merriman

Literal translation:

A thoice gan chríoch, nach chuimhin le táinte	Wench unmarried, do multitudes not remember
Olcas an tsíolraigh daoine ó dtángais,	The evil of the breed of people you came from,
Gan focal le maíomh ag do shinsir ghránna	Without a word to boast of by your ugly ancestors
Ach lópaigh gan bhrí, lucht míre 'is mála!	But louts without sense, bag-people and tramps!
Is aithnid dúinne an súmaire is athair duit,	We know the serpent who is father to you,
Gan chara, gan chlú, gan chúil, gan airgead,	Without a friend, without reputation, without shelter, without money,
Ina leibide liath, gan chiall, gan mhúineadh,	A grey clown, without sense, without education,
Gan mheidhir, gan mhias, gan bhia, gan anlann,	Without a cup, without a dish, without food, without sauce,
Gan faic ar a ghabhal 'is a dhrom gan chóta;	Without anything on his groin, and his back without a coat;
Gad ar a chom 'sa bhonn gan bhróga.	A cord around his waist and his soles without shoes.
Creidigí, a dhaoine, dá ndíoltaí ar aonach	Believe [it], people, if one would sell at a fair
Eisean 'sa mhaoin, d'éis íoc gach éilimh,	Himself and his property, after paying every demand,
Dar colainn na naomh! ba dhícheall mór dó	By the bodies of the saints! it would be a great effort for him
Pota maith dí lena fhuíollach a fhuascailt.	A good pot of drink to redeem with the surplus.
Nach mór an t-ábhacht 'san gleo idir dhaoine	Is it not great the drollery and chatter among people
Trudaire ded short gan bhó gan chaora;	[That] a stutterer of your kind, without a cow, without sheep;
Búclaí id bhróga agus clóca síoda ort;	[Has] buckles on your shoes and a silk cloak on you;
Ciarsúir phóca ag gabháil na gaoithe.	A pocket handkerchief moving in the wind.
Dallair an saol go léir le taibhse;	You deceive all the world with appearance;
Dob aithne dom féin tú i dtaobh le caidhp bheag.	I knew you myself having only a small cap.
Is deacair liom labhairt! Do lom is léir dom!	It is difficult for me to speak! your bareness is clear to me!
Is fada do dhrom gan chabhair ón léine;	Your back has been a long time without help from a shirt;
(Is togha drochdhuine do thuigfeadh ina gá tú!)	(It is the choice of bad people who would realise you to be in need of it!)
Agus feabhas do rufaí le do mhuinchillí *cambric*.	And the excellence of ruffs on your sleeves of cambric.
Tá canbhas saor chun sraod dod bhásta,	Canvas is cheap for the lining of your bodice,
Agus cá bhfios don tsaol nach *stays* bhí id fháisceadh?	And who in the world knows but that it was stays that were confining you?
Feiceann an tír ort frainsí 'is fáinní	The country sees on you fringes and rings
Agus ceileann do lámhainní gríos 'is gága.	And your gloves conceal blotches and cracks.
Aithris ar bord nó neosfad féin é	Relate at the [witness-] table or I myself will tell
An fada nár ólais deoir le do bhéile,	How long since you drank a drop with your meal,
A chonartaigh bhoicht na gcos gan ionnladh!	Poor vulgar woman of the feet without washing!
Dochar id chorp le *Bucks* gan anlann.	Harm to your body from potatoes without sauce.
Is furas, dar liom, dod chúl a bheith taibhseach,	It is easy, it seems to me, for your head of hair to be noticeable,

(The speaker in this selection is a man responding to the woman quoted above.)

> You slut of ill-fame, allow your betters
> To tell the court how you learned your letters!
> Your seed and breed for all your brag
> Were tramps to a man with rag and bag;
> I knew your da and what passed for his wife,
> And he shouldered his traps to the end of his life,
> An aimless lout without friend or neighbour,
> Knowledge or niceness, wit or favour:
> The breeches he wore were riddled with holes
> And his boots without a tack of the soles.
> Believe me, friends, if you sold at a fair,
> Himself and his wife, his kids and gear,
> When the costs were met, by the Holy Martyr,
> You'd still go short for a glass of porter.
> But the devil's child has the devil's cheek –
> You that never owned cow nor sheep,
> With buckles and brogues and rings to order –
> You that were reared in the reek of solder!
> However the rest of the world is gypped
> I knew you when you went half-stripped;
> And I'd venture a guess that in what you lack
> A shift would still astonish your back;
> And, shy as you seem, an inquisitive gent
> Might study the same with your full consent.
> Bosom and back are tightly laced,
> Or is it the stays that gives you the waist?
> Oh, all can see the way you shine,
> But your looks are no concern of mine.
> Now tell us the truth and don't be shy
> How long are you eating your dinner dry?
> A meal of spuds without butter or milk,
> And dirt in layers beneath the silk.
> Bragging and gab are yours by right,

Original: from 'Cúirt an Mheán-Oíche', by Brian Merriman (cont.)

Literal translation (cont.):

Do chonarc le mo shúile an chúil ina luíonn tú.	I saw with my eyes the nook where you lie.
Garbh ná mín ní shíntear fútsa,	Neither rough nor smooth is stretched under you,
Barrach ná líon dár sníomhadh le túirne;	Tow nor flax that was spun on a spinning-wheel,
Ach mata ina smoirt gan phluid, gan súsa,	But a dirty mat without a quilt, without a blanket,
Dealbh gan luid, gan chuilt, gan chlúda,	Bare without a stitch, without a covering, without a rag,
I gcúil bhótháin gan áit chun luí ann,	In a nook of a shack without a place for lying in it,
Ach sú sileáin agus fáisceadh aníos ann,	But soot shedding and rain pressing down on it,
Fiaile ag teacht go fras gan chuimse	Weeds flourishing without moderation
Agus rian na gcearc air trasna scríofa,	And the track of the hens written across it,
Lag ina dhrom 'is gabhla ar lúbadh	Weak at its top and props bending
Agus clagarnach dhonn go trom ag túir-ling.	And a heavy brown rain heavily pouring down.
A chumainn na bhfáidh! nach ard do labhair sí?	Fellowship of the seers! is it not loudly that she spoke?
Gustalach, gálbhach, gártha, gabhann sí	Well-to-do, testy, blushing she goes
I ndatha, i gcóir, is i gclóca síoda.	In colours, in gear, and in a silken cloak.
Faire go deo arú! Sceol cár fríth é.	But alas! where it was got is a story.
Aithris cá bhfaigheann tú an radharc so mhaígh tú!	Relate where you get this showy appearance you boasted of!
Agus aithris cár thuill tú an leadhb gan bhrí seo!	And relate how you earned this rag without substance!
Is deacair a shuíomh gur fríth é ar fónamh!	It is difficult to establish that it was well got!
Is gairid ó bhís gan síol gan órlach.	It isn't long since you were without seed, without an inch.
Aithris cá bhfuair tú luach do húda	Relate where you got the price of your hood
Agus aithris cá bhfuair tú luach do ghúna?	And relate where you got the price of your gown?
Ach ligimid uainn mar ghluais an cóta!	But we relinquish, for commentary, the coat!
Agus aithris cá bhfuair tú luach na mbróga?[51]	And relate where you got the price of the shoes?

Original:

Literal translation:

Céard a bheir scaoilte ó chuibhreach céile	What is it frees from the ties of a wife
In eaglais sinsir suim na cléire.	In our ancestors' church, the interest of the clergy.
Mo chrá gan leigheas! mo threighid dom' fháscadh!	My torment without cure! my pang pressing me!
Is láidir m'fhoighne agus laghad mo ráige,	Strong is my patience and small my anger,
An méid atá dínn ar díth gan éinneach	[About] the number of us who are in want, without anyone
Agus mian ár gcroí faoi shnaidhm na h-éide!	And the desire of our hearts under the bond of celibacy!
Nach bocht an radharc do mhaighre ghrámhar	Is it not a pitiful sight for a loving, robust beauty
A dtoirt 'is a dtaibhse, a mbaill 'is a mbreáthacht,	Their size and their appearance, their limbs and their fineness,
Bloscadh a n-aghaidh agus soilse a ngáire,	The radiance of their faces and the brightness of their laughter,
A gcoirp 'is a gcoim, a dtoill ar támhchrith.	Their bodies and their waists, their backsides sluggishly trembling.
Úireacht, áilleacht, bláth 'is óige,	Freshness, beauty, flower and youth,
Ramhadas cnámh agus meachain feola,	Stoutness of bone and weight of flesh,

But I know too where you sleep at night,
And blanket or quilt you never saw
But a strip of old mat and a bundle of straw,
In a hovel of mud without a seat,
And slime that settles about your feet,
A carpet of weeds from door to wall
And hens inscribing their tracks on all;
The rafters in with a broken back
And brown rain lashing through every crack –
'Twas there you learned to look so nice,
But now may we ask how you came by the price?
We all admired the way you spoke,
But whisper, treasure, who paid for the cloak?
A sparrow with you would die of hunger –
How did you come by all the grandeur,
All the tassles and all the lace –
Would you have us believe they were got in grace?
The frock made a hole in somebody's pocket,
And it wasn't you that paid for the jacket;
But assuming that and the rest no news,
How the hell did you come by the shoes?[52]

(The young woman speaks again, making at one point a spirited plea
for the end of celibacy.)

Has the Catholic Church a glimmer of sense
That the priests won't come to the girls' defense?
Is it any wonder the way I moan,
Out of my mind for a man of my own
While there's men around can afford one well
But shun a girl as they shun Hell.
The full of a fair of primest beef,
Warranted to afford relief;
Cherry-red cheeks and bull-like voices
And bellies dripping with fat in slices;
Backs erect and huge hind-quarters,
Hot-blooded men, the best of partners,
Freshness and charm, youth and good looks

Original: from 'Cúirt an Mheán-Oíche', by Brian Merriman (cont.)	Literal translation (cont.):
Martús trom agus drom gan suathadh,	A solid frame and a back without swaying,
Neart gan dabhat agus fonn gan fuaradh.	Strength without doubt and desire without cooling.
Bíonn sealbh gach só acu ar bhord na saoithe,	They possess every satisfaction at the table of the worthy,
Earra agus ór chun óil 'is aoibhnis,	Goods and gold for drink and delight,
Clúmh chun luí 'is saill chun bia,	Down for sleeping and salt meat for food,
Plúr 'is meidhir 'is milseacht fíona.	Flour and mirth and sweetness of wines.
Is gnáthach cumasach iomadach óg iad,	They are generally strong, proud, young,
'Is tá a fhios againn gur fuil 'is feoil iad!	And we know they are blood and flesh!

. . .   . . .

Is minic a bhuaitear buaibh 'is gréithe,	Often cattle and gifts are gained
Cuigeann 'is cruach de chuairt na cléire.	The contents of a churn and a rick from a visit of the clergy.
Is minic le mo chuimhne a maíodh a dtréithe	Often in my memory their qualities were praised
Agus iomad dá ngníomhartha fíorghlic féithe.	And a great number of their always-clever deeds of nerve.
Is minic a chualas ar fud na tíre	Often I heard throughout the land
Siosarnach luath á lua go líonmhar,	A frenzied whispering being mentioned strongly,
Agus chonarc go taibhseach roint dá rancaibh	And I saw clearly some of their romping
Agus uimhir dá gclann ar sloinnte falsa.	And a number of their children with false surnames.
Baineann sé fáscadh as lár mo chléibhe	It draws a tightening out of the center of my bosom
A gcaitear dá sláinte ar mhná treasaosta;	That their health is spent on women fairly advanced in age;
Is torann san tír chun díth na mbéithe	There is a report in the country, to the ruin of the women,
Ar cuireadh gan bhrí den síolrach naofa.	About the sowing without efficacy of the saintly seed.
Is dealbh an diachair dianghoirt d'Éirinn	It is miserable the very bitter trouble of Ireland
Ar chailleamar riamh le riall gan éifeacht.[53]	What we have always lost from a pointless rule.

Original: 'Is mebul dom imrádud'	Literal translation:

Is mebul dom imrádud
   a méit élas úaim:
ad-águr a imgábud
   i lló brátha búain.
	A shame is on my thoughts
	   how they stray from me:
	I fear great danger from them
	   on the day of lasting judgement.

Tresna salmu sétaigid
   for conair nád cóir,
reithid, búaidrid, bétaigid
   fíad roscaib Dé móir.
	Across the psalms they wander
	   on a road that is not right,
	they run, they trouble, they misbehave
	   in the presence of the eyes of great God.

Tre airechtu athlama,
   tre buidne ban mboeth,
tre choillte, tre chathracha –
   is lúaithiu ná in goeth.
	Through ready assemblies,
	   through companies of foolish women,
	through woods, through cities –
	   faster than the wind.

And nothing to ease their mind but books!
The best-fed men that travel the country,
With beef and mutton, game and poultry,
Whiskey and wine forever in stock,
Sides of bacon and beds of flock.
Mostly they're hardy under the hood,
And we know like ourselves they're flesh and blood.

. . .

Many a girl filled byre and stall
And furnished her house through a clerical call.
Everyone's heard some priest extolled
For the lonesome women that he consoled;
People I've known throughout the county
Have nothing but praise for the curate's bounty,
Or uphold the canon to lasting fame
For the children he reared in another man's name;
But I hate to think of their lonely lives,
The passions they waste on middle-aged wives
While girls they'd choose if the choice was theirs
Go by the wall and comb grey hairs.[54]

'A Prayer for Recollection'
(The original is dated to the tenth century.)

How my thoughts betray me!
    How they flit and stray!
Well they may appal me
    On great judgment day.

Through the psalms they wander
    Roads that are not right;
Mitching, shouting, squabbling
    In God's very sight.

Through august assemblies
    Groups of gamesome girls,
Then through woods, through cities,
    Like the wind in whirls.

Original: 'Is mebul dom imrádud' (cont.)	Literal translation (cont.):

Tresna séta sochraide
    ind ala fecht dó,
tre dimbíthe dochraide
    fecht aile, ní gó.

Along paths of loveliness
    at one time,
through gloomy, non-worlds
    another time, it is no lie.

Cen ethar 'na chloenchéimmim
    cingid tar cech ler;
lúath linges 'na oenléimmim
    ó thalmain co nem.

Without a ship in their perverse course
    they walk over every sea;
swiftly they leap in one bound
    from earth to heaven.

Reithid, ní rith rogaíse,
    i n-ocus, i céin;
íar réimmennaib robaíse
    taidlid dia thig féin.

They run, not a run of great wisdom,
    near, far;
after roamings of great folly
    they reach their own house.

Ce thrialltar a chuimrech-som
    nó geimel 'na chois,
ní cunnail, ní chuimnech-som
    co ngabad feidm fois.

Although one tries to bind them
    or chain their feet,
they are not constant, or mindful
    to undertake an act of rest.

Foebur ná fúaimm flecsbuille
    ní-traethat co tailc;
sleimnithir eirr n-escuinge
    oc dul as mo glaicc.

Neither weapons nor the sound of whip-blows
    keeps them down firmly,
they are as slippery as an eel's tail
    going out of my grasp.

Glas, nó charcar chromdaingen,
    nó chuimrech for bith,
dún, nó ler, nó lomdaingen
    nín astat dia rith.

Neither lock, nor vaulted dungeon
    nor any bond at all,
fort, nor sea, nor bleak fastness
    restrains them from their running.

Taet, a Chríst choím chertgenmnaid,
    dianid réil cech rosc,
rath in Spirta sechtdelbaig
    dia choimét, dia chosc.

Grant, O beloved, truly chaste Christ,
    to whom every eye is clear,
the grace of the seven-fold Spirit
    Keep them, check them.

Follamnaig mo chride-se,
    a Dé dúilig déin,
corop tú mo dile-se,
    co ndernar do réir.

Rule my heart,
    severe God the creator,
that you may be my love,
    that I may do your will.

Rís, a Chríst, do chétchummaid,
    ro bem imma-lle;
níta anbsaid éccunnail,
    ní inonn is mé.[55]

May I be, Christ, your perfect companion,
    may we be together;
you are not fickle nor inconstant,
    not as I am.

Now down lordly highways
　　　Boisterously they stride,
Then through desert pathways
　　　Secretly they glide.

In their whims unferried
　　　Overseas they fly,
Or in one swift motion
　　　Spin from earth to sky.

Lost to recollection
　　　Near and far they roam;
From some monstrous errand
　　　Slyly they slink home.

Where are ropes to bind them?
　　　Who has fetters fit?
They who lack all patience
　　　Cannot stand or sit.

No sharp sword affrights them,
　　　Nor any threatening whip;
Like an eel's tail, greasy,
　　　From my grasp they slip.

Lock nor frowning dungeon,
　　　Nor sentinelled frontier,
Townwall, sea nor fortress
　　　Halts their mad career.

Christ the chaste, the cherished,
　　　Searcher of the soul,
Grant the seven-fold spirit
　　　Keep them in control.

Rule my thoughts and feelings,
　　　You who brook no ill;
Make me yours forever,
　　　Bend me to your will.

Grant me, Christ, to reach you,
　　　With you let me be
Who are not frail nor fickle
　　　Nor feeble-willed like me.[56]

Original: 'Dírgidh bharr sleagha sealga'

Dírgidh bharr sleagha sealga · lé a ngonmaoís fearba fíre
    mar do bhámar re gaisgeadh · ní dhénmaoís aistear aoíne
Seólaidh bharr mbolcca corra · go borraibh loma Lochlann
    lé bhar gcraoíseachoibh go ndaíngne · ro gonsam Ráighni roscmall
Is mé Oisín gem ársaidh · do airrcis mé mná miolla
    léithi is goire don duinne · cruime is goire don dírge.[57]

Literal translation:

Lift up your hunting spears · with which we wounded true does
    when we were in arms · we did not make a journey of fasting
Steer your rounded hulls · to the bare castles of Scandinavia
    with your strong spears · we wounded slow-eyed Ráighni
I am Oisin, although I am old · I have met with gentle women
    greyness is nearest to brownness · stooped is nearest to straightness.

Original: from 'Úna Bhán'

A Úna Bhán is tú do mhearuigh mo chiall,
A Úna is tú chuaidh go dluth idir mé 'gus Dia,

Literal translation:

Fair Úna, it is you who set astray my senses,
Úna, it is you who went steadfastly between me and God,

Robert Farren
(1909–1984)

The verse translations of Robert Farren (Roibeárd Ó Faracháin), like those of his friend Austin Clarke, are constructed to reflect the patterns of assonance in Irish-language poetry. Farren was born in Dublin, into a working-class family, and spent much of his adult life working for Raidió Éireann. He worked closely with Clarke in the 1940s to establish a theatre in Dublin devoted to verse drama.

'Oisín's Exhortation'

(The original is attributed to Oisín, poet of the Fianna and son of the legendary Fionn Mac Cumhail, and is usually dated to the late Middle Irish period, from the tenth to the twelfth centuries.)

> Your hunting spears upfling
> remembering braver days.
> When Fenians served the king
> we trod no fasting ways.
>
> Your currachs' prows set straight
> for Lochlann's[58] rounded knolls,
> make fast the massive gate
> of Almhain's[59] ghosted halls.
>
> I am Oisín, though in age,
> who trysted queenly maids;
> I Oisín, bard and sage,
> who now keep tryst with shades.[60]

'The Love-Plaint of the O Costello'

'Tis Úna has hair looped and twisty like horns of the kine,
her two eyes cup quiet like dew, and drown fire like wine,
her arms sweep out white as the salmon leap light in the sun.
O my salt sea of grief! That my life and her life were one.

Original: from 'Úna Bhán'   Literal translation (cont.):
(cont.)

A Úna, a chraébh chubhartha, a lúibín   Úna, fragrant branch, small twisted tresses
    chasta na g-ciabh,   of the locks,
Nár bh'fhearr damh-sa bheith gan súil-   Would it not have been better for me to be
    iubh ná d'fheiceál ariamh.[61]   without eyes than ever to have seen
                                    you.

Original: from 'Ní sult leó   Literal translation:
muicfheóil ná fíon mar chuid'

Ní sult leó muicfheóil ná fíon mar chuid,   They do not enjoy pork or wine for a portion,
Ní sult leó puirt cheóil na saoithe glic,   They do not enjoy an air of music or clever
                                      wise men,

Ní sult leó bruit shróil ag caomhna a   They do not enjoy a garment of satin covering
    gcnis, –   their skin, –
Gan fir fós ní sult leó ní san mbith.[62]   Without men still, they do not enjoy anything
                                      in the world.

In what summer bloomed whin that could dim the gold floss of her
    hair?
What wave what swan-pinion laved wan as her white throat bare?
What strings upon streams ever tingled blood more than the breath
of her mouth, that has troubled, will trouble my birth and my death?

I sought west to Erris,[63] and east to the bawns of Meath;
I never saw maid for my love like my maid of the heath;
I never saw star without fault and alone in its light
but her beauty outstarred putting glory on roads o' night.

Ah, Úna, 'tis you made my mind like a trembling sod.
'Tis you that have leaped between my spirit and God.
A Úna 'rún,[64] looped, twisty, perfumed maze-head of curls,
had my eyes but lacked light when we met where the lake-tide
    swirls.[65]

'Women'

The fat and the lean of meat cannot please them, nor wine –
the agreeable tune nor the truth of a brooding mind –
the cool-touching, lustrous satin soothing their sides
delight them, quiet or beguile them, till men be by.[66]

Original: 'Scél Lemm
Dúib'

Literal translation:

Scél lemm dúib:
dordaid dam,
snigid gaim,
ro-fáith sam;

I have tidings for you:
the stag bells,
winter drips,
summer is departed ;

gáeth ard úar,
ísel grían,
gair a rith,
ruirthech rían;

wind high, cold,
low the sun,
short its course,
the sea running swiftly;

rorúad rath,
ro-cleth cruth,
ro-gab gnáth
giugrann guth;

very red the bracken,
shape wholly hidden,
it has become customary,
the wild-goose call;

ro-gab úacht
etti én,
aigre ré:
é mo scél.[67]

cold has seized
the wings of birds,
season of ice:
these are my tidings.

Flann O'Brien
(1911–1966)

Flann O'Brien (pseudonym of Brian O'Nolan, or Brian Ó Nualláin) grew up speaking Irish in his native Co. Tyrone. His best-known novel, *At Swim-Two-Birds* (1939), a wildly parodic work, includes a number of relatively literal translations of several poems from the twelfth-century *Buile Suibhne* (Frenzy of Sweeney), but O'Brien also composed a handful of poetic translations from the Irish.

'Scel lem duib'
(The original dates to the ninth century. For George Sigerson's version, see p. 143.)

Here's a song –
stags give tongue
winter snows
summer goes.

High cold blow
sun is low
brief his day
seas give spray.

Fern clumps redden
shapes are hidden
wildgeese raise
wonted cries.

Cold now girds
wings of birds
icy time –
that's my rime.[68]

Original: 'Dom-fharcai
fidbaide fál'

Literal translation:

Dom-fharcai fidbaide fál;
    fom-chain loíd luin, lúad nád
        cél;
úas mo lebrán ind línech,
    fom-chain trírech inna n-én.

A hedge of trees guards me;
    a blackbird's song sings to me, an uttering I
        will not hide;
above my lined book
    the trill of birds sings to me.

Fom-chain coí menn, medair
    mass,
    i mbrott glass di dingnaib doss –
dé bráth nom Choimmdiu coíma!
    cáin-scríbaimm fo roída ross.[69]

A clear-voiced cuckoo sings to me, a goodly
    speech,
    in a grey cloak from a fortress of bushes –
on the day of judgment may the Lord God keep me!
    I write pleasingly under the forest wood.

'Domforcai Fidhbaidae Fál'
(The original dates to the ninth century.)

A hedge before me, one behind,
a blackbird sings from that,
above my small book many-lined
I apprehend his chat.

Up trees, in costumes buff
mild accurate cuckoos bleat,
Lord love me, good the stuff
I write in a shady seat.[70]

<table>
<tr><td>

Original: 'Liam Ó Raghallaigh'

I.

An cumhan libhse an oíche úd, bhí an
   tsráid seo lán de eachraí
Ag sagairt is ag bráithrí agus iad ag trácht
   ar ar mbanais?
Bhí an fhidil ar clár ann agus an
   chláirseach dá spreagadh
Agus bhí triúr de na mnáibh bána ann le
   mo ghrá geal a chur ar leabaidh.

II.

'Mo bhaintreach is 'mo mhaighdean a
   fágadh mé go hóg,
Agus tabhair scéal ag mo mhuintir gur
   báthadh mo mhíle stór.
Dhá mbeinn ar an trá an lá sin agus mo
   dhá láimh bheith sa scód,
M'fhocal duit, a bhean Uí Raghallaigh, is
   deas a leigheasfainn do bhrón.

III.

Ní hionadh scéal cráite a bheith ag do
   mháthair is ag t'athair,
Is ag banaltra na gcíocha bán a bhíodh ag
   trácht[a] ort is tú 'do leanbh.
Ní áirím do bhean phósta nár chóirigh
   riamh do leabaidh,
Is ó chuaigh tú 'un na tráighe an lá sin, mo
   léan gur sháraigh ort a thíocht
   abhaile.

IV.

Is níor mhór liom do Liam Ó Raghallaigh a
   bheith 'na chliamhain ag an rí,
Agus cuirtíní geala gléigeala ar gach taobh
   de ins an oích';
Maighdean chiúin chéillí a bheith ag
   réiteach a chinn,
Agus ó luaidheadh sinn le chéile, is trua
   mar d'éag tú le mo linn.

V.

Tá do shúilí ag na péiste agus do bhéal ag
   na portáin,
Tá do dhá láimh gheala ghléigeala faoi
   ghéarsmacht na mbradán;
Cúig phunt a bhéarfainn don té a
   thóigfeadh mo dhianghrá,
Ach 'sé mo léan thú bheith t'aonraic, Neilí
   Ghléigeal Nic Shiúrtain.

</td><td>

Literal translation:

I.

Do you remember that evening, this street
   was full of horses,
With priests and with brothers and they trav-
   eling to our wedding?
The fiddle was on the board there and the
   harp encouraging it,
And there were three of the fair women there
   to lay out my bright love.

II.

I was left young, a widow and a maiden
And take the news to my people that my
   thousand-times love was drowned.
If I were on the strand that day and my two
   hands on the sheet,
My word to you, wife of Ó Raghallaigh, it is
   nicely that I would have cured your
   sorrow.

III.

It is no wonder that your mother and your
   father have a pitiful report,
And the nurse of the fair breasts who used to
   suckle you when you were a baby.
Not to mention your wedded wife who never
   arranged your bed,
And since you went to the strand that day, my
   sorrow that it failed you to come
   home.

IV.

And I did not begrudge Liam Ó Raghallaigh
   being a son-in-law to the king,
And bright, brilliant curtains on every side of
   him in the evening;
A quiet, sensible maiden to be combing his
   hair,
And since we were engaged to one another, it
   is a pity that you died in my time.

V.

The sea-serpents have your eyes and the crabs
   have your mouth,
Your two bright, brilliant hands are under the
   sharp rule of the salmon;
Five pounds I would carry to whomever
   would raise up my fond love,
But it is my grief you to be alone, Neilí
   Ghléigeal Nic Shiúrtain.

</td></tr>
</table>

Donagh MacDonagh
(1912–1968)

Perhaps known best for his ballad opera *Happy as Larry*, Donagh MacDonagh wrote out of a deep interest in folklore, and many of his verse translations draw on folk tradition. In reference to one of his translations, MacDonagh said, 'This, like the other poems "after the Irish", is rather an adaptation than a direct translation.'[71] MacDonagh was the son of Thomas MacDonagh.

'The Day Set for Our Wedding'

(The original, 'Liam Ó Raghallaigh,' is said to have been written in northwest Co. Mayo, probably in the eighteenth century, and concerns a man who was drowned in Sruwaddacon Bay while rowing home to his new bride, having taken the priest who married them back to his village.)

> The day set for our wedding
> The town was full of horses,
> There were priests and brothers murmuring
> The words of the marriage service,
> The feast upon the table,
> The harp and charming fiddle,
> Little the bridesmaids thought then
> That they'd lay out my darling.

> Take tidings to my people
> That the sea has widowed me
> And that my love who lightened
> The air at any meeting,
> Who would have been well mated
> With the King of France's daughter
> Is heavy on the bed
> They decked out for our bridal.

Original: 'Liam Ó Raghallaigh' (cont.)

Literal translation (cont.):

VI.

Beannacht Dé don triúr a chuaigh go Cill Eanainn

Ag íolacan an Athar Peadar bhí in aois a cheithre fichid.

Dhá dtigteá faoi cheann míosa – ach, mo léan choíche, ní thiocfaidh,

Agus nach trua sin bean san oíche, agus a caoifeach i mbarr toinne.

VI.

The blessing of God on the three who went to Cill Eanainn

As payment to Father Peadar who was eighty years old.

If you would come in a month's time – but, my love forever, will not come about,

And isn't it a pity for a woman in the evening, and her companion among the waves.

VII.

Mo mhallacht do na saortha a rinne an bád,

Nachar aithris dom féin go raibh an t-éag insna cláir!

Dá dtéitheá go Coill Tóchair agus an t-adhmad a cheannacht daor,

Ní báifí mo stórsa ar chóstaí *Malbay*.[72]

VII.

My curse on the craftsmen who made the boat,

You didn't tell me that death was in the boards!

If you had gone to Coill Tóchair to buy the wood dear,

My own love would not be drowned on the coast of Mal Bay.

---

[a] The literal translation assumes *a' tál* for *ag trácht*, as in *Blas Meala*.

Original: 'An Draighneán Donn'

Literal translation:

Síleann ceud fear gur leó féin mé nuair ólaim lionn,

'S téidhean dhá dtrian síos díom ag cuímhne ar do chomhrádh liom;

Sneachta séidhte 's é d'a shíor-chur ar Sliabh na mBan fionn,

'S tá mo ghrádh-sa mar bhláth na n-áirne ar an draighneán donn.

A hundred men think that I am theirs when I drink ale,

And two-thirds go down from me, remembering your conversation with me;

The blown snow and it forever falling on fair Sliabh na mBan,

And my love is like a sloe-blossom on the blackthorn.

Dá mbéinn am bhádóir is deas do shnámhfainn an fhairge anonn,

'S do sgríbhfinn chugat líne le bárr mo pheann;

Faraoir geur! gan mé a's tú a chráidh mo chroidhe

I ngleanntán sléibhe le h-éirghe gréine 's an drúcht 'na luighe!

If I were a boatman, it is well I would swim the sea over,

And I would write you a line with the tip of my pen;

Woe is me! heart torn with anguish, that you and I are not

In the small glen of the mountain at sunrise and the dew settling!

Cuirim féin mo mhíle slán leat, a bhaile na gcrann,

'S gach baile eile dá mbíodh mo thriall ann;

Is iomdha bealach fliuch, salach agus bóithrín cam

'Tá idir mé 'gus an baile 'na bhfuil mo stóirín ann!

I give my thousand farewells to you, town of the trees,

And every other town to which I used to journey;

Many is the wet, dirty way and twisted small road

That is between me and the town my little treasure is in!

The monsters have his eyes
And crabs the mouth that kissed me,
His two, bright, white hands
Devoured by the great salmon,
His curls tangled with salt
Are all the sea has spared me –
And may they rot, the botches
Who built the boat that drowned him.[73]

'A Hundred Men Think'

(The original, 'An Draigneán Donn' ['The Blackthorn'], occurs in many different versions. It has been argued that the poem originated in Co. Roscommon, in the area around Ballinlough, and in some versions, the name Sliabh Uí Fhloinn appears, apparently referring to a hill between Ballinlough and Castlerea to the east. But in other versions, the place-name Sliabh na mBan appears, which may refer to Slievenamon, just northeast of Clonmel, in Co. Tipperary. The poem has been dated to the beginning of the eighteenth century. For Padraic Colum's translation, see pp. 213–215.)

A hundred men think when I drink drink for drink with them,
Clink glasses, sing, laugh and talk, nod and wink with them,
That I'm in their company, one of the boys with them,
But always my darling can steal all my thoughts from them.

The snow that is light and is white on the mountain,
The sloe-blossom bright as the spray of the fountain
Are dimmed by my darling, and would we were skimming
Away on the ocean, or safe on the high hills.

One curse on your father and ten on your mother
Too bothered to learn how we must be together,
And curse them, that never taught sense to their daughter
To read in my hand-lines the scroll of her Charter.

Original: 'An Draighneán Donn' (cont.)	Literal translation (cont.):
Tabhair do mhallacht do t'athair 's dod' mháthairín féin,	Give your curse to your father and to your little mother herself,
Nár thug beagán tuigsiona dhuit mo láimh do léigheamh;	Who gave little understanding of your considering my hand;
Is moch ar maidin chuirfinn chughatsa brígh mo sgéil,	It is early in the morning I would send to you the meaning of my message,
Bíodh mo bheannacht agat go gcasfar ort i n-uaigneas mé.	My blessing on you that will meet me in a lonely place.
A Mhuire dhíleas! creud do dheunfadh má imthighean tú uaim!	Dear Mary! what will I do if you go from me!
Ní'l eolus chum do thighe agam, do theaghlaigh, ná do chlúid;	I don't know the way to your house, your family, or your bed;
Tá mo mháthairín faoi leath-trom 's m'athair san uaigh,	My little mother is under oppression and my father in the grave,
Tá mo mhuintir ar fad a bhfearg liom, 's mo ghrádh a bhfad uaim!	All my people are angry with me, and my love far from me!
Má's ag imtheacht atáir uaim anois, a mhúirnín, go bhfilleadh tú slan!	If you are going from me now, sweetheart, may you return safe!
Is dearbhtha gur mhairbh tú mo chroidhe in mo lár;	It is certain that you killed my heart in my breast;
Ní'l coite agam do chuirfinn ad' dhiagh, ná bád,	I haven't a skiff in which I would set out after you, or a boat,
Tá an fhairge na tuilte eadrainn 's ní h-eól dom snámh.[74]	The sea is in flood between us and I don't know how to swim.

Original: 'Jackeen ag Caoineadh na mBlascaod', by Brendan Behan	Literal translation:
Beidh an fharraige mhór faoi luí gréine mar ghloine,	The great sea will be under the setting sun like glass,
Gan bád faoi sheol ná comhartha beo ó dhuine	Without a boat under sail or a sign of life from a person
Ach an t-iolar órga deireanach thuas ar imeall	But the last golden eagle up on the edge
An domhain, thar an mBlascaod uaigneach luite . . .	Of the world, beyond the lonely, unused Blaskets . . .
An ghrian ina luí is scáth na hoíche á scaipeadh	The sun setting and shades of the night spreading
An ardú ré is í ag taitneamh i bhfuacht trí scamaill,	The rising moon and it shining in coldness through clouds,
A méara loma sínte síos ar thalamh	Its naked fingers stretched down to earth
Ar thithe scriosta briste, truamhar folamh . . .	On ruined, broken houses, pitiful, empty . . .
Faoi thost ach cleití na n-éan ag cuimilt thar tonna	In silence except for the feathers of the birds stroking over waves
Buíoch as a bheith fillte, ceann i mbrollach faoi shonas,	Thankful to be back, head in breast, happy,
Séideadh na gaoithe ag luascadh go bog leathdhorais	The blowing of the wind swinging gently a half-door,
Is an teallach fuar fliuch, gan tine, gan teas, gan chosaint.[75]	And the cold, wet hearth, without fire, without heat, without protection.

The village, the trees and the fields that surround you
Have my blessings and love as the spot where I found you,
For I'm led far astray from the spot that I'm bound to
By the damp, dirty roads and bohereens that I pound.

And what will I do if you go roving from me,
Or where find your new home, your town or your county?
The river is rising, the sea in flood round me
And I cannot swim to you. Come waves and drown me.[76]

'The Jackeen's Lament for the Blaskets'

(The original was written by Brendan Behan in 1948,
when he was in Mountjoy Gaol.)

The sea will be under the sun like an empty mirror,
No boat under sail, no sign of a living sinner
And nothing reflected but one golden eagle, the last,
On the edge of the world beyond the lonely Blaskets.

The sun will be setting, the shadows of night dispersing
As the rising moon shines down through the sea-cold night cloud,
Her long, bare fingers stretched down to the empty earth
And the houses fallen and ruined and broken apart.

The only sounds the hush of the birds' soft feathers
Skimming over the water, returning safe and together,
And the wind as it sighs and softly swings the half-door
Mourning a hearth that is cold for ever more.[77]

Contemporary
Ireland

Original: 'Duibhe id mhailghibh'

Duibhe id mhailghibh, gríos id ghruad-
   haibh,
   Gurma id roscaibh, réidhe it fholt,
Gaoth ag iomramh do chúil chraob-
   haigh,
   Úidh fhionnbhan an aonaigh ort.

Mná   fear   nach   aidmheóchadh
   t'fhéachain
   Ar h'aghaidh ag fighe a bhfolt;
Slighe   ag   méaraibh   tré   dhlaoi
   dhaghfhuilt
   Ag mnaoi ag déanamh amhairc
   ort.[1]

Literal translation:

Blackness in your eyebrows, embers in your
   cheeks,
   Blueness in your eyes, smoothness in your
   hair,
Wind coursing through your flowing head of
   hair,
   The attention of fair women of the fair on
   you.

Married women who would not acknowledge
   looking at you
   Over their faces plaiting their hair;
A path with fingers through a lock of pleasing
   hair
   By a woman taking a view of you.

Original: 'An bhean dob' annsa liom fán ngréin', by Piaras Feiritéar

An bhean dob' annsa liom fán
   ngréin,
   Is nárbh' annsa léi mé féin ar bith,
'Na suidhe ar ghualainn a fir féin,
   Ba chruaidh an chéim is mé istigh.

An guirtín branair do rinneas dom féin,
   Is mé bhfad i bpéin 'na bhun,
Gan ag an bhfear a tháinig indé,
   Acht a fhuirse dó féin 's a chur.

Má rinnis branar gan síol
   Is fear maith den tír uait 'na
   bhun
A fhreagras an Mhárta san am chóir
   Is a fhreastalas dóigh le n-a chur –

Literal translation:

The woman who was dearest to me under the
   sun,
   And to whom I myself was not dear at all,
Sitting at the shoulder of her own man,
   The position was hard and I inside.

The little fallow field that I made for myself,
   And I long in pain about it,
Only for the man who came yesterday,
   To harrow and sow for himself.

If you made a fallow field without seed
   A good man of the country around you is
   about it
Who responds to March at the proper time
   And prepares a way for his sowing –

Máire Mhac an tSaoi
(1933–)

Many of Máire Mhac an tSaoi's verse translations from the Irish reflect the theme of sexual passion in the Irish-language tradition. Born in Dublin, educated at University College Dublin and the Sorbonne, Mhac an tSaoi spent much time as a child in the Kerry Gaeltacht.

'Black Eye-Brow'

Black eye-brow and the cheek an ember glowing,
    Blue eye beneath the glossy head of hair,
Wind-ruffled now – O lad, 'tis easy knowing
    Whom women's glances follow at this fair.

And she whose wedded eye dares not to linger,
    Shaking the loosened locks about her face,
Lifts up the silken lattice with a finger,
    To gaze her fill, unguessed at by disgrace.[2]

'The Woman that I Loved the Most'

(The original is by Piaras Feiritéar, a seventeenth-century poet from the Dingle peninsula in Co. Kerry whose poetry draws on many of the courtly love conventions of Renaissance Europe.)

    The woman that I loved the most,
        Did never hold me worth a pin,
    But, by the shoulder of my host,
        Sat wed – harsh stroke! – and I within.

    The little fallow field I broke,
        Long labouring, for myself alone –
    Came yesterday one from the road,
        Harrowed and sowed it for his own.

    If you should leave the tilth unsown,
        Trust not your neighbour for the yield,
    Responsive to the call of March
        And prompt to set the crop in field –

Original: 'An bhean dob' annsa liom fán ngréin', by Piaras Feiritéar (cont.)

Literal translation (cont.):

Is mairg do-ní branar go bráth
    Is ná beir fás fada dá chuid féir,

Unhappy is [he who] makes fallow always
    And who does not bring long growth to his grass;

Is an tan do chuadhas-sa i bhfad
    Gur coilleadh mo nead thar m'éis.

It is the time that I went far away
    That my nest was robbed behind me.

Da mbudh duine mise raghadh i bhfad,
    Is d'fhágfadh mo nead thar m'éis,
Do chuirfinn anál fá n-a bruach
    Do chuirfeadh a fuath ar gach éan.

If I were a person who would go far away,
    And would leave my nest behind me,
I would put a breath around its edge
    That would make every bird abhor it.

Cumann go dté a sac i sac
    Ní dhéan feasta ar eagla an bháis;
Is é do bheir mo chroidhe 'na ghual
    An grá fuar a bhíos ag mná.

Until love goes packed in a sack
    I never again do [anything] for fear of death;
It is that which brought my heart to coal
    The cold love that a woman has.

Is mairg atá mar atáim,
    Is mairg do bheir grá leamh,
Is mairg do bheas gan mnaoi
    Is dhá mhairg ag ná bíonn ach bean.[3]

It is a pity that I am as I am,
    It is a pity that I gave soft-witted love,
It is a pity to be without a woman
    And two pities he who has only one woman.

Original: 'Bean an Fhir Rua'

Literal translation:

Tá siad á rá gur tú sáilín socair i mbróig,

They are saying that you are a quiet, little heel in a shoe,

Tá siad á rá gur tú béilín tana na bpóg,

They are saying that you are a thin little mouth of the kisses,

Tá siad á rá, a mhíle grá, go dtug tú dom cúl –

They are saying, thousand-times love, that you gave your back to me –

Cé go bhfuil fear le fáil, gur leis an dtáilliúir Bean an Fhir Rua.

Although a husband is available, that the Wife of the Red-Haired Man is with the tailor.

Do thugas naoi mí i bpríosún ceangailte cruaidh,

I spent nine months in prison bound tightly,

Boltaí ar mo chaolaibh agus míle glas as súd suas;

Bolts on my ankles and a thousand locks from there upward;

Thabharfainnse síog mar a thabharfadh an eala cois cuain

I would make a swath like that which the swan by a harbour would make

Le fonn a bheith sínte síos le Bean an Fhir Rua.

With longing to be lying down with the Wife of the Red-Haired Man.

Shaoileas-sa, a chéadsearc, go mbeadh aointíos idir mé agus tú,

I thought, a hundred-times love, that you and I would be living under one roof,

Agus shaoileas 'na dhéidh sin go mbréagfá mo leanbh ar do ghlúin;

And I thought after that that you would soothe my child on your knee;

Mallacht Rí Néimhe ar an té sin a bhain díom mo chlú,

The curse of the King of Heaven on that person who took from me my reputation,

Sin, agus uile go léir, lucht bréige[a] idir mé agus tú.

That, and entirely, who put a load of falsehood between me and you.

My curse on him who breaks a clod
      Nor leaves his green sod fallow lay,
For when that I was called abroad
      My nest of eggs was robbed away.

If I were wont abroad to go
      And leave my nest perforce behind,
About its edge a breath I'd blow
      Would make it loathed of birdly kind.

Till love like coal go packed in sack
      All pacts of love I do reprove;
My heart's turned cinder, burnt and black,
      On the cold slack of woman's love.

O pity him who must repent
      A love misspent as I have done,
Pity the man who goes unwed –
      Pity instead who loves but one.[4]

'The Red-Haired Man Reproaches His Wife Who Has Left Him'
(The original is a well-known folk poem from Connacht.)

They are saying your little heel fits snugly in the shoe,
They are saying your lips are thin, and saying they kiss well too;
You might have had many's the man, if what they are saying is true,
When you turned your back on your own, but only the tailor would do!

I'd have you know, nine months I was tethered in gaol,
Bolts on my ankles and wrists and a thousand locks on the chain,
And yet, my flight would be swift as the homeward flight of the swan
To spend but a single night with the Wife of the Red-Haired Man!

And I thought, 'One home we will share, Beloved, for you and for me,'
And I thought, 'Tis you will sit there and coax my babe on your knee.'
Heaven's King's curse be on him who has taken away my good name!
So that lies, in the end of it all, separate us in shame.

Original: 'Bean an Fhir Rua' (cont.)	Literal translation (cont.):
Tá crann insa ghairdín ar a bhfásann duilliúr is bláth buí,	There is a tree in the garden on which grow leaves and yellow blossom,
Is an uair a leagaim mo lámh air ritheann an fhuil óm' chroí;	And when I lay my hand on it, the blood runs from my heart;
Mo shólás go bás, is é 'fháil ó na flaithis anuas,	My solace until death, and to get it down from heaven,
Aon phóigín amháin is é 'fháil ó Bhean an Fhir Rua.	One small kiss only and, to get it from the wife of the Red-Haired Man.
Ach go dtig lá an tsaoil 'na réabfar cnoic agus cuain,	But a day of the world is coming in which hills and harbours will be torn asunder,
Tiocfaidh smúit ar an ngréin 's beidh na néalta chomh dubh leis an ngual,	Gloom will come on the sun and the clouds will be as dark as the coal,
Beidh an fhairrge tirim is tiocfaidh na brónta 's an trua,	The sea will be dry and sorrows and pity will come,
'S beidh an táilliúir ag scréachaigh i ngeall ar Bhean an Fhir Rua.[5]	And the tailor will be screaming because of the Wife of the Red-Haired Man.

[a] The literal translation follows HYDE, which has *lucht bréige chuir* and ND-I, which has , *lucht bréige a chuir.*

A green tree grows in the garden, I lay my hand on the bark,
The flowers that it bears are yellow and the life-blood drains from my
      heart;
It would console me till death, like His grace from above that can,
If one small kiss I could get from the Wife of the Red-Haired Man!

There's a day in store for the world when harbour and hill will be riven,
When dust will smother the sun and coal-black clouds cover Heaven,
And pity and grief there will be in that day when the sea will run dry,
And remorse for the Wife of the Red-Haired Man will be loud in the
      tailor's cry![6]

Original: 'Iar mBriseadh Mo
Choise Féin Isan bhFraingc', by
Pádraigín Haicéad

A chos bheag shiubhalach, fuiling i
gclúid faoi chléith,
ós cor ag druidim níos goire dom
mhuirnín é;
dob olc 'na choimhideacht mise, dá
sbiúntaoi mé,
's a chos sin brisde, mun mbrisfinn mo
chrúibín féin.[7]

Literal translation:

Little traveling foot, endure in a covering under
concealment,
since it is a condition bringing closer to me my
beloved;
I would be a bad companion, if I were exam-
ined,
and that foot broken, if I would not break my
own little hoof.

Pearse Hutchinson
(1927–)

Pearse Hutchinson has translated poetry from a variety of European languages, and has written poetry in English and Irish. Born in Glasgow to Irish parents, he was educated in Dublin, and studied Castilian at University College Dublin. He lives in Dublin.

'After Breaking My Own Foot in France'

(The original is by Pádraigín Haicéad [1600?–1654], from Co. Tipperary. Haicéad lived in France following the collapse of various rebellions in the wake of the Cromwellian conquest of Ireland.)

> My little wandering limb the splint must thole:
> it brings me nearer my dear one to console.
> How poor a friend I'd be, examined home,
> if, his bone broken, I broke not my own.[8]

Original: 'Do chuala inné ag maoth-
lach muinteardha', by Pádraigín
Haicéad

Literal translation:

Do chuala inné ag maothlach muin-
teardha
mar nuadhacht scéil ó chéile Chuinn is
Chuirc
gur duairc le cléir an Ghaeilge ghrinnsh-
litheach,
suairceas séimh na saorfhear sinseardha.

I heard yesterday from a friendly, good-
natured person,
As news of a story from the spouse of Conn
and Corc,
that dismal to the clergy is the thoroughly
fluent Gaelic,
the subtle wit of the ancestral noblemen.

Ní bhuaileabh féin i gcléith a gcointinne

ó chuaigh an ré 'narbh fhéidir linn friotal

gach   smuaineadh   d'éirgheadh   d'éirim
m'intinne,
uair fár bhaoghal faobhar m'intleachta;

I myself will not strike at the flank of their con-
tention
since the time has gone in which was possible
for us the utterance
of every thought that would rise from the
vigour of my mind,
a time in which the edge of my intellect was a
danger;

go suaithfeadh sé gan saobhadh slimfhuin-
nimh
fá thuairim thaobh na gcléireach gcinsealach
nó anuas fá a mblaoscaibh maola mill-
teacha
crua-ghlac ghéar do ghaethibh innlithe.

that it would toss about, without dissipating
pliant energy,
toward the flank of the dominant clerics
or down around their bald, pernicious
skulls
a sharp, hard fistful of ready darts.

Thomas Kinsella
(1927–)

No contemporary Irish poet has argued as forcefully for under-
standing Irish poetry as a dual tradition than has Thomas Kinsella.
Irish poetry, Kinsella has said, is always 'a matter of two linguistic
entities in dynamic interaction, of two major bodies of poetry asking
to be understood together as functions of a shared and painful
history'.[9] Perhaps because of this view, Kinsella's verse translations
tend to be relatively conservative; in the preface to his bi-lingual col-
lection *An Duanaire 1600–1900: Poems of the Dispossessed* (1981),
Kinsella says that the chief aim of the book 'is to demonstrate the
nature and quality of a part of the Irish poetic tradition', and his trans-
lations, he says, strive for 'the greatest possible fidelity of content'.[10]

Kinsella was born in Dublin and educated at University College
Dublin. He has taught at several universities in the United States, and
divides his time between Ireland and America.

'I Heard from a Decent Man the Other Day'

*On hearing it has been ordered in the chapterhouses of Ireland that the friars
make no more songs or verses.*

(The original is by Pádraigín Haicéad [1600?–1654], a Co. Tipperary
poet who supported various rebellions against the Cromwellian con-
quest of Ireland.)

> I heard from a decent man the other day
> a piece of news from the 'spouse of Conn and Corc':[11]
> that the Church condemns our Gaelic's subtle paths,
> the polished pleasure of our noble fathers.
>
> I will not spring at the flank of their argument
> now that the time is past when I could utter
> each thought erupting from the scope of my mind
> – when the edge of my intellect was a thing to fear
>
> showering with no loss of pliant force
> into the general flank of those arrogant priests
> or down on top of their bald malignant skulls
> a hard sharp fistful of accomplished darts.

Original: 'Do chuala inné ag
maothlach muinteardha',
by Pádraigín Haicéad (cont.)

Literal translation (cont.):

Fuaifidh mé mo bhéal le sring fhite
's ní luaifead réad dá bpléid bhig sprion-
laithe,
ach fuagraim tréad an chaolraigh chuim-
sithe
's a bhfuath, a Dhé, tar éis mo mhuintire.[12]

I will sew my mouth with a woven string
and I will not mention a thing of their small,
miserly wrangling,
but I denounce the herd of narrow extrem-
ists
and their hatred, Oh God, for my people.

Original: 'An cuimhin leat
an oíche úd'

Literal translation:

An cuimhin leat an oíche úd
    a bhí tú ag an bhfuinneog,
gan hata gan láimhe
    dod dhíon, gan chasóg? –
do shín mé mo lámh chughat
    's do rug tú uirthi barróg,
is d'fhan mé id chomhluadar
    nó gur labhair an fhuiseog.

Do you remember that night
    that you were at the window,
without a hat, without gloves
    for your protection, without a cloak? –
I stretched my hand to you
    and you gripped it tightly,
and I stayed in your company
    until the lark spoke.

An cuimhin leat an oíche úd
    a bhí tusa agus mise
ag bun an chrainn chaorthainn
    's an oíche ag cur cuisne,
do cheann ar mo chíocha
    is do phíob gheal á seinm? –
is beag a shíleas an oíche úd
    go scaoilfeadh ár gcumann.

Do you remember that night
    that you and I were
at the base of the rowan tree
    and the night getting a frost,
your head on my breasts
    and your bright pipe playing? –
it is little I thought that night
    that our love would come undone.

A chumainn mo chroí istigh,
    tar oíche ghar éigin
nuair luífidh mo mhuintir
    chun cainte le chéile;
beidh mo dhá láimh id thimpeall
    's mé ag insint mo scéil duit –
's gurb é do chomhrá suairc mín tais
    a bhain radharc fhlaithis Dé díom.

Love of my inner heart,
    come some night soon
when my people will be in bed
    to talk together;
My two arms will be around you
    and I telling my story to you –
and it was your pleasant, sweet, gentle conver-
    sation
    that took the sight of God's heaven from me.

Tá an tine gan coigilt
    is an solas gan múchadh,
tá an eochair faoin doras
    is tarraing go ciúin í,
tá mo mháthair 'na codladh
    is mise im dhúiseacht,
tá m'fhortún im dhorn
    is mé ullamh chun siúil leat.[13]

The fire is unraked
    and the light not extinguished,
the key is under the door
    and draw it softly,
my mother is asleep
    and I am awake,
my fortune is in my fist
    and I am ready to go with you.

I will stitch my mouth up with a twisted string
and say no word about their mean complaining,
merely condemn the herd of narrow censors
and the hate they bear my people, O my God.[14]

'Remember that Night'

(The original of this translation probably comes from Co. Clare or
Co. Limerick.)

Remember that night
    and you at the window
with no hat or glove
    or coat to cover you?
I gave you my hand
    and you took and clasped it
and I stayed with you
    till the skylark spoke.

Remember that night
    when you and I
were under the rowan
    and the night was freezing?
Your head on my breasts
    and your bright-pipe playing . . .
I little thought then
    that our love could sever.

My heart's beloved
    come some night soon
when my people sleep,
    and we'll talk together.
I'll put my arms round you
    and tell you my story
– O your mild sweet talk
    took my sight of Heaven!

The fire is unraked
    and the light unquenched.
The key's under the door
    – close it softly.
My mother's asleep
    and I am awake
my fortune in hand
    and ready to go.[15]

Original: 'Cé sin ar mo thuama?'   Literal translation:

Ise: 'Cé sin ar mo thuama   She: 'Who is that on my tomb
            nó an buachaill den tír tú?'   are you a boy of the country?'
Eisean: 'Dá mbeadh barr do dhá lámh He: 'If I could have the advantage of your
          agam   two hands
            ní scarfainn leat choíche.'   I would never release you.'
Ise: 'A áilleáin agus a ansacht,   She: 'Beauty and beloved,
            ní ham duitse luí liom –   it is not time for you to lie with me –
          tá boladh fuar na cré orm,   the cold smell of the clay is on me,
            dath na gréine is na gaoithe.'   the colour of the sun and of the wind.'

Eisean: 'Tá clog ar mo chroí istigh,   He: 'A blister is on my heart,
            atá líonta le grá duit,   which is filled with love for you,
          lionndubh taobh thíos de   a melancholy beneath it
            chomh ciardhubh le hairne'.   as jet-black as a sloe.'
Ise: 'Má bhaineann aon ní duit   She: 'If anything happens to you
            is go gcloífeach an bás tú,   and death would subdue you,
          beadsa im shí gaoithe   I will be a sudden blast of wind
            romhat thíos ar na bánta.'   before you down on the leas.'

Eisean: 'Nuair is dóigh le mo mhuintir He: 'When it seems to my people
            go mbímse ar mo leaba,   that I am in my bed,
          ar do thuama a bhím sínte   on your tomb I am stretched
            ó oíche go maidin,   from night until morning,
          ag cur síos mo chruatain   describing my hardships
            is ag crua-ghol go daingean,   and crying hard intensely,
          trí mo chailín ciúin stuama   for my gentle, modest girl
            do luadh liom 'na leanbh.'   who was pledged to me as a child.'

Ise: 'An cuimhin leat an oíche úd   She: 'Do you remember that night
            a bhíos-sa agus tusa   that I and you were
          ag bun an chrainn droighnigh   at the base of the blackthorn tree
            is an oíche ag cur cuisne?   and the night getting a frost?
          Céad moladh le hÍosa   A hundred praises to Jesus
            nach ndearnamar an mil-   that we made no spoiling,
          leadh,
          is go bhfuil mo choróin   and that my crown of maidenhood is
          mhaighdeanais
            'na crann soilse os mo   a beam of light before me.'
          choinne.'

'Who Is That on My Grave?'

(For a nineteenth-century version of the original, see 'From the Cold
Sod That's O'er You', by Edward Walsh, pp. 115–117.)

She: 'Who is that on my grave?
    A young man of this place?'
He: 'Could I touch your two hands
    I would never let go.'
She: 'My darling and sweet one
    this is no time to lie here:
I smell of cold earth,
    I am sun- and wind-coloured.'

He: 'There's a sore on this heart
    that is full of your love,
and a dark mood beneath it
    jet-black as the sloe.'
She: 'But if anything threatens
    and death overcomes you
a wind-gust I'll be
    on the fields out before you.'

He: 'When my people imagine
    that I'm in my bed
I am stretched on your grave
    from night until morning,
recounting my woes
    crying cruel and hard
for the gentle wise girl
    promised mine as a child.'

She: 'Remember that night
    when yourself and myself
were under the thorn
    and the night was freezing?
Hundred praises to Jesus
    we committed no harm
and my virginal crown
    is a bright light before me.'

Original: 'Cé sin ar mo thuama?' (cont.)

Eisean: 'Tá na sagairt is na bráithre
gach lá liom i bhfearg
de chionn a bheith i ngrá leat,
a Mháire, is tú marbh.
Dhéanfainn foscadh ar an ngaoith duit
is díon duit ón bhfearthainn,
agus cumha géar mo chroí-se
tú a bheith thíos ins an talamh.

'Tabhair do mhallacht dod mháithrín
is áirighse t'athair,
is a maireann ded ghaolta
go léireach 'na seasamh,
nár lig dom tú a phósadh
is tú beo agam id bheatha,
is ná hiarrfainn mar spré leat
ach mo léintín a ghealadh.'[16]

Literal translation (cont.):

He: 'The priests and the brothers are
every day angry with me
for being in love with you,
Máire, and you dead.
I would make a shelter from the wind for you
and protection for you from the rain,
and [it is] a sharp sorrow of my heart
for you to be down in the ground.

'Give your curse to your little mother
and include your father,
and your relations who are alive
all in their standing,
who did not allow me to marry you
and you alive with me in your life,
and I would not ask as a dowry for you
but my small shirt to brighten.'

Original: 'Ómos do John Millington Synge', by Máirtín Ó Direáin

An toisc a thug tú chun mo dhaoine
Ón gcéin mhéith don charraig gharbh
Bá chéile léi an chré bheo
Is an leid a scéith as léan is danaid.

Níor éistis scéal na gcloch,
Bhí éacht i scéal an teallaigh,
Níor spéis leat leac ná cill,
Ní thig éamh as an gcré mharbh.

Do dhuinigh Deirdre romhat sa ród
Is curach Naoise do chas Ceann Gainimh,
D'imigh Deirdre is Naoise leo
Is chaith Peigín le Seáinín aithis.

An leabhar ba ghnátha i do dhóid
As ar chuiris bréithre ar marthain;
Ghabh Deirdre, Naoise is Peigín cló
Is thug léim ghaisce de na leathanaigh.

Literal translation:

The circumstance that brought you to my people
From the fertile distance to the rough rock
Was identical with the living clay
And the hint escaping out of sorrow and regret.

You did not listen to the story of the stones,
Wonder was in the story of the hearth,
Head-stone or graveyard was of no interest for you,
Groaning did not come out of the dead clay.

Deirdre approached you in the road
And Naoise's currach turned Ceann Gainimh,
Deirdre and Naoise went off together
And Peigín cast reproach on Seáinín.

The book that usually was in your fist
Out of it you sent words that still live;
Deirdre, Naoise and Peigín took shape
And gave a hero's leap from the pages.

He: 'The priests and the friars
          are vexed every day
for my loving you, Mary,
          although you are dead.
I would shield you from wind
          and guard you from rain;
O my heart's bitter sorrow
          you are down in the earth.

'Give my curse to your mother
          and the same to your father
and all your relations
          left standing alive
who hindered our marriage
          while I had you in life
– I who'd ask no more dowry
          than to launder my shirt.'[17]

'Homage to John Millington Synge'

(The author of the original, Máirtín Ó Direáin [1910–1988], was a native of the Aran Islands.)

The thing that brought you among my people
from rich distance to rough rock
was something in the vital clay,
a trace escaping of woe and loss.

It was not from stone you took your stories,
but the wonders in stories by the fire;
not care for the stony cell or flag
– there are no groans out of dead ground.

Deirdre met you there on the road;
Naoise's *currach* turned Ceann Gainnimh.[18]
Deirdre and Naoise took their way
– and Pegeen was nagging at Shauneen.[19]

Always in your fist, that book . . .
You cast your words from it in a spell:
Deirdre, Naoise, Pegeen took shape
and gave a hero-leap from its pages.

Original: 'Ómos do John Millington
Synge', by Máirtín Ó Direáin
(cont.)

Literal translation (cont.):

Tá cleacht mo dhaoine ag meath,
Ní cabhair feasta an tonn mar fhalla,
Ach go dtaga Coill Chuain go hInis Meáin
Beidh na bréithre a chnuasaís tráth
Ar marthain fós i dteanga eachtrann.[20]

The practice of my people is declining,
Not a help henceforth is the wave as a wall,
But until Coill Chuain comes to Inis Meáin
The words that you gathered once will be
Alive still in a foreign tongue.

My people's way is failing fast,
the wave no longer a guarding wall.
But till Cuan Wood[21] comes to Inis Meán
the words you gathered here will be
alive still in a foreign tongue.[22]

Original: 'Mac ríg Múaide   Literal translation:
mid samraid'

Mac ríg Múaide mid samraid   The son of the king of the Moy in midsummer
fúair i fid úaine ingin: found in a green wood a daughter:
tucc dó mess ndub a draignib,   she gave him black fruit from blackthorns,
tuc airgib sub for sibnib.[23]   she gave an armful of strawberries on rushes.

Original: 'Ecne dergoir tarlastair'

Ecne dergoir tarlastair · lais tiar iar fuine ngréne
ra broinn Becnaiti baine · comba eisium a céle,
dia raibi ica fothracud il-Loch Lein.[24]

Literal translation:
A red-gold salmon came ·to the west after the setting of the sun
against the womb of fair Beccnat ·so that it was her husband,
the day she was bathing in Loch Lein.

John Montague
(1929–)

As cultural loss and dislocation are primary themes in John Montague's poetry, the tradition of translation from the Irish has a particular significance for him. 'What we find in the work of Mangan, Walsh, Ferguson, Callanan,' Montague has argued, 'is a racial sensibility striving to be reborn.'[25] Montague also says he came to see his local landscape of Co. Tyrone as 'a kind of primal Gaelteacht'.[26] Finally, Montague's interest in writing poetry about love and sexuality is rooted in the Irish-language tradition, which, as Montague has described it, approaches sexuality without inhibition, taking 'an enormous pleasure in the fact of sex'.[27]

Born in Brooklyn, New York, Montague was sent at the age of four to live with his aunts in Garvaghey, Co. Tyrone. He was educated at St. Patrick's College, Armagh, University College Dublin, and Yale University. In 1998 he was the inaugural occupant of the Ireland Chair of Poetry. He lives in West Cork.

'The son of the King of the Moy'
(The original dates to the seventh or eighth century.)

The son of the King of the Moy[28]
met a girl in green woods on midsummer's day:
she gave him black fruit from thorns
and the full of his arms
of strawberries, where they lay.[29]

'Sunset'

(The original comes from *Félire Óengusso Céli Dé* [*The Martyrology of Oengus the Culdee*], a calendar of saints' days composed by the monk Oengus in Tallaght, near Dublin, around the year 800. The *Félire* includes a quatrain for each day of the year. The text on which Montague's translation is based appears in a note to the quatrain for 7 April.)

In Loch Lene
a queen went swimming;
a redgold salmon
flowed into her
at full of evening.[30]

Original: 'Blodewedd', by Nuala Ní Dhomhnaill

Oiread is barra do mhéire a bhualadh orm
is bláthaím,
cumraíocht ceimice mo cholainne
claochlaíonn.
Is móinéar féir mé ag cathráil
faoin ngréin
aibíonn faoi thadhall do láimhe
is osclaíonn

mo luibheanna uile, meallta
ag an dteas
an sú talún is na falcaire fiain
craorag is obann, cúthail
i measc na ngas.
Ní cás duit
binsín luachra a bhaint díom.

Táim ag feitheamh feadh an gheimhridh
le do ghlao.
D'fheos is fuaireas bás
thar n-ais sa chré.
Cailleadh mo mhian collaí
ach faoi do bhos
bíogaim, faoi mar a bheadh as marbhshuan,
is tagaim as.

Soilsíonn do ghrian im spéir
is éiríonn gaoth
a chorraíonn mar aingeal Dé
na huiscí faoi,
gach orlach díom ar tinneall
roimh do phearsain,
cáithníní ar mo chroiceann,
gach ribe ina cholgsheasamh
nuair a ghaibheann tú tharam.

Suím ar feadh stáir i leithreas
na mban.
Éiríonn gal cumhra ó gach orlach
de mo chneas
i bhfianaise, más gá é a thabhairt
le fios,
fiú barraí do mhéar a leagadh orm
is bláthaím.[31]

Literal translation:

No more than the tip of your finger to touch me
and I blossom,
the chemical composition of my body
changes.
I am a meadow of grass maturing
under the sun
under the touch of your hand, ripen
and open

all my herbs, beguiled
by the heat
the strawberry and the scarlet pimpernels
blood-red and sudden, shy
in the midst of the stalks.
Well you may
a small bunch of rushes reap from me.

I have been waiting through the winter
for your call.
I withered and I died
back into the clay.
My sexual desire was lost
but under your palm
I rouse, as if it were out of a death-sleep,
and I come out of it.

Your sun shines in my sky
and a wind rises
that moves like an angel of God
the waters under it,
every inch of me ready
before your person,
goose-flesh on my skin,
every hair bristling, standing
when you go over me.

I sit for a spell in the toilet
of the women.
A fragrant whiff rises from every inch
of my skin
in evidence, if it is necessary to let it
be known,
laying even the tips of your fingers on me
and I blossom.

'Blodewedd'

(The original is by the contemporary poet Nuala Ní Dhomhnaill.)

At the least touch of your fingertips
I break into blossom,
my whole chemical composition
transformed.
I sprawl like a grassy meadow
fragrant in the sun;
at the brush of your palm, all my herbs
and spices spill open

frond by frond, lured to unfold
and exhale in the heat;
wild strawberries rife, and pimpernels
flagrant and scarlet, blushing
down their stems.
To mow that rushy bottom;
no problem.

All winter I waited silently
for your appeal.
I withered within, dead to all,
curled away, and deaf as clay,
all my life forces ebbing slowly
till now I come to, at your touch,
revived as from a deadly swoon.

Your sun lightens my sky
and a wind lifts, like God's angel,
to move the waters,
every inch of me quivers
before your presence,
goose-pimples I get as you glide
over me, and every hair
stands on end.

Hours later I linger
in the ladies toilet,
a sweet scent wafting
from all my pores,
proof positive, if a sign
were needed, that at the least
touch of your fingertips
I break into blossom.[32]

Original: 'Luibh na bhFear Gonta',   Literal translation:
      by Michael Davitt

Asal dall ag grágaíl –	A blind ass braying –
gach grág á saolú	delivering each bray
go mall anabaí.	slowly, prematurely.
Crúbálann leis	He paws on
i ngort síonbhriste	in a storm-broken field
ag b'lathaíl na bhfeochadán	smelling the thistles
is na neantóg	and the nettles
go n-aimseoidh luibh íce éigin	until some herb of healing will strike
a pholláire, á rá	his nostril, telling him
go bhfuil sí ann.[33]	that she is there.

'St John's Wort'
(The original is by the contemporary poet Michael Davitt.)

A blind ass brays –
each bray long delayed,
aborted.

He hobbles around
a weather-beaten field
snorting the thistles
and nettles

until some healing herb
will fill his nostril, announcing
she is there.[34]

Original: from 'Cois Taoibhe
Abhann Sínte', by Eoghan
Ruadh Ó Súilleabháin

Literal translation:

Mo mhíle creach, ba chneasta an stríapach í,

My thousand woes, she was the gentle harlot,

Do bhí sí i bhfad ag Art ag Niall 's ag Naois,

She was long with Art, with Niall and with Naois,

Do bhí sí seal ag fleadh na mBrianach ngroidhe,

She was a while at the feast of the spirited Brian,

Is ba mhín a cneas, gur chath an t-iasacht í.[35]

And her skin was smooth, until the foreigner used her.

Tom MacIntyre
(1931–)

Best known as a playwright and short-story writer, Tom MacIntyre published one collection of verse translations from the Irish, *Blood Relations*, in 1972. MacIntyre describes his translations, all of which are based on poems from the seventeenth and eighteenth centuries, as 'versions or adaptations'; his aim, he says, is 'to convey the gaiety of the poets in question clearly and faithfully'.[36]

MacIntyre was born in Co. Cavan and has taught at Clongowes Wood College and in the United States.

'Cathleen'

(The original is the final stanza – the *ceangal*, or binding – of an *aisling* [vision] poem by Eoghan Ruadh Ó Súilleabháin, the eighteenth-century Co. Kerry poet. In these poems, typically, a beautiful young woman representing the spirit of Ireland, and sometimes specifically identified as Caitlín ní Uallacháin, appears to the wandering poet, and prophesies the deliverance of Ireland from English rule.)

> Lovely whore though,
> Lovely, lovely whore,
> And choosy –
> Slept with Conn,
> Slept with Niall,
> Slept with Brian,
> Slept with Rory.
>
> Slide then,
> The long slide.
>
> Of course it shows.[37]

Original: 'Úr-Chnoc Chéin Mhic Cáinte', by Peadar Ó Doirnín

Literal translation:

A phlúr na maighdean is úire gné,
 Thug clú le scéimh ón Ádhamh-
chlainn,
A chúl na bpéarlaí, a rún na héigse,
 Dhúblaíos féile is fáilte;
A ghnúis mar ghréin i dtús gach lae
 ghil
Mhúchas léan le gáire,
Is é mo chumha gan mé is tú a shiúr,
 linn féin
San dún sin Chéin Mhic Cáinte.

Flower of the maidens of the freshest countenance,
 Who inherited honour with beauty from the
clan of Adam,
Head of the pearls, sweetheart of the poets,
 Who doubles hospitality and welcome;
Countenance like the sun at the start of every
 bright day
Who extinguishes grief with laughter,
It is my sorrow that you and I are not, sister, by
 ourselves
In that fortress of Cian Mac Cáinte.

Táim brúite i bpéin gan suan, gan
 néal,
De do chumha, a ghéag is áille;
Is gur tú mo roghain i gCúigibh
 Éireann –
Cúis nach séanaim ás de.
Dá siúlfá, a réalt gan smúid, liom féin,
 Ba súgach saor mo shláinte,
Gheobhair plúr is méad is cnuasach
 craobh
San dún sin Chéin Mhic Cáinte.

I am crushed in pain without repose, without sleep,
 From pining for you, most beautiful young
woman;
You are my choice in the provinces of Ireland
 –
A circumstance I don't deny a jot of.
If you would walk, star without mist, with me,
 My health would be cheerful, free,
You will get flour and mead and the fruit of
 branches
In that fortress of Cian Mac Cáinte.

Cluinfir uaill na ngadhar ar luas i
 ndéidh
Bhriain luaimnigh bhearnaigh mhá-
saigh,
Is fuaim guth béilbhinn cuach is smao-
lach
Suairc ar ghéaga in áltaibh;
I bhfuarlinn tséimh chífir sluabhuíon
 éisc
Ag ruagadh a chéile ar snámh ann,
Is an cuan gur léir dhuit uaid i gcéin
 Ón Úr-Chnoc Chéin Mhic Cáinte.

You will hear the howl of the hounds speeding
 after
Nimble, gap-toothed, large-thighed Brian,
And the sound of the sweet-mouthed voice of
 cuckoo and pleasant thrush
On branches in glens;
In a placid cold pool you will see a company of
 fish
Chasing each other swimming there,
And the harbour that will be clear to you in the
 distance
From the Green Hill of Cian Mac Cáinte.

A rún mo chléibh, is mar súd a b'fhearr
 dhuit –
Tús do shaoil a chaitheamh liom,
Is ní i gclúid faoi léan ag túirscín bréan
 I gcionn tuirne is péire cárdaí;
Gheobhair ciúl na dtéad le lúth na
 méar
Do do dhúscadh is dréachta grá fós,
Níl aon dún faoin ngréin chomh
 súgach aerach
Le hÚr-Chnoc Chéin Mhic Cáinte.

Sweetheart of my breast, it is this would be better
 for you –
The beginning of your life to spend with me,
And not in a nook under affliction from a foul churl
 Tending a spinning wheel and a pair of wool-
teasing cards;
You will get the music of the strings with the
 agility of fingers
For your awakening and songs of love yet,
No fortress under the sun as merry, airy
 As the Green Hill of Cian Mac Cáinte.

'On Sweet Killen Hill'

(The original is by Peadar Ó Doirnín, an eighteenth-century poet who
spent most of his life near Dundalk, Co. Louth. Killen Hill is just to
the northwest of Dundalk.)

Flower of the flock,
Any time, any land,
Plenty your ringlets,
Plenty your hand,
Sunlight your window,
Laughter your sill,
And I must be with you
On sweet Killen Hill.

Let sleep renegue me,
Skin lap my bones,
Love and tomorrow
Can handle the reins,
You my companion
I'd never breathe ill,
And I guarantee bounty
On sweet Killen Hill.

You'll hear the pack yell
As puss devil-dances,
Hear cuckoo and thrush
Pluck song from the branches,
See fish in the pool
Doing their thing,
And the bay as God made it
From sweet Killen Hill.

Pulse of my life,
We come back to – *mise*,
Why slave for McArdle[38] –
That bumbailiff's issue,
I've a harp in a thousand,
Love songs at will,
And the air is cadenza
On sweet Killen Hill.

Original: 'Úr-Chnoc Chéin Mhic
Cáinte', by Peadar Ó Doirnín
(cont.)

Literal translation (cont.):

A shuaircbhean tséimh na gcuachfholt
    péarlach,
    Gluais liom féin ar ball beag,
Tráth is buailte cléir is tuata i néal-
    taibh
    Suain faoi éadaí bána;
Ó thuaidh go mbéam i bhfad uathu
    araon
    Teacht nuachruth gréine amárach,
Gan ghuais le chéile in uaigneas
    aerach
    San uaimh sin Chéin Mhic Cáinte.[39]

Joyous, mild woman of the pearly curly
    locks,
    Come with myself in a little while,
The time the clergy and laity are overcome in
    clouds
    Of sleep under white cloths;
To the north until we both will be far from
    them
    At the coming of the new appearance of the
    sun tomorrow,
Without danger together in airy solitude
    In that grotto of Cian Mac Cáinte.

Gentle one, lovely one,
Come to me,
Now sleep the clergy,
Now sleep their care,
Sunrise will find us
But sunrise won't tell
That Love lacks surveillance
On sweet Killen Hill.[40]

Original: 'Marbhna Dhonnchadha Bháin'

Is ar an mbaile seo chonnaic sibh an t-iongnadh
Ar Dhonnchadh Bán is é dhá dhaoradh.
Bhí caipín bán air i n-áit a hata,
Is róipín cnáibe i n-áit a charabhata.

Tá mé ag teacht ar feadh na hoidhche
Mar bheadh uainín i measc seilbhe caorach,
Mo bhrollach fosgailte is mo cheann liom sgaoilte,
Is cá bhfuighinn mo dhearbhráithrín romham acht sínte?

Chaoin mé an chéad dreas ag gob an locha,
An dara dreas ag bun do chroiche,
An tríomhadh dreas os cionn do chuirp-se
I measg na nGall is mo cheann dá sgoilteadh.

Dá mbeitheá agam-sa san áit ar chóir dhuit,
Thíos i Sligeach nó i mBaile an Ródhba,
Brisfidhe an chroch, gearrfaidhe an rópa,
Is ligfidhe Donnchadh Bán a bhaile ar an eolas!

Literal translation:

It is in this town you saw the wonder
On Donnchadh Bán and he being condemned.
A small white cap was on him in place of his hat,
And a small rope of hemp in place of his cravat.

I've been coming through the night,
As a small lamb would be among a flock of sheep,
My bosom bared and my hair loosened,
And where would I find my dear brother before me but laid out?

I mourned the first bout at the mouth of the lake,
The second bout at the base of your gallows,
The third bout above your corpse
Among the foreigners and my head splitting.

If I had you in the place that was right for you,
Down in Sligo or in Ballinrobe,
The gallows would be broken, the rope would be cut,
And Donnchadh Bán would be allowed home on the knowledge!

Desmond O'Grady
(1935–)

Desmond O'Grady has translated from Irish, Welsh, Italian, Greek, Arabic, and Chinese, among others. His aim in translation has always been, he has said, to 'bring my Ireland into greater Europe and bring that greater Europe into Ireland'.[41] O'Grady knew Ezra Pound in Italy in the 1960s, and Pound's views on verse translation as a form of poetry in its own right, and on the verse translator as being free from scholarly constraints about literal accuracy, very much inform O'Grady's poetic translations. O'Grady has also cited the poetic translations of James Clarence Mangan as having exercised a strong influence on his work.

O'Grady was born in Limerick and educated at University College Dublin, and Harvard University. He has lived in Paris, Rome, and Cairo, and is currently living in Kinsale, Co. Cork.

'Donnagha White'

(The original is an elegy sung by a woman of the mountains for a young Connachtman hanged by the English. The identity of the victim is not known, although he has been associated both with the Fenians of the 1860s and with the White Boy movement of the late eighteenth century.)

This town has seen the wrong of a nation
In Donnagha White and his condemnation
His hat, the hood of those judged to die
And a hangman's noose, his collar and tie.

I've hurried all night without rest or sleep;
Like a spring lamb lost in a host of sheep;
With fear in my heart and fire in my head
To find my young brother[42] already dead.

I mourned you first at the mouth of the lake
And mourned you next at the gallows' stake,
I mourned again at the foot of your corpse
Among the British and the British curse.

If I only had you among your own
In Bally-na-Robe,[43] or in Sligo town,
The scaffold they'd break, the rope they'd sever
And you'd go home on your word of honour.

Original: 'Marbhna Dhonnchadha Bháin' (cont.)	Literal translation (cont.):

'S a Dhonnchadh Bháin, níorbh í an chroch badh dhual duit,
Acht dul chum an sgiobóil is t'easair do bhualadh,
An céachta d'iompódh deiseal is tuaithbheal,
'S an taobh dhearg de'n bhfód a chur i n-uachtar!

And Donnchadh Bán, it was not the gallows that was fitting for you,
But to go to the barn and do a spell of your threshing,
To turn the plough right and left,
And to put the red side of the sod on top!

A Dhonnchadh Bháin, a dhearbhráithrín dílis,
Is maith atá a fhios agam siúd do bhain díom thu,
Ag ól an chupáin, ag deargadh an phíopa,
'S ag siubhal na drúchta i gcuim na hoidhche.

Donnchadh Bán, fond dear little brother,
It is well I know those who took you from me,
Drinking the cup, reddening the pipe,
And walking the dew in the middle of the night.

A Mhic Uí Mhultháin, a sgiúrsa an mhí-áidh,
Ní laogh bó bradaighe do bhí in mo dhríotháir,
Acht buachaillín cruinn deas ar chnoc 's ar chnocán
A bhainfeadh fuaim go bog binn as camán!

Son of Ó Multháin, scourge of the bad luck,
No calf of a thieving cow was my brother,
But a perfect, fine, dear boy on mountain and on hillock
Who would take a sound softly, sweetly out of a hurley!

'S a Dhonnchadh Bháin, nach é sin an buaidhreadh,
'S a fheabhas is d'iomchróchthá spuir agus buatais!
Chuirfinn éadach faiseanta de'n éadach badh bhuaine
Is chuirfinn amach thú mar mhac duine uasail.

And Donnchadh Bán, is that not the sorrow,
How well it is you wore spurs and boots;
I would put [on you] fashionable clothes of the most enduring cloth
And I would send you out like a son of a nobleman.

A Mhic Uí Mhultháin, ná raibh do chlann mhac i bhfochair a chéile,
Ná do chlann inghean ag iarraidh spré ort! –
Tá dhá cheann an bhuird folamh, 's an t-urlár líonta,
Is Donnchadh Bán, mo dhearbhráithrín, sínte.

Son of Ó Multhán, may your sons not be in each other's company,
Or your daughters asking a dowry from you! –
The two tops of the table are empty, and the floor is full,
And Donnchadh Bán, my dear brother, laid out.

Tá spré Dhonnchadha Bháin ag teacht a bhaile,
Is ní ba, caoirigh é, ná capaill,
Acht tobac is píopaí is coinnealla geala,
Is ní dhá maoidheamh é ar lucht a gcaithte![44]

The dowry of Donnchadh Bán is coming home,
And it is not cattle, or sheep, or horses,
But tobacco and pipes and bright candles,
And those using them are not boasting about it!

If I only had you among your own
In Bally-na-Robe,[43] or in Sligo town,
The scaffold they'd break, the rope they'd sever
And you'd go home on your word of honour.

It was for no scaffold you were born –
But for cutting wheat and threshing corn,
For turning the plough both left and right
And turning the red clay into sight.

Dead brother Donnagha, honest and true
Well I know those who betrayed you;
Drinking the glass, sucking pipes bright
And stalking the dew in the middle night.

You, Mulhull, who struck this blow
My brother was no thieving cow,
But an honest man in thin and in thick
Who could knock a sweet tune from a hurling stick.

And Donnagha White – though the only truth
Was the grandeur and grace of buckets and boots –
We'll dress you up in fine home-spun
And send you out like a noble's son.

Mulhall, your sons were never united
And your daughters with dowries were never delighted!
The table is bare and the white boards full
With my brother, dead from a hangrope-pull.

The dowry of Donnagha is coming home
And it's not cattle nor spring crops sown,
But tobacco and pipes and candles bright –
And no boast dulls the candle light.[45]

Original: 'Clocán binn'   Literal translation:

Clocán binn   Melodious bell
benar i n-aidchi gaíthe: ringing on a windy night:
  ba ferr lim dola ina dáil   I would prefer to go in its company
indás i ndáil mná baíthe.[46]   than in the company of a wanton woman.

Original: 'Ba binne lium   Literal translation:
robháoi tan', from *Buile Suibhne*

        . . .   . . .

Ba binne lium robháoi tan   There was a time when more melodious to me
donálach na gcon alla,   was the yelping of the wild wolves,
ina guth cléirigh astoigh   than the voice of a cleric within
  ag meiligh is ag meigeallaigh.   bleating and whimpering.

Gidh maith libh-si i ttighibh óil   Although you like in drinking houses
bhar ccuirm leanna go n-onóir,   your ale-feast with pride,
ferr lium-sa deogh d'uisge i ngoid   I prefer a drink of water in theft
  d'ol dom bais asin tiopraid.   for drinking from my palm out of a well.

        . . .   . . .

Brendan Kennelly
(1936–)

Brendan Kennelly has argued that the English-speaking and Irish-speaking cultures of Ireland need to be seen 'as a compact imaginative unity',[47] and for Kennelly, translation provides an important means of trying to achieve that unity. A good translation, Kennelly says, 'is also a completely new, autonomous poem in English and is therefore an immediate and enduring part of the tradition.'[48]

Kennelly's interest in Irish-language poetry springs in part from his having been born and brought up in Co. Kerry. He has been Professor of Modern English at Trinity College Dublin since 1973.

'The Bell'

(The original is probably from the ninth century, and may have been written by a monk. For another version, see Robin Flower, p. 235.)

> I'd sooner keep my tryst
> With that sweet little bell
> The night of a bad winter mist
> Than risk a ravenous female.[49]

'The Wild Man and the Church'

(The original is one of the poems attributed to the madman Sweeney, in the medieval text *Buile Suibhne* (*Madness of Sweeney*). Suibhne, a king in Ulster, is put under a curse by a cleric named Ronan, and spends years living like a bird in tree-tops in various parts of Ireland while composing poems. For Robin Flower's translation of another of Sweeney's poems, see p. 235; for Seamus Heaney's version of still another, see pp. 343–345.)

> On the clean watercress
> I make a decent feast;
> Why should I sit at table
> With a bleating priest?
>
> I love the voices
> Of wolves in the dark glen;
> Not for me the gentle talk
> Of studious men.

Original: 'Ba binne lium robháoi   Literal translation (cont.):
tan', from *Buile Suibhne* (cont.)

Gidh maith libh-si an tsaill 's an fheóil   Although you like the bacon and the meat
caithter a ttighibh comhóil,   that are eaten in houses of carousal,
ferr lium-sa gas biorair ghloin   I prefer a bunch of clean watercress
d'ithe i n-ionadh gan chumaidh.[50]   for eating in a place without company.

With ceremony in their long halls
They drink and sing;
I cup cold water in my fist
From a pure spring.[51]

Original: 'Anocht is fúar an
snechta', from *Buile Suibhne*

Literal translation:

Anocht is fúar an snechta,
fodeachta is búan mo bhochta,
nidom neirt isin deabuidh
im geilt romgeoghuin gorta.

Tonight the snow is cold,
now my poverty is enduring,
there is not strength in me for conflict
in my madness famine wounds me.

Atchid cach nidom chuchtach,
as lom i snáth mo cheirteach,
Suibhne mh'ainm o Ros Ercain,
as misi an gealtán gealtach.

Everyone sees I am not powerful,
bare of thread are my rags,
Sweeney my name from Ros Earcain,
I am the crazed madman.

Nidom fois o thig aghaidh,
ni thaidlenn mo chois conair,
nocha bíu sonna a ccíana,
domeccad ialla omhain.

No rest for me when evening comes,
my foot does not touch a path,
I will not be here long,
bonds of fear come on me.

Mo bháire tar muir mbarcláin
ar ndol tar sáile soclán,
rogab time mo nertan,
as me gealtán Ghlinne Bolcáin.

My goal is beyond the sea full of boats
going over the sea full of prows,
fear has taken possession of my strength,
I am the madman of Glen Bolcain.

Seamus Heaney
(1939–)

Seamus Heaney's most substantial work in verse translation from the Irish consists of the poems in his version of *Buile Suibhne* (*Madness of Sweeney*), the medieval tale about an Ulster king who is put under a curse by a cleric named St. Rónán, and who spends years living like a bird in tree-tops in various parts of Ireland and composing poems. For Heaney, Sweeney can be seen as 'a figure of the artist, displaced, guilty, assuaging himself by his utterance', and *Buile Suibhne* as 'an aspect of the quarrel between free creative imagination and the constraints of religious, political, and domestic obligation'.[52]

Heaney's interest in the Sweeney story is also, in some ways, a product of personal geography. Born in the southeastern corner of Co. Derry, Heaney grew up near Sweeney's kingdom, supposedly in south Co. Antrim and north Co. Down. Heaney currently lives in Dublin.

'Tonight the snow is cold'

(For Robin Flower's translation of another of Sweeney's poems, see p. 235; for Brendan Kennelly's translation of still another, see pp. 339–341.)

> Tonight the snow is cold.
> I was at the end of my tether
> but hunger and bother
> are endless.
>
> Look at me, broken
> and down-at-heel,
> Sweeney from Rasharkin.[53]
> Look at me now
>
> always shifting,
> making fresh pads,
> and always at night.
> At times I am afraid.
>
> In the grip of dread
> I would launch and sail
> beyond the known seas.
> I am the madman of Glen Bolcain,[54]

Original: 'Anocht is fúar an snechta', from Buile Suibhne (cont.)	Literal translation (cont.):
Gaoth an reoidh ag mo rébadh, sneachta romleón go leige, as tsíon dom breith a n-éccuibh do géccuibh gacha geicce.	A frosty wind tearing at me, snow wounding me in the meantime, the storm bearing me to death from the branch of every limb.
Romgonsat géga glasa co rorébsat mo bossa, ni fargaibhset na dreasa damna creasa dom chossa.	Grey branches wound me they tear my palms, the briars do not leave material for a belt for my feet.
Ata crioth ar mo lámha tar gach mbioth fatha mbúaidre, do Slíabh Mis ar Slíabh Cuillenn, do Sléibh Cuillenn co Cuailgne.	A tremor is on my hands everywhere comes reason for confusion from Sliabh Mis to Sliabh Gullion, from Sliabh Gullion to Cooley.
As trúagh mo nuallán choidhche i mullach Cruachán Oighle, do Ghlinn Bolcain for Íle, do Chinn Tíre for Boirche.	My wail is wretched forever on the top of Cruachán Oighle, from Glen Bolcain to Islay, from Kintyre to Boirche.
Beg mo chuid o thig laa, ni thaét ar scath la noa, barr biorair Chluana Cille la gleorán Chille Cua.	Small my portion when day comes, it doesn't support for the good of a new day, a crop of watercress of Cluain Cille with the cuckoo-flower of Cill Cua.
An gen fil ag Ros Earcach ni thair imnedh na olcach, as edh dombeir gan nertach beith re sneachta go nochtach.[55]	The person who is at Rasharkin neither anxiety nor evil will come to him, what makes me without strength is being in snow in nakedness.

wind-scourged, stripped
like a winter tree
clad in black frost
and frozen snow.

Hard grey branches
have torn my hands,
the skin of my feet
is in strips from the briars

and the pain of frostbite
has put me astray,
from Slemish[56] to Slieve Gullion,[57]
from Slieve Gullion to Cooley.[58]

I went raving with grief
on the top of Slieve Patrick,[59]
from Glen Bolcain to Islay,[60]
from Kintyre[61] to Mourne.[62]

I waken at dawn
with a fasting spittle:
then at Cloonkill,[63] a bunch of cress,
at Kilnoo,[64] the cuckoo flower.

I wish I lived safe
and sound in Rasharkin
and not here, heartbroken,
in my bare pelt, at bay in the snow.[65]

Original: from 'Cúirt an Mheán-
Oíche', by Brian Merriman

Gan seilbh, gan saoirse ag síolrach
    seanda,
Gan cheannas i ndlí, gan chíos, gan
    cheannphort;
Scriosadh an tír agus níl ina ndiadh ann
In ionad na luibheanna ach fliodh 'is
    fiaile;
Na h-uaisle ab fhearr chun fáin mar
    leádar
Agus uachtar lámh ag fáslaigh saibhre,
Fealladh le fonn agus foghail gan
    féachaint,
Feannadh na lobhar 'san lom á
    léirscrios,
Is docharach dubhach mar d'fhúig gach
    daoirse
Go doilbhir dúr i ndubhcheart dlithe:

An fann gan feidhm ná faigheann ó aon
    neach
Ach clampar domhain agus luí chun
    léirscrios;
Fallsacht fear dlí agus fochnaoid airdnirt;

Cam 'is callaois, faillí 'is fábhar;
Scamall an dlí agus fíordhath fáinc-
    heart;
Dalladh le bríb, le fís 'is fallsacht.

. . .

Atá an chúirt seo seasmhach feasta san
    bhFiacail,
Siúl-se! freagair í! caithfidh tú triall ann,
Siúl gan tafann go tapa ar do phriacail,
Siúl nó stróicfead san lathaigh im
    dhiaidh tú!
Do bhuail sí crúca im chúl 'is im chába,
Do ghluais sí liom go lúfar láidir,
Do scuab léi síos mé trí na gleannta,
Cnoc Bháin Bhuí 'is go binn an teampaill.

Literal translation:

Without property, without freedom for an
    ancient race,
Without sovereignty in law, without rent,
    without a ruler;
The land destroyed and nothing after it there
In place of the herbs but chickweed and
    weeds;
The best nobility wandering as they faded
    away to nothing
And rich upstarts have the upper hand,
Deceiving with inclination and pillaging
    without looking,
Skinning the lepers, destroying them in their
    poverty,
It is distressing and sorrowful that every
    oppression is left
Darkly and unfeelingly to the severe justice of
    the law:

The weak without function get nothing from
    anyone
But great deceit and submitting to destruc-
    tion;
Falseness of the man of law and derision from
    high power;
Crookedness and fraud, neglect and favourtism;
A cloud is the law and straying justice
    absolutely nothing;
Blinding with bribe, with fees and falseness.

. . .

This court is established henceforth in
    Feakle,
Walk! attend it! you must travel there,
Walk quickly at your peril without complaining,
Walk or I will pull you in the mud after me!

She stuck a crook in my back and in my cape,
She moved me actively, strongly,
She swept me with her down through the glens
Of Cnoc Bháin Bhuí and to the gable of the
    church.

From *The Midnight Verdict*

(*The Midnight Verdict* brings together two translations, one based on
the story of Orpheus and Eurydice in Ovid's *Metamorphosis*, and the
other part of Brian Merriman's 'Cúirt an Mheán-Oíche' ['The
Midnight Court'], written in the latter part of the eighteenth century.
In Merriman's poem, the narrator falls into a dream-vision while
wandering through the countryside, and is taken to a court presided
over by a fairy-queen and entertaining complaints from Ireland's
young women about sexual frustration. In the following selection, the
woman who appears to the narrator complains of the condition of the
country, and then forcibly takes him to the court. For an eighteenth-
century version of parts of Merriman's poem, see under Denis Woulf,
pp. 27–33; for two modern versions, see under Percy Arland Ussher,
pp. 237–241, and Frank O'Connor, pp. 277–285; for another contem-
porary version, see under Ciaran Carson, pp. 387–393.)

> 'It's goodbye to freedom and ancient right,
> To honest dealing and leadership;
> The ground ripped off and nothing put back,
> Weeds in the field once crop is stacked.
> With the best of the people leaving the land,
> Graft has the under- and upper hand.
> Just line your pockets, a wink and a nod,
> And to hell with the poor! Their backs are broad.
> Alas for the plight of the underclass
> And the system's victims who seek redress:
> Their one recourse is the licensed robber
> With his legalese and his fancy slabber.
> Lawyers corrupt, their standards gone,
> Favourtism the way it's done,
> The bar disgraced, truth compromised,
> Nothing but kick-backs, bribes and lies.
>
> .   .   .
>
> Already at Feakle[66] the court's in session
> That you must answer. The pressure's on
> For you to appear. So move. And fast.
> Move or I'll make you move, you bast - .'
>
> With that she crooked her staff in my cape
> And hooked me behind and hauled me up
> And we went like hell over glen and hill
> To Moinmoy Church,[67] by the gable wall.

Original: from 'Cúirt an Mheán-Oíche', by Brian Merriman (cont.)	Literal translation (cont.):
Is deimhin go bhfaca mé ar lasadh le tóirsí	Indeed I saw ablaze with torches
An teaghlach taitneamhach maisiúil mórga	The pleasing, elegant, august household
Soilseach seasamhach lasúil lonrach	Luminous, steadfast, fiery, resplendent
Taibhseach dathúil daingean deadhóirseach.	Magnificent, colourful, solid, easily accessible.
Chonaic mé an tsí-bhean mhíonla bhéasach	I saw the gentle, well-mannered fairy woman
Chumais ina suí ar bhinnse an tsaorchirt.	Capable and sitting on the bench of noble justice.
Chonaic mé an garda láidir luaimneach	I saw the strong, nimble guard
Iomadach árracht tarraingthe suas léi.	Numerous, powerful drawn up around her.
Do chonaic mé láithreach lánteach líonta	I saw immediately a full house filled
Ó mhullach go lár de mhná 'is de dhaoine.	From top to middle with women and with people.
Do chonaic mé spéirbhean mhaorga mhallrosc	I saw a proud, languid-eyed beautiful woman
Mhilis bhog bhéaltais mhéarlag mheall-tach	Sweet, soft, soft-lipped, tender-fingered, beguiling
Thaitneamhach tháclach shásta fhionn	Pleasing, hair falling in tresses, willing, fair
Ina seasamh in airde ar chlár na mionn.	Standing up at the witness-table.
Bhí a gruaig léi scaoilte síos ina slaoda	Her hair was unbound down in layers,
Agus buaireamh suite fíor ina féachaint;	And true vexation settled in her look;
Fuinneamh ina radharc agus faghairt ina súile;	Energy in her vision and fire in her eyes;
'Is fiuchadh le draighean oilc aighnis fúithi;	And boiling with anger, rage and contention;
A caint á cosc le loisceadh a cléibhe	Her talk being hindered by her burning bosom
Gan gíog ina tost 'is tocht á traochadh.	Silent without a peep and a fit of grief exhausting her.
Dob furasta a rá gur bás ba rogha léi	It would be easy to say that death would be her choice
Agus tuile gan tlás ag tál go trom léi.	And a flood with unabated force pouring heavily from her.
Ina seasamh ar lár an chláir ina saighead,	Standing at the center of the table like an arrow,
Ag greadadh na lámh is ag fáscadh a ladhar;	Beating her hands and squeezing her fingers;
An uair do ghoil sí go foilitheach fíochmhar,	When she wept quietly, furiously,
D'fhuascail a h-osnaí a guthaí cainte.	Her sighs released her vowels of speech.
D'imigh an smúit agus d'iompaigh snó uirthi,	The gloom departed and her complexion changed,
Do thriomaigh a súile agus dúirt mar neosad:	She dried her eyes and said as I will tell:
Míle fáilte agus gairdeas cléibh romhat,	A thousand welcomes and heart's joy to you,
Aoibheall, a fháidhbhean ársa on Léithchraig!	Aoibheall, ancient woman prophet from Léithchraig!
A shoilse an lae 'is ré gan choimse!	Light of the day and moon without limit!
A shaibhreas shaolta i ngéibheann daoirse!	Wealth of life in bondage and servitude!
A cheanasach bhuach ó shlóite aoibhnis!	Powerful, victorious from hosts of pleasure!
Dob easnamh mór idTuan sa tír tú.	You were greatly wanted in Thomond in the country.
Cúis mo cháis agus fáth mo chaointe,	The cause of my concern and the reason for my lament,
Cúis do chráigh mé agus d'fhág mé cloíte,	The cause that vexed me and left me exhausted,
Do bhain dem threoir mé agus do sheol gan chiall mé	That took me from my way and that drove me senseless
Agus do chaith mar cheo mé, dóite i bpianta:	And that consumed me like a fog, burned in pains:
Na slóite míne gan chríoch gan chaomh-nadh	The gentle crowd, without fulfillment, without protection

And there (I'm sure) lit torches showed
A handsome, grand, well-built abode,
A stately, steadfast, glittering space,
Accessible and commodious.
And I saw a lovely vision woman
Ensconced on the bench of law and freedom,
And saw her fierce, fleet guard of honour
Rank upon rank in throngs around her.
I saw then too rooms filling full,
Crowding with women from wall to wall,
And saw this other heavenly beauty
With her lazy eye, on her dignity,
Seductive, pouting, with curling locks,
Biding her time in the witness box.
Her hair spilled down, loosed tress on tress,
And a hurt expression marked her face;
She was full of fight, with a glinting eye,
Hot on the boil, ill-set and angry –
Yet for all her spasms, she couldn't speak
For her hefts and huffing had made her weak.
She looked like death or a living death wish
She was so cried out; but straight as a rush,
She stood to the fore as a witness stands
Flailing and wailing and wringing hands.
And she kept it up; she raved and screeched
Till sighing restored her powers of speech.
Then her downlook went, her colour rose,
She dried her eyes and commenced as follows:

'A thousand welcomes! And bless your Highness!
Aoibheall of Crag,⁶⁸ our prophetess!
Our daylight's light, our moon forever,
Our hope of life when the weeping's over!
O head of all the hosted sisters,
Thomond⁶⁹ can thole no more! Assist us!
My cause, my case, the reason why
My plea's prolonged so endlessly
Until I'm raving and round the twist
Like a meanad whirled in a swirl of mist –
The reason why is the unattached
And unprovided for, unmatched
Women I know, like flowers in a bed
Nobody's dibbled or mulched or weeded

Original: from 'Cúirt an Mheán-
Oíche', by Brian Merriman (cont.)

Literal translation (cont.):

Ar fud an tsaoil seo d'fhíorscoth béithe,
Throughout this world, of the very best women,

Maslaithe i mbuairt gan suaimhneas oíche
Insulted in sorrow without peace at night

Ina gcailleacha dubha gan chumhdach
céile;
Melancholy celibate women without protec-
tion of a spouse;

Caite gan chlú gan chionta claonbheart.
Worn without reputation, without fault of evil
behaviour.

Is aithne dom féin san méid so dem shiúlta
I myself know in the amount I have walked

Bean agus céad nár méinn leo diúltadh
A hundred and one women who wouldn't
have a mind to refuse

Agus mise ina measc, mo chreach mar
tharla!
And myself among them, my ruin as it
happens!

D'imigh im spaid gan fear gan pháiste.
I am left a barren person without a man,
without a child.

Mo dhochar! mo dhíth! mo bhrón mar bhím
My harm! my destruction! my sorrow as I am

Gan sochar gan seoid gan só gan síoth
Without profit, without jewels, without
comfort, without rest

Go doilbhir duaiseach duamhar dítheach
Gloomy, cheerless, toilsome, destitute

Gan chodladh gan suan gan suaimhneas
oíche
Without sleep, without rest, without a night's
peace

Ar leaba leamhfhuar im shuathadh ag
smaointe.
On a lifeless cold bed disturbed by thoughts.

A Cháigh na Carraige! breathnaigh go
díreach
Cáig of Carraig! examine directly

Mná na Banba in anacrain sínte
The women of Ireland in affliction stretched

Ar nós má leanaid na fearaibh dá
bhfuadar,
So that if the men follow their tendency,

Och! mo lagar! go gcaithfeam a
bhfuadach![70]
Oh! alas! we will have to abduct them!

Original: 'A Shéamais, déan dam',
by Eoghan Ruadh Ó Súilleabháin

Literal translation:

A Shéamais, déan dam féinidh arm na bhfód:
Séamus, make for me a weapon of the sod:

Sciuirse ghléasta dhéanfas grafadh 'gus
romhar,
An equipped, industrious implement for grub-
bing and digging,

Stiuir ghlan éadtrom i bhfaobhar i dtathac
's i gcóir
A clean, light rudder in steel, in strength, in
proper condition

Nach tútach gné is bhéas néata tarraingthe
i gclódh.
Not uncouth in appearance, and will be neatly
drawn in form.

I gclódh an airgid bíodh tarraingthe gan
rian buille ar bith,
In the form of silver let it be drawn without a
trace of a blow at all,

Scóip fada aici is leabhaireacht 'na hiar-
rachtaibh,
A long stretch for it and flexibility in its
thrusts,

Sórd slaite bíodh leachuighthe ar a
riaghail-chiumhasaibh,
Let a kind of rib be embedded in the edge of
the spade,

'S is ró-thaitneamhach an t-arm liom faoi
dhíormaibh.
And the weapon is greatly pleasing for me
among the gang.

A ciumhasa má thígheann na bíodh ortha
sculib ná ruic,
Its edges, if they come, let there not be on them
a nick or a wrinkle,

Is feicim a tígheal sleamhain slím i bhfuirm
an tsuic,
And I see its smooth, slim wing in the form of
the sock of the plough,

Slighe an mhaide bíodh innti gan fuigheall
ná uir-easbaidh ar bith,
Let there be a contrivance of wood in it
without excess or deficit at all,

Is mar bharra ar gach nídh bíodh sí i mbin-
neas an chluig.[71]
And to top everything, let it have the sweet-
ness of the bell.

Or trimmed or watered or ever tended;
So here they are, unhusbanded,
Unasked, untouched, beyond conception –
And, needless to say, I'm no exception.
I'm scorched and tossed, a sorry case
Of nerves and drives and neediness,
Depressed, obsessed, awake at night,
Unused, unsoothed, disconsolate,
A throbbing ache, a dumb discord,
My mind and bed like a kneading board.
O Warden of the Crag, incline!
Observe the plight of Ireland's women,
For if things go on like this, then fuck it!
The men will have to be abducted!'[72]

'Poet to Blacksmith'

(The original is by the eighteenth-century Co. Kerry poet Eoghan Ruadh Ó Súilleabháin, and is addressed to a blacksmith named Séamus MacGearailt.)

Séamus, make me a side-arm to take on the earth,
A suitable tool for digging and grubbing the ground,
Lightsome and pleasant to lean on or cut with or lift,
Tastily finished and trim and right for the hand.

No trace of the hammer to show on the sheen of the blade,
The thing to have purchase and spring and be fit for the strain,
The shaft to be socketed in dead true and dead straight,
And I'll work with the gang till I drop and never complain.

The plate and the edge of it not to be wrinkly or crooked –
I see it well shaped from the anvil and sharp from the file;
The grain of the wood and the line of the shaft nicely fitted,
And best thing of all, the ring of it, sweet as a bell.[73]

Original: 'Aubade', by Nuala Ní Dhomhnaill

Literal translation:

Is cuma leis an mhaidin cad air a ngealann sí –

ar na cáganna ag bruíon is ag achrann ins na crainn

dhuilleogacha; ar an mbardal glas ag snámh go tóstalach

i measc na ngiolcach ins na curraithe; ar thóinín bán

an chircín uisce ag gobadh aníos as an bpoll portaigh;

ar roilleoga ag siúl go cúramach ar thránna móra.

Is cuma leis an ghrian cad air a n-éiríonn sí –

ar na tithe bríce, ar fhuinneoga de ghloine snoite

is gearrtha i gcearnóga Seoirseacha: ar na saithí beach

ag ullmhú chun creach a dhéanamh ar ghairdíní bruachbhailte;

ar lánúine óga fós ag méanfach i gcomhthiúin is fonn

a gcúplála ag éirí aníos iontu; ar dhrúcht ag glioscarnach

ina dheora móra ar lilí is róiseanna; ar do ghuaille.

Ach ní cuma linn go bhfuil an oíche aréir thart, is go gcaithfear glacadh le pé rud a sheolfaidh

an lá inniu an tslí; go gcaithfear imeacht is cromadh síos

arís is píosaí beaga brealsúnta ár saoil a dhlúthú

le chéile ar chuma éigin, chun gur féidir

lenár leanaí uisce a ól as babhlaí briste

in ionad as a mbosa, ní cuma linne é.[74]

It's all the same to the morning what it brightens on –

on the jackdaws quarreling and bickering in the leafy trees;

on the green drake swimming arrogantly

in the midst of the reeds in the marshes; on the small white backside

of the waterhen shooting up out of the bog hole;

on oystercatchers walking carefully on large strands.

It is all the same to the sun what it rises on –

on the brick houses, on windows of carved and cut glass

in Georgian squares; on the swarms of bees

preparing to make a raid on suburban gardens;

on young couples still yawning in harmony and the desire

of their coupling rising up in them; on dew glistening

in large tears on lilies and roses; on your shoulders.

But it is not all the same to us that last night is past, and that one must take whatever thing that

today will send on the way; that one must proceed and stoop down

again and draw the small, silly pieces of our lives

together in some way, so that it is possible

for our children to drink water out of broken bowls

instead of out of their palms, it is not all the same to us.

Michael Longley
(1929)

Michael Longley has written frequently about the landscape of Carrigskeewaun, near Kiladoon in Co. Mayo, part of the Mayo Gaeltacht. He was born in Belfast of English parents and educated in classics at Trinity College Dublin. He currently lives in Belfast.

'Aubade'
(The original is by the contemporary poet Nuala Ní Dhomhnaill.)

It's all the same to morning what it dawns on –
On the bickering of jackdaws in leafy trees;
On that dandy from the wetlands, the green mallard's
Stylish glissando among reeds; on the moorhen
Whose white petticoat flickers around the boghole;
On the oystercatcher on tiptoe at low tide.

It's all the same to the sun what it rises on –
On the windows in houses in Georgian squares;
On bees swarming to blitz suburban gardens;
On young couples yawning in unison before
They do it again; on dew like sweat or tears
On lilies and roses; on your bare shoulders.

But it isn't all the same to us that night-time
Runs out; that we must make do with today's
Happenings, and stoop and somehow glue together
The silly little shards of our lives, so that
Our children can drink water from broken bowls,
Not from cupped hands. It isn't the same at all.[75]

Original: 'Cinaed, cá cin ro buí
dúinn'

Literal translation:

Cinaed, cá cin ro buí dúinn
    cár n-innarba a críon Néill,
óir ní dingnainn re mnaí mín
    acht a ndingnainn rem mnaí
        féin?

Cinaed, what was the crime that was on us
    why are we expelled from the territory of Néill,
since I would not do with a gentle woman
    but what I would do with my own wife?

Fer liath ro lí orm a mnaí,
    ní ro tarbaige Dia dó
óir ní ragainn-si fó brat
    co n-ebad cat lemlacht bó,

It was a grey-haired man who misconstrued me
    regarding his wife,
    may God not benefit him
since I would not go under her covering
    until a cat would drink milk hot from the cow,

co linged os airbe n-aird
    co n-éirged eo a buinne bedg,
co ndernadh ben dolbad duilb,
    co n-ebtha cuirm a corn cerb.

until a deer would leap a high fence,
    until a salmon would rise from a rapid stream
        with a leap,
until a woman would make a dark deception,
    until ale would be drunk from a silver drinking-
        horn.

Cid isi ro léiced dam
    ní dingnainn ar apa a fir
co lenad torc trom a threoit
    co n-ebad leoit deoch do mil.

Although it is she who would allow me
    I would not do it on account of her husband
until a heavy boar would follow its leader
    until a human being would drink a drink of
        honey.

Seamus Deane
(1940–)

Seamus Deane has published several volumes of poetry as well as the acclaimed novel *Reading in the Dark* and numerous works of criticism. He also edited the three-volume *Field Day of Anthology of Irish Writing* (1991).

Born in Derry and educated at Queens University Belfast and Cambridge University, Deane was Professor of Modern English and American Literature at University College Dublin until 1993, when he moved to the University of Notre Dame in the United States.

'Why was I banished Cinaed, why?'
(The original has been dated approximately to the twelfth century.)

Why was I banished Cinaed, why?
Why sent out from Niall's country?

I would not, I tell you, do anything
With any decent woman, nothing,

That I would not do with my wife.
It was an old man who accused me

Of being intimate with his wife. Damn
Him! I'd no sooner go with her than

Would a cat drink new milk,
Than a deer jump a high fence,

Than a salmon leap from a stream,
Than a woman perform sorcery,

Than ale be drunk from a silver cup.
Even were she to allow me, I would

Not sleep with her, not even to spite
Her husband, not until a boar would

Follow its herd, a woman drink honey.
It was for a trivial reason

Original: 'Cinaed, cá cin ro buí
dúinn' (cont.)

Literal translation (cont.):

Fóill apa 'mar lied orm
    Gormfhlaith fhial ó Áth dá Rinn,
ar aoi gluasachta a dá les,
    meise 's mo lám des fó cinn.

Slight the reason that I was accused of violating
    warm-hearted Gormfhlaith from Áth dá Rinn,
on account of the movement of her two thighs,
    I with my right hand under her head.

Ar ar faicsin ima raen
    ar in raen fonnglas fér
fóill adbar d'innisin sceóil
    faicsin a beóil ar mo bél.

On our being seen on a path
    on the green-surfaced grassy path
a slight matter for telling a tale
    her mouth on my mouth being seen.

Nochar chert do Chinaed chain
    ar corn comóil, ce mad mid,
ingen ríg na n-étach ndrol
    d'écnach rim cen col cen cin.[76]

It is not right for fond Cinead
    because of a cup drunk in common, though it
    be mead,
regarding the king's daughter of the garments of
loops
    to accuse me who is without sin, without fault.

I was accused of violating Gormflaith.
Because of the way she was moving

Her slow thighs, because my hand
Was under her head, because we were

Seen together on the grassy pathway.
It was a trivial reason, I tell you.

Her lips on mine, they said!
It was not right for Cinaed,

Just because we had a drink together,
Even if it was mead, to accuse me,

I who am wholly innocent, without sin,
Of having been intimate with her,

The King's daughter, her of the fancy
Fringed garments. Not right, I tell you.[77]

Original: 'Mairg atá gan béarla binn', by Dáibhí Ó Bruadair

Literal translation:

Mairg atá gan béarla binn
ar dteacht an iarla go hÉirinn;
   ar feadh mo shaoghail ar chlár
      Chuinn
   dán ar bhéarla dobhéaruinn.[78]

Pity who is without sweet English
on the coming of the earl to Ireland;
   during my life on the plain of Conn
   I would give up poetry for English.

Original: 'Seirbhíseach Seirgthe', by Dáibhí Ó Bruadar

Literal translation:

I

Seirbhíseach seirgthe íogair srónach
   seasc
d'eitigh sinn is eibior íota im scórnaigh
   feacht
beireadh síobhra d'eitill í gan lón tar
   lear
an deilbhín gan deirglí nár fhóir mo
   thart.

I

A shriveled, touchy, nosy, barren servant
refused us once and the apex of thirst in my
   throat
may a fairy-child of flight bear her without
   provisions over the sea
the miserable figure without a ruddy com-
   plexion who did not relieve my
   thirst.

II

Dá reicinn í san bhfeileghníomh do
   gheobhadh ceacht
is beirt an tighe go leigfidís im scórsa
   casc
ó cheisnimh sí go bhfeirg linn is beoir
   na gar
don steiling í nár leige rí na glóire i
   bhfad.

II

If I would proclaim her in the treacherous
   act, she would get a lesson
it is the couple of the house who would
   allow on my tally a cask
since she grumbled angrily at us and beer
   near her
at the bench for barrels may the king of
   glory not let her be long.

Michael Hartnett
(1941–1999)

As a contemporary Irish poet writing in both Irish and English, Michael Hartnett identified particularly with the cultural ruin experienced by Gaelic culture in the seventeenth century, and he published important collections of translations of the works of Pádraigín Haicéad, Aoghagáin Ó Rathaille, and Dáibhí Ó Bruadair. Hartnett also translated the work of a number of contemporary Irish-language poets. In introductory comments to his collection of translations from Ó Bruadair, Hartnett says, 'A poet/translator, if he loves the original more than he loves himself, will get the poetry across: he may even get the whole poem across or, at second best, force his own version – within the strictures laid down by the original author – as close as possible to poetry.'[79]

Born in Croom, Co. Limerick, Hartnett lived in Dublin, Madrid, and London before moving to Newcastle West, Co. Limerick, in 1974.

'Pity the man who English lacks'
(The original is by Dáibhí Ó Bruadair.)

Pity the man who English lacks
      now turncoat Ormonde's[80] made a come-back.
As I have to live here, I now wish
      to swap my poems for squeaky English.[81]

'A shrivelled-up skivvy . . .'

(The original is by Dáibhí Ó Bruadair. For an earlier version, see under James Stephens, p. 225.)

A shrivelled-up skivvy, snappy, nosy, dry,
refused when a craving for booze ate my insides:
may she starve and a ghost over seas with her fly,
that wizened old midget who wouldn't one jorum supply.

I'd teach her a lesson if I really did pay her back
and the decent house-owners would give me on credit a cask:
though the beer was beside her I just got a bitter attack –
may the King of Glory not let her too long at her task.

Original: 'Seirbhíseach Seirgthe',
by Dáibhí Ó Bruadar (cont.)

Literal translation (cont.):

III

Meirgíneach bheirbhthe í gan
ceol na cab
do theilg sinn le greidimín san
bpóirse amach
gé cheilim ríomh a peidigraoi
mar fhógras reacht
ba bheag an díth dá mbeireadh sí
do ghósta cat.

III

A crabby, boiled woman [is] she, without
music in her mouth
who cast us with a gesture of hostile con-
tempt out through the porch
although I conceal an account of her pedi-
gree as law proclaims
little would be the harm if she would bear a
cat to a ghost.

IV

Reilgín an eilitín nach d'ord na
mban
is seisce gnaoi dá bhfeiceamaoid i
ród re maith
a beith na daoi ós deimhin dí go
deo na dtreabh
san leitin síos go leige sí mar
neóid a cac.[82]

IV

A club-footed person, the hind, not of the
order of women
the most barren face that we see on the road
of goodness
to be a dunce for certain to the end of the
tribe
in the gruel may she let down, like a miser-
able person, her excrement.

Original: 'Scéala', by Nuala Ní
Dhomhnaill

Literal translation:

Do chuimhnigh sí
go deireadh thiar
ar scáil an aingil
sa teampall,
cleitearnach sciathán
ina timpeall:
is dúiseacht le dord colúr
is stealladh ga gréine
ar fhallaí aolcloch
an lá a fuair sí an scéala.

She remembered
to the very end
the image of the angel
in the temple,
a fluttering of wings
around her:
and waking with a murmur of pigeons
and a splashing of a ray of sun
on limestone walls
the day she got the tidings.

É siúd
d'imigh
is n'fheadar ar chuimhnigh riamh
ar cad a d'eascair
óna cheathrúna,
dhá mhíle bliain
d'iompar croise
de dhóiteán is deatach,
de chlampar chomh hard
le spící na Vatacáine.

He
left
and I don't know if he ever
about what sprouted
from his thighs,
two thousand years
of carrying a cross
of fire and smoke,
of trouble as tall
as the spikes of the Vatican.

Ó, a mhaighdean rócheansa,
nár chuala trácht ar éinne riamh
ag teacht chughat sa doircheacht
cosnocht, déadgheal
is a shúile lán de rógaireacht.[83]

O, most gentle maiden,
There was never heard mention of anyone
coming to you in the darkness
barefoot, white-toothed
and his eyes full of roguery.

An over-done slut with no note in her throat,
she flung and two-fingered me out of the door:
as to where she came out of, I can say no more –
small harm if she pupped a cat to a ghost.

She's no woman at all, that club-footed bitch,
with the driest old face you could meet on a trip:
she talks apishly now and she always will
and like a fool in her gruel may she dribble her shit.[84]

'Annunciations'

(The original is by the contemporary poet Nuala Ní Dhomhnaill.)

She remembered to the very end
the angelic vision
in the temple:
the flutter of wings
about her –
noting the noise of doves,
sun-rays raining
on lime-white walls –
the day she got the tidings.

He –
he went away
and perhaps forgot
what grew from his loins –
two thousand years
of carrying a cross
two thousand years
of smoke and fire
of rows that reached a greater span
than all the spires of the Vatican.

Remember
o most tender virgin Mary
that never was it known
that a man came to you
in the darkness alone,
his feet bare, his teeth white
and roguery swelling in his eyes.[85]

Original: 'Is truagh 's géar an
sgéal . . .', by Páidrigín Haicéad

Literal translation:

Is truagh 's is géar an sgéal so malartaig-
    headh linn
(uaidh ní éisdim réad 's ní aithím poinn)
go luaidhfeadh Déirdre an réidhruisg
    mharbhrighin mhoill
buain fá chéile, i ngléas go sgarfadh sí is
    sinn.

It is pitiable and it is painful this destructive
    story about us
(because of it I don't hear a thing and I don't
    recognize much)
that Deirdre of the mild, languid, clear eyes
    would mention
taking a spouse, in such a way that she and we
    would separate.

Do luach an sgéil is baoghal nach mairfead
    mí acht tinn;
do ghluais mo sgéimh go léir gur athraigh
    sí sinn;
do nuaill ar n-éighmhe éirghid ealta
    chríoch Fhloinn,
is luas mo dhéar mar thréanrith ghaise faoi
    linn.

As a result of the news there is a danger I will
    not live a month, except sick;
my appearance went entirely, since she
    changed us;
from clamours of our crying, a flock of the ter-
    ritory of Floinn rises,
fast are my tears like the strong flow of a stream
    under a pool.

Monuar, ní béim don déidghil sheada
    shaoir shing,
suaimhneach shéaghain bhéilghlic bhlasda
    mhín bhinn,
buain go séimh do réir a carad bhíos
    grinn,
's a huaim le caomhthach saor ba cneasda
    dhí i gcuing.

Alas, it is not a flaw for the bright-toothed,
    slender, noble, thin,
tranquil, stately, clever-mouthed, well-spoken,
    smooth, sweet one,
to proceed gently according to her friends who
    are discerning,
and be united with a free companion who
    would be decent to her in marriage.

Sduadh na gcraobhfholt bpéarlach gcas-
    dadhlaoitheach gcruinn,
chuanna chéillidhe, an tsaoghlan chailce an
    taoibh shlim,
smuainim féin, gibé do mheasfadh í is
    inn,
gur cruaidh an céim, a Dhé, dá ngabhadh
    sí linn.

Graceful lady of the flowing, pearly, curly-
    locked, gathered tresses,
charming, sensible, the proud, chalk-white
    person of the smooth side,
I myself think, whoever would assess her and
    me,
That it would be a hard step, Oh God, if she
    went with me.

Is fuad bocht mé gan réad, gan aithris
    gníomh ngrinn;
ar thruas mo chléibh go léir go rachainn trí
    líon;
do chuaidh mo sbréidh, 's ní léigthear
    flaitheas faoim roinn;
's is uaisle Ó Néill i gcéim – dá mairfeadh
    Síol gCuinn.[86]

I am a poor wretch without a thing, without a
    vivid deed to recite;
my breast entirely lean so that I would go
    through a net;
my fortune went, and no sovereignty is left in
    my portion;
and Ó Néill is a noble in rank – if the Race of
    Conn had survived.

'A sad and bitter story . . .'

(The original is by Páidrigín Haicéad, whose love poetry often draws
on courtly love conventions.)

A sad and bitter story about us goes around –
it makes me blind to all things and deaf to every sound –
that Deirdre of the unrevealing eyes has said
that we must separate, for she intends to wed.

And thus I fear I'll not survive a month, but fade –
and my good looks are gone, so total is the change;
for my shrieks the birds of Ireland soar into the air,
my tears flow fast like undercurrents in a lake.

Alas, it is no fault of the slender noble svelte
sweet, silvertongued whitetoothed girl
to quietly take advice from her astuter friends
and be harnessed to a freeborn mate who'd treat her well
    when wed.

I think myself if anyone compared the two of us,
and she went with me, Oh God, they'd think it hard luck:
she, handsome graceful wise with twisting intricate hair,
a white-as-chalk and stately smoothflanked maid,

and I, poor wretch, without a daring deed to tell
no realm falls to my lot and I've lost all my wealth
and my body is so thin I'd go easily through a net –
and Ó Néill is of a noble clan – pity they're all dead![87]

Original: 'An Rás', by Nuala Ní Dhomhnaill

Literal translation:

Faoi mar a bheadh leon cuthaigh, nó tarbh fásaigh,
nó ceann de mhuca allta na Fiannaíochta,
nó an gaiscíoch ag léimt faoi dhéin an fhathaigh
faoina chírín singilíneach síoda,
tiomáinim an chairt ar dalladh
trí bhailte beaga lár na hÉireann.
Beirim ar an ghaoth romham
is ní bheireann an ghaoth atá i mo dhiadh orm.

As a raging lion would be, or a wild bull,
or one of the wild pigs of the Fenian cycle,
or the warrior leaping towards the giant
under his thinly lined silk crest,
I drive the car at speed
through the small towns of the midlands of Ireland.
I overtake the wind before me
and the wind that is behind me does not overtake me.

Mar a bheadh saighead as bogha, piléar as gunna
nó seabhac rua trí scata mionéan lá Márta
scaipim na mílte slí taobh thiar dom.
Tá uimhreacha ar na fógraí bóthair
is ní thuigim an mílte iad nó climéadair.
Aonach, Ros Cré, Móinteach Mílic,
n'fheadar ar ghaibheas nó nár ghaibheas tríothu.
Níl iontu faoin am seo ach teorainní luais
is moill ar an mbóthar go dtí tú.

As an arrow from a bow, a bullet out of a gun would,
or a red hawk through a crowd of small birds on a March day
I scatter the miles of road behind me.
There are numbers on the road signs
and I don't understand if they are miles or kilometres.
Nenagh, Roscrea, Mountmellick,
I don't know whether I did or did not go through them.
They are only by this time speed limits
and delays on the road to you.

Trí ghleannta, sléibhte, móinte, bogaithe
scinnim ar séirse ón iarthar,
d'aon seáp amháin reatha i do threo
de fháscadh ruthaig i do chuibhreann.
Deinim ardáin des na hísleáin, ísleáin des na hardáin
talamh bog de thalamh cruaidh is talamh cruaidh de thalamh bog –
imíonn gnéithe uile seo na léarscáile as mo chuimhne,
ni fhanann ann ach gíoscán coscán is drithle soilse.

Through glens, mountains, moors, bogs
I go quickly on a dash from the west,
on one rush of running in your direction
on a sudden dash to your room.
I make heights of the hollows, hollows of the heights
soft ground of hard ground and hard ground of soft ground –
all these marks of the map go out of my memory,
nothing remains there but a grinding of brakes and a sparkle of lights.

Derek Mahon
(1667–1745)

Although translation has often served Derek Mahon as a way of establishing a point of view outside the confines of the Irish experience – he has translated from French, Provençale, German, Latin, Russian, and Italian poetry – he has also produced several verse translations from the Irish. Mahon was born in Belfast, and educated at the Royal Belfast Academical Institution and Trinity College Dublin. He has worked as a teacher and a journalist in New York and London, and currently lives in Co. Cork.

'The Race'
(The original is by the contemporary poet Nuala Ní Dhomhnaill.)

Like a mad lion, like a wild bull, like one
of the crazy pigs in the Fenian cycle
or the hero leaping upon the giant
with his fringe of swinging silk,
I drive at high speed through
the small midland towns of Ireland,
catching up with the wind ahead
while the wind behind me whirls and dies.

Like a shaft from a bow, like a shot from a gun
or a sparrow-hawk in a sparrow-throng
on a March day, I scatter the road-signs,
miles or kilometres what do I care.
Nenagh, Roscrea, Mountmellick,
I pass through them in a daze;
they are only speed limits put there
to hold me up on my way to you.

Through mountain cleft, bogland and wet pasture
I race impetuously from west to east –
a headlong flight in your direction,
a quick dash to be with you.
The road rises and falls before me,
the surface changing from grit to tar;
I forget geography, all I know
is the screech of brakes and the gleam of lights.

Original: 'An Rás', by Nuala Ní Dhomhnaill (cont.)	Literal translation (cont.):
Chím sa scáthán an ghrian ag buíú is ag deargadh	I see in the mirror the sun yellowing and reddening
taobh thiar díom ag íor na spéire.	behind me on the horizon.
Tá sí ina meall mór craorag lasrach amháin	It is one great, blood-red, flaming ball
croí an Ghlas Ghaibhneach á chrú trí chriathar.	the heart of the Glas Gaibhneach being milked through a sieve.
Braonta fola ag sileadh ón stráinín	Drops of blood dripping from the strainer
mar a bheadh pictiúr den Chroí Ró-Naofa.	as a picture of the Most-Sacred Heart would be.
Tá gile na dtrí deirgeacht inti,	The brightness of three reddenings is in it,
is pian ghéar í, is giorrosnaíl.	it is a sharp pain, it is a short sighing.
Deinim iontas des na braonta fola.	I wonder at the drops of blood.
Tá uamhan i mo chroí, ach fós táim neafaiseach	There is dread in my heart, but still I am trivial
faoi mar a fhéach, ní foláir, Codladh Céad Bliain	as Sleeping Beauty must have looked
ar a méir nuair a phrioc fearsaid an turainn í.	at her finger when the spindle of the spinning-wheel pricked it.
Casann sí timpeall is timpeall arís í,	She turns it around and around again,
faoi mar a bheadh sí ag siúl i dtaibhreamh.	as if she were walking in a dream.
Nuair a fhéach Deirdre ar fhuil dhearg an laoi sa tsneachta	When Deirdre looked on the red blood of the calf in the snow
n'fheadar ar thuig sí cérbh é an fiach dubh?	I wonder if she understood who the dark raven was?
Is nuair is dóigh liom gur chughat a thiomáinim,	And when I consider that I am driving toward you,
a fhir álainn, a chumann na n-árann	beautiful man, love of my heart
is ná coinneoidh ó do leaba an oíche seo mé	and that nothing will keep me from your bed tonight
ach mílte bóthair is soilse tráchta,	except miles of road and traffic lights,
tá do chuid mífhoighne mar chloch mhór	your impatience is like a great stone
ag titim anuas ón spéir orainn	falling down from the sky on us
is cuir leis ár ndrochghiúmar,	and put with it our bad humour,
ciotarúntacht is meall mór mo chuid uabhair.	awkwardness and the great mass of my pride.
Is tá meall mór eile ag teacht anuas orainn	Another great mass is coming down on us
má thagann an tuar faoin tairngire	if the prophecy is fulfilled
agus is mó go mór é ná meall na gréine	and it is much greater than the mass of the sun
a fhuiligh i mo scáthán anois ó chianaibhín.	that bled in my mirror a little while a go now.
Is a mháthair ábhalmhór, a phluais na n-iontas	And great, immense mother, cave of the wonders,
ós chughatsa ar deireadh atá an spin siúil fúinn	since it is toward you in the end the spin under us is going
an fíor a ndeir siad gur fearr aon bhlaiseadh amháin de do phóigín	is it true what they say that one taste of your little kiss is better
ná fíon Spáinneach, ná mil Ghréagach, ná beoir bhuí Lochlannach?[88]	than Spanish wine, than Greek honey, than Scandinavian yellow beer?

Suddenly, in the mirror, I catch sight of the sun
glowing red behind me on the horizon,
a vast blazing crimson sphere like the heart
of the Great Cow of the Smith-God[89]
when she was milked through a sieve,
the blood dripping as in a holy picture.
Thrice red, it is so fierce it pierces
my own heart, and I catch my breath in pain.

I keep glancing anxiously at the dripping sun
while trying to watch the road ahead.
So Sleeping Beauty must have glanced
at her finger after the spindle
of the spinning-wheel had pricked her,
turning it round and round as if in a trance.
When Deirdre saw the calf's blood on the snow
did it ever dawn on her what the raven was?[90]

Oh, I know it's to you that I'm driving,
my lovely man, the friend of my heart,
and the only things between us tonight
are the road-sign and the traffic-light;
but your impatience is like a stone
dropping upon us out of the sky;
and add to that our bad humour,
gaucherie, and the weight of my terrible pride.

Another great weight is descending upon us
if things turn out as predicted, a weight
greater by far than the globe of the sun
that bled in my mirror a while back;
and thou, dark mother, cave of wonders,
since it's to you that we spin on our violent course,
is it true what they say that your kiss is sweeter
than Spanish wine, Greek honey, or the golden
    mead of the Norse?[91]

Original: 'Goinim thú, a naoídh bheg shíar', by Tadhg Ó Ruairc

Literal translation:

Goinim thú, a naoídh bheg shíar
   na bhfolt bfiar ar lí an óir;
's gach dúal díobh go fada fann
   nach gann do shín go barr feóir.

I wound you, little maid there
   of the twisted locks with the sheen of gold;
and every loop of them long, languid
   not restricted, that stretched to the top of the grass.

Na rosg líath, na bhféachan mall
   na maladh ngann mar sgríb phinn,
na ngrúadh ngeal, acht corcrós thríodh
   – ochón is tríod ataoím tinn!
     · · ·

The grey eyes, the slow glances,
   the narrow eyebrows like the line of a pen,
the white cheeks, except for rose-crimson through
   them
   – alas, it is because of you that I am sick!
     · · ·

An tenga bhlasda mhall bhfíor,
   is binne síons no guth téad;
ar chláirsigh, orgáin is liút,
   ní fríth riamh siúd mar ghléas.

The fluent, languid, true tongue,
   sweeter sings than the voice of a string;
for harp, organ and lute,
   never was found an instrument like it.

Na ngéag úr, na ngeallamh ngeal,
   na meór lag, na niongan ndonn,
do ní gach ceól sithbhinn síor
   bláth ro sgríobh faoilionn fionn.

The tender arms, the bright, white hands,
   the gentle fingers, the strong nails,
make continuous reed-music always
   a blossom that the fair quill wrote.

An uicht mar aól, na ccíoch ccruinn
   ariamh fós nar fhoirnigh fer;
an cuirp shéimhsheing, an táoibh báin,
   – ní seanuim dháoibh dáil mo
     sherc.
     · · ·

A bosom like lime, the round breasts
   that men never yet tumbled;
the slim, slender body, the white side,
   – I don't hide from them the matter of my love.
     · · ·

Do lairge caomh, do ghlún maol,
   do cholpa sáor, do thrácht glan,
do throigh mínbhán, mar uan tonn
   – dighbháil throm a bfaiscin damh.
     · · ·

Your beautiful thigh, your naked knee,
   your unrestrained calf, your white instep,
your smooth white foot, like the foam of a wave
   – a heavy injury for me to see.
     · · ·

Aón is dó iarrium ort
   – a ghnúis ettrocht, coisg mo bhrón! –
ná mill mo dhísle a ttáobh, a bhen,
   caithfead áon go cert is dó.

One and two I ask of you
   – brilliant face, prevent my sorrow! –
don't spoil my dice on your account, woman,
   I will throw a one rightly and a two.

Fear gonta od shaighdigh gráidh
   a chongmhail shuas ní dáil ghrinn;
gan caladh uaid dfosgladh dhó,
   más taiplios mhór imrir linn.

A man wounded from your arrows of love
   to hold up is not a matter of fun;
without a haven from you opening for him,
   if you play backgammon with us.

'A Game of Cards'

(The original is attributed to a seventeenth-century poet, Tadhg Ó Ruairc, who may have been from Co. Leitrim. In a note to his translation, Mahon says: 'At the time card games like "tables" often figured as erotic confrontations. Blánaid is otherwise unknown.'[92])

Blánaid, I face you, gorgeous foe,
girl of the wavy gold chevelure,
each curl long and provocative
reaching down to the forest floor.

Crazy about you, as you know,
your grey eyes and lingering looks,
your round cheeks where roses glow,
the eyebrows like two pen-strokes,

I listen to the languorous voice
where your superior nature sings,
a finer sound than organ pipe
or lute, sweeter than harp-strings,

and dote upon your skilful hands,
the long fingers and pink nails
designed to pluck a tremulous note
or draw ink from quivering quills;

the perfect opalescent breast
no knight or knave has ever known,
the slender body and slim waist:
Blánaid, I play for you alone.

The game is up if I should glimpse
a flash of knee or open side,
white ankle-flicker, pale instep,
toes creamy as the incoming tide;

but take me with a daring move,
bright woman of the devious mind.
Be generous with your secret love,
relieve me of my dubious hand.

Original: 'Goinim thú, a naoídh
bheg shíar', by Tadhg Ó Ruairc
(cont.)

Literal translation (cont.):

Mas tioc[a] díreach no tioc cam
   no maadh gemonn[b] ach mall bhíos;
laingmhír[c] chóir no brannamh cert,
   is trúagh nach léigir mfersa síos.

If it's straight backgammon or crooked backgammon
   or a trump board-game, I'm not slow;
an honest board-game or a correct game of chess
   it's a pity you do not throw my man down.

Ar t[d] a do, no accladh shíar,
   tabhair ionadh go dían, a shiúr;
don fhior ghonta ro cráidhis féin
   – ní iarruim é acht do thriúr.

On a line that is yours, or a bastion beyond,
   give a space quickly, sister,
to the wounded man whom you yourself tormented
   – I don't ask but your three men.

. . .

...

Ós tú Bláthnat, rún mo chléibh,
   aonghrádh cumhra séimh gan
      ghoimh,
saoilim, óm lot lé do ghrádh,
   nach olc leat mo lámh do ghoin.[93]

After you, Blánaid, sweetheart of my bosom,
   sweet, tender love without malice,
I think, since I'm injured by your love,
   that it is not bad for you to wound my hand.

---

[a] The literal translation follows Greene, who says *tioc* represents a form of backgammon.

[b] The literal translation follows Greene, who identifies *geamann* as a board-game.

[c] The literal translation follows Greene, who says *laingmhír* represents some kind of board game, possibly a form of chess.

[d] The literal translation follows Greene, who glosses *tí* as a line on a game-board.

It beats me you can keep in check
a rogue like me so quick to sin.
Strip poker, scrabble, snap, bezique:
whatever the game, we both can win.

So put your cards on the table, dear;
shuffle the deck and shake the dice.
It's serious stakes we play for here
and high time you showed your ace![94]

Original: 'Tusa', by Nuala Ní Dhomhnaill	Literal translation:
Is tusa, pé thú féin, an fíréan a thabharfadh cluais le héisteacht, b'fhéidir, do bhean inste scéil a thug cosa léi, ar éigean, o láthair an chatha.	You are, whoever you yourself are, the right person who would lend an ear, perhaps, to a woman telling a story who made her escape, barely, from the place of the battle.
Níor thugamair féin an samhradh linn ná an geimhreadh. Níor thriallamair ar bord loinge go Méiriceá ná ag lorg ár bhfortúin le chéile i slí ar bith ins na tíortha teo thar lear.	We ourselves did not take the summer with us or the winter. We did not travel on board a ship to America, nor were we seeking our fortune together in any way in the hot countries overseas.
Níor ghaibheamair de bharr na gcnoc ar chapall láidir álainn dubh. Níor luíomair faoi chrann caorthainn is an oíche ag cur cuisne. Ní lú ná mar a bhí tinte cnámh is an adharc á séideadh ar thaobh na gréine.	We did not go to the top of the hills on a strong, beautiful, black horse. We did not lie under a rowan tree and the night getting frosty. Much less were there bonfires and the horn being blown on the sunny side.
Eadrainn bhí an fharraige mhór atá brónach. Eadrainn bhí na cnoic is na sléibhte ná casann ar a chéile.[95]	Between us was the great sea which is sorrowful. Between us were the hills and the mountains that do not meet each other.

Eiléan Ní Chuillenáin
(1941)

Most of Eiléan Ní Chuillenáin's work in verse translation consists of versions of poems by her contemporary Nuala Ní Dhomhnaill, although she has also translated several traditional Irish-language poems. Ní Chuillenáin was born in Cork, and educated at University College Cork and at Oxford.

'You Are'
(The original is by the contemporary poet Nuala Ní Dhomhnaill.)

> Whoever you are, you are
> The real thing, the witness
> Who might lend an ear
> To a woman with a story
> Barely escaped with her life
> From the place of battle.
>
> Spring, the sweet spring, was not sweet for us
> Nor winter neither.
> We never stepped aboard a ship together
> Bound for America to seek
> Our fortune, we never
> Shared those hot foreign lands.
>
> We did not fly over the high hills
> Riding the fine black stallion,
> Or lie under the hazel branches
> As the night froze about us,
> No more than we lit bonfires of celebration
> Or blew the horn on the mountainside.
>
> Between us welled the ocean
> Waves of grief. Between us
> The mountains were forbidding
> And the roads long, with no turning.[96]

Original: 'Caoine Chille Chais'

Créad a dheunfaimuid feasda gan adhmad
    Atá deire na gcoillte ar lár?
Ní'l trácht ar Chill Chais ná a teaghlach,
    'S ní bainfear a clíng go bráth!
An áit úd 'na gcómhnuigheadh an dia-
    bhean
    Fuair gairm a's meidhir tar mná',
Bhíodh iarlaí ag tarraing tar toínn ann
    'S an t-Aifrionn bínn d'á rádh.

Is é mo chreach fhada 's mo léan ghoirt
    Do gheataí breagha néata ar lár!
An *avenue* ghreanta faoi shaothar
    'S gan fosg' ar aon taobh do'n *walk*!
An Chúirt bhreagh a' sileadh an bhraon di,
    'S an gasradh shéimh go tláth;
'S i leabhar na marbh do léaghtar
    An t-Easbog 's *Lady 'Veagh*.

Ní chluinim fuaim laca ná géi ann,
    Ná fiolar 'deunadh aedhir cois
    cuain,
Ná fiú na mbeacha chun saothair
    Thabharfadh mil agus céir do'n tslu-
    aigh!
Ní'l ceól binn milis na n-eun ann
    Le h-amharc an laé dhul uainn:
Ná'n chuaichín i mbárr na ngeug ann,
    Ó, 's í chuirfeadh an saoghal chun
    suain.

Nuair thigheadh na puic faoi na sléibhte
    'S an guna le n-a dtaobh, 's an líon,
Feuchan siad anuas le leun ar
    An mbaile fuair *sway* i ngach tír;
An fhaithche bhreagh aoibhinn 'na
    raobthacha,
    'S gan fosg' ar aon taobh ó'n tsín;
Páirc an *phaddoch* 'na *dairy*
    Mar a mbíodh eilit a' deunamh a sgíth.

Literal translation:

What will we do henceforth without timber
    The last of the woods are on the ground?
There is no mention of Kilcash or its house-
    hold,
    Its peal of bells will not be struck ever!
That place in which the goddess lived
    Who had acclaim and joy beyond women,
Earls used to come over waves there
    And the sweet Mass being said.

It is my lengthy ruin and my bitter anguish
    Your fine, neat gates on the ground!
The beautiful avenue under travail
    And without shade on any side of the
    walk!
The fine Court, the drop dripping on it,
    And the fine group of people weak;
And in the book of the dead one reads
    The Bishop and Lady Iveagh.

I don't hear the sound of ducks or geese there
    Or of an eagle taking the air by the
    harbour,
Or even of the bees at work
    Who used to give honey and wax to the
    crowd!
There is no sweet, melodious song of the birds
    there
    With the sight of the day going from us;
Or the cuckoo on top of the branches there,
    O, it is she who would put the world to
    sleep.

When the bucks come around the mountains
    And the gun near them, and the net,
They look down with grief on
    The place that had sway in every country;
The fine, pleasant green torn up,
    And without protection on any side from
    the weather;
The field of the paddock a dairy
    Where the doe used to take her rest.

'Kilcash'

(The original describes the ruin of a Big House belonging to a branch
of the Butler family at Cill Chais [Kilcash], a village in Co. Tipperary
at the foot of Slievenamon mountain.)

What will we do now for timber
With the last of the woods laid low –
No word of Kilcash nor its household,
Their bell is silenced now,
Where the lady[97] lived with such honour,
No woman so heaped with praise,
Earls came across oceans to see her
And heard the sweet words of Mass.

It's the cause of my long affliction
To see your neat gates knocked down,
The long walks affording no shade now
And the avenue overgrown,
The fine house that kept out the weather,
Its people depressed and tamed;
And their names with the faithful
    departed,
The Bishop[98] and Lady Iveagh!

The geese and the ducks' commotion,
The eagle's shout, are no more,
The roar of the bees gone silent,
Their wax and their honey store
Deserted. Now at evening
The musical birds are stilled,
And the cuckoo is dumb in the treetops
That sang lullaby to the world.

Even the deer and the hunters
That follow the mountain way
Look down upon us with pity,
The house that was famed in its day;
The smooth wide lawn is all broken,
No shelter from wind and rain;
The paddock has turned to a dairy
Where the fine creatures grazed.

Original: 'Caoine Chille Chais' (cont.)	Literal translation (cont.):

Atá ceó ag tuitim ar chraobha ann
    Ná glanan raé, grian, ná lá;

Fog is falling on branches there
    That neither the moon, the sun, nor the day clears;

Tá smúid ag tuitim ó'n spéir ann,
    'S a cuid uisge go léir ag trághadh:
Ní'l coll, ní'l cuilion, ní'l caor ann,
    Ach clocha 'gus maol-chlocháin,
Páirc an fhorghaois[a] gan craobh ann
    A's d'imthigh an *game* chun fáin!

Mist is falling from the sky there
    And all its water ebbing;
There is no hazel, there is no holly, there is no berry there
    But stone and bare, stony ground,
    The field of the rabbit-burrows without a branch in it,
    And the game departed to wander.

Anois mar bhárr ar gach mí-ghreann,
    Chuaidh prionnsa na nGaedheal tar sáil'
Anonn le h-ainnir na míne
    Fuair gairm sa bhFrainnc 's san Spáinn.
Anois tá a cualacht d'á caoine
    Gheibheadh airgead buidhe agus bán;
Is í ná tógfadh seilbh na ndaoine,
    Ach caraid na bhfíor bhochtán!

Now to top every displeasure,
    The prince of the Gaels went over the sea
Beyond with the young woman of the smoothness
    Who received glory in France and in Spain.
Now her clan is lamenting her
    Who used to get money yellow and white;
It is she who would not take the property of the people,
    But was a friend of the truly poor person.

Aitchím ar Mhuire 's ar Íosa
    Go dtagaidh sí 'rís chugainn slán!
Go mbeidh "raincí fada" ag gabháil timchioll,
    Ceól bheidhlín a's teinte cnámh;
Go dtógfar an bhaile-se ár sínsear,
    Cill Chais bhreagh arís go h-árd,
'S go bráth nó go dtiocfaidh an díleann
    Ní fhaicfear í 'rís ar lár![99]

I beseech Mary and Jesus
    May she come again to us safe,
That 'long dances' will be going around,

    Violin music and bonfires;
That this place of our ancestors will be built
    Fine Kilcash again up high,
And forever or until the flood will come
    Will it not be seen again laid low!

---

[a] The literal translation of *forghaois* as rabbit-burrows follows a gloss in PPM.

Mist hangs low on the branches
No sunlight can sweep aside,
Darkness falls among daylight
And the streams are all run dry;
No hazel, no holly or berry,
Bare naked rocks and cold;
The forest park is leafless
and all the game gone wild.

And now the worst of our troubles:
She has followed the prince of the Gaels[100] –
He has borne off the gentle maiden,
Summoned to France and to Spain
Her company laments her
That she fed with silver and gold:
One who never preyed on the people
But was the poor souls' friend,

My prayer to Mary and Jesus
She may come safe home to us here
To dancing and rejoicing
To fiddling and bonfire
That our ancestors' house will rise up,
Kilcash built up anew
And from now to the end of the story
May it never again be laid low.[101]

Original: 'An Tan D'Aistrigh go Duibhneachaibh Láimh le Tonn Tóime i g-Ciarraighe', by Aodhagán Ó Rathaille

Literal translation:

Is fada liom oidhche fhír-fhliuch gan suan, gan srann,
Gan cheathra, gan maoin, caoirigh, ná buaibh na mbeann;
Anfaithe ar tuinn taoibh liom do bhuaidhir mo cheannn,
Is nár chleachtas im naoidhin fioguig ná ruachain abhann.

It is long for me the truly wet night without sleep, without a snore
Without cattle, without riches, sheep or horned cows;
A storm on waves beside me vexed my head
And I was not accustomed in my young childhood to dogfish or periwinkles.

Dá maireadh an rí díonmhar ó bhruach na Leamhan
'S an gasrad bhí ag roinn leis ler thruagh mo chall,
I gceannas na gcríoch gcaoin gcluthair gcuanach gcam,
Go dealbh i dtír Dhuibhneach níor bhuan mo chlann.

If the protective king from the bank of the Laune was living
And the band of people who were sharing with him who pitied my loss,
In authority over the gentle, well-sheltered, twisted territory indented with harbours,
My family would not proceed poorly in the country of Duibhneach.

An Carrathach groidhe fíochmhar ler fuadhadh an meang,
Is Carrathach Laoi i ndaoirse gan fuascladh fann,
Carrathach rí Chinn Tuirc i n-uaig 's a chlann
'S is atuirse trím chroidhe gan a dtuairisc ann.

The strong fierce MacCarthy to whom guile was hateful,
And MacCarthy Lee in bondage without deliverance, weak,
MacCarthy king of Kanturk in the grave with his children,
And sorrow is through my heart without trace of them there.

Do shearg mo chroidhe im chlíteach do bhuaidhir mo leann;
Na seabhaic nár fríth cinnte, ag ar dhual an eang
Ó Chaiseal go Tuinn Chlíodhna 's go Tuamhuin tall,
A mbailte 's a maoin díth-chreachta ag sluaightibh Gall.

My heart withered in my breast, the humours of my body grieved;
The warriors who were not found stingy, who had the land by right
From Cashel to Tonn Chlíodhna and to Thomond beyond,
Their dwellings and their possessions destructively plundered by a host of foreigners.

Eavan Boland
(1945–)

Eavan Boland's verse translation of Aoghagán Ó Rathaille's early eighteenth-century poem appeared in Boland's first collection of poems, *New Territory*, published in 1967. The author of numerous volumes of poetry, Boland was born in Dublin and educated at Trinity College Dublin. She is currently teaching at Stanford University in the United States.

'After the Irish of Egan O'Rahilly'
(For James Stephens's version of Ó Rathaille's poem, see p. 223.)

Without flocks or cattle or the curved horns
Of cattle, in a drenching night without sleep,
My five wits on the famous uproar
Of the wave toss like ships,
And I cry for boyhood, long before
Winkle and dogfish had defiled my lips.

O if he lived, the prince who sheltered me,[102]
And his company who gave me entry
On the river of the Laune,[103]
Whose royalty stood sentry
Over intricate harbours, I and my own
Would not be desolate in Dermot's country.

Fierce McCarthy Mór[104] whose friends were welcome.
McCarthy of the Lee,[105] a slave of late,
McCarthy of Kanturk[106] whose blood
Has dried underfoot:
Of all my princes not a single word –
Irrevocable silence ails my heart,

My heart shrinks in me, my heart ails
That every hawk and royal hawk is lost;
From Cashel to the far sea
Their birthright is dispersed
Far and near, night and day, by robbery
And ransack, every town oppressed.

Original: 'An Tan D'Aistrigh go
Duibhneachaibh Láimh le Tonn
Tóime i g-Ciarraighe',
by Aodhagán Ó Rathaille (cont.)

Literal translation (cont.):

A thonn so thíos is aoirde céim go h-árd,
Meabhair mo chínn claoidhte ót bhéiceach tá;
Cabhair dá dtigeadh arís go hÉirinn bháin
Do ghlam nach binn do dhingfinn féin it
bhrághaid.[107]

Highest wave there below, proceeding loudly,
My mind is harrowed by your shouting;
If help would come again to fair Ireland,
Your howl that is not melodious I myself
would stuff in your throat.

Take warning wave, take warning crown of the sea,
I, O'Rahilly – witless from your discords –
Were Spanish sails again afloat
And rescue on your tides,
Would force this outcry down your wild throat,
Would make you swallow these Atlantic words.[108]

Original: 'An tSeanbhean Bhocht', by
Nuala Ní Dhomhnaill

Literal translation:

Féachann an tseanbhean orm le neamhshuim is uabhar	The old woman looks at me with indifference and arrogance
as a súile tréigthe atá ar dhath na mbugha	out of her faded eyes that are the colour of the hyacinth
ag cuimhneamh siar ar laethanta geala a hóige,	thinking back on the bright days of her youth,
gur thrua go raibh gach ní chomh buacach san aimsir ollfhoirfe.	that it was a pity that everything was so gay in the pluperfect time.
Canathaobh an uair úd nuair a chan éan	Why in that time when a bird sang
gurbh í an neachtingeal a bhí i gcónaí ann?	was it the nightingale that was always there?
Canathaobh fadó nuair a thug leannáin chúichi	Why long ago when lovers brought her
fleascanna bláth gurb iad na cinn 'orchidé en fleur'	garlands of flowers were they of the kind 'orchis in flower'
ab fhearr a fuaireadar? Nó b'fhéidir ar laethanta fuara	the best that they got? Or perhaps on cold days
sailchuacha cumhra. I gcónaí bhíodh buidéal seaimpéin	fragrant violets. A bottle of champagne was always
ar an gclár i mbuicéad ard leac oighre, bhíodh lása Charraig Mhachaire Rois	on the table in a tall bucket of ice, Carrickmacross lace used to be
ar chaola a láimhe is bhíodh diamaintí ar sileadh óna cluasa,	on her wrists and diamonds used to drip from her ears,
muince péarlaí casta seacht n-uaire thart faoina bráid,	a necklace of pearls wound seven times around her throat,
is ar a méireanta bhíodh fáinní luachmhara, go háirithe	and on her fingers used to be valuable rings, especially
ceann gur chuimhin léi a bheith an-speisialta – ceann	one that she remembered to be very special – one
ar a raibh smeargaidí chomh mór le húll do phíopáin.	on which there were emeralds as big as your Adam's apple.
Féachann sí orm anois leis an dtruamhéil fhuar	She looks at me now with the cold plaintiveness
a chífeá go minic i súile a bhí tráth óg is breá,	that you would often see in eyes that once were young and fine,
ag meabhrú di féin im' fhianaise, leath os íseal	recalling to herself, in my presence, half in a low voice
is leath os ard, gur mhéanar don té a fuair amharc	and half in a high voice, that fortunate was he who got a view
ar an gcéad lá a shiúil sí go mómharach síos an phromanáid	on the first day that she walked gracefully down the promenade
mar ríon faoina parasól; ar na céadta céadta gaiscíoch	like a queen under her parasol; the hundreds and hundreds of heroes
is fear breá a chuaigh le saighdiúireacht in arm na Breataine	and fine men who went soldiering in the British army
nó a theith leo ar bord loinge go dtí na tíortha teo,	or who fled on board a ship to the hot countries,
aon ní ach éaló ós na saigheada éagóra	anything only to escape from the arrows of injustice
a theilgeadh sí orthu de shíor faoina fabhraí tiubha.	that she cast on them constantly from under her thick eyebrows.
Caoineann sí, ag monabhar faoina hanáil go bog,	She laments, murmuring under her breath softly,
an tréimhse fhada, achar bliana is lae,	the distant time, a period of a year and a day,
ar thug sí an svae léithi mar bhanríon na bplainéad:	in which she held sway like a queen of the planets:

Ciaran Carson
(1948–)

Ciaran Carson brings to verse translation from the Irish not only a knowledge of the language – both his parents spoke Irish, and it was his first language growing up in Belfast – but also an interest in traditional Irish music. Of verse translation, he once said that a good translation should bear 'a sidelong metaphorical relation to the original'.[109]

Carson was educated at Queens University Belfast. He has worked as a teacher and civil servant, and is currently Professor of Poetry and Director of the Seamus Heaney Centre at Queens University.

'The Shan Van Vocht'

(The original is by the contemporary poet Nuala Ní Dhomhnaill.)

The faded cornflower blue of that old woman's eye
Stares through me – it's as if I wasn't there – back to where
The bright days of her youth shine through,
Lamenting all the halcyon monotony of that pluperfect time.
How come no common birds sang then,
Only nightingales?
How come her 'nice young men' would offer her,
Not just a bunch of flowers, but out-of-season orchids?
Or cold-weather, fragrant violets? And then, the eternal
Champagne on ice, the froth of lace at her wrists, diamonds
Dripping from her ears, pearls wound seven times
Around her neck, her fingers ponderous
With expensive rings, one with an emerald
As big as an Adam's apple.

That ice-blue pity stares through me, she
Whose eyes were radiant once with youth and blue fire –
How privileged they were, the poor unfortunates
Who caught a glimpse of her in all her majesty, gliding
On the promenade beneath a queenly parasol; the regiments
Of stricken youths who took to soldiering, who
Laboured in the White Man's Grave, anything
To flee the blue illicit lightning
She squandered from those eyes.

She's mumbling, babbling, murmuring
About that Long-Ago of a Year and a Day
When she held sway as Empress of the Zodiac;
And those who were born while she kicked and squealed

383

Original: 'An tSeanbhean Bhocht', by
Nuala Ní Dhomhnaill (cont.)

Literal translation (cont.):

na leanaí a bheirtí nuair a théadh sí faoi
loch

the children who were born when she was
submerged

i ndaigh uisce i lár na cistineach,

in a tub of water in the middle of the kitchen,

múchadh nó bá an chríoch bháis a bhíodh
orthu

suffocation or drowning the deadly end that
was on them

is dob é an chroch a bhí i ndán do gach n-
aon

and it was the gallows that was in store for
everyone

a raibh de mhí-ádh air teacht ar an saol

who had the misfortune to come into the
world

nuair a bhí lúb na téide tarraingthe ar a
muinéal.

when the loop of the rope was drawn on her
neck.

Is iad siúd a chéadchonaic solas an lae

And those who first saw the light of day

nuair a léimeadh sí sa tine gurbh é a
ndeireadh

when she leapt in the fire it was their end

a bheith dóite is loiscithe le teann grá di
féin,

to be burned and scorched with the force of
love for herself,

chun gur thit na céadta ina sraithibh deas is
clé

so that the hundreds fell in their rows right
and left

ní le grá bán nó breac ná grá pósta, mo léir

not for fair or middling love or married love,
alas

ach an grá dubh is an manglam dicé a
leanann é.

but the dark love and the worthless person
who follows it.

Anois tá sí cancarach, ag tabhairt amach dom
ar dalladh. Tá sí bréan bodhar badráilte
ó bheith suite ina cathaoir rotha. Gan faic
na ngrást le déanamh aici ach a bheith ag
féachaint
ar na ceithre fallaí. Rud eile,
níl na cailíní aimsire faoi mar a bhídís
cheana. Fágann siad rianta smeartha
ar an *antimacassar* lena méireanta salacha.
Fuair sí an píosa bróidnéireachta sin ó bhean
ambasadóra is bheadh an-dochma uirthi é a
scaoileadh
chun siúil nó tré dhearmhad ligint dóibh siúd
é a mhilleadh.

Now she is cantankerous, giving out to me
a lot. She is foul, confused, bothered
from being seated in her wheelchair. With
nothing
whatever for her to do except to be looking
at the four walls. Another thing,
the maids are not as they used to be
before. They leave trails of grease
on the antimacassar with their dirty fingers.
She got that piece of embroidery from the wife
of the ambassador and it would be a great
hardship on her to let it
go or through forgetfulness to allow those ones
to destroy it.

Tugaim faoi ndeara nach nguíonn sí
sonuachar maith chúchu nuair a thagann siad
isteach leis an dtrádaire líonta síos go talamh
le gréithre póirseiléine, taephota airgid
is ceapairí cúcumair. Táimse ar thaobh na
gcailíní,
is deirim léi cén dochar, go bhfuil siad fós
óg,
is nach féidir ceann críonna a chur ar
cholainn,
nach dtagann ciall roimh aois is gur mó
craiceann . . .
is gur ag dul i minithe is i mbréagaí atá gach
dream
dá dtagann: gach seanrá a thagann isteach i
mo chloigeann,
aon rud ach an tseanbhean bhaoth seo a
choimeád socair.[110]

I notice that she doesn't wish
them good fortune when they come
in with the tray laden down to the ground
with porcelain ware, a silver teapot
and cucumber sandwiches. I am on the side of
the girls,
and I say to her what is the harm, that they are
still young,
and that it isn't possible to put an old head on
a body,
that sense does not come before age and that
there are many phases . . .
and that getting more into swearing and more
deceitful is every crowd
that comes: every old saying that comes into
my head,
anything, only to keep this foolish old woman
quiet.

In a bath plonked down on the kitchen floor, well,
They were doomed to be drowned or smothered
And the ill-starred ones who came into the world
When the noose got tighter on her neck
Were doomed to be strung up
And those first smitten by the light of day
While she danced in the fire
Were doomed to be burnt-out, dazzled and frazzled
With all-consuming love for her
So that it came to pass that they were mowed down
In their hundreds, left and right, not with love
That you or I know, no, not with ordinary love
But with a gnawing, migraine-bright black lust
And galloping consumption.

She's getting to be cranky, cantankerous
And cancered, slabbering of this and that, straight-
Jacketed to her wheelchair, locked
Into self-pity, whingeing on and on – damn
All to do all day, but stare at these four walls.
And servants, of course, aren't what they used to be.
Look how these two chits of girls
Have smeared their greasy paws on the antimacassar.
And that embroidered tablecloth – you know the ambassador?
Well, his wife gave that to her. And she wouldn't like
To see it ruined by those same two hussies.

And here they come now, tinkling in
With an overloaded tray – china tea-set, silver pot,
The dreaded cucumber sandwiches. Not a word from her,
I notice, about *their* prospects. Well, I'm on their side
And I mutter something, that they're young yet, that wisdom
Only comes with age, that you can't put an old head on
      young shoul – . . .
Folly, I'm saying, gets worse with every generation:
Anything, every old cliché in the book, anything at all
To get this old bitch to shut the fuck up.[111]

Original: From 'Cúirt an Mheán-
Oíche', by Brian Merriman

Literal translation:

Ba gnáth me ag siúl le ciumhais na habhann

It was usual for me to be walking along the bank of the river

Ar bháinseach úr 's an drúcht go trom,

On the fresh green and the dew heavy,

In aice na gcoillte i gcoim an tsléibhe

Near to the woods in the middle of the mountain

Gan mhairg gan mhoill ar shoilse an lae.

Without oppression, without hindrance at day-light.

Do ghealadh mo croí an uair chínn Loch Gréine,

My heart lightened the time I would see Loch Gréine,

An talamh 's an tír is íor na spéire,

The ground and the country and the horizon,

Taitneamhacht aoibhinn suíomh na sléibhte

Pleasing, delightful the situation of the moun-tains

Ag bagairt a gcinn thar dhroim a chéile.

Brandishing their heads over each other's backs.

Do ghealfadh an croí bheadh críon le cianta

The heart would lighten that would be worn-out with the ages

Caite gan bhrí nó líonta 'o phianta,

Spent without strength or filled with pains,

An séithleach searbh gan sealbh gan saibhreas

The bitter, emaciated person without property, without riches

D'fhéachfadh tamall thar bharra na gcoillte

Who would look a while beyond the tops of the woods

Ar lachain 'na scuainte ar chuan gan ceo

At ducks in their clutches in a harbour without fog

Is an eala ar a bhfuaid 's í ag gluaiseacht leo,

And the swan among them and she moving with them,

Na héisc le meidhir ag eirghe in airde,

The fish with friskiness rising up,

Péirse im radhairc go taibhseach tar-rbhreac,

Perch in my view, striking, speckle-bellied,

Dath an locha agus gorm na dtonn

The colour of the lake and the blue of the waves

Ag teacht go tolgach torannach trom.

Coming strongly, noisily, heavily.

Bhíodh éanla i gcrainn go meidhreach mómhar

Birds used to be in trees, joyous, graceful

Is léimreach eilte i gcoillte im chóngar,

And leaping does in woods near me,

Géimreach adharc is radharc ar shlóite,

Sounding horn and a sight of crowds,

Tréanrith gadhar is *Reynard* rompu.

Dogs running hard and *Reynard* in front of them.

Ar maidin inné bhí an spéir gan ceo,

Yesterday morning the sky was without fog,

Bhí *Cancer* ón ngréin 'na caorthaibh teo

Cancer from the sun was a warm glowing mass

Is í gofa chun saothair tar éis na hoíche

And it harnessed for work after the night

Is obair an lae sin réimpi sínte.

And the work of that day stretched before it.

Bhí duilleabhar craobh ar ghéaga im thimpeall,

The leaves of the branches were on limbs around me,

Fiorthann is féar 'na slaodach taoibh liom,

Wheat grass and grass in swaths beside me,

From 'The Midnight Court'

(Carson based his verse translation of Brian Merriman's eighteenth-century satire on the rhythm of a jig tune, 'Larry O'Gaff', which he said he found 'not such a far cry from the prosody of "Cúirt an Mheán Oíche", with its internal rhymes and four strong beats to the line'.[112] In Merriman's poem, the narrator, while wandering through the country-side, falls into a dream-vision, and is taken to a court presided over by a fairy-queen and entertaining complaints from Ireland's young women of sexual frustration. For an eighteenth-century version, see under Denis Woulf, pp. 27–33; for Percy Arland Ussher's and Frank O'Connor's twentieth-century versions, see pp. 237–241 and pp. 277–285; for another contemporary translation, see under Seamus Heaney, pp. 347–351. The following selection is the opening of the poem.)

'Twas my custom to stroll by a clear winding stream,
With my boots full of dew from the lush meadow green,
Near a neck of the woods where the mountain holds sway,
Without danger or fear at the dawn of the day.
The sight of Lough Graney[113] would dazzle my eyes,
As the countryside sparkled beneath the blue skies;
Uplifting to see how the mountains were stacked,
Each head peeping over a neighbouring back.
It would lighten the heart, be it listless with age,
Enfeebled by folly, or cardiac rage –
Your wherewithal racked by financial disease –
To perceive through a gap in the wood full of trees
A squadron of ducks in a shimmering bay,
Escorting the swan on her elegant way,
The trout on the rise with its mouth to the light,
While the perch swims below like a speckledy sprite,
And the billows of blue become foam as they break
With a thunderous crash on the shores of the lake,
And the birds in the trees whistle bird-songs galore,
The deer gallop lightly through woods dark as yore,
Where trumpeting huntsmen and hounds of the hunt
Chase the shadow of Reynard, who leads from the front.

Yesterday morning, a cloudless blue sky
Bore the signs of another hot day in July;
Bright Phoebus arose from the darkness of night,
And got back to his business of spreading the light.
Around me were branches of trees in full leaf
And glades decked with ferns of a sylvan motif,

Original: from 'Cúirt an Mheán-
Oíche', by Brian Merriman (cont.)

Literal translation (cont.):

Original	Literal translation
Glasra fáis is bláth is luibheanna	Luxuriant greens and flowers and herbs,
Scaipfeadh le fán dá chráiteacht smaointe.	Would scatter astray thoughts however troubled.
Bhí mé cortha is an codladh dhom thraochadh	I was exhausted and sleep was wearing me out
Is shín mé thoram ar chothrom sa bhféar glas	And I stretched across on a level in the green grass
In aice na gcrann i dteannta trinse,	Next to the trees near a trench,
Taca lem cheann 's mo hanlaibh sínte.	A prop for my head and my limbs stretched.
Ar cheangal mo shúl go dlúth le chéile,	On fastening my eyes tightly together,
Greamaithe dúnta i ndúghlas néalta	Fixed shut in a firm lock of sleep,
Is m'aghaidh agam foilithe ó chuile go sásta	And my face hidden from flies satisfactorily
I dtaibhreamh d'fhuiling me an cuilithe cráite	In a dream I suffered the tormented whirlpool
Chorraigh do lom do pholl go hae me	Which moved me to distress, that pierced me to the heart
Im chodladh go trom gan mheabhair gan éirim.[114]	In a heavy sleep without consciousness, without intelligence.

Original:

Literal translation:

Original	Literal translation
Da mbeinnse silte mar thuilleadh dhom chomharsain,	If I were lazy like many of my neighbours,
Leadhbach liosta gan tuiscint gan eolas,	Silly, tedious, without understanding, without knowledge,
Gan radhairc gan gliocas in imirt mo chóra,	Without vision, without cleverness in playing for what is my due,
Mo threighid! cár mhiste me rith in éadóchas?	My bitter grief! what would be the harm of me running into despair?
Ní feacathas fós me i gcóngar daoine	I have not yet been seen in the vicinity of people
Ag faire ná ag tórramh óig ná chríonna,	Watching or waking, young or old
Ar mhachaire an bháire, an ráis ná an rince,	On the field of the match, the race or the dance,
I bhfarradh na dtáinte, ar bhántaibh líonta	In the company of the multitude, on crowded grasslands
Acht gofa go sámh gan cháim ar domhan	But was dressed pleasantly without any fault in the world
I gculaithe shásta ó bharr go bonn.	In agreeable clothes from head to sole.
Beidh a cheart im chúl do phúdar fillte,	The right amount of closely applied powder will be in my hair,
Starch is stiúir i gcúl mo chaidhpe,	Starch and a rakish angle in the back of my coif,
Húda geal gan ceal ribíní,	A bright hood with no lack of ribbons,
Gúna breac 's a cheart rufaí leis.	A speckled gown and the right amount of ruffs with it.
Is annamh go brách gan fásáil aerach	It is very seldom that without an airy floral design
Thaitneamhach bhreá lem cheárdán craorag	Pleasing and fine is my crimson cloak
Is an-iomdha luibheanna, craobhacha is éanla	And a great many herbs, branches and birds

With flowers and herbs so profusely in train
It would banish all thoughts of despair from your brain.
Beat out as I was and in need of a doze,
I laid myself down where a grassy bank rose
By the side of a ditch, in arboreal shade,
Where I stretched out my feet, and pillowed my head.
So I shut down my brain, and the lids of my eyes,
With my hat on my face to discourage the flies,
And I dropped off to sleep, quite composed and serene,
When I found myself sunk in a horrible dream
That jolted my senses, and grieved my heart sore;
Lying dead to the world, I was shook to the core.[115]

(The following passage is spoken by a young woman testifying to the
court about the lack of willing men in Ireland.)

And if I were inclined – like some neighbours I know –
To be laggard and lazy, with no brains to show,
With no gumption, or savvy, or sense of what's fair,
Then what odds if you saw me fall into despair?
But any reception, or party or spree,
At wedding or wake, of whatever degree,
At sports-field, or race-course, or on the fair green,
Where step-dancing punters in dozens are seen,
I'd be nicely turned out in an eye-catching kit,
From shoulder to hem of superlative fit,
My poll lightly powdered (too much is *de trop*),
My bonnet well starched, and adjusted just so,
The hood *à la mode*, trailing ribbons galore;
My gown of shot silk (that stuff I adore)
And its bodice befitting a well-made young maid,
Are enhanced by my cloak of the cardinal red;
There's a landscape embroidered, with branches and birds,

Original: from 'Cúirt an Mheán-Oíche', by Brian Merriman (cont.)	Literal translation (cont.):
Im aprún síogach ríogach *Cambrick*,	On my striped, startling apron of cambric,
Sála cumtha cúnga córach	Heels shapely, narrow, comely
Arda sleamhaine ar *Screw* fám bhróga,	A smooth height on a screw under my shoes,
Búclaí is fáinní is lámhainní síoda	Buckles and rings and gloves of silk
Is fonsaí, práslaí is lásaí daora.	And hoops, bracelets and high-priced laces.
Seachain ná síl gur scinnteach scáfar,	Beware, don't think that I am a timid, skinny girl,
Aimid gan ghaois ná naíondach náireach	A simpleton without intelligence or modest innocence
Eaglach uaigneach uallach fhiain me,	Fearful, lonely, scatter-brained, uncultivated,
Gealach gan ghuais gan stuaim gan téagar.	A brightness without enterprise, without good sense, without substance.
I bhfalach ní raghainnse ó radhairc na gcéadta,	In hiding I would not go from the views of the hundreds,
Is ceannasach taibhseach m'aghaidh agus m'éadan,	Commanding and proud are my face and my brow,
Is dearfa bhím dom shíorthaispeánadh	It is certain that I'm always displaying myself
Ar mhachaire mhín gach fíoriomána,	On the smooth field of every true hurling,
Ag rince, báire, rás is radaireacht,	At dance, match, race and courting,
Tinte cnámh is ráfla is ragairne,	Bonfires and gossiping and revelling,
Aonach, margadh is Aifreann Domhnaigh	Fair, market and Sunday Mass
Ag éileamh breathnaithe, ag amharc 's ag toghadh fir.[116]	Demanding observation, looking at and choosing men.

Original:	Literal translation:
Guím go hard tu, 'fháidhbhean tsíthe,	I beseech you loudly, prophetess of the fairies,
A shíolrach neámhdha 'o bharr na ríthe,	Heavenly seed from the branch of the kings,
A shoilse glóire, a choróin na sluaite,	Light of glory, crown of the crowds,
Eist lem ghlórsa, fóir is fuar dhúinn.	Listen to my voice, help and relieve us.
Meáigh an t'intinn díth na mbéithe	Weigh in your mind the deprivation of the women
Is práinn na mílte brídeach aonta	And the need of the thousands of single maidens
Is toicibh mar táid ar bhráid a chéile	And girls as they are present together
Ag borradh is ag fás mar ál na ngéanna.	Increasing and growing like a brood of geese.
An t-ál is lú atá ag siúl na sráide,	The smallest progeny who are walking the streets,
Garlaigh dhubha tá giúnnach gránna,	Dark urchins who are close-cropped, ugly,
An aga dá laghad má gheibhid a ndóthain	In a period of time, however small, if they get their sufficiency
Glasra, meidhg is bleaghdair, borrfaid	Of green stuff, whey and curdled milk, will grow
D'urchar nimhe le haois gan éifeacht,	Like a bolt from the blue with age without effect,
Tiocfaidh na cíocha, scinnfid, scéithfid.	The breasts will come, will start, will erupt.
Scalladh mo chléibh, is baoth mo smaointe	Scald of my bosom, foolish are my thoughts
Ag tagairt ar chéile i gcaorthaibh tinte,	Mentioning a spouse in fiery rages,
Is deacair dhom súil le subhachas d'fháil	It is difficult for me to hope to find joyfulness
Is gan fear in aghaidh triúir sa Mumhan dá mná.	And not a man for three of the women in Munster.
Ó tharla an ceantar gann seo gámhar,	Since it happens that this meagre district is needy,

My shoes have those new-fangled, screw-in high heels
(Not the best, I'll admit, for the jigs and the reels);
The essential accessories every girl loves;
But look out! don't assume I'm a bashful wee chit,
On my bright cambric apron, too lovely for words;
A simpering ninny, a twittering twit,
A flibbertigibbet, a bird-witted geck,
A loudmouth, a mope, or a gibbering wreck.I hold my head
high in the midst of the crowd,
My gaze self-assured, and my shoulders unbowed.
At races and dances I don't hide my figure;
At parties where jorums are poured into jiggers,
At junkets and suppers and bunfights and klatches,
At Mass or at market, and big hurling matches,
I show myself off, always looking my best;
When I size up the talent, I end up depressed.[117]

(In this selection, the young woman makes her final appeal to
Aoibheall, the fairy-queen presiding over the court.)

I beg and implore you, O All-knowing Vision!
Descended from heaven, give us a decision!
O Glorious Light! O Queen of the Nation!
Incline to my pleading, and further our station;
Weigh in your mind all our feminine needs,
The thousands of fields without husband or seed,
For the number of females is on the increase,
Falling over each other like flocks of young geese.
And the urchins you see running wild on the street –
Skinny wee lassies with dirty wee feet –
Will be healthy and fat in a month and a day
Should you feed them with greens and big mugfuls of whey,
Till they put on a spurt of unstoppable force,
And they blossom and bud as their blood takes its course.
It sickens my happiness! Look for a mate?
When I have to contend with a river in spate?
Hope for a tumble, a wee bit of fun,
When the girls are outnumbered by men three to one?
The province of Munster is utterly sunk,

Original: from 'Cúirt an Mheán-
Oíche', by Brian Merriman (cont.)

Literal translation (cont.):

Fáintibh fann 's an t-am seo práinneach,
Men enfeebled and this time urgent,

Fódla folamh is fothrom ag fiaile
Ireland empty and a commotion from upstarts

Is óige an phobail ag cromadh is ag liathadh,
And the youth of the people stooping and turning grey,

Aonta fada go dealamh ná foighnigh
Long single and destitute, don't have patience

Dh'éinne ar thalamh is fear éigin faighimse,
For anyone on earth, and get me some man,

Ceangail i dtráth go tláith fán úim iad
Bind them in time tenderly in harness

Is as sin go brách acht fágthar fúinne iad.[118]
And from then on just leave us to it.

And the wastrels of Munster are wasting their spunk;
The weeds are increasing, the country is spent,
Its youth growing feeble and agèd and bent.
Unmarried, impatient, deprived of coition,
I'm looking to you to improve my position:
So get me a man, and like birds of a feather
We'll make a fine couplet in harness together![119]

Original: 'Meabhraigh mo laoidh chumainnse'	Literal translation:

Meabhraigh mo laoidh chumainnse,
    a bhean an chumainn bhréige:
fuilngim feasta, is fulaingse
    bheith i bhféagmhais a chéile.

Teacht orm dá gcluinese
    i dtithibh móra ná i mbothaibh,
le cách orm ná cuiridhse,
    ná cáin mé is ná cosain.

I dteampall ná i mainistir,
    cé madh reilig nó réadmhagh,
dá bhfaice ná dá bhfaicearsa
    ná féach orm is ní fhéachfad.

Ná habair, is ní aibéarsa
    m'ainm ná fáth mo shloinnte;
ná hadaimh is ní aidéamhsa
    go bhfacas tú riamh roimhe.[120]

Remember my love song,
    woman of the false love:
I suffer henceforth, and you suffer
    to be without each other.

An account of me if you hear
    in big houses or in huts,
do not invoke me to everyone,
    don't censure and don't defend me.

In church or in monastery,
    though it be a graveyard or an open plain,
if you see [me] or if I see [you]
    do not look at me and I will not look [at you].

Don't say, and I will not say
    my name or an explanation of my family,
don't admit, and I will not admit
    that I ever saw you before.

Gabriel Rosenstock
(1949–)

Gabriel Rosenstock was one of the group of young Irish-language poets, which also included Nuala Ní Dhomhnaill and Michael Davitt, associated with the magazine *Innti* at University College Cork in the 1970s. Rosenstock has published poetry in Irish since the 1970s, and has also been a prolific translator, working with a wide range of traditions, including Arabic and Japanese as well as Irish.

Rosenstock was born in Kilfinane, Co. Limerick, and has worked as an editor at An Gúm, the government imprint for Irish-language books.

'Think Upon My Song of Love'
(The original dates to the seventeenth century.)

Think upon my song of love
    Lady in love untrue!
Let us suffer each other's loss,
    I and you.

Should they mention my name
    In houses big or small
Do not praise or blame me,
    Say nothing at all.

In a church, or abbey,
    The graveyard or open plain
Should I see you, or you me,
    Let it be with disdain.

Say not, nor shall I,
    Who my father is, my mother,
Don't admit, nor shall I,
    That we know one another.[121]

Original: 'An Casadh', by Nuala Ní Dhomhnaill	Literal translation:
Anois nó go bhfuil coiscéim choiligh	Now that it is a cock's step to
leis an oíche	the night,
ní féidir liom mo chasóg labhandair	it's not possible for me my lavender jacket
a chrochadh a thuilleadh	to hang any longer
le haon tsiúráil nó leath chomh neafaiseach	with any certainty or half as casually
ar na nga gréine	on the rays of sun
ar eagla go dtitfeadh sí ar an urlár romham	for fear that it would fall on the floor before me
ina glóthach frog.	like frog-spawn.
Tá an clog leis ar an bhfalla ag obair	The clock too on the wall is working
i mo choinne,	against me,
beartaíonn sé tréas de shíor	it brandishes treason constantly
lena lámha tanaí bruíne	with its thin hands of strife
a aghaidh mhílítheach feosaí	its pale, wizened face
ag stánadh orm gan stad	staring at me without stop
is bagairt shotalach óna theanga bhalbh.	and an arrogant threat from its inarticulate tongue.
Anois nó gur chac an púca	Now that the pooka shit
ar na sméara	on the blackberries
is go bhfuil an bhliain ag casadh	and the year is turning
ar a lúndracha	on its hinges
puthann siollaí gaoithe	puffs of wind blow
tríos na hinsí orainn	through the hinges on us
is séidimid fuar is te.	and we blow cold and hot.
Deineann ár gcnámha gíoscán	Our bones are creaking
ar nós doras stábla	like a stable door
atá ag meirgiú go mear cheal íle.	that is rusting actively for lack of oil.
Cuireann sé codladh grifín orainn is uisce faoinár bhfiacla	It puts numbness on us and water under our teeth
ag cuimhneamh dár n-ainneoin ar thránna móra	thinking actively in spite of ourselves of the large strands
an Earraigh go fuadrach is sinn	of the Spring and while we [are]
le linn taoidí móra an Fhómhair.	in the period of the great tides of Autumn.
Titfidh an oíche go luath sa tráthnóna	The evening will fall early in the afternoon
gan choinne	unexpectedly
mar shnap madra allta	like the snapping sound of a wild dog
i gcoinne an ghloine.	against the glass.
Ní chreidim an bearradh caorach	I don't believe the cirrus cloud
a iompraíonn an spéir a thuilleadh,	that the sky carries anymore,
níl ann ach dallamullóg,	there is nothing in it but deception
rud dorcha faoi bhréagriocht.	a dark thing under disguise.
Is ní haon mhaith	There's no use
'cuir do lapaí bána bána isteach'	in saying to the wind
a rá leis an ngaoth	'put your white, white paws in'

Medbh McGuckian
(1950–)

In addition to contributing several poetic translations to Nuala Ní Dhomhnaill's collection *Pharaoh's Daughter* (1990), Medbh McGuckian, along with Eiléan Ní Chuilleanáin, provided all the translations for a later Ní Dhomhnaill volume, *The Water Horse* (1999). She was born in Belfast and educated at Queens University.

'Nine Little Goats'
(The original is by the contemporary poet Nuala Ní Dhomhnaill.)

It's a cock's foot of a night:
If I go on hanging my lightheartedness
Like a lavender coat on a sunbeam's nail,
It will curdle into frogspawn.
The clock itself has it in for me,
Forever brandishing the splinters of its hands,
Choking on its middle-aged fixations.

Since the pooka fertilized the blackberries,
The year pivots on its hinges, breathing
Wintry gusts into our warmth.
Our bones grate like an unoiled
Rusty stable door,
Our teeth get pins and needles
As Autumn's looming tide drowns
The endless shores of Spring.

Darkness will be dropping in
In the afternoons without an appointment,
A wolf's bite at the windowpane,
And wolves too the clouds
In the sheepish sky.
You needn't expect the wind
To put in her white, white paws

Original: 'An Casadh', by Nuala Ní Dhomhnaill (cont.)	Literal translation (cont.):

sara n-osclaíonn tú an doras.
Tá neamhthoradh aici ort fhéin
is ar do chaint bhaoth, is léi
urlár na cruinne le scuabadh
mar is áil léi.
Is bí cinnte dho nach spárálfaidh sí
an bhruis orainn anois,
gheobhaimid ó thalamh an dalladh
má fuair éinne riamh,
tá nimh ina héadan inár gcoinne
is gomh ina guth
go háirithe le tamall
ó dh'imigh an bhliain ó mhaith.

before you open the door.
She has a disregard for yourself
and for your idle talk, she has
the floor of the world for scrubbing
as she desires.
And be certain of it that she will not spare
the brush on us now,
we will get from the ground plenty
if anyone ever got it,
poison is in her face against us
and venom in her voice
especially in the time
since the year went from the good.

Cad tá le déanamh ach meaits
a lasadh leis an móin fhuinte
atá ag feitheamh go patfhoighneach
sa ghráta le breis is ráithe,
na cuirtíní a tharrach go righin
malltriallach ag fógairt an donas amach
is an sonas isteach ar an dteaghlach,
suí síos le leabhar leabharlainne
le hais na tine
ag leathéisteacht le nuacht na teilifíse,
uaireanta dul i mbun cluiche fichille
nó dreas scéalaíochta
ag feitheamh le goradh na loirgne
is le róstadh na gcnap.[122]

What is there to do but light a match
to the compacted turf
which is waiting fairly patiently
in the grate for more than a season,
pull the curtains deliberately
sluggishly, driving the unhappiness out
and the happiness in on the household,
to sit down with a library book
by the fire
half-listening to the television news,
sometimes to go about a game of chess
or a spell of story-telling
waiting for the heating of the shins
and the roasting of the large potatoes.

Original: 'An Prionsa Dubh', by Nuala Ní Dhomhnaill	Literal translation:

Taibhríodh dom in aois coinlíochta
i mo leaba chúng sa tsuanlios aíochta
go rabhas i halla mor ag rince
i measc slua mór de mo dhaoine muin-
   teartha,
le prionsa dubh.

I dreamt when I was old enough
in my narrow bed in the dormitory
that I was in a great hall dancing
in the middle of a large crowd of my relations,

with a black prince.

Timpeall is timpeall do ghaibh an válsa,
bhí míobhán ar mo cheann le háthas,
ba mhear é a shúil, bhí a fhéachaint
   fíochmhar,
bhí bua gach clis i lúth is in aicillíocht
ag an bprionsa dubh.

Around and around went the waltz,
a dizziness was on my head with joy,
lively was his eye, his look was fierce,
excellence of every feat in movement and
   agility
had the black prince.

Before you open the door,
For she hasn't the slightest interest
In you or your sore throat:
The solar system is all hers
To scrub like a floor if she pleases,
She's hardly likely to spare her brush
On any of us, as the poison comes to a head
In the brow of a year
That will never come back.

So we might as well put a match
To the peat briquettes
That the summer gave the grate,
And draw the sullen curtains tight
On the family's bad luck,
And sit with a library book,
Half-dozed by the television news,
Or roused by a game of chess,
Or a story, until
We are our own spuds,
Roasting in the embers.[123]

'The Ebony Adonis'

(The original is by the contemporary poet Nuala Ní Dhomhnaill.)

At puberty I had a dream
in my all-too-single bunk in the school dorm,
of dancing the length of a public room
with the guts of my relatives looking on
in the arms of an ebony Adonis.

Round and round whirled the waltz
till my senses spun with joy
from the fiery, fierce glance of his eye.
Every achievement in fitness and sport
possessed my ebony Adonis.

Original: 'An Prionsa Dubh', by
Nuala Ní Dhomhnaill (cont.)

Literal translation (cont.):

Ach do plabadh oscailte an doras sa tsuan-
lios,
do chling soithí níocháin, do lasadh soilse,
bhí bean rialta ramhar ag fógairt 'Moladh
le hÍosa'
is do shuíos síos i lár an tsúsa is do ghoileas
i ndiaidh mo phrionsa dhuibh.

But the door in the dormitory was banged
open,
wash-basins rang, lights were lit,
a fat nun was declaiming 'Praise be to Jesus'
and I sat down in the middle of the blanket and
I wept
for my black prince.

A dhreach, a mharc ní dhearmhadfad
choíche,
a scáth ard baolach a bhíodh liom
sínte,
mo bhuachaill caol in éag do mhill mé,
mo rí, m'impire, mo thiarna,
mo phrionsa dubh.

His appearance, his authority I will never
forget,
his tall, dangerous shadow that had been
stretched by me,
my slender boy he ruined me forever,
my king, my emperor, my lord,
my black prince.

Is do m'iníon taibhríodh in aois a naoi di
gur oscail doirse in óstán draíochta
is duine éagsúil ag gach seomra acu á hiar-
raidh
is mar is dual máthar di (a chonách orm a
thóg í) roghnaíonn
is toghann an prionsa dubh.

And my daughter dreamt at the age of nine
that doors in a magic inn opened
and various people in every room seeking
her
and as she takes after her mother (serves me
right who raised her) chooses
and picks the black prince.

Is a iníon bháin, tóg toise cruinn dó,
ní maith an earra é, níl sé iontaofa,
is dúnmharfóir é, is máistir pionsa,
is sár-rinceoir é, ach cá ngabhann an
rince
ach trí thinte ifrinn leis an bprionsa dubh.

And, fair daughter, take an exact measure of him,
he is not the good article, he is not trustworthy,
he is a murderer, he is a fencing master,
he is an excellent dancer, but where does the
dance go
but through fires of hell with the black prince.

Cuirfear faoi ghlas tú i gcás gloine iata,
nó faoi mar a bheadh doras rothlánach in a
mbeifeá greamaithe
gan cead isteach nó amach agat ach an
suathadh síoraí
soir agus siar tré phóirsí an tsíce
má ligeann tú a cheann leis an bprionsa
dubh.

You will be put under lock in a closed glass case,
or as if there were a revolving door in which
you were stuck
without having permission to go in or out, but
turning constantly
east and west through the porches of the psyche
if you give the black prince his head.

Nó beir mar a bhíos-sa i néaróis sínte
ceithre bliana déag, is mé spíonta le pianta
faoi mar a thitfinn i dtobar ar chuma
Ophelia
gan neach beo i mo ghaobhar, ná éinne a
thuigfeadh
toisc gur thugas ró-ghean do mo phrionsa
dubh.

Or you will be as I was, stretched in neurosis
fourteen years, and I exhausted with pains
as if I had fallen in a well like Ophelia

without a living being near me, or anyone who
would understand
because I gave too much love to my black
prince.

Then the dormitory door caved in with a bang,
lights snapped on and wash-basins rang,
a well-fed sister was singing the praises of Christ,
and myself left amidst the bedclothes bereft
of my ebony Adonis.

His face and his touch I will never forget,
that high-powered shadow that with me slept,
that expert lover that spoiled me for dead,
my sovereign, imperial, absolute passion,
my ebony Adonis.

My daughter, in her turn, dreamed aged nine
of a door that led to a spellbound inn
where various chancers were coaxing her in
and, like mother like daughter, you'd know she was
    mine,
nothing would do her but the ebony Adonis.

Now, light of my soul, make no bones about it,
a no-good son-of-a-bitch can't be trusted,
with his murder record and black belt too,
this Lord of the Dance is headed where to?
Straight through the fires of hell, with the ebony
    Adonis.

You'll end up closed in an exhibition case,
under lock and key, or caught as it were in a
    revolving doorway,
unable either to get in or get out for the swish
back and forth, night and day, through the porches of
the psyche
if you give an inch to the ebony Adonis.

You'll be laid low as I was in a type of ME
at the dregs of a well like a sort of Ophelia,
tortured with symptoms for fourteen years
without a creature to speak to or a sympathetic ear
since I handed my cards to the ebony Adonis.

Original: 'An Prionsa Dubh', by
Nuala Ní Dhomhnaill (cont.)

Literal translation (cont.):

Nó gur shiúlas amach ar an nduimhche
    oíche duibhré

Until I walked out on the dune on a moonless
    night

is dar an Mháthair Mhór is dar déithe mo
    mhuintire

and by the Great Mother and by the gods of my
    people

a bhraitheas i mo thimpeall, do thugas
    móid agus briathar

that I felt around me, I vowed and promised

go dtabharfainn suas an ní ab ansa liom
    ach mé a shaoradh ón bpian seo –

that I would give up the thing dearest to me
    only to free me from this pain –

cén cás ach dob é sin mo phrionsa dubh.

what was the difficulty except that it was my
    black prince.

Mar dob é an bás é, ina luí i luíochán

Because he was death, lying in ambush

in íochtar m'anama, ins an bpaibhiliún

in the bottom of my soul, in the pavilion

is íochtaraí i mo chroí, de shíor ar tí

lowest in my heart, constantly about to

mé a ídiú gan mhoill is a shá ins an duib-
    heagán

destroy me without delay and thrust me in the
    abyss

mar sin é an saghas é, an prionsa dubh.

because that is the kind he is, the black prince.

Mar sin, a mhaoineach, dein an ní a deir do
    chroí leat,

So, my dear one, do the thing that your heart
    tells you,

toisc gur ghabhas-sa tríd seo leis ná bíodh
    aon ró-imní ort.

because I went through this with him, don't be
    too anxious.

Ní sháróidh an bás sinn, ach ní shaorfaidh
    choíche,

Death will not overcome us, but will not release
    us ever,

ní lú ná mar a aontóidh an saol seo le chéile

no less than this life will unite together

sinne, agus ár bprionsa dubh.[124]

us, and our black prince.

Till I walked out over the golf links to the moonless
    tide
and summoned up the Goddess and the spirits of my
    tribe
to gather around me, and I swore my solemn promise
to surrender what I loved most to exorcise the sickness –
all very well for a joke, except this was my ebony
    Adonis.

Who was all along Sir Death, lurking in ambush
in my womb's valleys, in the summer-house
and lowlands of my heart, forever alert
to decoy me into his desert, to destroy me in short,
being the ebony Adonis sort.

Still, my honeychild, since I've been there and done it,
you do your own thing and don't give a shit,
for Old Death will not get us, though he'll not let us go,
any more than this life will condone us
one kiss from our ebony Adonis.[125]

Original: 'An Taobh Tuathail', by
Nuala Ní Dhomhnaill

Literal translation:

Ar chuma na gealaí
in airde láin
seolann tú isteach
an seomra chugham.
Tánn tú i do mháistir
ar a bhfeiceann tú ann,
scáileanna an troscáin
is tonnlíonadh mo chroí bhig aitea
    saigh.

Like the moon
in the height of fullness
you sail into
the room to me.
You are master
of what you see there,
gleams of the furniture
and the filling wave of my small joyful
    heart.

Taoi ólta beagán,
tá leathmhaig ar do cheann,
do gheamaí is do gheaitsí
iomarcach.
Ní thugann tú faoi ndeara
go bhfuil do gheansaí bán
in aimhréidh is é iompaithe
taobh tuathail amach agat.

You are a little drunk,
your head is tilted,
your gestures and your antics
excessive.
You don't notice
that your white jersey is
disheveled and it is turned
inside out on you.

Tusa atá chomh cúramach
faoi do chom,
chomh feistithe is chomh néata
i do phearsain –
níl uaim le déanamh
ach siúl amach sa ghairdín
is suí ar an lána
is mo chumha a chaí leis an ngealaigh.

You who are so careful
about your covering,
so tidy and so neat
in your person –
there is nothing for me to do
but walk out in the garden
and sit on the lawn
and weep my loneliness to the moon.

Peter Fallon
(1951–)

Peter Fallon is the founder of the Gallery Press, which has published a significant amount of verse translation from the Irish, including three collections of Nuala Ní Dhomhnaill's poems translated by various contemporary Irish poets. Educated at Trinity College Dublin, where he was strongly influenced by Brendan Kennelly and Eiléan Ní Chuilleanáin, Fallon lives in Oldcastle, Co. Meath.

'Inside Out'
(The original is by the contemporary poet Nuala Ní Dhomhnaill.)

Proud as the new moon
in all its glory
you sail into
the room to me.
Master of all
you survey there –
the swelling of my happy heart,
the polish of my furniture.

So you've been drinking!
Your head's in a whirl,
your poses and postures
all aswirl –
it's crumpled, dishevelled,
but you don't even see,
it's inside out,
your white jersey.

You,
you who are generally
so set in your ways,
who dress impeccably.
What else could I do
but collapse on the lawn,
away from it all,
and howl at the moon?

Original: 'An Taobh Tuathail', by
   Nuala Ní Dhomhnaill (cont.)

Literal translation (cont.):

Mar ochón, mo chrá,
ach is fíor an rá
go bhfuil trí gháire
níos géire ná an bás fhéin –
gáire chú fhealltaigh,
gáire sneachta ag leá,
is gáire do leannáin
iar luí le bean eile dho.[126]

For alas, my torment,
but the saying is true
that there are three laughs
sharper than death itself –
the laugh of a deceitful dog,
the laugh of snow melting,
and the laugh of your lover
after lying with another woman.

Because it's true, I'm afraid,
it's true what they say.
There *are* three smiles
that will leave you astray:
the grin of a dog as it turns on you,
the glisten of melting ice,
and the smirk of your lover
and him after sleeping with somebody else.[127]

Original: 'An Bonnán Buí', by
Cathal Buí Mac Giolla Ghunna

Literal translation:

A bhonnáin bhuí, 'sé mo léan do luí
  is do chnámha sínte tar éis do ghrinn:
is chan easpa bídh ach díobháíl dí
  a d'fhág i do luí tú ar chúl do chinn.
Is measa liom féin ná scrios na Traí
  tú bheith 'do luí ar leaca lom',
's nach ndearna tú díth ná dolaidh sa
    tír
  's nárbh fhearr leat fíon ná uisce poll.

A bhonnáin álainn, 'sé mo mhíle crá
    tú
  'do chúl ar lár amuigh romham sa tslí,
's gurbh iomaí lá a chluininn do ghrág
  ar an láib is tú ag ól na dí.
'Sé an ní a deir cách le do dheartháir
    Cathal
  go bhfaighidh sé bás mar siúd, más fíor;
ach ní amhlaidh atá, siúd an préachán
    breá
  chuaigh in éag ar ball le díth na dí.

A bhonnáin óig, 'sé mo mhíle brón
  tú bheith sínte fuar i measc na
    dtom,
's na lucha móra ag triall 'un do thór-
    raimh
  le beith ag déanamh spóirt agus
    pléisiúir ann;
's dá gcuirtheá scéala faoi mo dhéinse

Yellow bittern, it is my grief your lying
  and your bones stretched after your mirth:
it is not lack of food but loss of drink
  that left you lying on the back of your head.
It is worse for me than the destruction of Troy
  [for] you to be lying on bare stones,
and you didn't do harm or destruction in the
    country
  and you didn't prefer wine to hole-water.

Beautiful bittern, it is my thousand-times sorrow
    you
  on your back on the ground out in front of me
    in the way,
and it was many a day I heard your croak
  on the mud and you drinking the drink.
It is the thing that everyone says to your brother
    Cathal
  that he will die like that, if it's true;
but it is not so, that fine crow there
  died a while ago for lack of the drink.

Young bittern, it is my thousand sorrows
  you to be stretched cold in the middle of the
    bushes,
and the large rats traveling to your wake

  to be making sport and pleasure there;
and if you had sent word for me

Gabriel Fitzmaurice
(1952–)

Gabriel Fitzmaurice is a prolific translator of poetry from the Irish, including poems in the historical tradition and the work of contemporary poets writing in Irish. In the introduction to *Poems from the Irish* (2004), Fitzmaurice says: 'A translator translates the whole poem, sound and sense. The translation must be a poem in its own right.'[128] Born in Moyvane, Co. Kerry, where he still lives, Fitzmaurice teaches in a local national school.

'The Yellow Bittern'

(The original is by the eighteenth-century poet Cathal Buí Mac Giolla Ghunna, probably born in south Fermanagh but generally associated with Co. Cavan. For another version of this poem, see under Thomas MacDonagh, p. 205.)

> Bitter, bird, it is to see
> After all your spree, your bones stretched, dead;
> Not hunger – No! by thirst laid low,
> Flattened here on the back of your head.
> It's worse than the ruin of Troy to me
> To see you stretched among bare rock
> Who never did harm nor treachery
> Preferring water to finest hock.
>
> My lovely bird, I sorely grieve
> To see you stretched beside my path
> Where you would swill and drink your fill
> And from the puddle I'd hear your rasp.
> Everyone warns your brother Cathal
> That the drink will kill him, to stop and think:
> But that's not so – observe this crow
> Lately dead for want of drink.
>
> My youthful bird, I'm so depressed
> To see you stretched among the gorse
> And the rats assembling for your waking
> To sport and pleasure by your corpse.
> And if you'd only sent a message

409

Original: 'An Bonnán Buí', by
Cathal Buí Mac Giolla Ghunna
(cont.)

Literal translation (cont.):

go raibh tú i ngéibheann nó i mbroid,
    gan bhrí

that you were in difficulty or in distress,
    without strength

do bhrisfinn béim duit ar an loch sin
    Bhéasaigh

I would break a slice for you from that Lake
    Vesey

a fhliuchfadh do bhéal is do chorp
    istigh.

that would wet your mouth and your body
    inside.

Chan iad bhur n-éanlaith atá mé ag
    éagnach

Not those birds of yours I am lamenting

an lon, an smaolach, nó an chorr ghlas,

the blackbird, the thrush, or the grey heron,

ach mo bhonnán buí a bhí lán den chroí,

but my yellow bittern who was full of heart,

    's gur chosúil liom féin é i nós is i
    ndath.

    and who was like myself in manner and in
    colour.

Bhíodh sé go síoraí ag ól na dí,

He used to be always drinking the drink,

    is deirtear go mbímse mar sin seal;

    and it is said that I am like that a while;

níl aon deor dá bhfaighinnse nach ligfinn
    síos

there isn't any drop that I would get that I would
    not let down [my throat]

ar eagla go bhfaighinnse bás den tart.

for fear that I would die of the thirst.

'S é d'iarr mo stór orm ligint den ól

It was my sweetheart asked me to give up the
    drink

    nó nach mbeinnse beo ach seal beag
    gearr;

    or I would not be alive but a little, short time;

ach dúirt mé léi gur thug sí an bhréag

but I told her that she lied

    's gurbh fhaide mo shaolsa an deoch
    úd d'fháil.

    and that my life would be longer [for] getting
    that drink.

Nach bhfeiceann sibh éan an phíobáin
    réidh

Do you not see the bird of the smooth throat

    A chuaigh d'éag den tart ar ball;

    that died of the thirst a while ago;

's a chomharsana cléibh, fliuchaigh bhur
    mbéal

bosom neighbours, wet your mouths

    óir chan fhaigheann sibh braon i
    ndiaidh bhur mbáis.[129]

    for you don't get a drop after your deaths.

Original: 'Mairg nach fuil 'na
dhubhthuata', by Dáibhí Ó
Bruadair

Literal translation:

Mairg nach fuil 'na dhubhthuata,
    Gé holc duine 'na thuata,
I ndóigh go mbeinn mágcuarda
    Idir na daoinibh duarca.

A pity that I am not a great boor,
    Although it is bad for a person to be a boor,
Since I would be going around
    Among dull people.

Mairg nach fuil 'na thrudaire
    Eadraibhse, a dhaoine maithe,
Ós iad is fearr chugaibhse,
    A dhream gan iúl gan aithne.

A pity that I am not a stutterer
    Among you, good people,
Since they are best for you,
    Oh crowd without direction, without
    knowledge.

That you were in a fix, and dry,
I'd have split the ice upon Lake Vesey,[130]
You'd have wet your mouth and your craw inside.

It's not for these birds that I'm mourning,
The blackbird, songthrush or the crane
But my yellow bittern, a hearty fellow,
Like me in colour, habit, name.
He was ever drinking, drinking
And so am I (they say I'm cursed) –
There's no drop I'm offered that I won't scoff
For fear that I might die of thirst.

"Give up the booze," my darling begs me,
"'Twill be your death." Not so, I think;
I correct my dear's delusion –
I'll live longer the more I'll drink.
Look at this smooth-throated tippler
Dead from drought beside me here –
Good neighbours all, come wet your whistles
For in the grave you'll drink no beer.[131]

'Just My Luck I'm Not Pig-Ignorant'

(The original is by the seventeenth-century poet Dáibhí Ó Bruadair, and was probably written after the Cromwellian plantations.)

Just my luck I'm not pig-ignorant
    Though it's bad to be a boor
Now that I have to go out among
    This miserable shower.

A pity I'm not a stutterer,
    Good people, among you
For that would suit you better,
    You thick, ignorant crew.

Original: 'Mairg nach fuil 'na dhubhthuata', by Dáibhí Ó Bruadair (cont.)

Dá bhfaghainn fear mo mhalarta,
　　Ris do reacfainn an suairceas;
Do-bhéarainn luach fallainge
　　Idir é 'gus an duairceas.

If I were to find a man to change with me,
　　To him I would sell the wit;
I would bring the price of a cloak
　　Between him and gloominess.

Ós mó cion fear deaghchulaith
　　Ná a chion de chionn bheith
　　tréitheach;
Truagh ar chaitheas le healadhain
　　Gan é aniogh ina éadach.

Since there is more respect for a well-clothed
　　man
　　Than respect for one being talented;
A pity what I spent on poetic art
　　Not having it today for clothes.

Ós suairc labhartha is bearta gach
　　buairghiúiste
　　Gan uaim gan aiste 'na theangain ná
　　suanúchas,
Mo thrua ar chreanas le ceannaraic cru-
　　aphrionta
　　Ó bhuaic mo bheatha nár chaitheas
　　le tuatúlacht.[132]

Since every rustic clown is content with speech
　　and deeds
　　Without alliteration, without meter on the
　　tongue or novelty of wit,
My pity what I spent on the strife of hard
　　print
　　From the beginning of my life, that I did not
　　spend on vulgarity.

If I found a man to swap, I'd trade
      Him verses that would cheer –
As good a cloak as would come, he'd find,
      Between him and despair.

Since a man is less respected
      For his talent than his suit,
I regret that what I've spent on art
      I haven't now in cloth.

Since happy the words and deeds that show no hint,
      On boorish tongues, of music, metre, clarity,
I regret the time I've wasted grappling with hard print
      Since my prime, that I didn't spend it on vulgarity.[133]

Original: 'An Scáthán', by
Michael Davitt

Literal translation:

I

Níorbh é m'athair níos mó é
ach ba mise a mhacsan;
paradacsa fuar a d'fháisceas,
dealbh i gculaith Dhomhnaigh
a cuireadh an lá dár gcionn.

Dhein sé an-lá deora, seirí,
fuiscí, ceapairí feola is tae.
Bhí seanchara leis ag eachtraí
faoi sciurd lae a thugadar
ar Eochail sna triochaidí
is gurbh é a chéad pháirtí é
i seirbhís Chorcaí/An Sciobairín
amach sna daicheadaí.
Bhí dornán cártaí Aifrinn
ar mhatal an tseomra suí
ina gcorrán thart ar vás gloine,
a bhronntanas scoir ó CIE.

I

He was not my father anymore
but I was his son;
a cold paradox that I embraced,
a figure in Sunday clothes
who was buried the next day.

It made a great day of tears, sherry,
whiskey, meat sandwiches and tea.
An old friend of his was telling
about a day's run that they took
to Youghal in the thirties
and that he was his first partner
in the Cork/Skibbereen service
back in the forties.
A handful of mass cards was
on the mantelpiece of the sitting-room
in a crescent around a glass vase,
his retirement present from CIE.

II

Níorh eol dom go gceann dhá lá
gurbh é an scáthán a mharaigh é . . .

II

I didn't know for two days
that it was the mirror that killed him . . .

Paul Muldoon
(1955–)

Although his work is often seen as inspired by a cosmopolitan post-modernism, Muldoon is in fact well grounded in the Irish-language tradition, and verse translations from the Irish appear in his work from the beginning of his career. Much of Muldoon's work in translation has been of the poetry of Nuala Ní Dhomhnaill – he is the sole translator of her collection *The Astrakhan Coat*, published in 1992 – and of Michael Davitt, two contemporary and congenial spirits.

Muldoon was born in Co. Armagh and educated at Queens University Belfast. He currently is teaching at Princeton University in the United States.

'The Mirror'

(The original is by the contemporary poet Michael Davitt.)

I

He was no longer my father
but I was still his son;
I would get to grips with that cold paradox,
the remote figure in his Sunday best
who was buried the next day.

A great day for tears, snifters of sherry,
whiskey, beef sandwiches, tea.
An old mate of his was recounting
their day excursion
to Youghal in the Thirties,
how he was his first partner
on the Cork/Skibbereen route
in the late Forties.
There was a splay of Mass cards
on the sitting-room mantelpiece
which formed a crescent round a glass vase,
his retirement present from C.I.E.

II

I didn't realize till two days later
it was the mirror took his breath away.

Original: 'An Scáthán', by Michael Davitt (cont.)	Literal translation (cont.):

An seanscáthán ollmhór Victeoiriach
leis an bhfráma ornáideach bréagórga
a bhí rhomhainn sa tigh trí stór

nuair a bhogamar isteach ón tuath.
Bhínn scanraithe roimhe: go scior-rfadh
anuas den bhfalla is go slogfadh mé
d'aon tromanáil i lár na hoíche . . .

The huge old Victorian mirror
with the ornate, mock-gold frame
that was there before us in the three-storey house
when we moved in from the country.
I used to be frightened of it: that it would slide
down from the wall and that it would swallow me
with one heavy breath in the middle of the night . . .

Ag maisiú an tseomra chodlata dó
d'ardaigh sé an scáthán anuas
gan lámh chúnta a iarraidh;
ar ball d'iompaigh dath na cré air,
an oíche sin phléasc a chroí.

Decorating the bedroom
he lifted down the mirror
without asking a helping hand;
in a little while he turned the colour of clay,
that night his heart burst.

III

Mar a chuirfí de gheasa orm
thugas faoin jab a chríochnú:
an folús macallach a pháipéarú,
an fhuinneog ard a phéinteáil,
an doras marbhlainne
a scríobadh. Nuair a rugas ar an scáthán
sceimhlíos. Bhraitheas é ag análú tríd.
Chuala é ag rá i gcogar téiglí:
I'll give you a hand, here.

III

As if a spell were put on me
I undertook to finish the job:
papering the echoing void,
painting the tall window,
the morgue door
scraping. When I took hold of the mirror
I took fright. I felt him breathing through it.
I heard him saying in a calm whisper:
I'll give you a hand, here.

Is d'ardaíomar an scáthán thar n-ais in airde
os cionn an tinteáin,
m'athair á choinneáil
fad a dheineas-sa é a dhaingniú
le dhá thairne.[134]

And we lifted the mirror back up
above the fireplace,
my father holding it
while I made to secure it
with two nails.

The monstrous old Victorian mirror
with the ornate gilt frame
we had found in the three-storey house
when we moved in from the country.
I was afraid that it would sneak
down from the wall and swallow me up
in one gulp in the middle of the night.

While he was decorating the bedroom
he had taken down the mirror
without asking for help;
soon he turned the colour of terracotta
and his heart broke that night.

III

There was nothing for it
but to set about finishing the job,
papering over the cracks,
painting the high window,
stripping the door, like the door of a crypt.
When I took hold of the mirror
I had a fright. I imagined him breathing
    through it.
I heard him say in a reassuring whisper:
I'll give you a hand, here.

And we lifted the mirror back in position
above the fireplace,
my father holding it steady
while I drove home
the two nails.[135]

Original: 'Lúnasa', by Michael Davitt	Literal translation:
másach mascalach stáidmhná	a big-bottomed, manly, stately woman
agus murúch fir	and a merman
chuaigh ag tiomáint an tráthnóna lúnasa soir	went driving east on an August evening along the abandoned strands
faoi na tránna tréigthe	
an breacsholas agus an dorchadas	the dappled light and the darkness
ag iompó isteach is amach	turning inside and out
idir gaineamh agus léas	between sand and light
taoscán vaidce agus toit	a drop of vodka and a cigarette
ruathar bóúil chun na taoide síos	a cow-like rush down to the tide
ina craiceann gealaí	in her skin of moonlight
eisean de thruslóga rónda ar teaintiví	he with dark bounding strides in hot pursuit
gur léim ar a muin de dhroim sobail	until jumping on her back on the back of a wave of foam
gur thiteadar i ngabhal a chéile ghoirt	until they fell thrown together in salt confusion
gur shnámh a chéile trí chaithir thonnchíortha	until swimming together through wave-combed pubic hair
faireoga tiarpacha le faireoga fastaímeacha	big-bottomed glands with pleasure glands
gur dhein pian amháin	until they made one pain
de phianta an tsaoil	of the pains of life
a shuaimhniú	tranquilised
dís débheathach	a pair of amphibians
i bhfreacnairc mhearcair[136]	in a present of mercury

'August'

(The original is by the contemporary poet Michael Davitt.)

a broad-beamed stately mannish woman
and a silkie man
took a spin of an august evening
along the empty strands

stippled light and shade
turning inside out
between silhouette and sand

a shot of Vladivar a cigarette

her rollicking down to the tide
in her moonstruck hide
his soft shoe shuffle at her hooves
till he bested her on the crest of a wave
and they set themselves up as pillars of salt
and swam through a swell of pubic hair
pleasure-gland to pleasure-gland

until at least one wound
among so many wounds
was salved

a pair of amphibians
in the oomph of quicksilver[137]

Original: 'An Traein Dubh', by Nuala Ní Dhomhnaill

Tagann an traein dubh
isteach sa stáisiún
gach oíche chomh reigleáilte
leis an gcóiste bodhar.
Bíonn na paisinéirí
ag feitheamh léi ag an ardán.
Aithnítear iad cé nach bhfuil réalt bhuí
fuaite ar aon cheann.

Tá cuid acu óg, lúfar
i mbarr a maitheasa.
Tá cuid acu críonna,
iad cromtha as a ndrom.
Tá cuid acu is níor dhóigh leat

go rabhadar marcáilte,
iad gealgháireach
le feirc ar chaipín is feaig fiarsceabhach.

Ach duine ar dhuine, bordálann siad
an traein chéanna
atá ag feitheamh leo go dúr
mar bheithíoch borb.
Tá gal á séideach aici
as polláirí a cuid píobán.
Bogann sí chun siúil ansan
gan glao fitéain ná doird.

Is maidir linne,
séanaimid a gcomhluadar.
Dúnaimid ár súile
is nímid ár lámha.
Ólamid caifé is téimid
i mbun ár ngnótha
ag ligint orainn féin
nach bhfuil siad ann.

Literal translation:

The black train comes
into the station
every evening as regularly
as the funeral hearse.
The passengers are
waiting for it on the platform.
One recognizes them although a yellow star is not
sewn on anyone.

Some of them are young, agile
at the peak of their prime.
Some of them are old,
bent from their backs.
There are some of them, and it wouldn't seem to you

that they were marked,
they are cheerful
with a tilt on a cap and a fag askew.

But one by one, they board
the same train
which is waiting for them grimly
like a coarse beast.
It is blowing steam
out of its nostril-passages.
It moves to set off then
without the sound of a whistle or a drone.

As for us,
we disavow their company.
We shut our eyes
and we wash our hands.
We drink coffee and we go
about our business
pretending to ourselves
that they are not there.

'The Black Train'

(The original is by the contemporary poet Nuala Ní Dhomhnaill.)

As surely as the Headless Horseman
came to Ichabod Crane,
into the station every night
comes the black train.
Waiting on the platform
are the passengers themselves,
easily distinguished though they wear
no yellow stars on their sleeves.

Some are young, in the prime
of life, still on the up and up,
some so well past their prime
their backs are bent like hoops.
Many of them, you'd hardly think
were marked for death,
what with smiles all round,
the jaunty cap, the fag in the mouth.

But one by one
they all will mount
the gangway of the Windigo
that stands there, adamant,
blowing steam
from its great nostril-valves
before slouching away
to the strains of no whistles nor fifes.

As far as the rest of us are concerned,
we wash our hands
of them. We give them a wide berth.
We bury our heads in the sand.
We grab another espresso
and, with renewed zest,
go about our business
as if they didn't exist.

Original: 'An Traein Dubh', by Nuala Ní Dhomhnaill

Literal translation (cont.):

Is mealltar sinn le spraoi,	We are enticed with fun,
le comhacht, le hairgead,	with power, with money,
leis an domhan gléigeal,	with the brilliant world,
le saol an mhada bháin	with the life of the idle dog
is dearmadaimid	and we forget
go bhfuilimid fós sa champa géibhinn	that we are still in the same prison camp
céanna is gan aon dul as againn	and there is no escape for us
ach tríd an ngeata cláir	except through the wooden gates
mar a bhfuil tiarnaí dorcha an bháis	where the dark lords of death are
ag feitheamh faoi éide.	waiting dressed in uniform.
Treoróidh siad láithreach sinn	They will direct us immediately
ar chlé, go dtí an traein.	to the left, to the train.
Níl éinne againn nach dtriallfaidh	There are none of us who will not travel
ann uair éigin.	there some time.
Níl éinne beo nach bhfuil sí dó	There is no one alive that it is not for him
i ndán.[138]	in store.

Original: 'Messe ocus Pangur bán'

Literal translation:

Messe ocus Pangur bán,	Myself and white Pangur,
cechtar nathar fria shaindán:	each of us with his particular art:
bíth a menmasam fri seilgg,	his mind is with hunting,
mu menma céin im shaincheirdd.	my mind a while with my particular craft.
Caraimse fos, ferr cach clú,	I still love, better than all fame,
oc mu lebran, leir ingnu;	to be at my book, scratching diligently;
ni foirmtech frimm Pangur bán:	not envious of me white Pangur:
caraid cesin a maccdán.	he loves his boyish art.
O ru biam, scél cen scís,	When we are, a story without weariness,
innar tegdais, ar n-oendís,	in our chamber, alone,
taithiunn, dichrichide clius,	we practice, a boundless sport,
ni fris tarddam ar n-áthius.	something set against our keenness.
Gráth, huaraib, ar gressaib gal	Usually, at times, because of attacks of fury,
glenaid luch inna línsam;	a mouse is stuck in his net;
os mé, du-fuit im lín chéin	as for me, sent into my net a while
dliged ndoraid cu ndronchéill.	a difficult principle with sound meaning.

We're so taken by the fun and games
of power and money – such is the allure
of the glistering world
and our wish for the life of Reilly –
we forget
we're all in the same holding-camp: we forget
there's no way out
but through the gateless gate

where the guards
are waiting in uniform
to herd
us down the platform
to the left and into the cattle-wagons
and on to Dachau or Belsen.
There's no one for whom it's not a foregone
conclusion.[139]

'Myself and Pangur'

(The original is dated to the early ninth century.)

Myself and Pangur, my white cat,
have much the same calling, in that
much as Pangur goes after mice
I go hunting for the precise

word. He and I are much the same
in that I'm gladly "lost to fame"
when on the *Georgics*, say, I'm bent
while he seems perfectly content

with his lot. Life in the cloister
can't possibly lose its luster
so long as there's some crucial point
with which we might by leaps and bounds

yet grapple, into which yet sink
our teeth. The bold Pangur will think
through mouse snagging much as I muse
on something naggingly abstruse,

Original: 'Messe ocus Pangur bán' (cont.)	Literal translation (cont.):

Fuachaidsem fri frega fál
a rosc, a nglése comlán;
    fuachimm chein fri fegi fis
    mu rosc reil, cesu imdis.
	He directs against the wall-fence
	his eye, bright and perfect;
	    I direct a while towards a keenness of
	        knowledge
	    my clear eye, although very weak.

Faelidsem cu ndene dul
hi nglen luch inna gerchrub;
    hi tucu cheist ndoraid ndil
    os me chene am faelid.
	He rejoices at the swiftness of motion
	when a mouse sticks in his sharp claw;
	    when I understand a difficult, beloved
	        question
	    in front of me, a length of time I rejoice.

Cia beimmi a-min nach ré
ni derban cách a chele:
    maith la ceachtar nár a dán;
    subaigthius a óenurán.
	Although we are thus at any time
	each does not hinder the other:
	    each of us likes his art;
	    a pleasure for himself.

He fesin as choimsid dáu
in muid du-ngní cach oenláu;
    du thabairt doraid du glé
    for mu mud cein am messe.[140]
	It is he who is master for himself
	in work done every single day;
	    giving clearness to difficulty
	    at my work a length of time I am.

then fix his clear, unflinching eye
on our lime-white cell wall, while I
focus, insofar as I can,
on the limits of what a man

may know. Something of his rapture
at his most recent mouse capture
I share when I, too, get to grips
with what has given me the slip.

And so we while away our whiles,
never cramping each other's styles
but practicing the noble arts
that so lift and lighten our hearts,

Pangur going in for the kill
with all his customary skill
while I, sharp-witted, swift, and sure,
shed light on what had seemed obscure.[141]

Original: 'Coillte Glasa an Triúcha', by Máire Nic a Liondain

Literal translation:

Dar mo láimh duit, a chailín, má ghluaisfir chun bealaigh
    Go bhfuighidh tú an uile shúgradh,
Céim, ól agus imirt, pléisiúr go deimhin
    Is féachaint mara agus cuain liom;
Níl traona nó truideog, smaolach nó fuiseog,
    Nó cuach bhinn bhlasta chumhra,
Nach mbeidh dhuit i gceiliúr, is téada dá seinm
    Fa choilltibh glasa an Triúcha.

By my hand, girl, if you will set out on the way
    You will get every diversion,
Stepping, drink and playing, pleasure indeed
    And a view of sea and harbour with me;
There is not a corncrake or a starling, a thrush or a lark,
    Or a melodious, fluent, sweet cuckoo,
That will not be singing for you, and strings being played
    Under the green woods of Triúch.

Ó Pharrthas ní aithin damh aon áit insan chruinne
    Is áilne is is deise cúirtibh –
Fonn agus fearann, coill agus abhaill,
    Toradh trom, piorraí is úlla;
Caora ar chrannaibh, cná buí ar choillibh,
    Ag dortadh le ceathaibh cnuasaigh,
An chóisir inár gcoinne, is na céadtaí dár gcineadh
    Fa choilltibh glasa an Triúcha.

Since Paradise I don't know any place on earth
    Of more beautiful and nicer palaces –
Land and field, wood and orchard,
    Heavy fruit, pears and apples;
Berries on branches, yellow nuts in woods,
    Spilling a shower of stores,
The festive party meeting us, and the hundreds of our race
    Under the green woods of Triúch.

(An Cailín)
Aidmhím gan scáth gur maith a bhfuil tú a' rá
    Fá thorthaibh is fá bhláth cnuasaigh;
'S gurb aoibhinn an áit atá againn le fáil

    Is nach eagal dúinn go bráth cumha ann.
Acht dá mbeadh seinm na ndán is gach éan dá raibh san airc
    Ag ceiliúir go bráth dúinne,
Char mhiste dhúinn cáil den arán a bheith i láthair
    I gcoilltibh glasa an Triúcha.

(The Girl)
I admit without pretence that it is good what you are saying
    About fruits and about blossoms in heaps;
And that beautiful is the place that is available to us
    And that fear of loneliness is never on us there.
But if there were playing of songs and every bird that was in the ark
    Singing always for us,
It would be no harm a share of bread to be present for us
    In the green woods of Triúch.

Moya Cannon
(1956–)

Moya Cannon was born in Dunfanaghy, Co Donegal, and educated at University College Dublin and Cambridge University. She has served as editor of *Poetry Ireland*, and lives in Co. Galway.

'The Green Woods of Triúch'

(There are numerous versions of the original. The version on which Cannon's translation is based has been attributed to Máire Nic a Liondain [fl. 1771], from Co. Louth, just north of Dundalk. *Triúch* means generally a district or territory.)

If you come with me, girl, I give you my word
            You'll have every kind of diversion,
Dance, drink and sport, pleasure of all sorts
            And viewing of bays and oceans.
There's no stare or corncrake, no thrush or lark
            Or clear-tuned, musical cuckoo
But will join in chorus when strings are struck
            Under the green woods of Triúch.

No place in the firmament save Paradise itself
            Has houses so fine and handsome –
Farms of good land, orchard and woodland
            Weighed down with pears and apples;
Berries on the branch, yellow nuts in the woods,
            Bowed low under clustered bounty,
A party out to greet us, our kin soon gathered,
            Under the green woods of Triúch.

(The Young Woman)
I'll admit straight away it is fine what you say
            About fruit and fruiting blossom;
That place we might have is pleasant for sure
            And there we would never fear sorrow.
Yet if the music of all arts and all the birds in the ark
            For us were singing in tune,
We would still have to have a little bread to hand
            Under the green woods of Triúch.

427

Original: 'Coillte Glasa an Triúcha', by Máire Nic a Liondain (cont.)

Literal translation (cont.):

(Eisean)

Tuig-se, a ghrá, iar gcruthú do Ádhamh,
  Nach arán a bhí i ndáil dúinne;
Cé go bhfuair sé gan spás compánach mná
  Is go ndeachaidh sé go Parrthas nua léi.
Acht dá gcongbhaidís a lámh ó aon úll amháin
  Ba é ár n-oiliúin cáil cnuasaigh,
Acht ní heagal dúinn cáin na haithne sin go bráth
  Fa choilltibh glasa an Triúcha.

Gheobhaimíd araon tigheadas dúinn féin
  Ar ealta an aeir san Triúcha,
Is ceatha dlúith' éisc ar easaibh go séimh,

  Is níorbh eagal dúinn ár mbeatha bheith dubhchroíoch.
Beidh duilliúr na gcraobh dár bhfolach ón ghréin,
  Agus ceiliúr na n-éan dár ndúisgeadh,
Uallghuth na ngadhar 'san bhforaois lenár dtaobh
  Agus an eilit ar a léim lúith leo.

(An Cailín)

A ógánaigh chaoimh, más deimhin gur fíor
  An méid sin a chuir tú i n-iúl damh,
Ar thorthaibh na gcraobh, 's ar áilne gach ní,
  Fán aird seo thíos don chúige,
Spré nó maoin ní ghabhfainn mar bhríb,
  Nó saibhreas ar rí mar chúitiú,
Gan bliain agus mí a chaitheamh do mo shaol
  Fá choilltibh glasa an Triúcha.

(Eisean)

A ainnir chiúin tséimh, is aithne damh féin
  Gach ní dá bhfuil do dhúil ann,
An saibhreas is fearr d'fhág mé mo dheaghaidh
  I n-oiliúin d'aireamh dhúchais.
Chífir cruithneacht mhaol, coirce geal na gcraobh,
  Is eorna ar gach taobh go dlúth ann,
Ná ceasnaigh go mbéir gan arán de phlúr déis
  Fá choillte glasa an Triúcha.

(He)

Understand, love, after the creation of Adam,
  It was not bread that was fated for us;
Although he got without delay a woman companion
  And he went to a new Paradise with her.
But if they had kept their hands from one apple
  Our nourishment would be a share of stores,
But we do not fear the rule of that commandment ever
  Under the green woods of Triúch.

We will both get husbandry for ourselves
  From the flocks of the air in Triúch,
And dense showers of fish from smooth waterfalls,
  And we would not fear our lives being joyless.
The leaves of the trees will be covering us from the sun,
  And the music of the birds waking us,
The crying voice of the hounds in the forest by our side
  And the doe leaping vigourously with them.

(The Girl)

Gentle youth, if indeed it is true
  That which you have let me know,
About the fruits of the branches, and about the beauty of everything,
  Below this height down in the province,
Wealth or prosperity I would not take as a bribe,
  Or the riches of a king as compensation,
Not to spend a year and a month of my life
  Under the green woods of Triúch.

(He)

Quiet, gentle girl, I myself know
  Everything that you desire there,
The best riches I left behind me
  In order to be a native ploughman.
You will see bread wheat, bright eared oats,
  And barley on every side densely there,
Don't complain that you will be without bread from corn flour
  Under the green woods of Triúch.

(The Young Man)
Oh, understand, dear, after Adam's creation,
      Bread was never intended as our share;
Though he was soon granted a female companion
      And they gained a new Paradise together.
But from that fated apple had they stayed their hands
      We would still be nourished on wild fruit,
Yet the weight of that command will not fall on us
      Under the green woods of Triúch.

Together we'll gain wherewithal for ourselves
      From the flocks of the air in Triúch.
Weirs will yield up dense showers of fish
      And there's no fear we'll ever face hardship.
The leaves of the trees will shield us from sun
      And the chorus of birds will rouse us,
There'll be baying of hounds in the forest nearby
      With the light leaping doe out before them.

(The Young Woman)
Oh, gentle young man, if it's true for sure,
      All of what you tell me
Of fruit on the branch and beauty all around
      In that place in the south of the province,
I'll accept no bribe of dowry or wealth
      Or the riches of a king in lieu,
But a month and a year of my life I will spend
      Under the green woods of Triúch.

(The Young Man)
Oh mild, tender girl, I know full well
      Everything you desire now,
I turned my back on the finest wealth
      To serve my time as a ploughman.
You'll see bread wheat, bright branching oats
      And barley on every side of you,
You'll never complain of lack of bread or grain
      Around the green woods of Triúch.

Original: 'Coillte Glasa an Triúcha', by
Máire Nic a Liondain (cont.)

Literal translation (cont.):

A spéirbhean bhreasnaí an déid ghil chailce
  Triall is bí ag teacht chun an Triúcha,
Is ní baol duit easbhaidh is mise ar mo
  mheisnigh
Nó ar léim dhá chos go lúfar;
Nuair a bheas céad bean go tuirseach beidh
  mise agus tusa
Le pléisiúr ag baint na n-úll ann,
Gheobhair mil ar gach cuiseog is líon geal
  'na shliseog
Fá choillte glasa an Triúcha.[142]

Lively beauty of the chalk-white teeth
  Proceed and be coming to Triúch,
And there is no danger for you of want and
  me with my vigour
Or the leap of two legs actively;
When a hundred women would be tired you
  and I will be
With pleasure picking the apples there,
You will get sweetness from every slender
  stalk and bright flax in its sheaf
Under the green woods of Triúch.

Oh, witty lady of the pearly teeth
     Come on away with me now,
You'll want for nothing for I have vigour
     And two limber legs for leaping;
Though a hundred women tire, you and I with pleasure
     Will still pluck apples together,
You'll have honey in hives and flax in sleighs
     Around the green woods of Triúch.[143]

Original: 'Mise', by Liam Ó Uirthile	Literal translation:
Díothódsa tusa fós i m'aigne,	I will eradicate you yet in my mind,
A bhean na beagmhaitheasa,	Woman of little good,
Ach tógann sé tamall an dealg nimhe	But it takes a while the thorn of poison
A chuir tú ionam a tharraingt go hiomlán;	That you put in me to pull out completely;
Ba dhóbair duit mé scrios gan oiread	You nearly destroyed me without so much as
Is súil a chaochadh le trócaire;	the flicker of an eye with mercy;
Agus cé go ndeirtear gur deacair	And although it is said that it is difficult
An croí a chneasú nuair a lúbtar	To heal the heart when it is warped
Cuimhním ar shamhail an rotha chairte	I remember the image of the cartwheel
A dheineadh m'athair aimsir an Chogaidh	That my father made in the time of the War

Is é ag rá: 'leamhán sa stoc, dair sna
      spócaí,
	And he saying: 'elm in the shaft, oak in the
	      spokes,

Agus leamhán arís amuigh sa bhfonsa.'	And elm again out on the rim.'
San áit a ndeisídís iad i gCorcaigh	In the place that they used to repair them in Cork
Chaithidís dul leis an snáithe	They used to have to go with the grain
Is an dair a scoilteadh le tua.	And to split the oak with an axe.
Bíse id dhair anois agus scoiltfead	Let you be the oak now and I will split
Tú ó bhun go barr leis an gceardaíocht	You from bottom to top with the craft
Is dual dom mhuintir, ainm nach	That is native to my people, a name
Bhféadfása is tú den stoc gur díobh tú	That you would not be able, and you of the stock that you are from,
A litriú: Ó Muirthile Carraige.[144]	To spell: Ó Muirthile Carraige.

Greg Delanty
(1958–)

Greg Delanty's verse translations have mostly been of the work of Irish-language poets of his generation. The original of the following translation was written by his contemporary Liam Ó Muirthile, who, like Delanty, was born in Cork. Delanty currently lives and teaches in Vermont, in the United States.

'Me'

I'll annihilate you yet from my mind,
Woman of little worth,
But it takes time
To withdraw your venomous dart.
You near destroyed me
Without a sliver of sympathy.

I fall back on the image of the cartwheel
My father made in Cork during the war
And him saying: 'Elm in the shaft, oak in the spokes
And elm again in the rim.'
They had to go with the grain
And split the oak with an axe.

And though it's said to be difficult
To mend a broken heart,
Let you now be oak and I'll split you in two
With the craft innate to my people,
Whose name, given your stock,
You couldn't even spell: Ó Muirthile Carraige.[145]

Original: 'I gClochar na Trócaire',   Literal translation:
by Michael Davitt

Raghainn níos faide anois dá ligfeá dom.   I would go further now if you would allow me.
Tá ár súile gafa cheana tríd ó bhun   Our eyes have already gone through it from
                                              bottom
go barr go tarr, dátheangach.   to top to belly, bilingually.
Nílim ag caint ar aon ní achrannach   I am not talking about anything deeply compli-
    doimhin   cated
ach ar rud éigin neamhachrannach doimhin   but about something deeply uncomplicated
nach mairfeadh ach fíche neomat,   that would not last but twenty minutes,
fiche cúig ar a mhéid: twenty-five at the most:
chasfainn an eochair le discréid   I would turn the key with discretion
d'iompóinn pictiúr an Easpaig   I would reverse the picture of the Bishop
choinneoinn mo ghuth umhal, a Shiúr,   I would keep my voice humble, Sister,
mo dhán go hard ag maistreach drúchta   my art churning dew mightily
i gcoim do shléibhe fraoigh.   in the middle of your heather mountain.
Eadrainn féin é mar chuigeann,   It is between ourselves as a churning,
ár dtriúrna amháin: tusa, mise, Eisean –   our only trinity: you, me, Him –
ní leáfadh an t-im inár mbéal.[146]   the butter would not melt in our mouths.

Dermot Bolger
(1959–)

A novelist and dramatist as well as a poet, Dermot Bolger founded Raven Arts Press in 1979, and edited *The Bright Wave/An Tonn Gheal: Poetry in Irish Now* (1986), a collection of contemporary verse translations. Bolger was born in Finglas, North Dublin, and currently lives in Dublin.

'In the Convent of Mercy'

(The original is by the contemporary poet Michael Davitt.)

> *Dieu me pardonnera, c'est son métier.*
> *– Heinrich Heine*

Now I'd go further than you would allow:
Our eyes having done it already from toe
To veiling cowl and back, bilingually.
I don't wish for such awkward intensity
But for sensations, overspilling naturally,
To eclipse us for just twenty minutes
Or a shocked twenty five at a stretch.
I would reverse the bishop's portrait,
I would twist the convent key discreetly,
Sister, I would lower my voice to you
And let my rhapsody churn the dew
From your depths of heatherfilled vales.
This will remain our secret churning,
Tasted only by the trinity of you, me and Him –
The butter will not melt in our mouths.[147]

Original: 'Súile Shuibhne', by Cathal Ó Searcaigh	Literal translation:
Tá mé ag tarraingt ar bharr na Bealtaine	I'm drawing near the top of Bealtaine
go dúchroíoch i ndorchacht na hoíche	disheartened in the darkness of the evening
ag ardú malacha i m'aistear is i m'aigne	ascending slopes in my journey and in my mind
ag cur in aghaidh bristeacha borba gaoithe.	setting against the fierce unsettled state of the wind.
B'ise mo mhaoinín, b'ise mo Ghort a' Choirce	She was my little treasure, she was my Gort a' Choirce
mise a thug a cuid fiántais chun mín-tíreachais	it was I who brought her wildness to cultivation
ach tá a claonta dúchais ag teacht ar ais arís	but her natural inclinations are coming back again
anocht bhí súile buí i ngort na seirce.	tonight there was weed-blossom in the field of love.
Tchím Véineas ansiúd os cionn Dhún Lúiche	I see Venus there above Dún Lúiche
ag caochadh anuas lena súile striapaí	winking down with her eyes of a harlot
agus ar ucht na Mucaise siúd cíoch na gealaí	and on the breast of Muckish there the breast of the moon
ag gobadh as gúna dubh na hoíche.	projecting out of the dark gown of the evening.
Idir dólas agus dóchas, dhá thine Bhealtaine,	Between sorrow and hope, two fires of Bealtine,
caolaím d'aon rúid bhuile mar leathd-huine.	I edge with one mad rush like a half-person.
Tá soilse an Ghleanna ag crith os mo choinne –	The lights of the Glen are trembling before me –
faoi mhalaí na gcnoc sin iad súile Shuibhne.[148]	Under the brows of the hills, those are the eyes of Sweeney.

Sara Berkeley
(1967–)

Sara Berkeley was born in Dublin and educated at Trinity College Dublin. Her first collection of verse appeared in 1986.

'Sweeney's Eyes'
(The original is by the contemporary Irish-language poet from Co. Donegal, Cathal Ó Searcaigh.)

I am making for the summit of Bealtaine[149]
My heart heavy in the black of night
Scaling the rockface of mind and matter
Defending myself in the wind's harsh fight.

She was my wealth, she my harvest.
Her wild country made fertile by my hand
But the natural barrenness creeps back once more
Tonight there were weeds choking the land.

I see Venus over Dún Lúiche[150]
Staring down with her whoring eyes
And the streak of the moon in Mucaise's[151] lap
Rents the black dress of the night's disguise.

Between horror and hope, two flames of Bealtaine
I swing in one movement as madmen will
The lights in the valley tremble before me
And Sweeney's eyes are below the hill.[152]

Original: 'Do Isaac Rosenberg', by Cathal Ó Searcaigh	Literal translation:
Le bánú an lae agus muid ag teacht ar ais	With the whitening of the day and we coming back
i ndiaidh a bheith ag suirí i mbéal an uaignis	after being courting on the edge of the deserted place
d'éirigh na fuiseoga as poill agus prochóga Phrochlais	the larks rose out of the holes and hollows of Prochlais
agus chuimhnigh mé ortsa, a Isaac Rosenberg,	and I thought of you, Isaac Rosenberg,
cathshuaite i dtailte treascartha na Fraince, ag éisteacht	battle-tired in the vanquished grounds of France, listening
le ceol sítheach na bhfuiseog le teacht an lae	to the peaceful music of the larks with the coming of the day
agus tú pilleadh ar do champa, thar chnámha créachta	and you returning to your camp, over the wounded bones
do chairde, ruaithne reatha na bpléascán, creathánach,	of your friends, the shimmering light of the explosive shells, trembling,
ag deargadh an dorchadais ar pháirc an chatha.	reddening the darkness on the field of battle.
Ag éisteacht le meidhir na bhfuiseog idir aer agus uisce	Listening to the gaiety of the larks between air and water
thaibhsigh do dhánta chugam thar thalamh eadrána na síoraíochta, líne,	your poems appeared to me over the no-man's-land of eternity, line,
ar líne, stadach, scáfar mar shaighdiúirí ó bhéal an áir	on line, faltering, fearful like soldiers from the mouth of the slaughter
agus bhain siad an gus asam lena gcuntas ar an Uafás:	and they took the spirit out of me with their account of the Horror:
as duibheagán dubh na dtrinsí, as dóchas daortha na n-óg, as ár	from the dark depths of the trenches, from the condemned hopes of the young, from slaughter
agus anbhás, d'éirigh siad chugam as corrabhuais coinsiasa –	and much death, they rose to me out of a confusion of conscience –
mise nach raibh ariamh sa bhearna bhaoil, nach dtug	I who was never in the gap of danger, who did not make
ruathar mharfach thar an mhullach isteach sa chreach,	a deadly charge over the top into the foray,
nár fhulaing i dtreascairt dhian na fola;	who did not suffer in a severe defeat of the blood;

Frank Sewell
(1968–)

In his preface to *Out in the Open*, the collection of poems by the contemporary Irish-language poet Cathal Ó Searcaigh for which he provided the translations, Frank Sewell argues that verse translation should strive 'to become a craft or art-form of its own, mirroring the standards of the original'.[153] Sewell was born in Belfast, and educated at Queens University and the University of Ulster.

'For Isaac Rosenberg'

(Isaac Rosenberg, the World War I poet, wrote a well-known poem entitled 'Returning, We Hear the Larks'. He was killed in battle in 1918. The original of this translation was written by Cathal Ó Searcaigh.)

> At dawn, we gave up our courting
> out in the wilderness. Larks soared
> from the bog-holes and hollows of Prochlais.[154]
>
> Then I thought of you, Isaac Rosenberg,
> war-weary in the 'torn fields of France',
> stunned by siren larks, one dawn
>
> as you returned to your camp over the ruined
> bones of friends, shaken, with bombs
> pouncing on the red and black battlefield.
>
> The larks' joy between air and water
> brought your poems across eternity's barricade, line
> by line, stutteringly, scared, like soldiers in battle,
>
> and they stopped me in my tracks with horror:
> the dark pits of trenches, youth's smashed-up
> hopes, the carnage wracked my conscience,
>
> I who was never within an ounce of my life,
> who never had to pile over the top and into battle,
> who never lost out in any of the bloodshed,

Original: 'Do Isaac Rosenberg', by
Cathal Ó Searcaigh (cont.)

Literal translation (cont.):

nach bhfaca saighdiúirí óga mar bheadh
sopóga ann, caite
i gcuibhrinn mhéith an áir, boladh bréan an
bháis
ag éirí ina phláigh ó bhláth feoite a n-
óige;

who did not see young soldiers, as if they were
handfuls of straw, thrown
into the fertile, enclosed fields of the slaughter,
the foul smell of death
rising in a plague from the withered blossom
of their youth;

nach raibh ar maos i nglár is i gclábar bhlár
an chatha,
nár chaill mo mheabhair i bpléasc, nár
mhothaigh an piléar
mar bheach thapaidh the ag diúl mhil
fhiáin m'óige.

who was not steeped in the silt and in the mud
of the field of battle,
who did not lose my mind in an explosion,
who did not feel the bullet
like a quick, hot bee sucking the wild honey of
my youth.

Ó ná hagair orm é, a Isaac Rosenberg,
d'ainm a lua,
mise atá díonaithe i mo dhánta i ndún seo
na Seirce
agus creach dhearg an chogaidh i gcroí na
hEorpa go fóill.

Oh don't hold it against me, Isaac Rosenberg,
mentioning your name,
I who am protected in my poems in this haven
of Love
and the red ruin of war in the heart of Europe
still.

Ach bhí mo chroí lasta le lúcháir agus
caomhchruth álainn
mo leannán le mo thaobh, gach géag, gach
alt, gach rinn,
gach ball de na ballaibh ó mhullach go
talamh mo mhealladh,

But my heart was lit with joy and with the
beautiful dear form
of my lover by my side, every limb, every joint,
every point,
every member of the body from top to ground
enticing me,

sa chruth go gcreidim agus muid i mbach-
lainn a chéile
go bhfuil díon againn ar bhaol, go bhfuil an
saol lán d'fhéile,
go bhfuil amhrán ár ngrá in a gheas ar gach
aighneas.

in such a way that I believe, and we in each
other's arms,
that we have a shelter from danger, that life is
full of generosity,
that the song of our love is an injunction
against every trouble.

Agus tá na fuiseoga ag rá an rud céanna
liomsa a dúirt siad leatsa
sular cuireadh san aer tú, sular réabadh do
chnámha –
is fearr cumann agus ceol ná cogadh agus
creach;

And the larks are saying the same thing to me
that they said to you
before you were shot into the air, before your
bones were shattered –
love and music are better than war and
ruin;

agus cé nach raibh mé ariamh i mbéal an
chatha
agus cé nach bhfuil caite agam ach saol
beag suarach, sabháilte,
ag daingniú mo choirnéil féin agus ag cúlú
ó chúiseanna reatha;

and although I never was in the mouth of
battle
and although I have not lived but a small,
insignificant, safe life,
securing my own corner and backing away
from current causes;

ba mhaith liom a dhearbhú duitse, a fhile, a
d'fhán go diongbháilte
i mbun d'fhocail, a labhair le lomchnámh
na fírinne ó ár an chatha –
go bhfuil mise fosta ar thaobh an tSolais,
fosta ar thaobh na Beatha.[155]

I would like to assure you, poet, who stead-
fastly kept
your word, who spoke the bare bones of truth
from the slaughter of war –
that I am still on the side of Light, still on the
side of Life.

I who never saw young soldiers torched
and dumped in an open field of slaughter,
their blighted bodies stinking with death,

I who was never plunged in the mud and mire,
never shell-shocked or stung by a bullet
sucking out my life like some crazy bee honey . . .

O, don't mind me, Isaac Rosenberg, calling you
from here, my safe-house of love poems,
while Europe still eats its heart out;

only mine was light with joy, my lover
beside me in all his glory, every limb,
joint, rim, every bit of him tempting me

to believe that we're safe together,
that life is for feasting
and love wards off trouble.

The larks tell me what they told you,
before you were blown to pieces –
that love and music beat war and empire;

and although I've never been in action,
though I've had a safe, ordinary life,
looking after my own and keeping out of it,

I want to assure you, poet whose truth
was bared to the bones in World War 1,
I too am on the side of light, and of life.[156]

Notes and references

INTRODUCTION

1 *The Penguin Book of Irish Verse* (London: Penguin, 1970, 1981), p. 27.
2 *Inventing Ireland: The Literature of the Modern Nation* (1995; Cambridge, Mass.: Harvard Univ. Press, 1996), p. 624.
3 See Michael Cronin, *Translating Ireland: Translation, Languages, Cultures*. Cork: Cork Univ. Press, 1996, p. 2, for this argument. Also see Kiberd, *Inventing Ireland*, p. 66, for the argument that to revert to the traditional in any way in Ireland has generally been, at least since the sixteenth century, to act subversively, to challenge England's political and cultural domination.
4 *The Field Day Anthology of Irish Writing*, Vol. III (Derry: Field Day, 1991), p. 633.
5 'The Kings of the Race of Eibhear', a verse translation of a fourteenth-century poem recording the kings of Cashel from the earliest times up to the Norman invasion, and ascribed to Seán Ó Dubhagáin (? –1375), a member of a learned family associated with Ballydoogan, Co. Galway. For the text of the original and of Kearney's translation, see John Daly, ed., *The Kings of the Race of Eibhear* (Dublin: John Daly, 1847). The other candidate for the distinction of being the first verse translation from Irish to English is a five-line translation possibly done by a Shropshire Englishman named Meredith Hanmer (1543–1604), who spent time in Ireland in the last dozen years or so of his life. The text of the translation is in Robert Pentland Mahaffy, ed., *Calendar of the State Papers Relating to Ireland. 1601–3. (With Addenda. 1565–1654.) And of the Hanmer Papers. Preserved in the Public Record Office* (London: Public Record Office, 1912; rpt. Nendeln/Liechtenstein: Kraus Reprint, 1974), pp. 681–682.
6 *Reliques of Irish Poetry* (Dublin: George Bonham, 1789), pp. vii–viii.
7 Kiberd has described *Reliques of Irish Poetry* as 'perhaps the first attempt at a narrative that accorded "parity of esteem" to both island traditions' (*Irish Classics* [London: Granta, 2000], p. 619).
8 Robert Welch has said that Walsh's *Reliques of Irish Jacobite Poetry* 'helped to establish eighteenth century Irish political poetry as a definite tradition in its own right' (*A History of Verse Translation from the Irish: 1789–1897* [Gerrards Cross, Bucks: Colin Smythe, 1988], p. 132).
9 *Bards of Gael and Gall* (London: T. Fisher Unwin, 1897; Dublin and Belfast: Phoenix Publishing, n. d.), p. 91.
10 *Bards of Gael and Gall*, p. 21.
11 *The Poem-Book of the Gael: Translations from Irish Gaelic Poetry into English Prose and Verse* (London: Chatto and Windus, 1913), p. xxxiii.
12 As Declan Kiberd has put it, Hyde's translations implicitly argued that 'the songs of the country people should never have been put into well-bred Tennysonian metrics' (*Inventing Ireland*, pp. 314–315).
13 Quoted in A. Norman Jeffares, *Ango-Irish Literature* (New York: Schocken Books, 1982), p. 271.
14 'Preface', *Abhráin Grádh Chúige Connacht: Love Songs of Connacht* (London: T. Fisher Unwin; Dublin: Gill, 1893), n. p.
15 *Twice Round the Black Church: Early Memories of Ireland and England* (London: Routledge and Kegan Paul, 1962), p. 16.
16 Merriman's poem was shocking enough in its day, but as Kiberd has observed, there is in O'Connor's version of it a 'will to transgress' not found in the original (*Irish Classics*, p. 200).

17 'Preface', *Kings, Lords, & Commons: Irish Poems from the Seventh to the Nineteenth Century* (1959; Dublin: Gill and Macmillan, 1991), p. xii.

18 Kathleen Shields has said that translation by contemporary poets 'is done to redress the balance between the two literatures and to create a modern cultural climate which will incorporate the Irish language tradition' (*Gained in Translation: Language, Poetry and Identity in Twentieth-Century Ireland* [Oxford: Peter Lang], p. 9).

19 Kiberd has made this argument in *An Crann Faoi Bhláth: The Flowering Tree: Contemporary Irish Poetry with Verse Translations*, ed. Kiberd and Gabriel Fitzmaurice (Dublin: Wolfhound, 1991), p. xvii.

20 'Introduction', *Sweeney Astray* (1983; New York: Farrar Straus Giroux, 1984), n. p.

21 *Translating Ireland*, p. 184.

22 This argument has been made by Shields, in *Gained in Translation*, p. 120.

23 Cronin, *Translating Ireland*, has argued that medieval translations into Irish were 'source texts rewritten for an Irish audience, initially for Gaelic chieftains and Anglo-Norman lords, monasteries and native schools of learning, and violated free/literal distinctions' (p. 22).

24 'Introduction', *O Bruadair* (Oldcastle, Co. Meath: Gallery Press, 1985; 2000), p. 13.

EIGHTEENTH CENTURY

1 This view is advanced in an appendix on Turlough Carolan in Joseph Walker's *Historical Memoirs of the Irish Bards* (Dublin: Luke White, 1786), p. 81.

2 Alan Harrison, *Ag Cruinniú Meala: Anthony Raymond (1675–1726), ministéir Protastúnach, agus léann na Gaeilge i mBaile Átha Cliath* (Baile Átha Cliath: An Clóchomhar, 1988), p. 116.

3 See Harrison, *Ag Cruinniú Meala*, pp. 116–120, for evidence that Anthony Raymond, an antiquary and translator, gave Swift specific help with the translation, and supplied a prose version that Swift worked from.

4 From *uisce beatha*, meaning whiskey (literally water of life).

5 The Irish *meadar* means a wooden drinking vessel.

6 Harold Williams, ed., *The Poems of Jonathan Swift*, Vol. I (Oxford: Clarendon Press, 1958), glosses 'kercher' as 'a cloth used by women to cover the head'.

7 Williams (*Poems of Swift*), quotes the editor of the 1735 edition of Swift's poems who glossed 'Yean' as 'Another Irish Name for a Woman.' The vocative of the Irish *bean*, meaning a woman, is *a bhean*. The original text refers to a woman named Áine.

8 Charles Vallencey, *A Grammar of the Iberno-Celtic, or Irish Language* (1781; Dublin: R. Marchbanks, 1782), pp. 128–131. This version was published side-by-side with Swift's translation. Also consulted were the texts in Charles Henry Wilson, *Select Irish Poems, Translated into English* (n.d [1782?]), pp. 69–72; *Ag Cruinniú Meala*, p. 119–120; Tomás Ó Máille, ed., *Amhráin Chearbhalláin: The Poems of Carolan* (London: Irish Texts Society, 1916), pp. 205–207; Douglas Hyde, *Amhráin Chúige Chonnact: The Songs of Connacht*, ed. Breandán Ó Conaire (1893; Blackrock, Co. Dublin: 1985), pp. 146–150; and ND–II, pp. 12–13. Only the parts of the poem translated by Swift are included here.

9 From *scian*, meaning knife.

10 A town just north of Dublin.

11 Slane Castle, in Co. Meath.

12 *Cora Droma Rúisc* (Carrick-on-Shannon), Co. Leitrim.

13 Williams says this is possibly a reference to Gerald Fitzgerald, the eleventh Earl of Kildare, who died in 1585.

14 *Poems of Swift*, pp. 243–247. Williams's text is based on that which appeared in Vallencey, *Grammar*, pp. 128–131. See Harrison, *Ag Cruinniú Meala*, pp. 119–120, for a slightly different version based on the manuscript papers of Anthony Raymond. See also Edward Bunting, *A General Collection of the Ancient Music of Ireland* (London: Clementi, [1809]), for still another slightly different version, under the title 'O'Rourke's Noble Fare Will Ne'er Be Forgot' (p. 9).

15 *The History of Ireland*, Vol. I, ed. and tran. by David Comyn and P.S. Dineen,

(London: Irish Texts Society, 1902), p. 160. Also consulted was the text in P. W. Joyce, *Keating's History of Ireland. Book I. Part I* (Dublin: M. H. Gill, 1880), p. 68.

16 Harrison, *Ag Cruinniú Meala*, p. 115.

17 Quoted in Diarmuid Ó Catháin, "Dermot O'Connor, Translator of Keating," *Eighteenth-Century Ireland: Idir an dá chultúr*, Vol. 2 (1987), pp. 84–85. Seán Ó Neachtain, a dominant figure in the community of Irish-language writers and scholars in Dublin at the time, wrote two poems accusing O'Connor of deceit and fraud. (For texts of the two poems, see M. H. Risk, "Two Poems on Diarmuid Ó Conchubhair," *Éigse: A Journal of Irish Studies*, 12 [Spring 1967], pp. 37–38.) In 1831, James Hardiman, the editor of the influential collection *Irish Minstresly*, called O'Connor's Keating 'a burlesque on translation' (IM, Vol. II, p. 378).

18 Robert Welch (*A History of Verse Translation from the Irish: 1789–1897* (Gerrard's Cross: Colin Smythe, 1988), praises O'Connor's verse translations of the poems in Keating for their 'easy musical quality, accommodating what the Irish says with a degree of effortlessness which was not to be seen again for a long time' (p. 16).

19 Dermod O'Connor, translator, *The General History of Ireland*, by Jeoffrey Keating, Vol. I (1723; Dublin: J. Christie, 1809), pp. 40–41.

20 Comyn and Dineen, *History of Ireland*, Vol. II (1908), pp. 18–19.

21 *General History*, p. 104.

22 Comyn and Dineen, *History of Ireland*, Vol. II, pp. 342–344.

23 *General History*, p. 427.

24 Justin McCarthy, ed., *Irish Literature*, Vol. 3 (Philadelphia: John Morris, 1904), p. 841.

25 Andrew Carpenter, ed., *Verse in English from Eighteenth-Century Ireland* (Cork: Cork Univ. Press, 1998), says Dawson's version was "based loosely on the Irish words of Carolan" (p. 299). Welch mentions the poem in his *History of Verse Translation* (p. 32–33), and Walker, who included the poem in *Historical Memoirs of the Irish Bards*, said that Carolan's poetry has been 'lost in the splendour of the facetious Baron Dawson's paraphrase' (p. 71).

26 William Salkeld (1671–1715) and Sir Peyton Ventris (1641–1691), legal commentators. In Oliver Goldsmith's *Citizen of the World* (1762), Salkeld and Ventris are described as 'two lawyers who, some hundred years ago, gave their opinions on cases similar to mine' (1762; Bungay, J. and R. Childs, 1820, Vol. I, p. 195). According to MacCarthy, *Irish Literature*, Dawson was 'a shrewd and witty lawyer' (p. 841).

27 Galen (131[?]–201AD) was a Greek physician who lived most of his adult life in Rome, and was considered an authority on medicine.

28 'Appendix', in Walker, *Historical Memoirs*, pp. 72–75.

29 Russell K. Alspach, *Irish Poetry from the English Invasion to 1798* (Philadephia: Univ. of Pennsylvania Press, 1943), pp. 110–111.

30 *Reliques of Irish Poetry* (Dubliln: George Bonham, 1978), p. 268.

31 Walker, 'Appendix', *Historical Memoirs*, pp. 91–92. A version of the original that is quite close to that attributed by Brooke to McCabe is included in Ó Máille's edition of Carolan's poems, *Amhráin Chearbhalláin*, pp. 162–163, under the title 'Uaill-Chumha Chearbhalláin Os Cionn Uaighe Mhic Cába' ('Sorrow-Lament over the Grave of MacCabe'), and Ó Máille, in a note, retells the story told in Walker (p. 302).

32 *Reliques*, p. 311. Also consulted were the texts in Ó Máille, *Amhráin Chearbhalláin*, pp. 162–163; Walker, 'Appendix', *Historical Memoirs*, p. 92; and ND–II, p. 5. In Walker and ND–II, the poem is entitled 'Feart-Laoi', meaning Epitaph.

33 *Reliques*, pp. 21–23.

34 *Reliques*, pp. 225–226.

35 Alspach, *Irish Poetry*, p. 109.

36 'Appendix', *Historical Memoirs*, p. 93. The title means 'Elegy for His Wife'. Also consulted was the text 'Marbhnadh Chearbhalláin air Bhás a Mná, Máire ní'g Uidhir' ('Carolan's Elegy on the Death of His Wife, Mary Maguire') in Ó Máille, *Amhráin Chearbhalláin*, pp. 161–162.

37 'Appendix', *Historical Memoirs*, pp. 94–95.

38 *Verse in English*, p. 446. On the other hand, Liam P. Ó Murchú, in *Cúirt an Mheon-*

Oíche (Baile Átha Claith: An Clóchomhar, 1982), says Woulfe was working in Clare and Limerick between 1817 and 1826, and that his translation of Merriman was made about forty years after the original was composed (p. 84).

39   Ó Murchú, *Cúirt*, pp. 24–25. Also consulted was the text in Patrick C. Power, trans., *Cúirt an Mhean-Oíche: The Midnight Court* (Cork: Mercier Press, 1971), pp. 27–28.

40   Carpenter, *Verse in English*, glosses this as an 'old stick'.

41   Carpenter glosses this as 'a tough old rope', referring to the Irish word *gad*, meaning a twisted twig, a tie or a cord.

42   Ó Murchú, *Cúirt*, pp. 89–90.

43   Ó Murchú, pp. 31–33. Also consulted were the texts in Power, pp. 44–48, and AD, pp. 232–234.

44   Ó Murchú, pp. 95–96.

45   There is some confusion as to when the book, which carries no publication date, was published. Séamus Ó Casaide, *A Rare Book of Irish and Scottish Gaelic Verse* (Wexford: The Bibliographic Society of Ireland, 1928), notes that James Hardiman set the date as 1792, and Ó Casaide says Wilson published an earlier collection in 1782, entitled *Poems, translated from the Irish language into English*, although no copy of this book seems to be extant. Wilson's translation of 'Pléaráca na Ruarcach' certainly was known by 1786, when Joseph Walker mentioned it in his *Historical Memoirs of the Irish Bards*, but it is not known whether the version he saw was in print, and, if so, where. Although Ó Casaide concludes that *Select Irish Poems* was probably published in 1792, he concedes that Hardiman's date of 1792 may have been a misprint, and that the book might in fact have been published in 1782.

46   *Historical Memoirs*, p. 81.

47   IM, Vol. I, p. 171.

48   Quoted in Ó Casaide, p. 69.

49   The Irish for whiskey is *uisce beatha*, literally water of life.

50   The Irish *meadar* means a wooden drinking cup.

51   *Select Irish Poems*, pp. 69–72. Also consulted were the texts in Ó Máille, *Amhráin Chearbhalláin*, pp. 205–207; Vallencey, *A Grammar*, pp. 128–131; Harrison, *Ag Cruinniú Meala*, pp. 119–120; Hyde, *Amhráin Chúige Chonnact*, pp. 146–150; and ND–II, pp. 12–13.

52   An idle, lazy fellow (*OED*).

53   The Irish for Carrick-on-Shannon, Co. Leitrim, is *Cora Droma Rúisc*.

54   Probably Moynalty (Maigh nEalta), near Kells, in Co. Meath.

55   Wilson glosses this as 'an instrument for sprinkling the holy water'. The Irish for aspergillum is *speirgeas*.

56   Possibly a reference to a medieval cycle of tales, said to be of Eastern origin, about a young prince whose life is saved by seven sages who tell stories over the course of a week until the prince, who has been sentenced to silence for seven days, is allowed to speak and reveal a plot against him by one of the king's wives. The wife had tried but failed to seduce the prince, and then sought to have him killed. The tales appear in many European languages, including English.

57   Wilson, *Select Irish Poems*, , pp. 73–77.

58   IM, Vol. I, p. 171.

59   There follows a passage of twenty lines, principally referring to other famous Irish families in the same way, not represented in Wilson's translation.

60   *Select Irish Poems*, pp. 78–80. Also consulted was the text in IM, Vol. I, pp. 146–152.

61   *Select Irish Poems*, pp. 81–83.

62   *Transactions of the Gaelic Society of Dublin* (Dublin: John Barlow, 1808), pp. 8–10, 34.

63   O'Flanagan glosses this as a 'poetic appellation given to Ireland', referring to the sovereignty of 'Feilim the Lawgiver', who was, he says, its monarch at the beginning of the second century.

64   *Transactions*, pp. 31–33, 53–54.

65   Mushera is a mountain in the Boggeragh range north of Macroom, in Co. Cork.

66   Loch Leane is the largest of the lakes near Killarney.

67 *Amhráin Dhiarmada Mac Seáin Buidhe Mac Cárthaigh* , ed. Tadhg Ó Donnchadha (Baile Átha Cliath: M.H. Mac Goill, 1916), pp. 17–18, 25. The title means 'Powerful Noble Judge'.

68 Heber, or *Eibhear* or *Eibhir* in Irish, is the son of the legendary Milesius who supposedly reigned in the southern half of the country.

69 *The Journal of the Royal Historical and Archaeological Association of Ireland* (July 1882), pp. 735, 739.

70 *Uileacán dubh ó* is a refrain often found in Irish poetry of keening, and means, literally, 'dark lament, oh!'

71 Bunting, *A General Collection*, p. 4.

NINETEENTH CENTURY

1 IM, Vol. II, pp. 208–210. The title means 'Reminiscence of Mac Liag on Brian Ború'.

2 On the banks of the Shannon in Co. Clare, Kincora was home to the celebrated Dál gCais, or Dalcassians, and the site of Brian Ború's palace.

3 Identified by Hardiman as one of the nobles of Brian Ború's court.

4 Hardiman glosses this as the Hebrides, where Mac Liag supposedly retired after Brian Ború's death.

5 Identified by Hardiman as a member of Brian Ború's court, and a cousin to Morrogh.

6 Identified by Hardiman as a son-in-law to Brian Ború and the highest-ranking prince to have survived the battle of Clontarf.

7 IM, Vol. II, pp. 209–211.

8 *Céad mile fáilte* means, literally, a hundred thousand welcomes.

9 IM, Vol. I, pp. 140–144.

10 *Uisce beatha*, literally water of life, means whiskey.

11 IM, Vol. I, pp. 141–145.

12 IM, Vol. II, pp. 212–216. Also consulted was the text in DÁNGRÁ, pp. 26–28. The title means 'Carroll O'Daly and the Echo'.

13 IM, Vol. II, pp. 213–217.

14 IM, Vol. I, pp. 66–68. Also consulted was the text 'Seorsa Brún,' in Tomás Ó Máille, ed., *Amhráin Chearbhalláin: The Poems of Carolan* (London: Irish Texts Society, 1916), pp. 210–211. The title in the IM version means 'Margaret, Daughter of George Brown'.

15 Hardiman, 'Memoir of Thomas Furlong', IM, Vol. I, p. lxxviii.

16 Desmond Ryan, *The Sword of Light: From the Four Masters to Douglas Hyde: 1636–1938* (London: Arthur Barker, 1939), p. 113.

17 IM, Vol. I, pp. 67–69.

18 *The Irish Poems of J. J. Callanan*, ed. Gregory A. Schirmer (Gerrards Cross, Bucks.: Colin Smythe, 2005), pp. 88–90.

19 AD, pp. 330–332. There are a number of occasionally overlapping versions of 'Príosún Chluain Meala', and although this one corresponds more closely to Callanan's translation than do others, it doesn't appear to be the specific text that Callanan was working from.

20 A pattern or festivities connected with a patron saint's day.

21 *Poems of Callanan*, pp. 92–93.

22 DG, Vol. I, pp. 69–70. Also consulted were the texts in FG, p. 18; AD, p. 310; SONGS, p. 143; and O-C, p. 15.

23 ND-III, p. 3. Also consulted was the text in IM, Vol. II, p. 145.

24 *Poems of Callanan*, p. 95.

25 Lough Leane is the largest of the lakes around Killarney, Co. Kerry.

26 *Poems of Callanan*, p. 94.

27 IM, Vol. II, pp. 20–22. Also consulted was the text in *Filidheacht Sheagháin Uí Neachtain*, ed. Úna ní Fhaircheallaigh (Baile Átha Cliath: Conradh na Gaedhilge, 1911), pp. 22–24. The title means "Lament on the Death of the Wife of James II'.

28 IM, Vol. II, pp. 21–23.

29   *The Giantess, from the Irish of Oisin, and the War of Donomore, with Other Poems and Translations* (Belfast: Simms and M'Intyre, 1833), p. xiii.

30   *The Giantess*, p. 182.

31   *Peadar Ó Doirnín: Amhráin*, ed. Breandán Ó Buachalla (Baile Átha Cliath: An Clóchomhar, 1969), pp. 36–37. There is a final stanza in Ó Doirnín's poem not represented in Graham's version.

32   The foe, the gauger [exciseman]; the friend, Captain Whiskey (Graham's note).

33   *Giantess*, pp. 182–184.

34   *Autobiography*, ed. James Kilroy (Dublin: Dolmen Press, 1968), p. 23.

35   An anglicisation of *a ghrá*, the vocative form of 'love'.

36   *The Irish Penny Journal*, Vol. I, No. 9 (29 August 1840), pp. 68–69; this version accompanied Mangan's translation. Also consulted were the texts in FG, p. 176, and Ó-C, pp. 94–96.

37   Munster's.

38   Mythical ancestor of the sept that dominated Munster in the medieval period.

39   The third Viscount of Clare, Domhnhall Ó Briain, whose two sons died in exile after the Treaty of Limerick.

40   An angilicization of *mo bhrón*, meaning 'my sorrow'.

41   Domhnall Ó Súilleabháin Béarra (1560–1618), whose castle, Dún Buidhe, or Dunboy, stood on the sea just west of Castletownbere, in Co. Cork. It was destroyed in 1602, in the fighting that followed the Battle of Kinsale.

42   Probably Brian Óg Ó Ruairc and Brian Maghuidhir, both comtemporaries and associates of Domnhnall Ó Súilleabhán Béarra.

43   Probably the influential O'Carroll family, who lived near the Tipperary-Offaly border.

44   Mangan gives 'forsooth' as the meaning.

45   *The Collected Works of James Clarence Mangan. Vol. II: Poems: 1838–1844*, ed. Jacques Chuto, et. al. (Dublin: Irish Academic Press, 1996), pp. 201–202.

46   ND-I, p. 84. Also consulted were the texts in DG, Vol. I, p. 65; Ó-C, pp. 12–13; and AD, p. 308. Several stanzas of the version that Mangan seems to have been translating from are included in PPM, pp. 256–258, under the title 'Rois Gheal Dubh', and translated by Mangan there as 'Black-Haired Fair Rose'. But 'Dark Rosaleen' is very different from 'Black-Haired Fair Rose.'

47   *Collected Works. Vol. III: Poems: 1845–1847* (1997), pp. 167–170.

48   The land given to the Israelites in Egypt, and which was spared the plague.

49   A knightly hero.

50   DG, Vol. II, pp. 2–5. Also consulted were the texts in *The Irish Miscellany*, ed. John O'Daly (Dublin: John O'Daly, 1876), pp. 45–47; and Ó-C, pp. 108–110. The title means 'Meditation of the Melancholy Man, or Lament of Teach Molaga'.

51   *Collected Works. Vol. III*, pp. 221–223.

52   An anglicisation of *mo bhrón*, meaning 'my sorrow'.

53   West Munster.

54   Possibly a tribe settled in parts of Meath, Sligo, and Cavan.

55   DG, Vol. III, pp. 20–22.

56   A bardic name for Munster.

57   'A concluding stanza, generally intended as a recapitulation of the entire poem' (Mangan's note). *Amhrán* means song or poem, or, more specifically, a concluding set of lines, often referred to as a *ceangal*, or binding.

58   *Collected Works. Vol. III*, pp. 111–113.

59   A range of mountains about fifteen kilometres east of Killarney, in Co. Kerry, the area in which Ó Rathaille grew up. The name 'Sliabh Luachra' is also given to the area.

60   PPM, pp. 28–30; this version was accompanied by Mangan's translation. Also consulted were the texts in *Dánta Aodhagáin Uí Rathaille: The Poems of Egan O'Reilly*, ed. Patrick S. Dineen and Tadhg O'Donoghue, 2nd ed. (London: Irish Texts Society, 1911), pp. 18–20; FG, p. 64; and AD, pp. 150–152.

61   *Collected Works of Mangan, Vol. IV*, pp. 143–144.
62   PPM, pp. 14–5; this version was accompanied by Mangan's translation. Also consulted was the text in *Éigse na Máighe*, ed. Risteárd Ó Foghludha (Baile Átha Cliath: Oifig an tSoláthair, 1952), pp. 108–109.
63   An anglicisation of *mo bhrón*, meaning 'my sorrow'.
64   *Collected Works of Mangan, Vol. IV*, pp. 141–142.
65   *Irish Popular Songs* (Dublin: James McGlashan, 1847), pp. 12, 29.
66   *Reliques of Irish Jacobite Poetry*, ed. John O'Daly (Dublin: Samuel J. Machan, 1844), pp. 10–12. Also consulted were the texts in *Amhráin Seagháin Cláraigh Mhic Dhomhnaill*, ed. Pádraig ua Duinnín (Baile Átha Cliath: Connradh na Gaedhilge, 1902); and DG, Vol. II, pp. 43–44. The title means, literally, 'The Wild-Buck Walker', but the phrase can be taken to mean an Englishman, a tyrant, or, more specifically, James II.
67   A poetic name for Ireland, literally a large district of territories.
68   *Reliques*, pp. 11–13.
69   *Irish Popular Songs*, pp. 72–74. Also consulted were the texts in PPM, pp. 344–346; and ND-I, p. 76.
70   *Irish Popular Songs*, pp. 73–75.
71   'Flower of the young, brown-haired maidens.' In the next stanza, the refrain translates as 'Said the flower of the young, brown-haired maidens.'
72   *Irish Popular Songs*, pp. 90–94. Also consulted was the text in DG, Vol. II, pp. 48–49. A version entitled 'Úilleacán Dúbhach Ó!', and with a different refrain, is attributed to Turlough Carolan; see *Amhráin Chearbhalláin*, ed. Ó Máille, pp. 223–225.
73   *Irish Popular Songs*, pp. 91–95.
74   *Irish Popular Songs*, pp. 144–148. Also consulted were the texts in AD, pp. 312–314; and ND-I, pp. 79–80.
75   *Irish Popular Songs*, pp. 145–149.
76   *The Irish Penny Journal*, Vol. I, No. 44 (1 May 1841), p. 352, which accompanied Fox's translation. Also consulted were the texts in DG, Vol. I, pp. 59–60; IM, Vol. I, pp. 337–338; and CEÓL, p. 41.
77   In the original, Iar-Umhall. The districts of Umhall Íochtarach and Umhall Uachtarach are the baronies of Burrishoole and Murrisk, respectively, in Co. Mayo.
78   *The Irish Penny Journal*, p. 352. Although this is the version widely attributed to Fox, it was published here anonymously.
79   Probably the *Lighe* (gen. *Lighean*, also known in English as the Swilly Burn), a river near Raphoe in eastern Co. Donegal, about ten kilometers northwest of Strabane.
80   IM, Vol. II, pp. 102–108. Also consulted was the text in *Measgra Dánta*, Part II, ed. Thomas F. O'Rahilly (Cork: Cork Univ. Press, 1927), pp. 144–147. Ó Gnímh's poem contains another ten stanzas not translated by Ferguson. The title means 'On the Downfall of the Gael.'
81   *Lays of the Western Gael and Other Poems* (London: Bell and Daldy, 1865), pp. 181–185.
82   IM, Vol. I, p. 60. Also consulted were the texts in *Amhráin Chearbhalláin*, ed. Ó Máille, pp. 109–110; and *Reliques of Irish Poetry*, trans. by Charlotte Brooke (Dublin: George Bonham, 1789), pp. 316–317. The original contains two stanzas not translated by Ferguson.
83   Based on the text in IM, Vol. I, pp. 238–240. Quite different versions, except for the first stanza, appear in ND-I, p. 82, and AD, pp. 278–280.
84   *Lays of the Western Gael*, pp. 199–200.
85   *Lays of the Western Gael*, pp. 209–210.
86   IM, Vol. I, p. 262. Also consulted were the texts in DG, Vol. I, p. 39; ND-III, pp. 62–63; AD, p. 284; and FG, p. 87.
87   *Lays of the Western Gael*, p. 216.
88   *The Celt, a Weekly Periodical of Irish National Literature*, Vol. I, No. 2 (8 August 1857), pp. 29–30; this text appeared with Joyce's translation. Also consulted were the texts in *Amhráin Phiarais Mhic Gearailt*, ed. Riseárd Ó Foghludha (Baile Átha Cliath: Conradh na Gaedhilge, 1905), pp. 23–24; FG, p. 25; and DG, Vol. II, pp. 27–28.
89   *The Celt*, pp. 30–31.

90   *The Adventures of Donnchadh Ruadh Mac Con-Mara, a Slave of Adversity* (Dublin: John O'Daly, 1853), pp. 20–24. Also consulted was the text in *Donnchadh Ruadh Mac Conmara*, ed. Risteárd Ó Foghludha (Baile Átha Cliath: Oifig Díolata Foillseacháin Rialtais, 1933), pp. 22–23.

91   The Power family were patrons of Mac Conmara when he was living in Co. Waterford.

92   *Adventures of Donnchadh Ruadh*, pp. 21–25.

93   *Adventures of Donnchadh Ruadh*, pp. 24–26; *Donnchadh Ruadh Mac Conmara*, p. 24.

94   *Adventures of Donnchadh Ruadh*, pp. 25–27.

THE LITERARY REVIVAL

1   *Medieval Irish Lyrics*, ed. James Carney (Dublin: Dolmen, 1967), pp. 10–12. Also consulted were the texts in MURPHY, p. 160; and *Four Old Irish Songs of Summer and Winter*, ed. Kuno Meyer (London: David Nutt, 1903), p. 14.

2   *Bards of the Gael and Gall* (1897; Dublin and Belfast: Phoenix, n.d.), p. 23.

3   *Bards of Gael and Gall*, p. 130.

4   *Oidhe Chloinne Lir: The Fate of the Children of Lir* (Dublin: M. H. Gill, 1883), pp. 24–25.

5   The Straits of Moyle, the name given to the sea between northeast Ireland and southwest Scotland.

6   *Bards of Gael and Gall*, pp. 155–156.

7   *The Dean of Lismore's Book: A Selection of Ancient Gaelic Poetry*, ed. Thomas M'Lauchlan (Edinburgh: Edmonston and Douglas, 1862), pp. 75–77; Sigerson cites this as his source. Also consulted was the text in *Irish Bardic Poetry*, ed. Osborn Bergin (Dublin: Dublin Institute for Advanced Studies, 1970), pp. 207–208.

8   *Bards of Gael and Gall*, p. 194.

9   *Aislinge Meic Conglinne: The Vision of Mac Conglinne*, ed. Kuno Meyer (London: David Nutt, 1892), pp. 35–39; Sigerson cites this as his source.

10   *Bards of Gael and Gall*, pp. 210–213.

11   *Oidhe Chloinne Lir*, p. 22.

12   *The Banshee and Other Poems* (Dublin: Sealy, Bryers, and Walker, 1888, 1891), p. 45.

13   Preface, *The Irish Poems of Alfred Perceval Graves: Songs of the Gael and a Gaelic Story-Telling* (Dublin: Maunsel, 1908), p. vii.

14   Based on the text in MURPHY, pp. 86–88. Also consulted were the texts in NEESON, pp. 52–54; and *A Golden Treasury of Irish Poetry A. D. 600 to 1200*, eds. David Greene and Frank O'Connor, eds. (London: Macmillan, 1967), pp. 78–80. Graves said he drew on Kuno Meyer's literal translation, in MEYER, pp. 63–64. The literal translation here draws on that in MURPHY, pp. 87–89.

15   This probably refers to Kilmacduagh (Mac Duach's Church), on the Galway-Clare border, a few miles southwest of Gort, Co. Galway. Mac Duach's full name was Colmán Mac Duach.

16   *The Book of Irish Poetry* (London, Dublin, Belfast: Gresham, n.d. [1914]), pp. 81–82.

17   In his preface, Ó Flannghaile says Mac Conmara's poem is indebted to Virgil's *Aeneid* (*Eachtra Ghiolla an Amaráin, or The Adventures of a Luckless Fellow* [Dublin: Seary, Bryers and Walker, n.d. (1897)], p. ix).

18   Aodh Buidhe Mac Cruitín (1680?–1755), a poet and prominent member of Seán Ó Neachtáin's group of Gaelic scholars in Dublin in the eighteenth century.

19   *Eachtra Ghiolla an Amaráin*, pp. 54–66. Also consulted was the text in *Donnchadh Ruadh Mac Conmara*, ed. Risteárd Ó Foghludha (Baile Átha Cliath: Oifig Díolata Foillseacháin Rialtais, 1933), pp. 32–36, 40–42. The title means 'Adventure of the Unfortunate Fellow'.

29   Heber, or Eber, was one of the two legendary Milesian kings of Ireland. Eber supposedly controlled the southern half of the island.

21   *Eachtra Ghiolla an Amaráin*, pp. 55–67.

22   *Christian Inscriptions in the Irish Language*, eds. George Petrie and M. Stokes, Vol. I (Dublin: Royal Historical and Archaeological Association of Ireland, 1872), p. 5. Rolleston's translation represents the first five stanzas of a lengthy poem. Also

consulted was *A Literary History of Ireland*, ed. Douglas Hyde (New York: Scribners, 1899), p. 206, which provides the text of the first two stanzas.

23 St. Ciarán is said to have founded a monastery at Clonmacnoise in the middle of the sixth century.

24 Conn Cétchathach, or Conn of the Hundred Battles, a legendary king of Tara in pre-Christian Ireland.

25 Probably Cairbré of the Liffey, a great-grandson of Conn of the Hundred Battles.

26 An ancient territory roughly equivalent to Co. Longford.

27 An ancient territory roughly equivalent to Co. Meath.

28 *Sea Spray: Verses and Translations* (Dublin: Maunsel, 1909), p. 47.

29 *The Poem-Book of the Gael: Translations from Irish Gaelic Poetry into English Prose and Verse* (London: Chatto and Windus, 1913), p. xxxiii.

30 *Four Old Irish Songs of Summer and Winter*, ed. Kuno Meyer (London: David Nutt, 1903), p. 18; Hull cites this as her source.

31 MURPHY, p. 168. Also consulted were the texts in *Duanaire Finn: The Book of the Lays of Fionn*, Part I, ed. Eoin MacNeill (London: Irish Texts Society, 1908), p. 80; *Measgra Dánta*, Part II, ed. Thomas F. O'Rahilly (Cork: Cork Univ. Press, 1927), pp.184–185; and DG, Vol. III, p. 75.

32 *Reliques of Irish Poetry*, ed. Charlotte Brooke (Dublin: George Bonham, 1789), p. 232; Hull cites this as her source. Also consulted were the texts in AD, p. 276; and DG, Vol. I, p. 27.

33 *Poem-Book of the Gael*, p. 82.

34 *Poem-Book*, p. 91.

35 *Poem-Book*, p. 265.

36 HYDE, pp. 8–10.

37 HYDE, pp. 9–11.

38 HYDE, pp. 28–30. Also consulted was the text in DG, Vol. I, pp. 31–32.

39 HYDE, pp. 40–42. Also consulted was the text in DG, Vol. I, p. 33.

40 HYDE, pp. 29–31.

41 Literally small treasure, generally used for sweetheart.

42 HYDE, pp. 41–43.

43 HYDE, pp. 134–136. The title means 'The Lover at His Being Refused'.

44 Anglicisation of *rún*, often translated as secret love, or sweetheart.

45 HYDE, pp. 135–137.

46 Douglas Hyde, *Abhráin Diadha Chúige Chonnacht: or The Religious Songs of Connacht*, Part I (Dublin: M. H. Gill, n.d. [1906]), pp. 274–282. *Mallacht* means a curse.

47 *Abhráin Diadha Chúige Chonnacht*, pp. 275–283.

48 Loch Leane is the largest of the lakes near Killarney, Co. Kerry.

49 *Ancient Music of Ireland*, ed. George Petrie (Dublin: Society for the Preservation and Publication of the Melodies of Ireland, 1855), Vol. I., pp. 182–183; McCall cites this as his source.

50 The Irish for harp is *cláirseach*.

51 *A stór* is the vocative form of *stór*, meaning treasure or sweetheart.

52 *Pulse of the Bards* (Dublin: M. H. Gill, 1904), pp. 52–53.

53 Femen is a plain in Co. Tipperary, in the vicinity of Cashel, and Bregon a place on it. St. Rónán died in 664.

54 MURPHY, pp. 74–82. Also consulted was the text in *A Golden Treasury of Irish Poetry A. D. 600 to 1200*, eds. David Greene and Frank O'Connor (London: Macmillan, 1967), pp. 48–52. Only the stanzas represented in Gwynn's translation are included here. The order of stanzas in Gwynn's translation does not always follow that in in the versions in MURPHY and *Golden Treasury*, and Gwynn's fourth stanza is not represented in either. The literal translation draws on that in MURPHY.

55 *A Lay of Ossian and Patrick with Other Irish Verses* (Dublin: Hodges Figgis, n.d. [1903]), pp. 20–23.

56 HYDE, pp. 4–6. Also consulted were the texts in AD, pp. 292–294; DG, Vol. I, p. 48; and FG, p. 94.

57   Thomas Boyd, *Poems* (Dublin: M.H. Gill, 1906), pp. 19–21.
58   *Dánta Amhráin is Caointe: Sheathrúin Céitinn*, ed. Eoin Cathmhaolach Mac Giolla Eáin (Baile Átha Cliath: Connradh na Gaedhilge, 1900), p. 60. Also consulted were the texts in ND-I, pp. 15–16; and DÁNGRÁ, pp. 133–134. Synge's translation is of the first and third stanzas of Keating's poem.
59   Quoted in Michael Cronin, *Translating Ireland: Translation, Languages, Cultures* (Cork: Cork Univ. Press, 1996), p. 141.
60   Review of *Dánta Amhráin is Caointe: Sheathrúin Céitinn*, ed. Rev. J. C. MacErlean, *The Speaker*, 8 Dec. 1900; rpt. in *J. M. Synge: Collected Works: Vol. II: Prose*, ed. Alan Price (London: Oxford Univ. Press, 1966), p. 357.
61   Based on the text in CEÓL, p. 50. Also consulted were the texts in ND-I, p. 90; and *Collected Works of Padraic H. Pearse: Songs of the Irish Rebels* (Dublin: Phoenix, n.d.), p. 114. None of these seems to be the text that MacDonagh was working from, but the version in CEÓL is the only one that contains the material in MacDonagh's fourth stanza.
62   Preface, *Literature in Ireland: Studies Irish and Anglo-Irish* (Dublin: Talbot Press, 1916), p. viii.
63   Literally small treasure, generally used as for sweetheart.
64   *Songs of Myself* (Dublin: Hodges, Figgis, 1910), pp. 43–44.
65   Lough Macnean (Upper and Lower), situated where Cos. Fermanagh, Leitrim, and Cavan meet.
66   *Lyrical Poems* (Dublin: The Irish Review, 1913), pp. 39–40.
67   *Cathal Buí: Amhráin*, ed. Breandán Ó Buachalla (Baile Átha Cliath: An Clóchomhar, 1975), pp. 77–83. This is the second of two versions of the poem given by Ó Buachalla, who says there are many different versions extant. Only those stanzas represented in MacDonagh's translation are included here. Also consulted were the texts in ND-II, pp. 47–48; AD, pp. 132–134; Ó-C, pp. 47–49; and SONGS, p. 124. None of these, including Ó Buachalla's, seems to be precisely the text that MacDonagh was working from.
68   *Literature in Ireland*, pp. 83–84. Also consulted was the text in NEESON, p. 62.
69   *Lyrical Poems*, p. 43. This translation was also included in *Literature in Ireland*, p. 84.
70   PPM, pp. 264–266. This version contains several stanzas not represented in Pearse's translation. Also consulted were the texts in SONGS, p. 150; and Ó-C, pp. 66–68.
71   *Poem-Book of the Gael*, pp. 202–203.
72   *Collected Works of Padraic H. Pearse: Songs of the Irish Rebels*, ed. Desmond Ryan (Dublin: Phoenix, n.d.), p. 34.
73   *Collected Works: Songs of Irish Rebels*, p. 35.
74   Quoted in A. Norman Jeffares, *Ango-Irish Literature* (New York: Schocken Books, 1982), p. 271.
75   *Linn* is Irish for a lake or pond.
76   HYDE, pp. 30–32; Colum cites this as his source. Also consulted were the texts in PPM, pp. 286–290; ND-I, pp. 77–78; FG, pp. 94–95; DG, Vol. I, pp. 37–38; AD, pp. 298–300; and CEOL, p. 18. The title means 'The Blackthorn'.
77   HYDE, p. 138; Colum cites this as his source. Also consulted was the text in DÁNGRÁ, pp. 132–133.
78   *Wild Earth and Other Poems* (1916; New York: Macmillan, 1927), pp. 38–39.
79   *Wild Earth*, pp. 48–49.
80   HYDE, pp. 20–22; Colum cites this as his source. The original contains one stanza not represented in Colum's translation. The title means 'The Brow of the Red Mountain'.
81   *Dramatic Legends and Other Poems* (New York: Macmillan, 1922), pp. 13–14.
82   *Reincarnations* (London: Macmillan, 1918), p. 61.
83   *Dánta Amhráin is Caointe: Seathrúin Céitinn*, p. 60. Also consulted were the texts in ND-I, pp. 15–16; and DÁNGRÁ, pp. 133–134. In some versions, the original contains two final stanzas not represented in Stephens's translation.
84   *Abhráin agus Dánta an Reachtabhraigh*, ed. Dubhglas de hÍde (Baile Átha Cliath: Oifig Díolta Foillseacháin Rialtais, 1933), p. 72.

85 *Reincarnations*, pp. 1–2.

86 *Reincarnations*, p. 14.

87 *Dánta Aodhagáin Uí Rathaille: The Poems of Egan O'Reilly*, 2nd ed., eds. Patrick S. Dineen and Tadhg O'Donoghue (London: Irish Texts Society, 1911), pp. 26–28. Also consulted were the texts in AD, p. 140; and *Aogán Ó Rathaille: Dánta*, ed. Dáibhí Mac Conmara (n.p.: Aquila, 1969), pp. 34–35. Only the final three stanzas of this five-stanza poem are represented in Stephens's translation. For the full version of the original, see under Eavan Boland's translation. The title means 'The Time of Moving to Duibhneacaibh, beside Tonn Tóime in Kerry'. According to AD, Tonn Tóime is near the mouth of Castlemaine Harbour, Co. Kerry, but Dineen says Duibhneachaibh is near a waterfall that courses down the side of Tomies Mountain, on the western edge of Lough Leane, near Killarney.

88 The head of the MacCarthy clan.

89 The Earl of Clancarty, who had a residence in Blarney, Co. Cork, near the Lee, in the seventeenth century.

90 MacDonogh MacCarthy, Lord of Duhallow, built Kanturk Castle, in Co. Cork, early in the seventeenth century.

91 The Wave of Cliona, or *Tonn Clíodhna*, is often associated with Glandore Harbour, Co. Cork. In Ó Rathaille's poem, it is mentioned in a list of places in Munster.

92 *Reincarnations*, pp. 28–30.

93 *Duanaire Dháibhidh Uí Bhruadair*, ed. John C. Mac Erlean, Part II (London: Irish Texts Society, 1913), p. 221. Also consulted were the texts in ND-I, p. 54; and AD, p. 116. There is a fourth stanza not translated by Stephens; for the full text, see under Michael Hartnett.

94 *Reincarnations*, pp. 37–38.

95 *Duanaire Uí Bhruadair*, Part III, pp. 202, 206. The title means 'Time for an easy step.'

96 *Reincarnations*, pp. 52–54.

MODERN IRELAND

1 DÁNGRÁ, pp. 70–71. Flower wrote the introduction to this collection.

2 *Love's Bitter-Sweet: Translations from the Irish Poets of the Sixteenth and Seventeenth Centuries* (Dublin: Cuala Press, 1925) , p. 7.

3 DÁNGRÁ, pp. 10–11. Flower wrote the introduction to this collection. There is one stanza in the original not translated by Flower.

4 *Buile Suibhne: The Adventures of Suibhne Geilt*, ed. J. G. O'Keeffe (London: Irish Texts Society, 1913), p. xvii. The poem is not actually part of O'Keeffe's text of *Buile Suibhne*, but is cited in his introduction as a poem attributed to Sweeney. Also consulted was the text in MURPHY, p. 112.

5 NEESON, p. 58. Also consulted was the text in MURPHY, p. 4.

6 *Love's Bitter-Sweet*, pp. 9–11.

7 Gerard Murphy says *Túaim Inber* is glossed by the ninth-century scribe whose manuscript he was working from as *barr edin*, meaning ivied tree-top (MURPHY, p. 113)

8 Murphy, noting that *gobbán* is a common noun meaning artisan, says *Gobbán* could be a reference to the divine artisan, or God (MURPHY, p. 224). In Irish folklore, Gobán Saor is a stone-mason who travels around the country building castles, monasteries, and round towers.

9 *Poems and Translations* (London: Constable, 1931), p. 115.

10 *The Irish Tradition* (Oxford: Clarendon Press, 1947), p. 49.

11 *Cúirt an Mheán-Oíche: The Midnight Court*, ed. and trans. Patrick C. Power (Cork: Mercier Press, 1971), pp. 14–18.

12 *The Midnight Court and The Adventures of a Luckless Fellow*, trans. Percy Arland Ussher (London: Jonathan Cape, 1926), pp. 16–18.

13 Power, *Cúirt an Mheán-Oíche*, pp. 26–28.

14 Power, pp. 60–62.

15 *Midnight Court*, pp. 23–24.

16 *Midnight Court*, pp. 44–45.

17   SONGS, p. 2.

18   SONGS, pp. 73–74.

19   SONGS, pp. 73–44.

20   *Collected Plays* (Dublin: Dolmen Press, 1963), p. 398.

21   ND-I, p. 8. Also consulted were the texts in AD, p. 16; and Ó-C, pp. 18–19.

22   DG, Vol. III, pp. 63–65. Also consulted were the texts in AD, pp. 40–42; and Ó-C, p. 40.

23   *Collected Poems*, ed. Liam Miller (Dublin: Dolmen Press; London: Oxford Univ. Press, 1974), p. 162.

24   *Collected Poems*, pp. 203–204.

25   IM, Vol. I, pp. 60–62. Also consulted were the texts in *Amhráin Chearbhalláin: The Poems of Carolan*, ed. Tomás Ó Máille (London: Irish Texts Society, 1916), pp. 109–110; and *Reliques of Irish Poetry*, trans. by Charlotte Brooke (Dublin: George Bonham, 1789), pp. 316–317.

26   IM, Vol. I, pp. 66–68. Also consulted was the text in *Amhráin Chearbhalláin*, pp. 210–211.

27   *Collected Poems*, pp. 295–296.

28   *Collected Poems*, p. 297.

29   SONGS, pp. 187–190. In a note to his translation, Clarke refers to O'Sullivan's reprinting of Charles Henry Wilson's eighteenth-century translation in this collection, and O'Sullivan included this version of the original along with Wilson's translation. Also consulted were the texts in Charles Henry Wilson, *Select Irish Poems, Translated into English*. n.p., n.d (1782?), pp. 69–72; *Amhráin Chearbhalláin*, pp. 205–207; Charles Vallencey, *A Grammar of the Iberno-Celtic, or Irish Language*, 2nd ed. (Dublin: R. Marchbank, 1782), pp. 128–131; Alan Harrison, *Ag Cruinniú Meala: Anthony Raymond (1675–1726), ministéir Protastúnach, agus léann na Gaeilge i mBaile Átha Cliath* (Baile Átha Cliath: An Clóchomhar, 1988), pp. 119–120; and Douglas Hyde, *Amhráin Chúige Chonnact: The Songs of Connacht*, ed. Breanán Ó Conaire (1893; Blackrock, Co. Dublin: 1985), pp. 146–150.

30   *Collected Poems*, pp. 300–301.

31   *The Silver Branch: A Collection of the Best Old Irish Lyrics, Variously Translated* (New York: Viking, 1938), p. 9.

32   *Érui*, Vol. II, eds. Kuno Meyer and John Strachan (1905; Dublin: Royal Irish Academy, 1971), pp. 55–56; O'Faolain cites this as his source. O'Faolain's translation represents eight of the fifteen stanzas in the original. Also consulted was the text in MURPHY, pp. 19–22. The literal translation here draws on that in Meyer and Strachan.

33   *Irische Texte*, Vol. I, ed. Ernst Windisch (Leipzig: Verlag von S. Hirzel, 1880), p. 224; O'Faolain cites this as his source. The literal translation here draws on that by Jeffrey Gantz in *Early Irish Myths and Sagas* (New York: Penguin, 1981), pp. 175–176.

34   Kuno Meyer, 'Notes on Irish Texts', *University of Illinois Studies in Language and Literature*, II, Part 4 (1916), p. 44; O'Faolain cites this as his source. The literal translation here draws on that in Meyer.

35   *Silver Branch*, p. 34.

36   *Silver Branch*, p. 86.

37   *Silver Branch*, p. 131.

38   *Poems from the Irish* (Dublin: Hodges, Figgis; Oxford: B. H. Blackwell, 1944), p. ix.

39   DÁNGRÁ, pp. 55–59.

40   There follow twenty lines praising Costello in terms of heroic figures from Ireland's legends and history.

41   *More Poems from the Irish* (Dublin: Hodges, Figgis; Oxford: B. H. Blackwell, 1945), pp. 23–27.

42   *The Bardic Poems of Tadhg Dall Ó hUiginn*, ed. Eleanor Knott, Vol. I (London: Irish Texts Society, 1922), pp. 260–261.

43   *The Dove in the Castle: A Collection of Poems from the Irish* (Dublin: Hodges Figgis; Oxford; Blackwell, 1946), pp. 152–153.

44 See Diane Wong, 'Literature and the Oral Tradition', in *The Cambridge History of Irish Literature*, Vol. I, eds. Margaret Kelleher and Philip O'Leary (Cambridge: Cambridge Univ. Press, 2006), pp. 657–662, for a discussion of the arguments against attributing the poem to Ní Chonaill.

45 *Caoineadh Airt Uí Laoghaore*, ed. Seán Ó Tuama (Baile Átha Cliath: An Clóchomhar, 1993), pp. 33–36.

46 *Dánfhocail: Irish Epigrams in Verse*, ed. Thomas F. O'Rahilly (Dublin: Talbot, 1921), p. 22. The two stanzas that O'Connor is translating are two different epigrams in O'Rahilly's collection, one following the other.

47 *Kings, Lords, and Commons* (New York: Knopf, 1959), pp. 110–112. The translation was first published, in a slightly different form, in *The Wild Bird's Nest: Poems from the Irish* (Dublin: Cuala Press, 1932), then included, in a version closer to this one, in *The Magic Fountain* (London: Macmillan, 1939), and finally published as *The Lament for Art O'Leary* (Dublin: Cuala Press, 1940).

48 *Kings, Lords, and Commons*, p. 81. The first stanza was published separately in *Lords and Commons: Translations from the Irish* (Dublin: Cuala Press, 1938); both stanzas appeared, under the title 'Fathers and Children', and in slightly different form, in *Magic Fountain*, p. 54.

49 Power, *Cúirt an Mhean Oíche*, pp. 24–28.

50 *Kings, Lords, and Commons*, pp. 141–143. An earlier, slightly different version of the translation was published as *The Midnight Court* (London, Dublin: Maurice Fridberg, 1945).

51 Power, pp. 38–42.

52 *Kings, Lords, and Commons*, pp. 146–148.

53 Power, pp. 68–72.

54 *King, Lords, and Commons*, pp. 159–160.

55 *A Golden Treasury of Irish Poetry A. D. 600 to 1200*, eds. David Greene and Frank O'Connor (London: Macmillan, 1967), pp. 144–146. Also consulted were the texts in MURPHY, pp. 38–42; and NEESON, pp. 78–80. The literal translation here draws on those in MURPHY and NEESON.

56 *Kings, Lords, and Commons*, pp. 10–11.

57 *Duanaire Finn: The Book of the Lays of Fionn*, Part I, ed. Eoin MacNeill (London: Irish Texts Society, 1908), p. 82.

58 Scandanavia.

59 The Hill of Allen, Co. Kildare, where Fionn Mac Cumhaill is said to have had his headquarters.

60 *Thronging Feet* (New York: Sheed and Ward, 1936), p. 84.

61 HYDE, p. 58. Also consulted were the texts in DG, Vol. I, p. 49; and ND-I, pp. 71–72. Only this one stanza, appearing in all three versions, is represented in Farren's translation.

62 *Búrdúin Bheaga: Pithy Irish Quatrains*, ed. Thomas F. O'Rahilly (Dublin: Browne and Nolan, 1925), p 7.

63 Erris Head, on the Belmullet peninsula, Co. Mayo.

64 *A rún* is the vocative of *rún*, meaning sweetheart.

65 *Thronging Feet*, p. 88.

66 *Rime, Gentlemen, Rime* (New York: Sheed and Ward, 1945), p. 34.

67 *Medieval Irish Lyrics*, ed. James Carney (Dublin: Dolmen, 1967), pp. 10–12. Also consulted were the texts in MURPHY, p. 160; and *Four Old Irish Songs of Summer and Winter*, ed. Kuno Meyer (London: David Nutt, 1903), p. 14.

68 *The Lace Curtain*, Vol. 4 (Summer, 1971), p. 47.

69 *Golden Treasury of Irish Poetry*, p. 84. Also consulted was the text in MURPHY, p. 4.

70 *The Lace Curtain*, p. 46.

71 *The Hungry Grass* (London: Faber and Faber, 1947), p. 69.

72   *Amhráin Chlainne Gael*, eds. Micheál and Tomás Ó Máille (Indreabhán: Cló Iar-Chonnachta, 1905, 1991), pp. 76–77. Also consulted were the texts in AD, pp. 334–336; *Blas Meala: Sips from the Honey-Pot*, ed. Brian O'Rourke (Blackrock, Co.

Dublin: Irish Academic Press, 1985), pp. 94–96; and in the liner notes to the album "Reacaireacht an Riadaigh" (Gael-Linn).

73 *Hungry Grass*, p. 12.

74 CEÓL, p. 18. Also consulted were the texts in FG, pp. 94–95; DG, Vol. I, pp. 37–38; HYDE, pp. 30–32; PPM, pp. 286–290; ND-I, pp. 77–78; and AD, pp. 298–300.

75 Brendan Behan, *Poems and a Play in Irish* (Dublin: Gallery Press, 1981), p. 17. The ellipses are in Behan's text.

76 *Hungry Grass*, p. 36.

77 *A Warning to Conquerors* (Dublin: Dolmen Press, 1968), p. 63.

CONTEMPORARY IRELAND

1 *Trasládáil* (Belfast: Lagan Press, 1997), p. 18. Also consulted was the text in ND-I, p. 9.

2 *Trasládáil*, p. 19. The poem was originally published in *A Heart Full of Thought* (Dublin: Dolmen Press, 1959) under the title 'Duibe id Mhailghibh'.

3 *Trasládáil*, p. 14. Also consulted was the text in *Dánta Piarais Feiritéir*, ed. Pádraig Ua Duinnín (Baile Átha Cliath: Connradh na Gaedhilge, 1903), pp. 33–36. There are fifteen stanzas in the version in *Dánta Piarais Feiritéir* not represented in the text in *Trasládáil*, or in Mhac an tSaoi's translation.

4 *Trasládáil*, p. 15.

5 *Trasládáil*, p. 22. Also consulted were the texts in HYDE, pp. 92–94; and ND-I, p. 85.

6 *Trasládáil*, p. 23.

7 *Filíocht Phádraigín Haicéad*, ed Máire Ní Cheallacháin (Baile Átha Cliath: An Clóchomhar, 1962), p. 13. Also consulted was the text in AD, p. 94. The title means 'After Breaking My Own Foot in France'.

8 *Done into English: Collected Translations* (Oldcastle, Co. Meath: Gallery Press, 2003), p. 87.

9 'Introduction,' *The New Oxford Book of Irish Verse* (Oxford: Oxford Univ. Press, 1986), p. xxvii.

10 AD, p. xxxv.

11 Conn was a king of ancient Ireland, and Corc of Munster.

12 AD, p. 92. Also consulted was the text in Ní Cheallacháin, *Filíocht Phádraigín Haicéad*, p. 63.

13 AD, pp. 294–296.

14 AD, p. 93.

15 AD, pp. 295–297.

16 AD, pp. 312–314. Also consulted was the text in ND-I, pp. 79–80.

17 AD, pp. 313–315.

18 *Ceann Gainimh* [Sandy Head] is on the east coast of Inis Meáin, the middle island of the three Aran Islands.

19 Deirdre and Naoise, legendary lovers in the pre-Christian Irish saga tradition, are characters in Synge's play *Deirdre of the Sorrows*. Pegeen and Shauneen are characters in Synge's *The Playboy of the Western World*.

20 *Máirtín Ó Direáin: Dánta 1939–1979* (Baile Átha Cliath: An Clóchomhar, 1980), p. 55.

21 Cuan Wood, or *Coill Chuain*, is one of the places in Scotland where Deirdre lived with Naoise.

22 *New Oxford Book of Irish Verse*, p. 358.

23 *Early Irish Literature*, ed. Myles Dillon (Chicago: Univ. of Chicago Press, 1948), p. 155.

24 *Félire Óengusso Céli Dé: The Martyrology of Oengus the Culdee*, ed. Whitley Stokes (London: Henry Bradshaw Society, 1905), p.112.

25 *The Book of Irish Verse: An Anthology of Irish Poetry from the Sixth Century to the Present* (New York: Macmillan, 1974), p. 21.

26 'A Primal Gaeltacht', *The Figure in the Cave*, ed. Antoinette Quinn (Dublin: Lilliput Press, 1989), p. 44.

27 Dennis O'Driscoll, 'An Interview with John Montague,' *Irish University Review* (John Montague Special Issue), 19, No. 1 (Spring 1989), p. 62.

28 Moy (*An Maigh*), Co. Tyrone, 10 kilometres north of Armagh City.

29 *Book of Irish Verse*, p. 89.

30 *The Great Cloak* (Dublin: Dolmen Press, 1978), p. 55.

31 Nuala Ní Dhomhnaill, *Pharaoh's Daughter* (Oldcastle, Co. Meath: Gallery Press, 1990; Winston-Salem, N.C.: Wake Forest Univ. Press, 1993), pp. 116–118.

32 *Pharaoh's Daughter*, pp. 117–119. The title, from Old English, means 'blood oath'.

33 Michael Davitt, *Freacnairc Mhearcair: The Oomph of Quicksilver: Rogha Dánta 1970–1998* (Cork: Cork Univ. Press, 2000), p. 128. The title means, literally, 'herb of the wounded men', but generally refers to bedstraw.

34 *Freacnairc Mhearcair*, p. 129.

35 *Amhráin Eoghain Ruaidh Uí Shúilleabháin*, ed. Pádraigh Ua Duinnín (Baile Átha Cliath: Connradh na Gaedhilge, 1901), p. 41. The title means 'Stretched by the Side of the River'.

36 *Blood Relations: Versions of Gaelic Poems of the 17th and 18th Centuries* (Dublin: New Writers' Press, nd [1972]), p. 35.

37 *Blood Relations*, p. 34.

38 Supposedly a rival for the affections of the young woman from Co. Armagh to whom Ó Doirnín's song is addressed. He was nicknamed, according to one account, *Úcaire Mac Ardghoile*, meaning 'spawn of the large appetite' (note quoted in *Peadar Ó Doirnín: Amhráin*, ed. Breandán Ó Buachalla [Baile Átha Cliath: An Clóchomhar, 1969], p. 85.)

39 *Peadar Ó Doirnín: Amhráin*, pp. 69–70. Also consulted were the texts in ND-II, pp. 37–38, and SONGS, p. 64. In the versions in *Ó Doirnín* and ND-II, there is a sixth stanza not represented in Mac Intyre's translation. Killen Hill is called in Irish *Úr-Cnoc Chéin Mhic Cáinte*, as it is said to be the burial place of Cian Mac Cáinte.

40 *Blood Relations*, pp. 29–30.

41 'Preface', *Trawling Tradition: Translations 1954–1994* (Salzburg: University of Salzburg, 1994), p. xii.

42 The woman is not necessarily the youth's sister; the terms brother and sister were commonly used in Gaelic culture, at the time the poem was written, to refer to people with the same last name, whether they were related or not.

43 Ballinrobe, Co. Mayo.

44 *Collected Works of Padraic H. Pearse: Songs of the Irish Rebels and Specimens from an Irish Anthology* (Dublin: Phoenix, n.d.), pp. 96–100. Also consulted were the texts in AD, pp. 336–338; and Ó-C, pp. 74–76. The title means 'Elegy for Donnachadh Bán'.

45 *Off Licence* (Dublin: Dolmen Press, 1968), pp. 19–20.

46 NEESON, p. 58. Also consulted was the text in MURPHY, p. 4.

47 *The Penguin Book of Irish Verse* (London: Penguin, 1970, 1981), p. 26.

48 *Penguin Book*, p. 27.

49 *A Drinking Cup: Poems from the Irish* (Dublin: Allen Figgis, 1970), p. 15.

50 *Buile Suibhne: The Adventures of Suibhne Geilt*, ed. J.G. O'Keeffe (London: Irish Texts Society, 1913), p. 152. Kennelly's translation represents three stanzas from a poem spoken by Sweeney that begins, 'Ba binne lium robháoi tan' ['There was a time when more melodious to me']. Although it begins with the same line, the first stanza represented in Kennelly's translation is not the first stanza of the original.

51 *A Drinking Cup*, p. 16.

52 'Introduction,' *Sweeney Astray* (1983; New York: Farrar Straus Giroux, 1984), n.p.

53 In Co. Antrim, about 15 kilometres northwest of Ballymena, and close to the border with Co. Derry.

54 The precise location of Glen Bolcain is not clear. J. G. O'Keeffe, the editor of *Buile Suibhne*, says it's probably in North Antrim; there is a ridge, he says, called Dunbolcain just north of Rasharkin. Other authorities have suggested that Glen Bolcain may be in Co. Louth, either near Ardee or in the area of Carlingford.

55 *Buile Suibhne*, ed. O'Keeffe, pp. 28–32; Heaney cites this as his source.

56 Mountain of Mis, in Co. Antrim.

57 In Co. Armagh, just southwest of Newry.

58 The Cooley Peninsula is in the northern part of Co. Louth, bordering Carlingford

Lough to the north. This is where the famous brown bull of the *Táin Bó Cualinge* presumably roamed.

59　Croagh Patrick, near Westport, Co. Mayo.

60　Island off the southwest coast of Scotland.

61　Peninsula on southwest coast of Scotland, the closest point between Scotland and Ireland.

62　Mourne Mountains, Co. Down.

63　O'Keeffe, *Buile Suibhne*, says Cluain Cille is on the border between Tír Conaill (Tyrconnel) and Tír Boghaine (Bannagh) in Co. Donegal.

64　In Co. Down, on the northern side of the Mourne Mountains.

65　*Sweeney Astray*, pp. 17–18.

66　In east Clare, where Merriman ran a hedge school.

67　In the parish of Feakle.

68　Aoibheall is a local queen of the *sídh*. The placename in the original is Léithchraig, translated by Power as Creglee. Crag has also been identified as Craig Liath, a rock associated with Aoibheall, near Killaloe, Co. Clare. There is also a place called Cragroe, about 10 kilometres southwest of Feakle.

69　Thomond is an anglicisation of *Tuamhain*, or *Tuadh-Mhumhain* [north Munster].

70　*Cúirt an Mheán-Oíche: The Midnight Court*, trans. Patrick C. Power (Cork: Mercier Press, 1971), pp. 18, 22–26. Also consulted was the text in *Cúirt an Mheon Oíche*, ed. Liam P. Ó Murchú (Baile Átha Cliath: An Clóchomhar, 1982), pp. 21–24.

71　*Amhráin Eoghain Ruaidh Uí Shúilleabháin*, p. 53.

72　*The Midnight Verdict* (Oldcastle, Co. Meath: Gallery Press, 1993, 2000), pp. 25–29.

73　*District and Circle* (London: Faber and Faber, 2006), p. 25.

74　*Pharaoh's Daughter*, p. 148.

75　*Pharaoh's Daughter*, p. 149.

76　*The Field Day Anthology of Irish Writing*, Vol. IV (Cork: Cork Univ. Press, 2002), p. 224.

77　*Field Day Anthology*, p. 224.

78　*Duanaire Dháibhidh Uí Bhruadair*, ed. John C. Mac Erlean, Part I (London: Irish Texts Society,1908), p. 18.

79　'Introduction,' *O Bruadair* (Oldcastle, Co. Meath: Gallery Press, 1985; 2000), p. 13.

80　This is usually taken to refer to James, the twelfth earl of Ormond, appointed Lord Lieutenant of Ireland in 1643 and again in 1661 .

81　*Ó Bruadair*, p. 24.

82　*Duanaire Uí Bhruadair*, Part II (1913), p. 221. Also consulted were the texts in ND-I, p. 54; and AD, p.116. The final line of the poem appears in ND-I and AD, but not in *Duanaire Uí Bhruadair*

83　Nuala Ní Dhomhnaill, *Selected Poems: Rogha Dánta*, trans. Michael Hartnett (Dublin: Raven Arts Press, 1991), p. 44. The title means tidings or news.

84　*Ó Bruadair*, p. 21.

85　*Rogha Dánta*, p. 45.

86　Ní Cheallacháin, *Filíocht Pháidrigín Haicéad*, p. 2.

87　*Haicéad* (Oldcastle, Co. Meath: Gallery, 1993), p. 16.

88　*Pharaoh's Daughter*, pp. 94–96.

89　Probably Goibhniu, one of the three craft-gods of the legendary Tuatha De Danann. Goibhniu was also the provider of sacred feasts for the gods.

90　According to the story of Deirdre and Naoise, in the Ulster cycle of pre-Christian Irish tales, when Deirdre sees a raven drinking the blood of a slaughtered calf in the snow, she knows that the man she desires will have black hair, a ruddy complexion, and a white body. When she later sees Naoise, she recognizes these qualities in him, and they flee together to Scotland.

91　*Pharaoh's Daughter*, pp. 95–97.

92　*Harbour Lights* (Oldcastle, Co. Meath: Gallery Press, 2005), p. 35.

93　*Field Day Anthology: Vol IV*, pp. 417–418. The poem was published earlier in David Greene, 'Un Joc Grossier in Irish and Provençal', *Ériu*, Vol. 17 (1955), pp. 10–11. Five of the original sixteen stanzas are not represented in Mahon's translation in *Harbour Lights*.

94   *Harbour Lights*, pp. 35–36. Mahon published a longer and substantially different translation of this poem in *Field Day Anthology of Irish Writing: Vol. IV*, p. 418.

95   Nuala Ní Dhomhnaill, *The Water Horse*, trans. by Medbh McGuckian and Eiléan Ní Chuilleanáin (Oldcastle, Co. Meath: Gallery Press, 1999), p. 96.

96   *Water Horse*, p. 97.

97   Margaret Butler, Viscountess Iveagh.

98   Identified in PPM as Bishop Butler of West-Court, Callan, Co. Kilkenny.

99   CEÓL, pp. 49–50. Also consulted were the texts in Ó-C, pp. 79–81; PPM, pp. 238–244; AD, pp. 328–330, and ND-I, pp. 86–87.

100   Identified in PPM as the exiled Duke of Ormond.

101   *The Girl Who Married the Reindeer* (Winston-Salem, N.C.: Wake Forest Univ. Press, 2002), pp. 42–43.

102   Probably Eoghan MacCarthy, who may well have educated Ó Rathaille.

103   The MacCarthys built a castle on the River Laune, near Killarney, Co. Kerry.

104   The head of the MacCarthy clan.

105   The Earl of Clancarty, whose chief residence was at Blarney, Co. Cork, near the River Lee, in the seventeenth century.

106   MacDonagh MacCarthy, Lord of Duhallow, built Kanturk Castle, in north Cork, early in the seventeenth century.

107   *Dánta Aodhagáin Uí Rathaille: The Poems of Egan O'Reilly*, 2nd ed., eds. Patrick S. Dineen and Tadhg O'Donoghue (London: Irish Texts Society, 1911), pp. 26–28. Also consulted were the texts in *Aogán Ó Rathaille: Dánta*, ed. Dáibhí Mac Conmara (n.p.: Aquila, 1969), pp. 34–35; and AD, p. 140. The title means 'The Time of Moving to Duibhneacaibh, beside Tonn Tóime in Kerry.' According to AD, Tonn Tóime is near the mouth of Castlemaine Harbour, Co. Kerry, but Dineen says Duibhneachaibh is near a waterfall that courses down the side of Tomies Mountain, on the western edge of Lough Leane, near Killarney.

108   *New Territory* (Dublin: Allen Figgis, 1967), pp. 24–25.

109   'Foreward', *The Midnight Court* (Oldcastle, Co. Meath: Gallery Press, 2005), p. 15.

110   *Pharaoh's Daughter*, pp.128–130. The title means 'The Poor Old Woman'.

111   *Pharaoh's Daughter*, pp.129–131.

112   *Midnight Court*, p. 11.

113   In northeastern Co. Clare, just north of Feakle, where Merriman lived for a time, running a hedge school and a small farm.

114   Ó Murchú, *Cúirt an Mheon-Oíche*, pp. 19–20; Carson says he relied on on this edition. Also consulted was the text in Power, *Cúirt an Mheán-Oíche*, pp. 14–16, which Carson says occasionally influenced him.

115   *Midnight Court*, pp. 19–20.

116   Ó Murchú, pp. 25–26. Also consulted was Power, pp. 28–30.

117   *Midnight Court*, pp. 26–27.

118   Ó Murchú, pp. 41–42. Also consulted was Power, pp. 72–74.

119   *Midnight Court*, pp. 50–51.

120   *Treasury of Irish Love Poems, Proverbs, and Triads*, ed. Gabriel Rosenstock (New York: Hippocrene Books, 1998), p. 39. Also consulted was the text in DÁNGRÁ, p.127.

121   *Treasury of Irish Love Poems*, p. 38.

122   *Pharaoh's Daughter*, pp. 110–112. The title means 'The Turning'.

123   *Pharaoh's Daughter*, pp. 111–113.

124   *Water Horse*, pp. 22–24. The title means 'The Dark Prince'.

125   *Water Horse*, pp. 23–25.

126   *Pharaoh's Daughter*, p. 124. The title means 'The Wrong Side'.

127   *Pharaoah's Daughter*, p. 125.

128   *Poems from the Irish: Collected Translations* (Cork: Merino, 2004), p. 14.

129   *Poems I Wish I'd Written: Translations from the Irish* (Indreabhán: Cló Iar-Chonnachta, 1996), pp. 16–18. Also consulted were the texts in *Cathal Buí: Amhráin*, ed. Breandán

Ó Buachalla (Baile Átha Cliath: An Clóchamhar, 1975), pp. 75–83; AD, pp. 132–134; and ND-II, pp. 47–48.

130   Probably a small lake in Co. Cavan or Co. Leitrim.

131   *Poems I Wish I'd Written*, pp. 17–19.

132   *Poems from the Irish*, p. 16. Also consulted were the texts in Mac Erlean, *Duanaire Dháibhidh Uí Bhruadair*, Part I, pp. 130–132; AD, pp. 112–114; and ND-I, p. 49.

133   *Poems from the Irish*, p. 17.

134   Michael Davitt, *Selected Poems/Rogha Dánta 1968–1984* (Dublin: Raven Arts, 1987), pp. 12–14.

135   *Quoof* (London: Faber and Faber, 1983), pp. 12–13.

136   Davitt, *Selected Poems/Rogha Dánta*, p. 10.

137   *Selected Poems/Rogha Dánta*, p. 11.

138   Nuala Ní Dhomnhnaill, *The Astrakhan Cloak* (1992; Winston-Salem, N.C.: Wake Forest Univ. Press, 1993), pp. 28–30.

139   *Astrakhan Cloak*, pp. 29–31.

140   MURPHY, p. 2. Also consulted was the text in NEESON, pp. 66–68.

141   *Hay* (New York: Farrar Straus Giroux, 1998), pp. 74–75.

142   *Field Day Anthology*, Vol. IV, pp. 436–437.

143   *Field Day Anthology*, pp. 437–438.

144   *An Crann Faoi Bhláth: The Flowering Tree: Contemporary Irish Poetry with Verse Translations*, eds. Declan Kiberd and Gabriel Fitzmaurice (Dublin: Wolfhound, 1991), p. 276.

145   *An Crann Faoi Bhláth*, p. 277.

146   *The Bright Wave/An Tonn Gheal: Poetry in Irish Now*, ed. Dermot Bolger (Dublin: Raven Arts, 1986), p. 56.

147   *Bright Wave*, p. 57.

148   *Bright Wave*, p. 190. Also consulted was the text in Cathal Ó Searcaigh, *Out in the Open* (Indreabhán: Cló Iar-Chonnachta, 1997), p. 50.

149   Cnoc na Bealtaine, in Co. Donegal.

150   At the foot of Errigal Mountain, in Co. Donegal.

151   Muckish Mountain, in the northern part of Co. Donegal.

152   *Bright Wave*, p. 191.

153   *Out in the Open*, p. 13.

154   Townland in Co. Donegal near Falcarragh.

155   *Out in the Open*, pp. 240–242.

156   *Out in the Open*, pp. 241–243.

Bibliography

Anthologies of verse translations by various translators

Bolger, Dermot, ed. *The Bright Wave/An Tonn Gheal: Poetry in Irish Now*. Dublin: Raven Arts, 1986.

Bunting, Edward, ed. *A Collection of the Ancient Music of Ireland, 1840. A General Collection of the Ancient Music of Ireland, 1809. A General Collection of the Ancient Irish Music, 1796*. Dublin: Walton's, 1969.

Fitzmaurice, Gabriel, ed. *Irish Poetry Now: Other Voices*. Dublin: Wolfhound Press, 1993.

Graves, Alfred Perceval, ed. *The Book of Irish Poetry*. London, Dublin, Belfast: Gresham, n.d. [1914].

Hardiman, James, ed. *Irish Minstrelsy, or Bardic Remains of Ireland*. 2 vols. London: Joseph Robins, 1831.

Hull, Eleanor, ed. *The Poem-Book of the Gael: Translations from Irish Gaelic Poetry into English Prose and Verse*. London: Chatto and Windus, 1913.

Kiberd, Declan, and Gabriel Fitzmaurice, eds. *An Crann Faoi Bhláth: The Flowering Tree: Contemporary Irish Poetry with Verse Translations*. Dublin: Wolfhound Press, 1991.

Maclean, Malcolm, and Theo Dorgan, eds. *An Leabhar Mór: The Great Book of the Gaelic*. Edinburgh: Canongate, 2002.

O'Daly, John, ed. *The Irish Miscellany*. Dublin: John O'Daly, 1876.

O'Faoláin, Seán, ed. *The Silver Branch: A Collection of the Best Old Irish Lyrics, Variously Translated*. New York: Viking, 1938.

Petrie, George, ed. *Ancient Music of Ireland*. 2 vols. Dublin: Society for the Preservation and Publication of the Melodies of Ireland, 1855.

Rosenstock, Gabriel, ed. *Treasury of Irish Love Poems, Proverbs, and Triads*. New York: Hippocrene Books, 1998.

Transactions of the Gaelic Society of Dublin. Vol. I. Dublin: John Barlow, 1808.

Walker, Joseph C., ed. *Historical Memoirs of the Irish Bards*. Dublin: Luke White, 1786.

Verse translations by individual authors

(Note: this list includes only works containing a substantial amount of verse translation from the Irish; for individual verse translations, see endnotes.)

Brooke, Charlotte. *Reliques of Irish Poetry*. Dublin: George Bonham, 1789.

Carson, Ciaran. *The Midnight Court*, by Brian Merriman. Oldcastle, Co. Meath: Gallery Press, 2005.

Drummond, William Hamilton. *Ancient Irish Minstrelsy*. Dublin: Hodges and Smith, 1852.

Ferguson, Samuel. *Lays of the Western Gael and Other Poems*. London: Bell and Daldy, 1865.

Fitzmaurice, Gabriel. *Poems I Wish I'd Written: Translations from the Irish*. Indreabhán: Cló Iar-Chonnachta, 1996.

Fitzmaurice, Gabriel. *Poems from the Irish: Collected Translations*. Cork: Mercier Press, 2004.

Flower, Robin. *Love's Bitter-Sweet: Translations from the Irish Poets of the Sixteenth and Seventeenth Centuries*. Dublin: Cuala Press, 1925.

Flower, Robin. *Poems and Translations*. London: Constable, 1931.

Graham, Matthew. *The Giantess, from the Irish of Oisin, and the War of Donomore, with Other Poems and Translations*. Belfast: Simms and M'Intyre, 1833.

Graves, Alfred Perceval. *The Irish Poems of Alfred Perceval Graves: Songs of the Gael*. Dublin: Maunsel, 1908.

Gwynn, Stephen. *A Lay of Ossian and Patrick with Other Poems*. Dublin: Hodges Figgis, n.d. [1903].

Hartnett, Michael. *O Bruadair*. Oldcastle: Co. Meath: Gallery Press, 1985.

Hartnett, Michael. *Portrait of the Artist as an Abominable Snowman*, by Gabriel Rosenstock. London: Forest Books, 1989.

Hartnett, Michael. *Selected Poems: Rogha Dánta*, by Nuala Ní Dhomhnaill. Dublin: Raven Arts Press, 1991.

Hartnett, Michael. *Haicéad*. Oldcastle, Co. Meath: Gallery, 1993.

Hartnett, Michael. *O Rathaille*. Oldcastle: Co. Meath: Gallery Press, 1998.

Heaney, Seamus. *Sweeney Astray*. 1983; New York: Farrar Straus Giroux, 1984.

Heaney, Seamus. *The Midnight Verdict*. Oldcastle, Co. Meath: Gallery Press, 1993.

Hyde, Douglas. *Abhráin Grádh Chúige Connacht: Love Songs of Connacht*. London: T. Fisher Unwin; Dublin: Gill, 1893.

Hyde, Douglas, *Amhráin Chúige Chonnacht: The Songs of Connacht*. Ed. Breandán Ó Conaire. 1893; Blackrock, Co. Dublin: Irish Academic Press, 1985.

Hyde, Douglas. *Abhráin atá leagtha ar an Reachtúire, or, Songs ascribed to Raftery*. Baile Átha Cliath: Gill, 1903.

Hyde, Douglas. *Abhráin Diadha Chúige Chonnacht: or The Religious Songs of Connacht*. Cuid I, II. Dublin: M. H. Gill, n.d. [1906].

Kennelly, Brendan. *A Drinking Cup: Poems from the Irish*. Dublin: Allen Figgis, 1970.

Kennelly, Brendan. *Love of Ireland: Poems from the Irish*. Cork and Dublin: Mercier Press, 1989.

Kinsella, Thomas. *An Duanaire: 1600-1900: Poems of the Dispossessed*. Mountrath, Portlaoise: Dolmen Press, 1981.

Longford, Earl of. *Poems from the Irish*. Dublin: Hodges, Figgis; Oxford: B. H. Blackwell, 1944.

Longford, Earl of. *More Poems from the Irish*. Dublin: Hodges, Figgis; Oxford: B. H. Blackwell, 1944.

Longford, Earl of. *The Dove in the Castle: A Collection of Poems from the Irish*. Dublin: Hodges Figgis; Oxford: B. H. Blackwell, 1946.

MacIntyre, Tom. *Blood Relations: Versions of Gaelic Poems of the 17th and 18th Centuries*. Dublin: New Writers' Press, n.d. [1972].

Mangan, James Clarence. *The Poets and Poetry of Munster: A Selection of Irish Songs*. Dublin: James Duffy, 1849.

McCall, Patrick Joseph [Cavellus]. *Irish Nóiníns*. Dublin: Sealy, Bryers and Walker, 1894.

McCall, Patrick Joseph. *Pulse of the Bards: Songs and Ballads*. Dublin: M. H. Gill, 1904.

McCall, Patrick Joseph. *Irish Fireside Songs*. Dublin: M. H. Gill, 1911.

McGuckian, Medhb [co-trans.]. *The Water Horse*, by Nuala Ní Dhomhnaill. Oldcastle, Co. Meath: Gallery Press, 1999.

Mhac an tSaoi, Máire. *A Heart Full of Thought*. Dublin: Dolmen Press, 1959.

Mhac an tSaoi, Máire. *Trasládáil*. Belfast: Lagan Press, 1997.

Montague, John. *A Fair House: Versions of Irish Poetry*. Dublin: Cuala Press, 1972.

Muldoon, Paul. *The Astrakhan Cloak*, by Nuala Ní Dhomhnaill. 1992; Winston-Salem, N.C.: Wake Forest Univ. Press, 1993.

Ní Chuilleanáin, Eiléan [co-trans.]. *The Water Horse*, by Nuala Ní Dhomhnaill. Oldcastle, Co. Meath: Gallery Press, 1999.

O'Connor, Frank. *The Wild Bird's Nest: Poems from the Irish*. Dublin: Cuala Press, 1932.

O'Connor, Frank. *Lords and Commons: Translations from the Irish*. Dublin: Cuala Press, 1938.

O'Connor, Frank. *The Fountain of Magic*. London: Macmillan, 1939.

O'Connor, Frank. *A Lament for Art O'Leary*. Dublin: Cuala Press, 1940.

O'Connor, Frank. *The Midnight Court*, by Brian Merriman. London, Dublin: Maurice Fridberg, 1945.

O'Connor, Frank. *Kings, Lords, & Commons: Irish Poems from the Seventh to the Nineteenth Century*. 1959; Dublin: Gill and Macmillan, 1991.

Ó Flannghaile, Tomás. *Laoi Oisín ar Thír na n-Óg: The Lay of Oisín in the Land of Youth*, by Micheál Coimín. Dublin: M. H. Gill, 1896.

Ó Flannghaile, Tomás. *Eachtra Ghiolla an Amaráin*, or *The Adventures of a Luckless Fellow and Other Poems*, by Donnchadh Ruadh MacConmara. Dublin: Sealy, Bryers and Walker, n.d. [1897].

O'Grady, Desmond. *Off Licence*. Dublin: Dolmen Press, 1968.

O'Grady, Desmond. *A Limerick Rake: Versions from the Irish*. Dublin: Gallery Press, 1968, 1978.

O'Grady, Standish Hayes ['S. Hayes']. *The Adventures of Donnchadh Ruadh Mac Con-Mara, A Slave of Adversity*, by Donnchadh Ruadh Mac Con-Mara. Dublin: John O'Daly, 1853.

O'Sullivan, Donal. *Songs of the Irish*. Dublin: Brown and Nolan, 1960.

Pearse, Padraic H. *Collected Works of Padraic H. Pearse: Songs of the Irish Rebels and Specimens from an Irish Anthology*. Dublin: Phoenix, 1910; Dublin: Maunsel, 1918.

Sewell, Frank. *Out in the Open*, by Cathal Ó Searcaigh. Indreabhán: Cló Iar-Chonnachta, 1997.

Sigerson, George ['Erionnach']. *The Poets and Poetry of Munster: A Selection of Irish Songs. Second Series*. Dublin: John O'Daly, 1860.

Sigerson, George, *Bards of Gael and Gall*. London: T. Fisher Unwin, 1897; Dublin and Belfast: Phoenix Publishing, n. d.

Stephens, James. *Reincarnations*. London: Macmillan, 1918.

Ussher, Percy Arland. *The Midnight Court and The Adventures of a Luckless Fellow*. London: Jonathan Cape, 1926.

Walsh, Edward. *Reliques of Irish Jacobite Poetry*. Dublin: Samuel J. Machan, 1844.

Walsh, Edward. *Irish Popular Songs*. Dublin: James McGlashan, 1847.

Wilson, Charles Henry. *Select Irish Poems, Translated into English*. [n.d. 1792].

Index by first line of
Irish-language poems translated

Index by title of Irish-language poems translated

Index by first line of poetic translations

Index by title of poetic translations